Beyond the Sidewalks

A chronicle of the ups and downs, struggles and dreams, of one man, his farm, and his magazine — Countryside

By Jerome D. Belanger

ISBN: 978-0615972855
Copyright 2014 B-Hive Books

Philosophy does not promise to secure anything external for man; otherwise it would be admitting something that lies beyond its proper subject matter. For as the material of the carpenter is wood, and that of statuary bronze, so the subject matter of the art of living is each person's own life.
— *Epicetus, Greek sage and Stoic philosopher*

Belanger Homestead Eras:
The Creamery: 1964-1973
The Farm: 1973-1978
The Dome: 1978-1990

4

6

Foreword

1969: In Viet Nam, U.S. forces peaked at 543,000, while 240,000 anti-war protestors marched on Washington. The top song was Aquarius, *and 400,000 people gathered at Woodstock. Neil Armstrong became the first man to walk on the moon; gas was 36¢ a gallon; a first class stamp was 6¢. U.S. population had just reached 200,000,000; the world, 3.6 billion.*

And a young fellow scraped together $25 to place a classified ad in *Organic Gardening & Farming* magazine offering a newsletter devoted to people seeking an antidote to the insanity of the Industrial Establishment through self-sufficient country living. Communal hippies with similar ideas were saying, "Never trust anyone over 30." He was 31, married, with four children, eking out a living with a small print shop in a village in rural southern Wisconsin.

At one time I was that man. Now he's a stranger to me: a younger man (31 years vs. my 76) in another time and place; a man with similar ideas but in a different world. I in turn laugh at him, envy him, pity him, and sometimes admire him. And again and again, I'd love to offer him some sound advice!

This collection of his thoughts and experiences, while often quite personal, also reflects the times in which they were written. Comparing those times with today also prompts comments: if he could have known in 1970 what *we* know in 2014, would it have made any difference? Most of the time he had his own ideas and apparently was quite certain of them, but he was also searching for something just out of his reach. Maybe, just maybe, I can help with that, by the end of this book.

His life (and mine) seems to be divided into 15-year segments. It might be significant that the first one was aimed toward a monastic lifestyle, with its attendant simple living. He left the seminary at age 15.

Part 2 started when he met his future wife, Diane. She was 14. This was the "growing up" phase: high school, the Marine Corps, college, marriage, children, several writing jobs, and starting the home business. Part 3 covers the 15 years we're about to look at: the ups and downs of business, farming, and family life. Part 4 was to be more of the same, with even lower lows, although with a fairly bright ending. Part 5 covers retirement, from 2000 to the present. While all five are distinctly unique, they are all interrelated in many ways, especially regarding a love of nature and simple living — and thinking and writing about them.

He had started a magazine—*The Wisconsinite*—in 1961. It didn't even bring in enough money to pay the printer, so he bought his own offset press (actually, a newfangled office offset duplicator). That led to other printing and publishing projects. One, serving small independent (non-Bell) telephone companies around the country, was his home business and main source of income. (*Telco Call* lasted 14 years.) With that background, starting a newsletter about homesteading was almost a reflex action that required little thought or planning.

Obviously, with a subscription price of $1 a year, his goal was not to become a publishing tycoon. He wanted to collect information on simple old-fashioned country living, especially from the elderly, before it was swept under the rug of modern progress and lost forever. That accounted for the additional subscription requirement: a letter with a question, an answer, or at least a comment that would help others.

When it was time to butcher a pig, he wanted to cure and smoke the bacon. He called a meat expert at the University of Wisconsin for information on how to do it. There was a long pause. Then the expert laughed and said, rather incredulously, "*People* don't make bacon; *Oscar Mayer* makes bacon!"

Belanger not only got the information from an 80-year-old neighbor: neighbors also went to their attics and lent him a bell hog scraper, lard press, sausage stuffer, and more advice.

That's how it began. What happened over the next 15 years —well, that's what we're about to discover.

These essays might be considered autobiographical, even though they cover only 1/5th of a lifetime (so far) and they don't come close to fully exposing even that brief period. Some readers might consider them history; others, philosophy (more on this in the final chapter). But whatever the harmonics, the main tune is a personal glimpse of running a small family business, and a small family farm, in the 1970s and early '80s.

I'll tag along to make occasional comments I added between 1995 and 2014 (yes, it took that long for this to come together), and after we cover 1985 I'll quickly fill you in on the next 30 years. But first, here's an introductory word from the kid. —*Jerome D. Belanger (The Elder)*

In the beginning
Jerry Belanger (The Younger)

One of my goals was to *avoid* becoming a "magazine" that would require collating, stapling and trimming, among other tasks that didn't appeal to me: they either required expensive machinery or mind-numbing hand labor. We had done that with *The Wisconsinite*. And I was not the least interested in selling advertising. (It's true that, as Irwin Cobb said, "If writers were good businessmen, they'd have too much sense to be writers.") Little did I realize at the time that keeping a business small and *staying* in business would be as difficult as managing a business for growth.

The first issue of COUNTRYSIDE was merely one 12" x 18" sheet of paper, folded down to 6" x 9": in format, eight digest-size pages. The press run was about 200 copies, of which less than half were sold. But that was enough to recoup my $25 investment in the ad in *OGF*, pay for the printing (paper and ink only, labor was donated) and postage (6¢), with enough left over to put out #2.

And that was it. While the "experts" said it took at least half a million dollars to start a magazine, that $25 (and the print shop) was our total grubstake.

The newsletter didn't actually have a name. I simply used the return address from the Countryside Print Shop, including the stylized rooster logo, and merely blocked out the "Print Shop." Later, when I asked readers if they couldn't think of a better name for our newsletter, the consensus was that COUNTRYSIDE was just fine; that said it all. This became apparent almost 20 years later when the giant Hearst Corporation started a magazine they called "Countryside" — but that's another story (related on page 422).

After two issues, one sheet wasn't enough to contain the letters from readers. By the fourth, we were forced to produce a 6" x 9" stapled booklet. By the 7th, our hand stapler wouldn't go through the number of pages required and the "book" was too thick to go through our primitive el cheapo addressing machine, so it became an 8-1/2" x 11" 20-page magazine. Putting it together was a family project. I stacked the folded sheets on the dining room table and we all marched around the table, collating them. They were still stapled by hand, and trimmed on the hand-operated paper cutter.

There is more... much, much more... leading up to this point. In some ways, it all began when I was still in grade school: my interests and attitudes had changed little since then. But this collection of essays is about what happened after that. Here I'll just mention that we wound up with a very well-equipped print shop, including machinery for putting magazines together (collating, folding, stapling and trimming in one operation), and at one time we published, produced and mailed seven different titles, all related to country living: COUNTRYSIDE, *Dairy Goat Guide, Backyard Poultry, sheep!, Rabbit World, National Stock Dog*, and *Homegrown*. In addition, we operated a retail and mail order business, the Countryside General Store, which became a tourist attraction in downtown Waterloo, Wisconsin. An old drugstore provided the picturesque fixtures, complete with soda fountain and neon signs. The store offered everything imaginable devoted to serious homestead living including spinning wheels, kerosene lamps, and woodstoves. In spite of all this, the main attraction often seemed to be the very well-stocked, nostalgically old-fashioned candy counter! At one point we had 24 employees.

But mainly, I was a farmer. That's what I wrote about.

COUNTRYSIDE always was a personal magazine. In the beginning, of course, with less than a hundred subscribers, it was more like a round robin letter than a magazine: how could it *not* be personal, for both the editor and the reader/writers? Many *Beyond the Sidewalks* columns were little more than personal notes and comments written to those few dozen friends, who responded in kind. *(2014 note: Some readers might have trouble envisioning stacks of personal letters and postcards in this age of Facebook and Twitter, neither of which I have ever used.)*

In spite of that, a great deal was left unsaid. In this collection, I have filled in some of those gaps in an attempt to tell a more detailed story... a story about one person, one family, and one small business, against a background of sweeping social and economic change that now seems to have been forgotten by most of the world.

In those first issues the masthead said, "COUNTRYSIDE is published in the countryside, by and for countrysiders, whenever the other chores are done." Since there were no set publication dates, the issues were numbered, rather than dated.

When we applied for second class mailing status the U.S. Post Office didn't approve of this lackadaisical attitude. Already we were forced to become more "businesslike." (Incidentally, after COUNTRYSIDE merged with *Small Stock Magazine*, the combo used SSM's second class mailing permit, which was issued in January, 1918, making it one of the oldest publications in the country.)

When the first issue of *The Mother Earth News* appeared in the spring of 1970 I gave serious consideration to dropping out. It was obviously much better financed, more "professional," and considerably more marketable than what we had. But as interesting letters continued to pour in ("pour" being a relative term, since *TMEN* already had thousands of readers while we remained with a few hundred), I just never got around to pulling the plug. Several years later, John Shuttleworth told me his TMEN got off to a running start by distributing free copies in "head shops." I had no idea what a head shop was. Score one for the kids who said, "Never trust anyone over 30."

It got easier when well-known goat lady Judy Kapture joined me to start *Dairy Goat Guide.* Diane and I bought the venerable *Small Stock Magazine* (circulation: 2,000). I was then printing and mailing three homestead publications plus the telephone periodical, when all I really wanted to do was care for my animals and garden!

Apparently the time was ripe for such innovations. In 1969-70 The *Whole Earth Catalog* was new and exciting. We celebrated the first Earth Day. John Shuttleworth of *TMEN* and I were joined by a host of others. Most were even smaller than COUNTRYSIDE and didn't last long. It was several years before Blair & Ketchum's *Country Journal* and other really professional, well-financed magazines came along, and country living became what the publishing and advertising trades call "upscale."

But then, they all folded. Even *Mother Earth News* went bankrupt at one time. (Not that I'm vindictive, but I couldn't resist framing a check from TMEN stamped "insufficient funds".)

COUNTRYSIDE struggled on, more from the publisher's bull-headed perseverance than from any grand business plan or certainly ability.

The following pages retell the story as it unfolded in the editor's column, *Beyond the Sidewalks,* from 1970 to 1985. But bear in mind the backdrop: high inflation, wage and price controls, fears of The Bomb, globalization, drawn-out recessions, and the attempt to have both guns *and* butter (wars in Viet Nam and on poverty) and a growing awareness of ecology. What some economists call "the disastrous decade" is reflected in many of these essays, but there is also a strong undercurrent of even more disturbing and more permanent change... as well as a wonderful sense of living close to nature.

It's a nostalgic trip. I hope you enjoy it.

Part I: "The Disastrous Decade"

2014: It often takes writers a while to get warmed up. Editors are aware that killing the first few sentences, paragraphs, or even pages, can improve many stories. In this case, I have eliminated the first six issues — an entire year. But bear in mind, several of these were only a single sheet of paper, with little that would interest us here and now. You're not missing anything important.

Here's a taste of what life is like as we begin our story in 1970: the Dow Jones Industrial Average drops to 631 (but ends the year at 838); inflation is high, at 5.84%; average cost of a new house: $23,450; AMC Gremlin, $1,879; average annual income, $9,400; 600,000 attend the largest-ever rock festival (Isle of Wight); Concorde (SST) makes its first supersonic flight; first Earth Day celebration; EPA established; U.S. population is 203 million, world, 3.63 billion; U.S. invades Cambodia; 100,000 anti-war demonstrators gather in Washington, D.C.; National Guard troops kill four demonstrators at Kent State; Boeing 747 goes into service.

And in 1971: North Sea oil production begins (Norway); Greenpeace organizes to question resource management (and governments); Intel releases first microprocessor (start of the Digital Age); new stock exchange begins (NASDAQ); U.S. voting age lowered to 18; Walt Disney World opens in Florida; Federal Express begins; cigarette advertising banned on U.S. tv; The New York Times prints parts of the Pentagon Papers showing the U. S. government had been lying to the people; The Sharp Company releases the pocket calculator, and IBM, the floppy disk.

With this background, let's join the conversation already in progress.

1. February/March 1971

"A letter to old friends I haven't met yet"

(After some chit-chat about the print shop—including the debut of
Dairy Goat Guide—*and the arrival of the new pig...)*

Obviously I've been busy lately. It seems most of you have been too. I haven't heard from anybody who's actually tried the things we've been talking about. But talking without *doing* makes this all something of a fantasy. If we get some first-person accounts (and pictures) of the pitfalls, techniques, etc., it seems reasonable to expect that others who haven't the time or inclination or finances to experiment would be more willing to get started.

Although we have no definite plans yet, I think it would be great to have an experimental homestead. We'd dig, drive and drill wells just for the pictures and first-hand report. *(This issue features wells.)* We'd experiment with keeping animals on a small scale. We'd set up a solar heater and a wind generator and then tell you what we did wrong.

As for animals and crops, which many of us are now working with, we still need better methods for accomplishing what we want to accomplish without becoming "farmers."

Had quite a few calls and comments about the solar piece in the last issue. The main query could be summarized as "Does it really work?" And as Diane put it, "If it works, why don't we hear more about it?"

The reason is simply that nobody stands to make money on it. Nobody counts sunshine in the gross national product. Therefore, you can't expect anyone with a financial interest in the current way of doing things to spend time and money developing something that won't pay a return. That doesn't mean it won't work. It *is* working, right now, but we don't hear about it.

(This idea accounts for the "advertisements" you'll find in COUNTRYSIDE. If nobody else will promote clean air, or blades of grass, or rain or snow or earthworms, then *we* will!)

This brings up another letter we received from a real skeptic. He was sour about several things, but mentioned that methane-from-manure was a big farce. But this too has been in operation in several places.

True, we don't want to grab at every scheme that comes along. But if the sources of information are at least as reliable as those we believe daily as a matter of course, why, we should check them out.

We have several feet of snow here now, but the seed catalogs are beginning to arrive, so you know spring is on the way!

That reminds me: I was digging carrots under two feet of snow in January. With all the snow, the ground is frozen only an inch or so deep (in spite of some 20-below temperatures) and the layer of straw and leaves I put on the carrot rows last fall protected them pretty well.

Actually, to back up a few months, we ate pretty well from the garden long after some light frosts. We made whole meals of salads. Jerusalem artichokes, Brussels sprouts, carrots, endive, turnips, winter radishes, and lots more lasted well into November. Those fall gardens can be one of the most profitable and enjoyable projects you can undertake, I think. It takes planning to have fresh produce when everybody else's garden is lost in the weeds, but it's worth it.

The unemployment rate is going up every month. Seems everybody who's not on strike is talking about it or has just been on one.

On top of that, the agribusiness people are softening us up for major food price increases due to the corn blight. (Less feed means less milk, less meat, fewer eggs.)

Sounds like a good year to read those seed catalogs even more carefully than usual. Likewise, if you've been hankerin' to get some chickens or rabbits, 1971 is the year. (Don't forget to plant some feed for them too, just for insurance. Some farmers are planting milo instead of corn, and of course, homesteaders should be planting sunflowers, mangle beets, etc., blight or no blight.)

Busy days ahead... beyond the sidewalks!

Notes, 2014: This was low-tech solar energy: not photovoltaic production of electricity, but running water through pipes or tubes in a box on the roof to heat it. It predated the 1973 energy crisis.

Yes, seed catalogs really did arrive in spring, then. Now we start getting them before Christmas.

That last item—about unemployment and the corn blight—was typical of the references to relevant current news in those early issues. Part of my reason for homesteading — and one big reason I didn't set a conventional business course for the magazine — was that I honestly felt that by 1980 it would all be over: the world as we had known it would be gone, and nobody would be reading magazines. While it took longer than I'd expected and not quite the way I envisioned it, that's pretty much what happened.

2. April/May 1971
Speaking of economics...

It's March. There's a promise of spring in the air that makes the still below-freezing temperatures bearable, at least. All the anticipation that goes into those few short days called "spring" is almost ridiculous, and yet, at this time of the year it's just about impossible to keep from looking forward to it.

It looks like I'm going to prove something I thought had been proven long ago: It's not possible to be a full-time homesteader and have a full-time job too. My 1971 garden is already behind schedule!

Usually by this time I have the tomatoes, peppers, eggplant, and all the other tender bedding plants safely tucked into flats in a spare room. But now the seeds are still in the packages. I keep telling myself I usually get over-anxious, plant too soon, and the plants get leggy before I set them out anyway... but the time is getting closer.

We do have one compost heap working, though. Cleaned out the goat barn. Do you suppose there's something wrong with somebody who takes such delight in the aroma of a steaming compost heap? I can't help myself: it just smells great.

The first kids are due next week, we have a new beehive all assembled (but not painted yet) and the seeds are here. When it warms up the henhouse will have to be cleaned, we'll start turning the mulch piles regularly, and the place sure needs a post-winter general cleanup. There will be trees to transplant and a fence to paint, but that can wait 'til school's out. There's little doubt that the busiest days of the year are just ahead.

E conomics, to me, has always been a dull (and useless) subject. But the January issue of the *Whole Earth Catalog* had an article that really hit home, and it wasn't until I finished it that I realized it was about economics.

It was written by Gary North of the History Dept. of the University of California. The title was "Inflation and the Return of the Craftsman."

He starts out by predicting that more inflation is likely (giving reasons, if anybody needs them) and goes on to say:

"The man who plans carefully at this stage stands to survive the wage-price squeeze, the shortages, and the defective workmanship that are on their way. The hobbyist has one item that will rise in value, will be marketable, and will be in heavy demand: specialized knowledge. In some cases that knowledge will become so valuable that a hobby may become a new occupation for those men who take advantage of new conditions. For white collar workers or those associated with heavy industries that will be hard hit by the economic controls, their skills in the home shop may be more profitable than their skills in the factory or office.

"Why? Because the official lines of supply will be increasingly empty of the desired goods and services. The black market —an inevitable effect of price controls — will begin to absorb the goods most in demand."

He goes on to explain that a startling effect is produced: the price differential between new and old goods begins to narrow. Used refrigerators or washing machines will go up in price, and the person who can repair them will be in great demand.

"This has led me to a strange conclusion (for a college instructor)," North said. "The young man who has mechanical skills would be wise to stay out of college... there will be a glut of people holding college degrees... the skilled craftsman is about to have his day. The man who can produce a thing of beauty or of use through his own genius, with simple tools and common materials, would find the coming decade exceptionally profitable."

2014 note: In 1995, when I started toying with these essays as a possible book, I noted that Gary North got his PhD in U.S. economic history a year after the above was written. I said he wrote an investment newsletter that recommends (among other things) moving at least 75 miles from major cities that "will be hit hardest by the coming apocalypse."

By 1998-99 I could add that Dr. North ran one of the most popular and comprehensive websites on the Y2K computer situation, which provided much of the Y2K information that appeared in COUNTRYSIDE at that time.

Today — 2014 — he's still putting out an interesting "contrarian" investment newsletter.

And we might ask any unemployed college graduate with a horrific student loan about that "glut of people holding college degrees" North referred to, 43 years ago.

As for economics, I have discovered what a fascinating subject it is, especially when combined with other disciplines. I have enjoyed taking several college-level econ courses since retiring.

A note about style: COUNTRYSIDE has always capitalized "Earth" and lower-cased "tv." The reasons should be obvious... and telling.

3. June/July 1971

Hog butchering

2014 note: I was surprised to re-read this column and discover that for many years I've been telling a fib. Whenever anyone asks how or why COUNTRYSIDE got started, I tell the story about butchering our first pig. I wanted to cure and smoke the hams and bacons but couldn't find out how. So I called the Meat Science Dept. at the University of Wisconsin.

After a moment of stunned silence, the "expert" laughed and said, "People don't make bacon; Oscar Mayer makes bacon!"

And so, I've been saying, I started COUNTRYSIDE *to get the answer from the real experts: the people who do it.*

It's a good story, but alas, according to this column, COUNTRYSIDE *had eight issues under its belt before I butchered my first pig.*

So many things to talk about this time, I don't know where to begin. Anybody who thinks country life is dull should just spend a few days around *this* place.

The most memorable event of spring, 1971, was butchering our first pig. The afternoon of the day I wrote the piece on vegetarianism for this issue.

Although I was rather fond of the creature (it was named Pepper), the actual killing didn't raise any qualms. We encountered no major problems. It seemed like an awful lot of work, but maybe that's because I'm used to butchering chickens and rabbits. Even the goats we put in the freezer were nothing compared with the pig.

In the first place, he was big. The goats we butchered weren't much over 50 pounds: Pepper went 250. The book said slitting the throat without shooting or stunning is the best and most humane way to kill a pig, but to me, it seemed too personal. I shot him.

Now, in case you've never butchered a pig, let me point out that you don't skin them. The process is more akin to plucking chickens, and that's where the work comes in. You dunk the pig in hot water, and pull and scrape and shave the hair off. The government booklet on slaughtering hogs on the farm says to have the water at 140 to 144 degrees and the Morton Salt booklet *The Complete Guide to Home Meat Curing* advised a temperature of 150 to 160 degrees. Not trusting a government recommendation, we followed the higher one. We took water from the furnace boiler, from the water heater, and boiled a big canning kettleful on the stove, and managed to get the 50 gallon barrel about half full.

The barrel was tilted at about a 45 degree angle against a sturdy table. Two of us lifted the hog up on the table, and doused him in the water, and believe me, that's different from scalding a chicken. After soaking about five minutes, we hauled him out and started working with the bell scrapers. I have no idea where a body could pick up something like this today: I borrowed a couple from a neighbor, Ernie Blaschka, and even got his advice and assistance in the bargain.

Anyway, the hair didn't come out all the way. We stuck him back in the water and waited. Again, nothing. By that time, I could have had any normal skinned animal finished, but we decided the water had gotten cold (it was a windy, chilly day) so we had to heat more.

To make a long story short, that still didn't help so we built a fire under the barrel, got the water steaming, and the hair came out with no problems. Next time I'll do that in the first place.

Right here is the first indication of a problem that concerned COUNTRYSIDE, rather than Pepper, throughout the operation: it's just about impossible to do a job like this and be a scientific reporter at the same time. How hot was the water when we finally got it to work? You'd want to know if you're contemplating such an operation yourself. I don't know. I was so busy scraping and dunking I really didn't give it more than a passing thought. I didn't get any pictures for the same reason, or because you can't haul a 250 pound pig out of the barrel with one hand and take a photo of what you're doing with the other. Or my hands were, uh, too messy to handle a camera.

It took over two hours just for this first operation.

Removing the intestines wasn't particularly difficult, in spite of the fact that we had no means of hanging the carcass. But this was finished in short order, and we took it to Blaschka's garage and hung it from the beams to cool overnight.

This cooling was something that had concerned me, because we can get some pretty warm nights in May. Without even knowing it, the day we chose to butcher was the feast of the Ice Saints. I'd never heard of them, but I later read of the tradition that says there's a cold spell the 11th, 12th, and 13th of May. There was. Got down below freezing, no flies, and by morning the meat was chilled.

So I started cutting it up according to the pictures in Morton's booklet.

Did you ever notice how a fresh carcass laying on a table bears no resemblance to the pictures in the how-to manuals? And after I finish cutting it up, it doesn't bear any resemblance to much of anything. If homesteading ever affects my marriage, it will be because of butchering. Witness this dialog:

Jd (wrapping meat): "You can put these packages in the freezer now."

Diane: "What's in them? You don't even have them marked. Label the packages, for pete's sake, or I won't have any idea of what's in them."

Jd writing carefully on lumpy freezer paper: "Pig meat."

Diane: "Pig meat! What's that going to tell me! Is it loins or ribs or chops or what? How could I make dinner with a package labeled 'pig meat'!"

But it all looked the same to me. Like I said, I'm used to butchering chickens, and drumsticks are rather distinctive.

What do you do with the hams and bacons when you butcher your own pig? Have them cured and smoked, by whom, pray tell, with all the new regulations for meat inspection? Blaschkas just had a hog butchered one place and smoked another, and they were told they couldn't even transport the meat between the two establishments: the smokehouse had to pick it up at the slaughterhouse, or they'd contaminate it or something.

So I mixed up a sweet-pickle brine: 8 pounds of salt, 2 pounds of sugar, 2 ounces of saltpeter and 4-1/2 gallons of water. I put the hams and bacon into my good old 20 gallon crock and poured the brine over all. A weight keeps the meat from floating. I'll have to repack it on the 7th, 14th and 28th days. A 15 pound ham should take about 60 days, at 4 days per pound.

Then it was back to the lard. The kitchen became a rendering plant, as I cut up the fat and cooked it in a canning kettle. The first batch, cooked slowly, took 6 hours. The second was done in about three, at a higher temperature, but both were cooked too much and the lard is not as white as it should be. At any rate, we got 10 three-pound lard cans filled.

The caul and ruffle fats from internal organs were rendered, and saved for soap. And that's where things stand right now: we have a freezer loaded with "pig meat," a crock of ham and bacon that nobody is too sure about, and a pot of soap-making lard and a lifetime supply of cooking lard. And the goats are back in the pig yard.

Almost forgot: Also from Blaschkas, we borrowed a lard press and a sausage grinder. The press did save some lard, by squeezing out the cracklin's, but I don't think it was an appreciable amount. That might have something to do with my overcooking it.

The sausage grinder, on the other hand, was indispensable. I'm not sure if I put too much sausage meat in the freezer, or what happened to it, but I only got a few pounds. What there was, was great (and I don't usually care for pork sausage). We used about 5 pounds of trimmings (1/3 fat and 2/3 lean); 5 teaspoons of salt, 4 teaspoons of ground sage; 2 teaspoons of ground pepper; 1 teaspoon of sugar; and 1/2 teaspoon of ground cloves.

With a breakfast of homemade bread, fresh eggs from your own hens, milk from your own goats, and fresh, homemade pork sausage from a pig you butchered yourself, a fellow gets to feeling a little like a homesteader.

While the pig was the homesteading highlight here since COUNTRYSIDE No. 8, that was by no means the only activity. Matter of fact, since I typed that last paragraph (this afternoon), we spent some time with a typewriter salesman (our 8-year-old one finally bit the dust. We had to pull a string tied to a watchamacallit to turn it on, among other little quirks and foibles, and that's no way to put out a magazine... even one like this). Then the hatchery called to say our chicks were ready, so I had to dust off and check out the brooder. That was interrupted by calls from the high school about the commencement programs we're printing and another local printing customer, plus a few other pressing office matters that came up. We ate supper quickly and picked up the chicks, and not until they were safely installed did we get to the milking and other chores. And now, back to the typewriter. If there is such a thing as tranquil country life, it somehow passed us by!

Ordered some geese too, but they weren't hatched out yet. I love a Christmas goose... and since we've had some inquiries about them, this provided a perfect excuse to raise some.

The business side of COUNTRYSIDE hasn't been dull either. We bought out *Small Stock Farmer* magazine (another one of those rabbit journals with a crazy name) and we're in the process of incorporating it into *Rabbit World*. This now makes us by far the biggest rabbit magazine in the country, which is kind of funny when you consider how just a year ago, I was sitting here chatting with a few of you COUNTRYSIDE readers, doing a little printing, and running the homestead. Period. *Rabbit World* circulation has doubled (even without the consolidation) in the past six months, which is gratifying: maybe there really is a place in the straight world for an odd fellow like me!

With *Rabbit World* and *Dairy Goat Guide* going the way they are, I figured it was time I got on the ball and got back to my chosen trade in earnest. So I played journalist, with a trip to Oregon. It was interesting and enlightening in many little ways, and although I didn't pick up anything specifically for COUNTRYSIDE, there were dozens of chance encounters and casual observations that I hope will make me a better editor of this magazine.

For example, I was impressed by the trailer parks, of all things. Here in Wisconsin, trailer parks (or mobile homes courts or whatever fancy name they can dream up) are invariably dull, junky-looking parking lots. Come to think of it, some junkyards look better: at least they have grass and weeds growing around. But in Oregon, at least the ones I noticed, were so surprising simply because they were so different. They reminded me of cottages in little villages, with trees in blossom, flowers and shrubs, and a general appearance of being fit for human habitation. I've seen some pretty dumpy homesteads, and some perfectly charming places, and these trailer parks just struck me with what wonders a little planning and work can achieve.

Oregon seems full of homesteaders, even though most don't call themselves by any special name. Many places are several acres: too small to be farms, but much larger than lots. And people raise rabbits and goats and chickens without thinking too much about it.

I spent most of my time down around Grants Pass where the unemployment rate is close to 20%, which might have something to do with it. Us poor folk seem more amenable to homesteading. Land prices surprised me. I talked with several Realtors, and found that the average is about $1,000 an acre, which will get you some pretty good land here in Wisconsin.

One funny thing happened. I tried to rent a car, but I don't have any credit cards. Just cash, but it wasn't any good. No identification, except for my driver's license. I went to four different places, and got the same story. Finally, one gal said "Do you have some employment identification?" and I happened to think of the sample copies of COUNTRYSIDE I had with me. So I showed her my picture and my name in the magazine, and my driver's license, and got the car.

I told you lots was happening here: that still isn't all.
Early this spring I started clearing rocks off a portion of our 20-acre future homestead in hopes of getting a few crops in. One afternoon with a crowbar was all I needed to convince me that wasn't the way to pick rocks.

I had been looking for a small tractor, but the rocks and boulders presented a real problem. I thought I found the solution when I ran across a 10-year-old bulldozer at a pretty reasonable price. And I had some mad money from my first book, *Country Living.*

Now, operating a bulldozer is quite a bit different from running a typewriter or a printing press. It's certainly different from milking a goat. There, beginners seem to have too many hands and fingers, but on a dozer you don't have enough. And while I was getting the hang of it, a track fell off.

This machine weighs three tons, so when a track falls off you have a problem. I got some professional help. They put it back on and tightened it up.

Then the battery went dead, and the diagnosis was a short in the wiring someplace, but before they could find it, I threw another track. They had to cut a link out. In the process, they got mine buried in the swamp, brought out another bigger one to pull me out and promptly sunk that one too. You might say I haven't had a whole lot of luck with my bulldozer so far.

But there are some COUNTRYSIDE lessons here too. In the first place, I had the thing running long enough to learn that those rocks I was poking at with the crowbar were as big as pianos once the dozer shoved them out. All I could think of was those pioneers doing the job with a team of oxen! We have a dandy pile of stone now, and with my proclivity for masonry, we should have some interesting building projects ahead.

Part of the land I wanted to clear was covered with hummocks as much as two feet high. We had to knock them down before the land could even be plowed, but a crawler with a bucket just couldn't do the job. I later borrowed one with a blade, and was much more successful.

The machine pulls a three-bottom plow, but the combination of stone, sod, and muck is just too much: after breaking a couple of hitches, the tractor drawbar finally cracked. About that time, I left for Oregon.

So right now the place is a disaster area. I've only torn up an acre or so, but it's a narrow strip the entire length of the property, and it looks like we're building a superhighway through the place. With time, a little more practice, and the bugs out of the bulldozer, I think we'll make a homestead out of it. But I'd hate to try it with oxen.

Why a bulldozer? The rocks, which I mentioned. It would've cost $15 an hour to have someone come in with the equipment to clear them out. That might've been a bargain, if it weren't for all the other projects I have in mind. We need a road. We'll be digging a couple of ponds. The machine has power take-off which, added to the increased flotation provided by the tracks, makes it a pretty good tractor for our muckland. And, we can use it to dig a basement, the root cellar, and similar construction projects. But first we have to get it running.

Our bees arrived the first week of May, and seem to be doing much better than last year. We have one hive at Stony Brook, which is woodsy and wild, and one hive here in the village, and it will be interesting to compare the production of the two. Our post office closes at 5 P.M., so I wasn't prepared when the postmaster called me at 7 to ask me to come and get the bees because some were loose and buzzing around the post office. He had stopped in on some kind of hunch, because the mail truck doesn't usually bring such cargo to Marshall.

Anyway, being caught unawares, I couldn't find my bee veil, so I installed them with no protection. No trouble at all. Practice really does make perfect: there was much less fumbling with the queen cages this year. And they're starting to make brood comb, while last year at this time they hadn't even arrived yet.

Back to the garden. Our Stony Brook neighbors, the Lillies, offered to let us use some of their land. That's where our COUNTRYSIDE experiments in small grains will take place. We got some oats planted, but pretty late: there isn't a whole lot of hope there. We'll put in barley and millet, to get the story on growing small grains on a small scale.

All the garlic and Jerusalem artichokes we didn't dig last fall came up eightfold, so with some transplanting we got a good start on these. My bedding plants never did take off like they should have, so I guess I'll have to buy some, but everything else is just about on schedule.

We've had a number of visitors here lately to see the homestead, and expect a lot more, but that's kind of embarrassing. I don't really know what they expect to see or learn, or maybe I write about COUNTRYSIDE in terms that are a bit too glowing, but the place really is a mess. I have a lot of ideas on how things should be, but there's neither the time nor the money to bring them to fruition. We manage to do all right, but this is far from the ideal homestead. So if you do drop by on your vacation, please don't think you'll get much in the way of inspiration or enlightenment here! Don't the shoemaker's children go barefoot?

Each season has its own special charm, but I sorta suspect Heaven must have about nine months of spring. Work? Sure, but with the garden still weedless, the kid goats weaned but still cute and playful, the orchard in blossom, the chicks still cuddly, the goats eating cheap grass instead of hay and in the peak of production, the homesteader's work is more enjoyable than most people's play! Maybe that's the reason more and more people are looking for the good life, beyond the sidewalks.

2014: Several readers informed me that you can indeed skin a hog—and it's much faster and easier. You do lose quite a bit of lard, and the hams are said to not keep as well, but since most people don't use much lard any more anyway and nowadays hams are kept in freezers rather than attics, maybe it doesn't matter. We did skin several hogs later and it was much easier, but for some reason I still prefer scalding and scraping. Which, other readers have told me, has still other variations! For example, you can burn off the hair and scorch the skin with burning straw, or even a blowtorch.

We also learned (from readers, naturally) that lard rendered in the oven rather than on the stovetop results in much less odor, much better lard, and delicious "cracklins'."

And in yet another development, a reader led us to a manufacturer of bell hog scrapers, which in a way led to the Countryside General Store, which eventually overshadowed the magazine as a profitable business.

As for the "reasons" for the bulldozer... shucks, what red-blooded American male wouldn't want a toy like that?

4. August/September 1971

The summer lull: a goat show, more work, and celebrating the 4th of July country-style

2014: The highlight of this piece is the mention of solar and wind power. In 1971, well before the "energy crisis" of 1973, such topics were pretty radical. But, as was to be expected, several readers pitched in with information on the 32-volt systems they'd used in the '30s, before the REA brought electric power to the countryside.

I never did finish building the wind generator described here, and since I'm a mechanical klutz, I'm sure it wouldn't have worked anyway. Later, when knowledgeable people started tinkering with the concept, Mother Earth News *beat us all to heck with their far superior coverage and alternative energy became a hot topic even in the mainstream press,* COUNTRYSIDE *ceded the field: we simply didn't have the resources to compete. It would be more than 25 years before we installed a hybrid wind/solar system that allowed us to brag that the magazine was "printed on recycled paper with soy ink and powered by the wind and sun."*

The pace I told you about last time has slackened a bit, with the heavy spring schedule behind us. Just a bit, though. Here's a rundown on some of the latest activities at COUNTRYSIDE:

In early June, I was show superintendent at the Kid and Buck Show put on by the Wisconsin Dairy Goat Association... and it was fun! As you know, showing goats or rabbits isn't really my cup of tea, even though I write about such shows for Countryside Publications' *Rabbit World* and *Dairy Goat Guide*. I do think showing has much to recommend it, especially for people who are really into goats or rabbits (or any other animals, for that matter). There just never seemed to be much relationship between homestead animals and show animals so far as I was concerned. Anyway, actually getting involved makes something like this more interesting, and I'm sure I learned a few things too. Might even try it again.

Those late oats planted at Lillie's are growing, but it's too soon to tell if they'll beat the heat. (Oats are a cool-weather crop.) We have the scythe all sharpened up, so if they amount to anything, we'll have some information on harvesting grain on a small scale. The way it looks now, though, we'll be lucky to get as much as we planted. We never did get anything else planted there, so the other small grains will have to wait another year.

The potatoes, beans, Jerusalem artichokes and a few other things we planted among the rocks at Stony Brook (the bulldozer still isn't running) are going fine, and for some reason, the garden here at COUNTRYSIDE is unusually weed-free this year. We need rain badly... it's been a very dry season right here, although rain has fallen all around us... but we're in good shape anyway.

I don't know if I mentioned this, but the chicks we got this year were a grab-bag... guaranteed to be heavy breeds, but that's it. And I'm thinking of starting a chicken zoo.

We have birds I've only seen in pictures. Red ones, white ones, black ones, brown ones, chickens colored like pheasants, chickens with feathers on their feet, and the prize has a big mop on its head. That's a Polish. There are Buff Orpingtons, Barred Rocks, and Heaven knows what else. All purebred, but a really motley assortment. Actually, it makes the chicken yard very interesting. How they shape up for the table and feed conversion remains to be seen.

My sister Gretchen was here for a while, helping out with the gardening in the morning, and doing a little writing afternoons. Man, what a life! That's the way I started out here, but the "business" got to be too much. I'd get bored stiff in the garden all day long, I'm afraid, and sitting at a typewriter for 40 hours a week is a ridiculous way to spend your life, so my ideal was (is) to work a few hours a day in the barn or garden or shop, work a few hours at the desk, then have some time for a swim or other relaxing exercise, and wind up the day with some non-business type reading or just plain contemplation. We manage that on a weekly basis, but not daily. Anyway, I just wanted to warn you that if you read anything this time that doesn't quite sound like me, it's Gret.

She was doing something on homemade noodles, which interested me because I guess I just never thought that much about noodles. I was surprised to learn you don't bake them or anything like that: they're just dried. We were discussing this when Judy Ramsdale piped up from her corner that she makes noodles all the time. So, Gret and Judy ended up in the kitchen making noodles. Sometimes it's a wonder how we ever get any magazines published around here, let alone three of them.

Unfortunately, Diane had homemade from scratch pizza on the menu that night. We made chicken noodle soup for a midnight snack. It was good. The recipe is in this issue.

We got our geese, but I don't know what to tell you about them, except that they need a pen. We bought six embdens, put them in the chicken brooder for a couple of days, then decided it was just as warm out in the sun. I put together a temporary pen, but they made it even more temporary than I had planned. It's a shame to keep them cooped up, actually, the way they go waddling around eating grass instead of expensive store-bought feed. But man, are they messy. "Loose as a goose" is no idle expression. Sasha (the collie) got a mite too playful with one a few days after we left them out, and killed it. Another one died just the other day, from unknown causes. So on a percentage basis — 2 out of 6 mortality — I'm not much of a goose farmer, either. They are kinda fun, though, and if Sasha and the chickens wouldn't eat their feed, I don't think we would have made much of a dent in the 50 pound sack yet, so they're fairly maintenance-free. They do take a lot of water, especially since they seem to prefer drinking while standing in it with their muddy webbed feet and we try to keep it clean.

Our neighbors, who have access to the river behind us, have geese and they look like swans when they go floating on the mill pond. Stony Brook, with the stream and the ponds, will be a much better place for these birds, I think.

I like geese, but nobody's going barefoot around here this summer.

I've been working on an article on solar energy for *Organic Gardening & Farming* magazine (an interview with Dr. Farrington Daniels, one of the pioneers of direct use of the sun's energy) so logically my shop time should have been spent on the solar water heater I've been toying with for a year now. But for practical reasons, wind-generated electricity interests me more, as a first homestead power project, anyway. The solar energy will come later.

I'm using an old bicycle to do some experimenting. After a couple of months of spare time (which means an hour or so a week) I have a six foot blade fastened to the pedal sprocket. Sounds simple, but it took four tries. My frame didn't work because the blades, made out of 1/4 inch plywood, bend quite a bit in a heavy wind and they bang against the frame. I'm going to tilt them out a bit, which seems like a good idea anyway to catch more air, and then even if they do give they'll still clear the superstructure.

Following the 1:6 ratio, each of the two-blade propellers is six inches wide and 36 inches long. It takes a good breeze to get it started, but once it goes it really moves. Darn near cut my leg off with it when I was up on the roof testing it out. (What did the neighbors think? They're used to us by now.)

I intend to use the bicycle chain, connect it to the smaller sprocket, and after seeing how many rpm's I get, use the proper (I hope) gear ratio to drive the auto generator I scrounged up. After that, it's all touch-and-go, but at least we'll have some how-to (or maybe just how-not-to!) information for you. This experimental model will put lights in the hen house this winter, if it works. One at Stony Brook will power lights and a radio. If it works — and there's no reason why it shouldn't, with time and patience — there's a whole list of 12 v. goodies that could be connected to the system, including a device for charging more than one battery but only drawing on one at a time; a converter to change D.C. to A.C. so a car battery can run such things as light power tools; a 12 v. refrigerator; motors; and more.

On the Fourth of July, when it seemed like the entire world was cooped up in autos, when the state police detoured traffic off the Interstate Highway near Madison because the road couldn't handle it, we were sitting at home. Somebody suggested that we camp out at Stony Brook, and by the time the boys had the chores done, the girls had the tent and sleeping bags in the car.

For newcomers, I should mention that Stony Brook is hopefully the site of our ideal homestead: 20 acres of oak covered hill, a stream and two springs, and marsh. It's only about four miles from COUNTRYSIDE, so it's ideal for a spur-of-the-moment outing like this.

We climbed the hill and set up a camp, built a fire and threw some foil-wrapped potatoes in it, then just wandered around the woods eating black raspberries, checking the bee hives, and looking over the rough garden. We saw a young raccoon a few yards ahead of us. He looked at us and we looked at him, and when I said "Hi" he scampered away. Didn't see any deer, but we saw tracks.

It was getting dark when we trudged back up through the woods. We sat around the fire until the potatoes were done, then everyone had a hot potato for a "treat." In that setting, a potato went over better than a bag of crispy crunchies in front of the tv set.

We had just settled down in our nests when a little screech owl sat in the tree right over our heads, so we all had to get up to take a look. Anne-marie, especially, was impressed to learn that such a tiny thing could make such a loud and eerie noise... but I'll bet she's just a little more at home with Mother Nature for the experience.

It would have been nice to have made breakfast over the campfire, but we slept late and had to get home for chores again. Five minutes after we were in the car, we were home.

All of us are looking forward to the day when we can live out there full-time. Not only will there be camping right in our own backyard, but we'll be living with the raccoon and the deer and the owl... and all the other wildlife... with the sounds and chance encounters that heighten the thrill and tingle of living in the woods. This place is by no means isolated, or remote. Just unspoiled. We plan to keep it that way. It's not far from school or the fire department, not really removed from pollution or politics or the world's strife... but it's way beyond the sidewalks.

2014: We never did build or live at Stony Brook. We moved to a real, 80-acre (and later 170-acre) farm instead. The village-edge homestead is now well inside the town (with an additional house where we had our garden), and Stony Brook is pretty much a suburb. Gretchen later became a full-time COUNTRYSIDE writer before going on to publish a successful magazine of her own, the Salt Lake City *Catalyst*. And of course, my clumsy efforts at harnessing wind power were obviously ridiculous.

5. October/November, 1971

Searching for a farm

2014: One note really dates this piece: land for $100 an acre! However, you must remember that in 1971 doctors earned around $15,000 a year, editors and reporters got closer to $7,000... and editor/printers of magazines like COUNTRYSIDE were far below average (I mean in salaries, of course).

One interesting fact isn't mentioned here. We bought this 8,000 square-foot three-story brick building on one acre with city water and sewer in

1964 for $5,000. And the bank wouldn't lend us even that much. We borrowed the money from a relative.

The sky was darkening, there was a chilly wind from the east, and I was out on the barn roof, trying to get it closed in before the rain came. And Judy II, (as distinguished from Goat Lady Judy Kapture) who was laying out this issue of COUNTRYSIDE, came out and hollered up, "Hey, you didn't write *Beyond the Sidewalks* yet!"

So here I am. Hello. (Never would've finished the roof before dark anyhow.)

As usual, life on the Belanger homestead is sometimes sad, sometimes hilarious, sometimes maddening, and always busy. The barn is all that wrapped into one, and our life will probably center around it in more ways than one.

To begin with, let's get this "barn" image straight: it's not a barn-type barn, but a homestead barn. It's about 15 by 30 feet, which, according to the *Dairy Goat Guide's* recommendation of 20 square feet per animal, is big enough for 22-1/2 goats. Moreover, it fills the gap between the print shop and the hen house, so it's really more like an addition than a new building. But there's an interesting story or two behind it. Let's go way back.

As most of you charter members of this get-together might recall, our home is an old creamery. It's big. We have ample room for the printing equipment, and a good-sized paper storage area. Then we put the goats in the paper room during the winter, which worked out fine because we didn't even have to go outside to milk or feed them. But that was when we had four.

Now we have 11. They wouldn't fit in the paper room. We could get rid of some of them, especially since we're only milking four (the rest are kids and dry yearlings) and actually we'd get enough milk with the two best. But I have some kind of crazy intuition that makes me want to keep all of them. But where?

We considered moving. Not just because of the goats, of course, but for a variety of little reasons. And brother, does *that* give me some insight into some of the problems prospective homesteaders face! We rejected Stony Brook, the 20 acres we've been dreaming about (and already own) and which some of you have been asking about. There's no road, no water, no housing, no nothing... and we simply don't have the time or the money to start from scratch. We would if it weren't for the magazines... or is that rationalization? At any rate, we were looking for a farm.

We found it, in the area I've told you about before, in western Wisconsin. This is the famous driftless region, untouched by the glaciers that pretty well leveled out most of the rest of the state. It's hills and woods, with few real highways, no major cities, springs on almost every tract of land, and even the farms are sparse because the land is too rough. There's beautiful soil though in the valleys, and land prices are about $100 an acre, compared with an average of perhaps $300-$400 around here, 70 miles to the east.

This place was one of two farms that were on a side road that was off a gravel road that was off a class B highway. It had one of the most picturesque barns I've ever seen, a comfortable home in good repair, and a gushing, frigid spring, complete with springhouse, between the two. A huge garden was beyond the house, and the whole was nestled in a valley overlooked by rocky bluffs that must have been 300 feet above the homestead.

No one was home, so we did some exploring while waiting. We found butternut trees, which I hadn't seen since I was a boy. We watched the ducks puddling in the spring among the willow trees, and envisioned how our geese would look floating on the pond that we'd build between the house and the road. We inspected the vines hanging heavy with grapes, checked the garden and the texture of the soil, the corn fields and the timbers in the barn. Spent a whole afternoon there, and nobody showed up.

But we were sold. And on the way home, Diane remarked how noticeable the "return to civilization" was... more houses, more cars, more crossroads... even though we consider COUNTRYSIDE and Stony Brook "remote" in comparison to Madison, where you can see smog hanging when you dip down into the four lakes basin even though Madison is by no means an industrial city.

At any rate, we got to work. We couldn't buy another place without selling ours, so we got an ad in the paper, and put in an offer to purchase on the other place. We got the first call by 9 A.M. the day our ad appeared, the couple came out that afternoon, and called back that same evening to say they'd take it. And that's when we started to have some doubts.

More background: When we moved here, seven years ago, the place had been abandoned for at least three years. The downstairs was still fitted out as a creamery, and there were two bedrooms, a kitchen, a huge living-dining room, bath, and an unfinished room upstairs. There wasn't a tree on the place (except for one apple, which blew down within a month after we moved in). Half the place was gravel, for driveways for the six milk trucks that used to operate out of here, and the rest was cinders thrown out from the boiler room.... and broken milk bottle glass. The chimney is about 40 feet high and six feet square on the inside, and when I cleaned it out, there were six feet of ashes in there. That's 216 cubic feet.

Well, to make a long story short (it's too late for that... maybe I should go back out on that barn roof?) we made a home out of the place. I hauled in 16 tons of stone and built a 14 foot high waterfall in the old boiler room, complete with a pond and fish. I excavated around that huge chimney and built a sunken fireplace conversation pit... a 21 foot curved couch, facing a six-foot fireplace that will suck you out if you get too close. We tore out walls, put up new ones, raised the floors and lowered the ceilings, made the upstairs into four bedrooms, a loft, and two other rooms, and the downstairs became the atrium, the conversation pit, a living room, dining room, kitchen, utility room, darkroom (the former cooler), print shop (with tile floor and walls: it used to be a butter-making room), and paper-storage-turned-goat barn. This place has about 8,000 square feet, by the way.

And I planted trees. Apple trees, walnut trees, plum trees, cherry trees, pear trees, pines and maples and blue spruce. We got the garden into shape. Put up a suburban-type white fence, built a hen house.

And now to leave it all? Well, don't I always tell COUNTRYSIDE readers to take the rabbit by the ears, do what you *really* want, and forget the past if you decide you got off the track somewhere?

So with our place sold, the coast was clear. We went back to the farm... and found that despite our offer, it had already been sold. Two salespeople were involved, and the paperwork got mixed up, somehow.

Then came a seemingly endless round of Realtors, of trekking in and out of farmhouses that ranged from mediocre to hopeless. The whole situation got to be such a blur that when somebody wanted to discuss the relative merits of one place, nobody else could figure out which place he was talking about. What it boiled down to was, none of them "fit."

And so far as that insight I said I gained to share with you... when I sat down and coldly calculated things, I began to realize that on most of these places, only a quarter of the land was good for anything at all. The rest was too steep, too rocky, too sandy, too dry, even for trees. On a dollars and cents basis, a place that costs $100 an acre there is really no less expensive than one for $400 an acre here.

So you like the privacy and solitude? On one of the best places we found, the taxes were as high as they are here in Marshall, but with not nearly the opportunity of getting the cash to pay those taxes. Heating bills in most of the houses were as high as ours, even though they had only a fraction of the square footage.

And then to be completely realistic, how would we get paper in over those roads for our printing operation? I used to like to brag that I could make a living wherever I had a mailbox... but we get paper in semitrucks that aren't allowed on those gravel back roads. We make at least two trips a day to the post office, to give our readers good service. How much time and travel would that entail? Our kids were starting band, they take piano lessons, they're Girl and Boy Scouts... what does living in the boondocks do to those activities? I used to say homestead living was more exciting and rewarding than other, outside activities, but my children don't always back me up. If I believe in free choice, am I right, or wise, to limit their activities?

These are all questions that came up, were pondered, and didn't get any real answers, because we just didn't find the right place. I liked one, but the house would have required more labor than I've stuck into this one, and with the magazines and other chores, it just wouldn't be possible to keep on any sort of schedule and rebuild a house too.

Putting it all together, we decided Countryside (the homestead) wasn't so bad after all, and we backed out of the sale.

Back to the original dilemma: Get rid of some goats, or build more housing? In view of our experience in the realty business, I thought it would be a good idea to build a two-car garage on one side of the house. It would surely be easier to sell a house, especially an unusual one like this, with three garages than with a goat barn!

The estimates we got all ran over $2,000. Hah, seen my savings account lately? Just wait, I said, the fates will provide. And they did.

We've been going through about a bale of hay a day, picked up on a weekly basis from a neighbor, who charges the going rate. It's about 35¢ a bale in the flush season, and goes up to 90¢ in late winter. But we're using a lot more than we were a year ago, and I hate to impose on him, so I've been looking for a supply at a low price that would carry us through to next spring at least.

There aren't many auctions around here this time of the year, but I found one just on the other side of Stony. The hay was timothy... no good for dairy goats. But, they had piles and piles of lumber and poles. (I had been thinking of a pole building as a cheap construction method.)

Nobody bid on the first pile, and I got it for 25¢. There were 2 x 4's, 2 x 6's, 4 x 4's, and boards. In all, I bought eight piles, at a total cost of... are you ready?... five dollars. I borrowed Ernie Blashka's truck from the feed mill, loaded it to the hilt, and brought home four loads of wood. (Thank goodness it was a dump truck... took an hour to load, and 30 seconds to unload it.)

It wasn't until I got to sorting it out that I really found out what I had bought. There were mostly beams and studs, and very little lumber, but I sure got my five dollars' worth! I started building a barn.

To date, I spent $5 on lumber, $40 on 1/2 inch exterior plywood for part of the roof and a wall, $3.90 on nails, and $20 for four rolls of roofing. And I'll probably have $15 worth of firewood left over. No doubt you'll hear more about this project as it progresses.

Why room for 20 goats? Well, when we made the decision to stay here, I got the idea that it would be interesting to show just what you can do on one acre. We won't have 22-1/2 goats... I hope. But how about a steer for beef? Oh heavens, I'm sure we'll find a use for the space.

We brought our new pig home Saturday night. Put him in the snow fence enclosure Pepper lived in up to his 250 pound butchering weight... and the little rascal got out before we finished chores. Fortunately, we bought him from Blashkas, who live just across the road, and he went straight home to mama (Mabel).

We took some of the posts from the auction and blocked up the bottom of the fence. We brought him back. I wanted to name him Carcass, but the kids ganged up on me and called him Irving. We're not sure if he stayed overnight the second time or not, but he got up awful early if he did, because he was back with Mabel when I went out, at 6 A.M.

I accused Ernie of teaching the thing to fly, so it would come home and he could sell it again, but since he sells feed, he wished I'd keep it here and start feeding it myself.

The course is clear-cut: build a hog-tight pen. Goodness knows we have the lumber! Now we have to find the time.

Actually, we should have started on the new pig right after putting the last one in the freezer, and for a steady supply, we'll even have to double up at times. This is one of those interesting little things you run into on the homestead: how many people know how many pigs (or anything else) they consume in a year? I would have guessed that two would be plenty for our family of six, but we went through one in about three months. Maybe we used a little more pork than usual, but we'd need three a year in any event. Keeping them roughly six months, that means we need facilities for two at a time for at least part of the year.

Bits of information like this are mighty important on a self-sufficient place, and sometimes it seems like the only way to learn is by experience.

About a year ago, when we talked about raising chickens, I voiced my opinion that bargain basement chickens are no bargain. I should have taken my own advice. The motley assortment of meat birds we got this year are still scratching, when any good ones would have been in the freezer long ago. Last year, the chicks we got from Sears were nice plump fryers at 12 weeks, but these (from a local source) aren't big enough to butcher at twice that age. Even the Rhode Island Reds, which we've had good luck with before, aren't worth a darn. Same breed, but different breeding.

The geese are big, and getting mean. There's something about those birds that really turns me on. We won't be letting them run all over the place next year (no point in cooping them up now... the place is hopeless already anyway) but the way they grow without boughten feed is sort of fascinating. Grass, weeds, even corn stalks, seem to be preferable to the grain we put out for them, and that's just fine with me.

Our beehives were only slightly less disappointing than last year. I hadn't checked the one at Stony Brook since a week or so after installing the bees, and was pretty surprised to find not a single bee nor a drop of honey. I doubt if it had anything to do with pesticides, out there, and there was no evidence of disease in the brood comb. Looks to me like a queen problem.

The hive here at COUNTRYSIDE did a little better, but not by much. But we don't expect a whole lot here, surrounded by gardeners with insecticides, and acres and acres of nothing but corn, oats, and hay that's cut before blossoming. Good for the cows and goats, bad for the bees.

As an editor, I'd dearly love to make this Oct-Nov issue a harvest issue... thanksgiving and all that. Here, beyond the sidewalks is where you can really appreciate the meaning of the traditional Thanksgiving. What do city dwellers know about harvests, about the real meaning of fall? What do they know of the anxiety of wondering if you have enough hay and grain to last the winter, how long the cabbages will keep, how to ration out the potatoes to last 'til spring?

But it looks like I'm more of a homesteader than editor, at times at least, and it just isn't in me to sit down and fake a magazine when there's so much to be done around here. There are a few pears left in the orchard, but many more in the freezer. We haven't canned anywhere near the 200 quarts of tomatoes we usually like to see in the root cellar, the dry weather wreaked havoc with a lot of other crops, but all in all, we don't have much to complain about. We're getting a dozen eggs and six quarts of milk a day, the Jerusalem artichokes look fabulous, the freezer is full of green peppers, beans, summer squash, berries, beets, cauliflower, asparagus, and lots of other goodies, the navy beans have been pulled and are drying, we'll mulch the carrots any day now that the nighttime temp has been dipping near freezing, and it looks like we're pretty well set for winter.

And believe me, next year will be better! Eternal hope, my friends, is one of the attributes you pick up out here, beyond the sidewalks.

1995: Chickens... from Sears, as in Roebuck, the catalog company? Oh yes indeed, they sold chickens back then. Our first beehives came from Sears, too. And when we bought the farm a few years later, we learned that the farmhouse was a Sears & Roebuck catalog product!

Businesses must change to keep up with the times, but that's not always easy. Changes ("improvements") in COUNTRYSIDE invariably caused dissent... and look at Sears, today.

Part II: 1972

Gas/gal: 55¢; average annual income, $11,800; Ford Pinto, $2,078; ground beef, 98¢/lb; Frisbee, 98¢. Arab gunman kills 11 Israeli athletes at Munich Olympics. Five White House operatives are arrested for burglarizing the Democratic National Committee offices (Watergate); Digital watch introduced; Apollo 17 lands on the moon, ending that program.

6. December 1971/January 1972

Winter

I like winter. The evergreens about an arm's length away from my window are drooping under the 9-inch load of snow and the whole scene looks just like an old-fashioned Christmas card.

And while the radio is telling about closed roads, people are slipping and sliding to work and cussing the white stuff, I'm sitting here enjoying the view and a cheery oak fire. We have plenty of hay and feed, plenty of food and fuel, and I wouldn't really mind being snowed in all winter!

(Judy didn't make it to work today, so I'm writing this directly on the composer. Any typing mistakes are mine.)

Just got the latest issue of *The Mother Earth News*, and found a two-page article on COUNTRYSIDE. Diane read it and said "Gosh, that sounds like a nice place to live." I thought so too... but it isn't always like that. Maybe that's the reason I tend to bend over backwards sometimes giving the dreary side of things. It's just too easy to give an unrealistic, story-book impression of a homestead! Nothing is a bed of roses, I suppose, and I sure prefer the thorns here to some of the others I've been pricked with.

This really comes to life when I think over the last year. Quite a year. A dismal failure, so far as the homestead is concerned. I'm in deep enough that this could be a full time job, but the magazines just wouldn't let it happen. I don't really know how we got this involved in publishing again, after being out of the business for three years. But that's not worth talking about, because the only one I'd even consider giving up is *Rabbit World*, and we're pretty well stuck with that. The two other rabbit magazines have been for sale for some time, with no results, and with magazines, it costs more to go out of business than it does to keep pluggin' away losing money. Since ours is the biggest (and best) of the three... well, it's better than working at a "normal" job.

But there's gonna be some changes made. "Physician, heal thyself" sort of changes. We have to cut financial losses on the magazines, because we need the money in other areas, and because I'm becoming less convinced all the time that it's honorable to work for nothing.

And then we have to streamline things to cut down on these ridiculous 80 and 90 and 100-hour work weeks. (Wonder why it makes me mad to read about union people getting $7 or $8 an hour for 35 or 40 hours a week?)

Then... it'll be back to the land, to start up again where we left off. The nice thing is, this should actually benefit COUNTRYSIDE magazine. There are so many things I want to do, so much to learn, so many ideas to experiment with... But then, that's why I started that little one page newsletter in the first place! Didn't really mean for it to become a 20-page magazine. That slowed me down a bit.

You'll be hearing a lot more about Stony Brook. I'd enjoy sharing some of my plans with you now, but rather than falling into the trap of writing about dreaming (as opposed to doing) I'll try to control myself. (Our motto is "Tell me what you *did*, not what you're *going* to do.")

But I did get some work done out there this fall, after a complete overhaul on the dozer. Fall plowing of that sod should help considerably by next spring. And I got a lot of stone moved, too. With any luck at all — and with proper planning to have the time available at the *right* time — we'll have some land to plant.

Bob and Ginny Lillie have offered us part of their garden, which must span an acre or so. They didn't even use half of it this year. And they have plans for running some steers on a cooperative basis, too.

So with the garden here, Lillies, and a few acres at Stony Brook for crops, we'll have plenty of gardening to do next spring. We should be milking ten goats (if they're all bred), we'll have geese at Stony even if the pond I started doesn't get dug any deeper (a project cut short by the snow... and the treachery of operating the bulldozer in oozy clay), and the steer. I think our pig operation is going to be all right here at Countryside. We'll need two next time around, but I can't see any problems there.

If I keep chinking the new goat barn every time the wind blows snow in from a different direction, that should be in pretty good shape come spring. I think I ruined the henhouse by building an "addition" right in front of it and cutting off the light, but I'll put the hens in the addition and use the original house for something else.

That's something that might interest you. Our hens were laying pretty well, and some of them were two and three years old. Then I built the new building, just about the time the days seemed to dwindle down to just a few hours out of 24. I thought the skylight might help, but it doesn't do much good unless the sun is really bright.

And egg production fell. Plummeted. We had culled down to about 30 birds, but some days we were lucky to get 3-4 eggs. Our egg customers didn't even bother calling anymore.

So I put the chickens in the new shed. It has windows on three sides, so it's plenty light. Didn't make any difference. I left the lights on in the house. No eggs. We now have the most expensive eggs in town. $1 a dozen just for feed.

That doesn't set very well with me. I hate to think of plucking those scrawny leghorns en masse... but I have an order in for 50 ready-to-lay pullets. It'll be all out-all in (except for the Bantams and the Black Majorcas, which are in a class by themselves).

What happened? Could be age, although I've had birds older than this that still layed pretty well. And these weren't all the same age, so why would the younger ones quit at the same time as the old ones? Moult? Nope.

The lighting certainly makes a difference, and maybe the combination of short days and the blocked daylight was enough to do them in. I was sort of hoping they might come back, or at least some of them, but I can't afford to wait any longer just to experiment.

Half a dozen hens are enough to supply our needs, but I find it's no more work to take care of 50. Even a hundred might not be any worse, but then I think I'd run into marketing problems. We know enough people to take care of our surplus with 50 or so... and there are even a couple of salesmen calling on the print shop who always leave with a few dozen farm fresh eggs. If we had to sell eggs wholesale, it wouldn't be worth it. I should have gotten new chicks six months ago, but that's only one of many, many things that didn't get done here six months ago.

Judy asked why we always turn on the chicken lights when it gets dark. In case you don't know either, here's a very sketchy explanation:

Light entering the eyes stimulates activity in the pituitary and pineal glands, and possibly other areas of the mid-brain, in addition to enabling vision to function. And for some reason I know nothing about, that makes hens lay more eggs. Light affects other animals too. *Rabbit World* ran an article on its effect on rabbits.

And some research I ran across claims that pink florescent light tends to make eggs infertile, while daylight white light doesn't have that effect. We could go into the stories from people who swear blue light in the buck barn produces doe goat kids, while red light produces buck kids, but that's a little too far afield for now.

But the idea with chickens is to simulate the natural lighting conditions present if we weren't messing around trying to make them lay when ordinary birds aren't supposed to. Commercial egg people have completely controlled lighting and claim to get 5% to 6% more egg production, with 12 to 15 more eggs per hen per year, and bigger eggs during the pullet stage. They have the hen house lighted for eight hours a day while the birds are growing, then up it to 13 hours when they start laying. This is increased 15 minutes a week, so that the birds are in the light for 20 hours when they're 60 weeks old. Then they keep it steady at 20 hours a day.

There are other, more complicated schedules for growers that make use of natural light, but all I'm trying to point out is that when the sun comes up at seven, and is gone by four, you don't get many eggs without lights in the hen house.

Good grief, some people get carried away when they talk about chickens. Forgot what I was talking about.

I guess the main point is that in the winter, on the homestead, all the year's mistakes are behind us. After Christmas the new seed catalogs will be arriving, and we'll be doing all the planning and dreaming that event brings. I for one will be trying to cram five acres worth of plantings on a half-acre plot, like I do every year... at least until I total up the bill and start cutting back on the frills!

It's a season of rest, for the most part. A time to reflect. But somehow, reflecting isn't nearly as much fun as planning. I have a bunch of new books to read, to get new homestead ideas. The magazines will be gone over more carefully, the garden will be plotted out on paper, and plans will be made for livestock and other projects.

Then by January we'll have a pig to butcher, in February the goats start kidding, in March the bedding plants get started... and we're off and running again.

No wonder I like winter. Even if we have snow from November to April, real winter only lasts from Thanksgiving to Christmas out here, beyond the sidewalks.

Footnote on the above: The new birds arrived. And here's some information worth sharing.

I never bought started pullets before, but I kept good records on day-old chicks. They show it costs me $1.64 per bird to raise them to laying age.

The birds we got are 18 weeks old, and cost $1.70.

The extra few cents seems like a small enough price to pay for the 18 weeks of feeding, watering and cleaning I got out of. Chicks are much more fun, of course, but we're out of eggs *now.*

2001: Nowadays we usually get an egg a day per hen right through the winter, and without lights. But we only keep the birds for two years. (And in 2014, *day-old* chicks cost more than $2.50.)

7. February 1972

Let the doomsaying begin

2001: This appears to be one of the first real "doomsaying" pieces I wrote. (But note how I was egged on by a reader!)

When other readers disagreed, I backed off... until another doomsaying reader would get me started again. My own apprehension about the future was more-or-less constant, but it was reader reaction that determined what I put in the magazine. (The good news/bad news in the daily papers also played a role.) This pattern was to be repeated often, until I felt like a bent paper clip: ready to break.

Dear Jerry: We enjoy your thoughts and find they often parallel our own. However, we feel the problems will not be solved in time as the populace of the world will not be willing to make the necessary sacrifices. Therefore, nature will make the decision, and away we go! —*Virginia Moore, Terre Haute, Ind.*

You could very well be right. And if you are, I know how it will happen, having figured it out one day while picking strawberries.

Up to the end, people were belittling the prophets of doom. We'll never run out of oil, they laughed, driving their high powered cars two blocks to the drug store for cigarettes. We can always drill deeper water wells, they shrugged as they poured phosphates and sewage into the streams. Who gives a hoot about a couple of crummy brown pelicans they said, as they spread DDT on their crops.

Man is a very adaptable creature, they said, and they adapted to the pall hanging over the cities, to the millions of acres of fertile farmland turned into superhighways and parking lots, to additives in their food. They took pills for nutrition, got up and stretched every half hour to change tv channels for exercise, read the newspapers to add excitement to their drab lives... and they were content.

They complained when the price of gasoline went up, but they adapted. The cost of electricity rose and they grumbled. And they paid more for many goods and services because the people who provided them said they were trying to clean up the environment and that was good, because it was a way of adapting.

But it didn't seem to help. Oh, the people still used throwaway bottles, because it was so much bother to take them back, and what difference did a few bottles a week make anyway? They still used plastics and other disposables because the neighbors did, so a little more didn't make much difference. And when taxes went up because the sanitary landfill was more filled than sanitary, and the sky seemed to get darker, they adapted and were proud of themselves.

They read about the emphysema rate and tsked, they watched dead fish wash ashore on tv and sadly shook their heads, they watched the price of lumber soar, and they said, "Why doesn't somebody DO something?" but nobody did.

And little by little, over the land, there was sickness and death. Some people said it was from the chemicals in food, others said it was because of foreign matter in the air and water, and still others said it was a communist plot. "But we have good doctors and scientists and drug companies. We will adapt."

But the doctors and the scientists and the chemists couldn't find out what was wrong, and some of them got sick and died too. And the truck drivers who brought food to the cities couldn't work, and when some of them could, they couldn't get through because the roads weren't kept in repair because the repair crews were sick or their trucks wouldn't run and the mechanics were sick and the well ones couldn't get parts because the people who made *those* were sick and the people who did make some parts couldn't ship them because the trucks couldn't run without drivers and road repair crews and mechanics.

"Let's adapt to this," the people said. So they formed a committee.

Some people on the committee thought they should clean up the environment. But others said, "No, that would hurt business" or "That would cost too much." So they did nothing.

By this time, the cities were deserted, because there were no jobs and no food, and because with so many deaths and no medical help and no sanitation many new diseases appeared, killing even more. So after a time there were just a few widely scattered people left, living as best they could.

The aerospace engineers and mathematicians and embalmers who were left had to learn to provide their own food. Even the farmers who had done the job before had to learn new techniques, because they had no tractors or machinery, no electricity, no chemicals. But they adapted.

And in the evenings, the mathematicians and computer operators and airline pilots told their sons about how the world used to be. The sons listened with awe, and years later, when they told their own sons, the stories got a little mixed up. The ideas lived on, but it was more important to learn the things necessary to keep alive.

A tin can rusting in the garden will disappear in a few years, turned back into the soil it came from. It takes a little longer for buildings of glass and steel to disappear, but they did. Bridges, roads, machinery, buildings: all crumbled or rusted and the particles were blown away until not a trace remained. And the old stories, having lost any semblance to reality, were retold in terms people could understand, and the inhabitants of the old world became as gods.

"This is the way the world ends:" T. S. Eliot said, "not with a bang, but a whimper."

But man is adaptable, and he slowly climbed back. He rediscovered all the things that had been forgotten. He built cities and bridges and vehicles that could go out into space and universities and weapons of great destruction. He discovered everything that had been learned millions of years before: except one. He didn't learn that — man is not as adaptable as he thought.

This happened many times. There seemed to be a plateau beyond which mankind could not evolve. But one time, there happened to be a large number of people who were not like the rest, which is the basis for improvement of a species in all evolution. They did not try to accumulate as many material goods as possible, because they saw that this meant their brothers would have less, and they realized that merely owning things added nothing to their pleasure or well-being. They did not work for the sake of working, but for the joy; they did not accumulate goods indiscriminately, but gathered only what was needed. The center of their lives was not labor, but living.

Not only did they not try to dominate other people, they did not try to dominate nature just to show that they were as gods, and they observed

*her as they would a loving mother, and tried to live in the pattern of her
teachings. And when they pursued the arts and sciences in this frame of
mind (rather than in the quest of gaining more wealth and power than
their brothers) they made a further amazing discovery:*

**Human beings actually *were* more godlike than even the most
advanced thinkers of previous levels had guessed. The dreams of
countless utopians in previous eons could come true: with no greed
and small thinking, there is no war; no "bad times." If the measure
of a man is not what he has but what he is, the measure of a nation
(or a world) should be the same.**

Is this the point in the cycle? Time will tell.

If it is, some people are ready. If it isn't... it doesn't make a whole lot
of difference, as long as we've done our part to make a big enough
impression to secure a place in the myths and legends that will be
carried on. That way, maybe *next* time...

**2014: There is a certain amount of naiveté here, along with a
basic theme that the magazine never did address head-on; viz., in
cosmic time, humans appeared on Earth only moments ago, and
while we act as if we have achieved perfection, in reality we have
barely begun to evolve to achieve our potential. Not until re-
reading these essays did I discover what was really bugging me all
those years! There's more on this in the final chapter, but it could
fill a book by itself.**

Part III: 1973

Inflation hits 6.16%; average income, $12,900; year-end Dow, 850; dozen
eggs, 45¢; men's paisley slacks, $23.95; OPEC restricts flow of crude oil to
countries supporting Israel; oil prices increase by 200%; Roe vs. Wade
makes abortion a constitutional right; Closing auto plants idle 100,000
workers; World Trade Center becomes tallest building in the world; Jet ski
and barcodes introduced; Endangered species Act signed; US troops
withdrawn from Viet Nam.

8. January 1973

A winter project

Ah yes, homesteading's the life! Work hard in the warm summer
sun, and then when winter comes you just relax around the
fireplace drinking hot cider and maybe carding a little wool or
something to keep from getting bored.

If you're a homesteader, you know what a fairy tale *that* is! I suspect we Belangers are pretty close to average, and here's what we've been up to lately.

As soon as the Nov./Dec. issue of the magazine was in the mail, I picked up my tool box and started looking for all the tools that were taken from it and left in the garage, the print shop, the machine shed, and under the seat of the truck. And then I tackled phase II of our remodeling project.

In case you're new here, we live — and work — in a recycled creamery. We had done a lot of work on the place already, but there were still bedrooms without closets, bare light bulbs dangling from the ceiling where fixtures should have been, and various walls, floors, ceilings, doors and windows that needed work.

I'm no carpenter. But when you buy an abandoned building and try to make a home out of it even though you don't have much money, you learn. It's amazing what you can do when you have to.

So I sawed and hammered and plastered and did some wiring and Diane painted and papered and Bob Lillie helped with some cabinet work... and that was our vacation for the month we don't publish.

Part of the project involved moving the office out of the living room to a spare room upstairs. Naturally, when we got back in here with new surroundings, with piles of books stacked from floor to ceiling, with wall to wall boxes of letters and pictures and magazines and even unopened mail, I didn't really feel like I'd been on vacation.

Of course, as is to be expected on any normal homestead, about this time our faithful but rusty old car refused to start at all, Sasha (one of our collies) had 13 puppies, and John got the measles. Is it any wonder my lambs' tails seldom get docked and my meat chickens lay eggs?

Somehow, it all seems funnier now than it did two weeks ago.

We had a nice Thanksgiving dinner here. Almost all the dinner, including of course the goose, was grown right here, there were some dandy hickory logs from our woodlot in the fireplace, and three guitars, a piano, mandolins and other assorted noisemakers (plus singing) after dinner.

And we had as much fun as the city cousins when we took a troop of goats for a hike down the road later on.

Then winter hit.
      Every year about this time I tell you how much I like winter. I

don't mind the cold. I love snow. It's the truth, but there's one qualification: I hate watering animals in freezing weather!

It's been 13 below here and everybody seems thirstier than they were when it was 90 in the shade. I use very warm water but everything is frozen solid by noon. I usually try to give everybody all they want, then take the containers away so they don't freeze, but this involves twice as much running around, even if it means I don't have to thaw out goat buckets, sheep buckets, chicken and rabbit and goose fountains.

Winter would be a lot more fun on the homestead if water didn't freeze.

R emember a few issues ago when Bob Bennet was talking about his watch rabbit? We have one here that I think might win out over Bob's.

He's a cull who just sort of hangs around. He spends his days visiting the pigs, the chickens, the geese and the goats. And he chases dogs.

He must have learned from Mellow, a collie who loves to play. She'd paw at him, egging him on, he'd run after her and they both loved the game.

But Mellow is in heat and we keep her in the house. Mr. Rabbit has no one to play with. So when a stray dog wandered onto the place, Mr. Rabbit took off after him lickety split!

This has happened more than once, and I'll bet those dogs are as amazed as the neighbor who told me, rather slack-jawed, that unbelievable as it was, he swore he saw a rabbit chasing a dog!

A pparently some of our readers think rabbits—or goats or pigs— are pretty dumb animals. No personality, no individuality, just blah beasts.

Could it be because they've never known a goat or a rabbit personally?

In a magazine like this, where our primary concern is something other than animal's personalities, we take it for granted that you know how lovable they are.

Everybody knows how fuzzy and cute an Easter bunny is, but only rabbit breeders know about pranksters like Mr. Rabbit. Fewer people are aware of just how delightful goats are. You have to see them in action to appreciate them, I suppose, but for my part, when it comes to companionship, intelligence, entertainment or you-name-it, I'd take a goat even in preference to a dog.

This means that our animals are not just machines, to be maintained for production. They aren't plants, to be cared for and harvested. They act and react and interact in such a way that they provide much more than just meat, milk or eggs to the people who care for them . . . and about them.

A homestead without animals is just a garden. Gardens are all right if you're a vegetable, but barns are much more interesting and full of life. And I, personally, love life. There's a big difference between the meaningless whirlwind we associate with the ratrace, and the fulfillment-action we have here.

Just last weekend, Judy Kapture was here working on the goat section, my sister Gretchen came to record the sound of a printing press for a choreography class at the university, somebody came to have a kid goat disbudded, other homestead friends dropped by to show us their funky new 1955 pickup truck, we got a call from a health food store for more Jerusalem artichokes, two people came to buy goat milk, Dave was butchering rabbits, there were a couple of phone calls about the magazine, and we ended up with ten people eating supper here.

Later, Judy, Diane and I were sitting around the fireplace, talking goats and magazines and homesteading, and the events of the day, of all past days, began to drift by like the smoke being wafted out the chimney. Is any life "perfect?" What really is the criteria for "making it?"

We have a roof over our heads, enough to eat, we have each other... and a dream. An afternoon of convivial fellowship followed by a quiet evening of discussion around a cheery oak fire makes me think that maybe it isn't such a bad world after all.

Not with the joys and pains, the values and rewards, beyond the sidewalks!

Afterword: This was when I learned (from readers) that warm water freezes faster than cold water, and that even Aristotle knew that! It is now called the Mpemba effect.

9. February 1973

It's time for vinegar pie, and valentines

((The only good thing about February is that it's short."

Oh, in gentler climes the early gardens are getting started, but up here our biggest heating bill of the year comes in February. The seed catalogs, now getting pretty dog-eared, are approached like some kind of fairy tale. Is there really a warm sun, and grass and flowers?

Why certainly, there will be a spring. The bees will fly, the plum blossoms will perfume the whole area, the snow will disappear from the garden and that hard-as-a-rock soil will once more be soft and crumbly. And this year we're going to have the biggest, most productive, most weed-free garden ever!

Seems like I've said that before. Probably in another February.

Ever wonder what this time of the year was like for the real, old-time pioneers? Our apples are shriveled like prunes, the potatoes are starting to get soft, the winter squash is in the last stages of edibility, the hens wouldn't be laying at all without the electric lights, most of the goats are dry in preparation for kidding, we lost way too many baby rabbits in the cold, and in general, the larder that was filled with good things to eat just a short time ago now looks more like a warehouse for empty glass jars. What did the pioneers who didn't have grocery stores nearby eat at this time of the year?

Well, for one thing, they had vinegar pie.

In late winter, when all the canned and dried fruit was gone, housewives made use of what they had. To tell the truth, I had never heard of vinegar pie, but a newspaper columnist who writes about his grandmother's old recipes recently said he couldn't find her recipe for vinegar pie, and could his readers help him out? He got 103 recipes.

Diane made two of them. One had a vinegary taste, although it was more like the acid of lemon and certainly wasn't as objectionable as "drinking vinegar" would seem to be. The other honestly didn't taste anything at all like vinegar. **(Note: Switchel, a traditional haying drink, actually is made with vinegar; some people consider it quite refreshing in hot weather. Try 2 Tbs cider vinegar, 4 tsp sweetener such as honey or maple syrup, ¼ tsp ground ginger and 1 cup water. You can add lemon juice, fresh berries, mint leaves, etc.)**

Diane's super-flaky pie crust, made with home rendered lard, can make any pie a delight, I admit, but these really were good.

All of which adds just a little more evidence to the nagging suspicion that the old-timers didn't really have it so rough after all: we've been brainwashed into thinking we can't survive without tv dinners and instant this or that.

Here are the recipes.

Vinegar Pie No. 1

Beat well:

One egg

One heaping tablespoon flour

One teacup sugar (3/4 cup?)

Add:

One tablespoon sharp vinegar

One teacup cold water

Flavor with nutmeg and bake with 2 crusts.

Vinegar Pie No. 2

One cup of sugar, one-half cup of vinegar, two teaspoons of flour, one teaspoon butter, one teaspoon of cinnamon, two cups of water. Boil all together 'til thick, and bake as you would a custard pie. (Note: The columnist said he didn't think it would thicken with two teaspoons of flour, so he used two tablespoons, and "In a taste test at the *Wisconsin*

State Journal, three out of five said they liked this pie the best." Diane cooked hers too long, waiting for the filling to get thick, but it doesn't thicken until it cools. This filling is very dark, almost like jelly.)

Aside from making and eating vinegar pies and planning the new garden, homestead activity is pretty much at a standstill in February. There are a lot of things that should be done… the rotary tiller was acting up last fall and should be checked out, we really should draw up some plans for the new hog pen we're going to build this spring, I'd like to get an incubator for the goose eggs this year, and the brooder, the sheep shears, the kid pens and 1001 other things should be checked out before the spring rush… but then, February is so short there really isn't time to do all that anyway, is there?

The fireplace is the heart of our homestead at this time of year. We don't heat with wood because we have a "modern" house — which means that when the fuel oil dealer runs out of fuel, we'll have to freeze. (That's happening this year, which amazes even me although I've been writing about the energy crisis for a couple of years now. I didn't think I meant *now*.)

I know many people will argue against my fireplace. In fact, I heard a rumor not long ago that fireplaces were going to be banned under air pollution regulations.

Yet, one of the sharpest pleasures of living in the North is being outside in zero degree air splitting wood and hauling hay or ice skating, then coming inside to a roaring fire and a cup of hot chocolate. To my nose, the pungent aroma of good wood smoke is no more "pollution" than the odor of new-mown hay. There's more entertainment in an evening of watching the dancing, ever-changing flames of a good fire, than a week of tv programs. There's more to contemplate in a glowing fire than in a half-dozen of most modern books.

And whoever heard of a family cracking walnuts and singing songs while sitting around a gas furnace? Our woodlot keeps us well supplied with oak, and getting the wood is almost as much fun as basking in its warmth. When there's so little to do outside, it's a pleasure to have an excuse for spending time in the woods.

Since the only thing of note that happens in February is Valentine's Day, this seems like a good month to tell you about someone who's very important to the magazine, but who doesn't get mentioned very often.

My own Valentine, Diane. Without Diane, there probably wouldn't be a COUNTRYSIDE & SMALL STOCK JOURNAL, because I'd most likely be bumming around on a tramp steamer or something.

But even more important, she does a fantastic amount of work on the magazine. She's the one who opens all the mail and reads every word of it. She takes care of all the subscriptions, all the book orders, and all the little complaints and problems that seem to crop up no matter how hard we try to avoid them. Since the two of us are the entire full-time "staff," she gets to do a little of everything.

All this, of course, is in addition to being the mother of four children and a homestead wife. She bakes bread, makes cheese, weeds the garden, cans hundreds of quarts of good things to eat and freezes more... and she's the one who gets stuck with the pin feathers after everybody else gives up after a chicken butchering session.

She's been active in Girl Scouts for several years, and her favorite pastime, sewing, too often falls by the wayside as she tends to the demands of the rest of us.

Diane lived on a farm for awhile, but was never as excited as I was about homesteading. In fact, although we'd been talking about it since the mid-50's, it wasn't until she started reading COUNTRYSIDE and found that other seemingly sensible women enjoyed homesteading that she showed any real enthusiasm for it.

She's always in charge of the kid goats, and has been taking a special interest in the rabbits. She can unstick stuck zippers that I can't budge, untangle balls of string I would throw out in disgust, find things that everybody else is 1000 per cent positive the fairies stole, and being a registered nurse, is at her best when somebody's sick and needs a little TLC, be it family, neighbor or livestock.

She hates ironing, loves flowers and newborn goats, gets very upset with people who send money for subscriptions or books and don't include their addresses, and wistfully wishes we could take a real vacation at least once in our lifetime.

Women's lib leaves her cold, she says. She's a woman, and likes it. Of course, that doesn't keep her from driving the bulldozer, helping to build a shed, load hogs, castrate goats, dock lambs' tails... just so long as nobody sees her with her hair mussed, her hands rough and dirty, or manure on her shoes. Nor does it prevent her from allowing me to do the cooking, the dishes or the laundry once in awhile.

She is also the best proofreader I've ever worked with—and you'd be surprised at how many errors can creep into 64 pages when only two people get to check them. She won't be proofing this because if she sees it before it gets in print she won't let me run it.

Happy Valentine's Day.

Looking at the snow-covered garden, the barren trees and the tightly closed house and barns, everything seems to be in hibernation. But there's always an undercurrent of life on the homestead. Next month we start the bedding plants. The first kids and lambs are due any day now.

Even in the "dead" season, life goes on, beyond the sidewalks.

Afterwords (2001 note): Today of course, fireplaces are out, but there were no decent wood stoves in early 1973. (A short time later there would be about 400 different manufacturers in the U.S., and they became much more efficient.) Now we have not only an airtight stove insert in the old-fashioned fireplace, but also a thermostatically controlled wood-burning furnace in the basement... and an 80-acre woods that provides plenty of firewood as well as maple syrup and much more. (We also have some grandsons who love to split and stack wood!)

2014 update: This was the winter from hell: bitter cold that made the polar vortex familiar even to those who never studied meteorology or climatology; and a shortage of the LP gas many rural homes are heated with, due in part to high demand last fall for drying corn. Those of us with wood heat were encouraged to use it to conserve gas because not only did the price triple within days: for some people it was unavailable at any price. How does this mesh with The American Dream?

10. March 1973
The homestead comes alive in spring

Here in the north, March is the month when the homestead starts to come alive.

And brother, is ours jumpin'.

By March, the celery, tomatoes, peppers, cabbage, broccoli and a few odds and ends are starting to sprout in the flats. We're keeping the bedding plants in the print shop this year, since our old "greenhouse" is now the office.

I know I'm getting to be a better gardener: this year I didn't have to go out and scrape up frozen dirt in February to get the plants started. We had a few boxes of soil tucked away in a corner of the machine shed.

Starting seeds in flats while it's still way below zero outside is fun, but there are perils to this kind of gardening too. Some people worry about dampening off, but a bigger problem for us is the cat, who thinks a flat is a sandbox.

Among other winter activities here is my back-to-school experience. Dairy science. We talk about goats quite a lot: it's surprising how interested those cow dairymen are in goats.

This adult class is a lot like college. Maybe you don't learn much in class, but the rap sessions afterwards are most enlightening. For example, there are guys who snort at organic farming, but still think feeds today don't have the nutrition they used to, or that some unknown factor in overfertilized hay causes health problems, and so on. Very interesting.

Outside, of course, it's still winter, more or less. What we're experiencing now is just a two-month January thaw.

This weather is going to be awfully tough on some of the overwintering plants, like alfalfa, and the plowed land that's frozen underneath and thawing on top is taking a beating. I don't recall that Faulkner even mentioned this type of damage in *Plowman's Folly.*

On the other hand, the weather has been terrific for ice skating.

With not a flake of snow for months, and the alternate thawing and freezing, the ice on the mill pond just across the road is as smooth as glass. The pond is usually snow-covered, and we skate in little circles (as big as the neighborhood kids care to clear off) and it's about like skating in Rockefeller Plaza. But this year, we can skate for miles upstream.

I love to skate at night, myself. With a full moon shimmering on the ice, the temperature just brisk enough to firm up the ice and put a little sparkle in your lungs, the sensation of skimming over the center of the Maunesha River is something to experience. I'm always amazed that more people aren't out there: could they be sitting watching tv when such pleasures await them just outside their doors?

All six of us have skates, and we've been using them. And I'll bet we have the biggest hot chocolate bill in town!

For some reason, I was expecting a real old-time winter. I spent a couple of hours last fall putting the snowblower and tire chains on the garden tractor, and I have yet to use it. The one day it did snow here, the battery was dead, naturally.

About this time of the year I always look back to last year's records to help decide what to plant. Seems like finally, after 10 years in the country with large gardens, we hit on the right formula. We still have plenty of potatoes, tomatoes, honey and other staples on the shelves and in the freezer.

But was it our planning, or the weather and other factors? After awhile you get too smart to feel proud about being lucky.

This year it'll probably snow in July and louse everything up just because I think I'm finally learning something.

We have all our seed ordered (and some should be growing in those flats by the time you read this), the order for package

48

bees has been sent, and I'm about ready to order some new chicks, so we're itching for spring to arrive.

And this year, spring holds a special excitement for us: it's sure to be one we'll never forget.

We're moving. To a farm. (I didn't want to start this chat with the big news, because I knew I'd never get to anything else!)

It's not *"the"* farm, the homestead of my dreams for the past 15-20 years. It's a working, 80 acre hog and beef operation. Of course, it will be a homestead once the Belangers get at it! And with better facilities for the goats, rabbits and chickens, as well as room to grow our own feed, I expect to be able to do a better job of raising small stock and consequently of editing the magazine.

The livestock aspect of Countryside Homestead just sort of got tacked together as the need arose. The only way to salvage it would be to tear everything down and start all over. But we did want more room anyway. There are a bunch of new houses going up down the road... and the time has come to move on.

We'll miss this place. We've put untold hours of labor into it, and we've learned a lot. In fact, before we leave, I'd like to share some of those experiences with you. So in one of the upcoming issues you'll be invited to a farewell visit through the magazine.

The new place has a Waterloo, Wisconsin address, but it's only about six miles east of here on the same Highway 19 we're almost on now, so it isn't a major relocation. We get possession of the farm in March, but won't be moving until the middle of June, when the sellers' new home is finished. (That means a six-mile commute to do chores.)

There is absolutely no doubt that you'll be hearing lots more about it in the months to come. Watch for more, from way beyond the sidewalks.

2014: The homestead on the edge of the village was the last house on the block and literally, just beyond the sidewalks. Today there are dozens of homes beyond it, but so far as I know, no sidewalks. Nobody uses them anymore.

11. April 1973

Shopping for farm machinery

S pring seems to be taking forever to get here this year. Oh, the weather is fine so far—but spring on the homestead is a very special season in ways that have no relation to the weather.

Spring is newborn goats and lambs, for one thing ... and we don't have a single one of either, yet. Nor do we have fluffy chicks or goslings. Matter of fact, the first goose egg arrived only yesterday.

On the other hand, we know spring is coming because the yard is a sea of mud, and we have a pile of work that boggles the mind.

One of the time-consuming tasks I've had to take care of lately was shopping for machinery in anticipation of the full-scale farming we'll be involved in shortly. And after looking at tractors, plows, discs, drags, grain drills, corn planters, mowers, conditioners, wagons, balers, manure spreaders, combines and silo fillers and on and on, you begin to appreciate the quip that farmers never have any money until they're dead and their estates are settled.

We've also acquired two homestead-type items that might be of interest to you: an incubator, and a garden seeder. Neither is very high on the list of absolute necessities, I'll admit.

The incubator was purchased for the goose eggs, primarily— assuming we have a gander, which I'm still not certain of! We have a batch of chicken eggs in it right now, partly to check it out, and partly because we didn't have any goose eggs nor the patience to let it stand idle.

Steve is in charge of turning the eggs and the one he dropped yesterday had a little chick inside, so it looks like it's going to work.

This came from Sears, by the way, for $31.25. It's supposed to hold 100 chicken eggs, 80 turkey or duck eggs, or 40 goose eggs. We must have large eggs: we couldn't possibly get 100 in it.

The seeder is something else: a regular Rube Goldberg contraption. It's a two-wheeled affair (lined up like a motorcycle) with a handle with a seed box. You push it like a lawnmower. It opens a furrow, plants the seeds with the proper spacing and covers them up, all in one operation. There are six different seed plates, for everything from carrots to corn. You can space seeds 1-1/2, 2-1/2, 3 or 8 inches apart.

I don't know how it'll work in actual practice, but the mechanism was so fascinating we were "planting" beans all over the living room carpet the day it came. In a garden the size of ours, it should save some labor but the thing that interested me most was the automatic spacing of those tiny seeds. I always tend to pile them up, which results in a tedious amount of thinning later, which means a waste of seeds and labor.

Got this from Sears, too. If you haven't seen their farm catalog, get a copy.

Feed prices continue to be a prime factor in livestock raising. Ernie Blaschka lists feed prices at his mill on a chalk board, and the eraser is really getting a workout these days. In fact, he said the price on one protein supplement jumped $17 a ton from one order to the next, and before he got the bill he was selling it below cost.

The price of hay has come down, but the quality is so poor you simply must use more protein supplements. And those prices are ridiculous.

Purina Rabbit Chow is selling for $8 a hundredweight here now.

There are some new corn problems, too. A lot of it is moldy. In fact, some of it that looks all right has some kind of fungus that's killing pigs and causing abortions.

Up to now corn was just plain old corn at the auctions around here. But lately, the sellers have been providing an analysis of the moisture content and the bushel weight, both indicators of whether this mold might be present. Some farmers won't touch corn that weighs less than 52 lbs. per bushel.

I haven't seen any technical data on this, but apparently the mold doesn't affect beef cattle. Obviously then we don't know what effect it might have on our rabbits and goats.

The spring workload is picking up tempo already, and when it peaks this year we might as well take the hands off the clock. But who needs a clock anyway, when you live and work beyond the sidewalks?

2002: I still have, and use, the Esmay seeder, and wouldn't bother planting carrots in particular without it. But only later did I learn that a similar tool was popular way back in the 1800s.

And while we've been commenting on price inflation in the past 30 years, I was rather surprised to see the price of Purina Rabbit Chow. Until I realized that the $8 I paid recently was for a 50-lb. bag, not a hundredweight! *(2010 note added: Now make it 40 years... and $15 and up for 50 pounds.)*

Since Ernie Blaschka appears to be a regular in the cast of players in these accounts, you might be interested in knowing that a son and daughter now run the feed mill—which might be the only water-powered mill still operating in Wisconsin—and that Ernie still shows up at work, in his eighties. (2014 note: He died last year at age 94.)

12. May/June 1973

The lull before the storm

"Well, Jer, how's the farming going?"

Funny you should ask. I was sort of trying to forget about it.

Last week I was probably the only guy in the whole world with a broken-down tractor hooked up to a broken-down manure spreader. The spreader was loaded, of course: they only break down when they're loaded.

Just about everybody else in the township was planting oats while I put a new generator on the tractor and a new PTO shaft on the spreader. And then, although it sounds made-up I swear it's the truth, a track came off the bulldozer I was using to load manure, and a tire went flat on the tractor.

Is it any wonder I like animals better than machinery? Of course, along about then was when the hog market had dropped $11 since I bought my pigs.

If it sounds like things have been in an uproar on the farm, you're right. But that's only a part of what goes on around here, and everything else seems to be in almost as much turmoil.

And yet, this is the lull before the storm, so far as the homestead is concerned. All the sheep and goats have lambed and kidded, but the kids are still getting the milk so we don't have to make cheese yet. The tomatoes are growing lustily in the flats, the peppers look great, and the other bedding plants are doing well, but it's been too wet to do anything outside.

This is in contrast to letters we've been getting from people in more sensible climates, where the sunflowers are two inches high already. That's all right, we'll catch up.

(That was written last week. Would you believe we have eight inches of snow now, and the forecast is for a foot by tonight.)

No doubt you've noticed the change in our appearance the last few issues. This is due to Lynn Grosz, who is doing the layout now so I can be a tractor mechanic. Lynn and her husband, Ron, have a few goats, chickens and rabbits, she's been talking about doing a craft column, and she does a nice job with the art. Same old magazine — just a bunch of us farmers sitting around chatting — so I told her not to get *too* uptown. But it doesn't hurt to have a little class.

Speaking of chatting, we've had a few letters lately from folks who are a mite peeved at one thing or another that gets said here. One of them put it rather succinctly: "What makes you think you know so much?" (Funny: That's what my mother says.)

For the benefit of newcomers, let's get something straight: I don't claim to know much of anything (although I'd like to think I'm as smart as you about some things). This would be a pretty dull magazine if we only said things nobody could disagree with.

And I don't think that's even possible. No matter how qualified the expert who puts something in writing, another expert who is just as qualified will come along and prove him wrong. This is in addition to the people who will disagree if you say the sun rises in the east and sets in the west.

What I'm trying to do is to provide a wide enough spectrum of opinion so you can look it all over and make up your own mind, just as it would be if we were sitting around that pot-bellied stove I so often talk about. That other kind of journalism, where you just sit there and get spoon-fed pap, is not only out-of-date: it would be pretty useless in our particular fields of interest, where so few things are "right" or "wrong."

What we want to know most about the methods and ideas we discuss is "does it work?" and "is there a better way?"

So if you see something here you can't agree with, don't just get mad at the writer or the magazine. Let us hear your story, and maybe we'll all learn something.

Sure, we're all biased. I make no apologies for most of mine. If I didn't have them I wouldn't waste my time with COUNTRYSIDE and we could all read some big-farm magazine, or none at all.

Those biases are mainly rabbits, goats, backyard poultry, doing-it-yourself, doing more-with-less, and doing without.

All of this adds up to another personal opinion. This magazine really deals with the fun and economy and spiritual rewards of homesteading, but for the past few years I've also been suggesting that it may some day be a necessity. Not everybody agrees yet, but I'm winning support.

Just in this morning's paper, in addition to the meat boycott news (and I wish I had a dozen extra pages to sound off on *that!*) there was an item about Colorado ranchers losing 50% of their calf crop in a storm, hundreds of thousands of acres of farmland flooded in the highest flood levels in 129 years, the power blackouts in Florida, the shortage of gas and diesel fuel in some areas (which affects farming, and future food supplies... and prices...), the shortage of rail cars to haul fertilizer, and on and on.

As Diane said while reading the paper, "Golly, everything is either in short supply or it causes cancer!"

If George Meany's solution is put into effect—raising workers' salaries so they can afford to buy meat—the farmers won't be able to afford the tractors and clothes and food and everything else the union people make and handle, and they'll quit in even greater numbers.

Many people still carry on as if high prices were the only problem. Holy cow, if there ain't none there *ain't* none. I can't help but feel we're only seeing the beginning.

If this adds a bittersweet quality to homesteading... well, that's life. If the world is hectic and tumultuous, at least you don't have to go far to get away from it if you live on a homestead.

For instance, the other day I went out in the rain to do chores. I checked the hogs, gave the heifers some grain, then sat on a gate in the barn to watch them clean it up so I could give them their hay. The rain dripping from the eaves added a moody background to the sounds of cattle eating.

It was relaxing. Certainly nothing to write home about, but it seemed like an oasis of peace in a busy, hectic day. And since some days I do the same thing with the rabbits, or the goats, or the pigs or the pigeons, I'm sure you do it too.

In the end, it's the kind of simple thing that makes it all worthwhile.

On somewhat the same line of thought, neighbor Tom Sowle, and sons Dave and Steve and I spent a couple of strenuous hours in the slime and mud on a cold, windy, misty day, and got the track back on the bulldozer. That job is a sonuvagun, but the elation you feel at success makes it worthwhile. Back in the house, drying out and warming up by the fireplace, I couldn't help but think that's like almost everything. The harder the climb, the better the view from the top.

Homesteaders meet plenty of obstacles. The climbing is often difficult. But mastering the pinnacle makes it all worthwhile, out here beyond the sidewalks.

2014: The comment about readers writing most of the magazine, what I called "participatory journalism," sounds an awful lot like much of what we see on the Internet today. But while we heard from a few bozos, they weren't nearly as bad as many of those mouthing off on the web, and we did a lot more editing: that kept conversations on track, mostly, and improved grammar. (Foul language was not a problem in 1973.)

Some readers thanked me for editing their letters, while others complained that average people weren't experts and weren't worth listening to. I disagreed, but also pointed out that reader participation was a key element in the old-time farm publications I tried to pattern COUNTRYSIDE after. The fact that we had no money to pay writers, that I wrote and edited for nothing but made a few nickels by doing the printing, never came up.

13. July 1973

The excitement of moving... to a real farm!

At least once a year I write about how the homestead closes in on itself in a sort of hibernation during winter. But as I look out the window now—in June—we seem to be getting closed in literally! Last month I could see for a couple of miles, but now that the trees in Jerry's Jungle have leafed out, we have our own oasis of privacy.

This brings up many thoughts. In the first place, this is the last *Beyond the Sidewalks* I'll be writing looking out this window, since we're moving to the farm as soon as this issue is in the mail. Since this place was a virtual desert when we moved here nine years ago, there's a bit of nostalgia out there. The apple trees bought with pennies scrimped and hoarded are just beginning to bear fruit. The pears, cherries and evergreens we splurged on when we got a windfall from taking odd jobs or working the printing press overtime are becoming a natural part of the landscape. The black walnuts are growing lustily, the plums I transplanted are loaded with blossoms, and even the maples, Chinese elms and honey locusts I started from seed just for fun are much taller than I am and make the place look like a forest preserve.

And nine years ago the place looked like an airfield. May the new owners appreciate half the trees as much as I appreciate all of them, knowing each one personally.

Of all the things we have here that will be hard to leave, the trees will be among the hardest. So we started over again.

We planted 500 pine trees in the woods, which had been grazed. The grazing effectively prevented all new growth. We planted apples, pears, cherries, plums, hazelnuts, and a few black walnuts. Our order for 500 black walnut seedlings wasn't filled because of the weather: the nursery couldn't dig them. And there are plenty of arbor vitae and poplars for screens around the grain bins and hen house. I just couldn't live without trees, it seems.

I really didn't expect to find time to do all this planting and transplanting this spring, but you can plant trees when it's too wet to plow... and it's been too wet to plow. We still have ducks swimming in one of our corn fields.

Only about half of our 80 acres are planted, and most of that was plowed last fall. Even on the fields that are planted there are odd corners and patches that I couldn't get on with the tractor. Naturally, all the farmers in this area (and a mighty big area it is) are in the same boat, and you can take that literally. Think feed prices are going down much next fall?

Everything else concerning the move is pretty much on schedule. We've already moved out Caesar, our buck goat, and this year's crop of keeper kids, as well as the geese and 12 rabbits which are housed in brand new cages in the old corn crib. Since I have to go out every day to take care of the cows and pigs, moving some of the stock helped to ease the crowded conditions here somewhat.

We're making progress on converting an old shed into a magazine office, and I have some bred gilts in a corner of the machine shed, so facilities for the milking goats are the only major project left.

And planting those other 40 acres, of course.

We've made a start on the garden. Come to think of it, I'll miss the garden as much as the trees.

The soil here wasn't in bad shape to begin with, having been unused for many years. And after dumping loads and loads of goat, rabbit, pig, sheep, chicken, goose and pigeon manure on it, as well as countless trailersful of leaves, grass cut by the highway crews along the road, sawdust from the local mill, ground corncobs, and even cow manure I got for cleaning a neighbor's barn, this one-third acre garden is rich and friable.

The new garden is in a cornfield which has probably been cropped for 100 years. It looks sick. It feels sick. I expect this year's crops to be sick.

That will change. It will take time, and plenty of work, and better management than the haphazard system I used here, but we'll do it.

One of the saddest things about moving is not starting over, but wondering what will happen to the garden we have here.

Thirty acres just down the road from us have been sold. And the other day, as the new spring growth of alfalfa was shaking the morning dew from its succulent leaves, three big roaring monsters crawled off trailer trucks and tore into it like wolves ripping into an unsuspecting lamb. They built roads. Very soon, there will be 60 houses standing where we used to glean corn in the fall or take the goats for a romp, fields that grew the hay we bought to feed our livestock. Never again will that land feed anyone.

How long will it take for the bulldozers to snort into "my" garden and rape that fertile soil that virtually fed a family of six for so many years?

Some people call that progress.

Big story coming up on comfrey. The interest in this forage plant is amazing, and largely unexplainable.

One of our readers sent a clipping from a state farm magazine saying comfrey was worthless, and asked for my comments. I don't comment on factual matters without facts, so we proceeded to dig them out.

The search took us through the National Research Council, the Agronomy, Horticulture, Biochemistry and Agriculture Departments of the University of Wisconsin, the Wisconsin Alumni Research Foundation (WARF), the University of Guelph in Canada, the offices of *Organic Gardening and Farming,* and even to England. We're having some of our comfrey analyzed in the interests of good journalism (and will have to sell 27 new subscriptions to pay for it) so we expect to come up with a blockbuster of an article. Don't miss it.

I had always known that homesteading was less "efficient" than farming... which is why few factory farmers, if any, bother to make cheese, grind wheat or even bake bread, do their own butchering, and many of the other things we take for granted as a normal part of homesteading.

Their goal is living the same kind of life their city cousins live, and that means their major aim in farming is to create a cash flow.

But, as with most areas of life, there is more grey here than black or white.

This thought was especially poignant the other day when I was plowing. The red-wing blackbirds and grackles were following in my furrow and pouncing on worms and bugs much like seagulls in the wake of a garbage scow. Field mice scurried out of my path. Never harmed a one of them, and no doubt they'll be eating my seeds and will survive next winter thanks to the grain I'll spill when harvesting.

I derived enjoyment from watching these fellow creatures, from sharing "my" land with them. And there was satisfaction in envisioning the full granaries that would hopefully result from my labors, granaries that will keep my goats and rabbits and other livestock well-fed even when the snow lies deep over the Wisconsin fields and the "unexploited" animals have rough going.

All this was in addition to feeling the warm spring sun on the back of my neck, the interest generated by watching (from the top of a high hill) a black and threatening storm move in from the west, and the sense of contentment inspired by the evening call of a mourning dove as I walked, dusty and weary, from the hot but silent tractor.

I'm sure there are farmers who could never be classed as homesteaders who are still mighty close to us in many ways.

As for the efficiency part, I never realized just how much work we make for ourselves by raising a little of everything. My hogs are a perfect example. We have automatic waterers, heated in winter, so the only watering chore involves checking to make certain everything is working properly, and occasionally cleaning out the fountains.

The feed mill picks up corn from our bin, grinds and mixes it with protein supplement, and delivers it to the feed hoppers with a bulk truck and auger. All the miller does is push buttons, and all I do is write checks.

When the pigs are ready for market, we call the trucker who can haul a pen at a time (50 hogs). I pay the trucker, and take what's left of the check from the slaughterhouse and buy more pigs, pay the miller again, grow more corn.

Contrast that with a dozen rabbits. I'm not about to have a heated building for a dozen or so rabbits, so in this climate automatic watering is pretty useless. Each rabbit is watered individually. They are fed individually—grain, pellets, alfalfa, salt, minerals. They have to be bred. I have to put in nest boxes, and clean them.

I spend as much time in a day taking care of the rabbits as I do in two weeks taking care of the pigs! And while the price of live rabbits is 32¢ a pound, the price of hogs is 36¢ or more.

What's time to a hog? Maybe nothing. But it's money to a hog farmer.

Most of us homesteaders aren't too rational about this, simply because we love our stock and we enjoy what we're doing. But when we start to think of homesteading as something more than a hobby, we have to realize we're competing with an agricultural system that has us far outclassed. How can we justify working 18 hours a day just to provide our food, when with a city job and a union contract we could work a fraction of that, buy groceries, and still have enough left over for vacations, cars, boats, snowmobiles, and more?

The justifications are there, of course. But they are often personal, they often don't fit in with the usual concepts of success and good living, and that's why it's all but impossible to explain our reasons for homesteading to anyone who hasn't already convinced himself.

Efficiency, in itself, is nothing bad. Just because we disagree with certain big farm practices is no reason to break our backs needlessly!

As we've said before, saving one minute a day on chores adds up to six hours a year... and on most homesteads six hours would be a virtual vacation. If we look over our operations carefully, we might be able to place a gate more conveniently, use a better latch, run a water line a few more feet or install a float valve, or combine several similar jobs to make each one take less time.

We'll still be organic. We'll still be homesteaders. But we'll be a lot less pooped at the end of the day.

Just talked with Judy Kapture on the phone. Told her we have a goat producing 14 lbs. a day. She claims it's beginner's luck. I think she's jealous.

Actually, I'm quite pleased with our production this year. Three of our milkers are producing more than a gallon a day apiece, a far cry from what we were doing just a couple of years ago.

The rabbits, on the other hand, need some help. The biggest problem has been unusually small litters from stock that up to now had been doing pretty well.

And on the third hand, those bred gilts I mentioned earlier farrowed since I started writing this. One had seven pigs, the other had 10. I was hoping for at least six each. That was beginner's luck.

Seems like I wandered even more than usual this month. Couldn't help it. There are so many things to think about, so much to reflect on, not only because of leaving the old Countryside homestead but because of all the new experiences we've already had with the farm.

Next time we get together, we'll be in the old-machine-shed/new-office, overlooking the hog barn, the more than one acre garden, the new orchard where I installed the bees just yesterday, the grassy patch where the goat kids already kick up their heels when I let them out of their pen... and a brand new adventure for the Belangers.

I hope you join us so we can share our new joys and problems with you as we delve into new adventures, even farther beyond the sidewalks.

Afterword: Only a few years passed before that productive organic garden in the village sprouted... a house. Naturally, most of my trees disappeared as well.

The gist of that comfrey article was that somebody at the University of Wisconsin Extension set out a few comfrey plants in the experimental garden many years ago, "just for fun." Based on that, somebody wrote a bulletin claiming that comfrey wasn't a viable crop for livestock farmers. That bulletin got picked up, and spread, by other universities. Presto, instant facts, "backed by major universities."

Somehow that seemed to fit in with my "People don't make bacon; Oscar Mayer makes bacon!" experience. I've met some Extension people who are really cool as individuals, but I don't have much use for Extension as a whole.

That includes the Master Gardener program. The bigwigs in Madison wanted us to sign a statement that we wouldn't bring guns, alcohol or drugs to meetings or functions. A bunch of mostly old women talking about flowers, and they're worried about drugs and guns? Hilarious. Also insulting, bureaucratic, and stupid. I quit.

14. August 1973

The big move

Our first post-college move—from a Madison apartment to a rented farmhouse—was easily accomplished with our Nash Rambler station wagon. We had hardly anything to move.

The move from the farmhouse to the creamery was a bit more demanding, since by then we had acquired the small printing press and a few other tools.

But moving from the creamery to the farm... that was an operation that required calling in a local livestock hauler with his truck. And not for the livestock! We put the furniture and other belongings on that truck: the goats, sheep, rabbits, poultry and the rest went in our battered pickup. It took many trips.

There were also two printing presses, a very large and heavy paper cutter and a great deal of paper and other printing supplies, and all the records etc. associated with the magazine.

The people who were moving in (with professional movers and their professional semi-trailer moving van) were there before our cattle truck was loaded... and it was raining.

Man, am I beat. Moving, after nine years in one place, was a traumatic experience and the adrenaline was really flowing, but trying to get organized on the new homestead has left me adrenalineless. Numb. I always knew "simple country living" was just a pretty phrase, but this is ridiculous.

Moving the household stuff was bad enough, but the office was even worse, the animals and equipment posed additional problems, and the print shop just about did me in. We had to take the presses and some of the other large equipment apart to get them out the door and quite frankly, I doubt whether I'll ever get some of that machinery put together again. Besides that, I had a deadline for another book breathing down my neck (this one to be published by Rodale Press), 18 acres of hay to get in, the planting to finish up and of course the garden, milking, and other "must" chores.

More than a few friends have suggested that I'm taking on too much, especially when the cows get in the garden or the baler breaks down and I hit another low in my manic-depressive cycles. But doggone it, cows aren't *supposed* to get out on a good farm, and the baler isn't supposed to break down on every circuit of the field. As we lick these problems one by one, we'll climb back up to the efficiency level and more-or-less sane living we enjoyed before.

Sometimes I reflect on the amount of work I've been doing the past few years and wonder not only how, but why. The answer to both questions is pretty much the same. I not only love what I'm doing (in spite of the frustrations) but there's enough variety that none of it really seems like work. This, I feel, is one of the main concepts of homestead living: work is play and play is work and since you're either working or playing all day long anyway, it just seems like I get a lot more accomplished than the average person. A farmer making hay is working, but a writer making hay might be having more fun than if he were on a golf course. A writer putting out a magazine or a book is working, but a farmer who is writing might well be playing.

And I still haven't decided what I want to be when I grow up.

This whole concept is what makes homesteading such a pleasant way of life. Taking care of a few chickens and rabbits, a couple of goats and a pig and a steer and a huge garden certainly isn't "efficient" when compared with raising pigs or cows or goats or rabbits by the ton, but by golly, it's a lot more fun! So instead of figuring out our labor costs and deciding we'd be better off going to the supermarket, we add up what we save on "entertainment" expenses and decide we're not so bad off after all. Even if a homesteader does do a little boating, or plays a round of golf every so often or bowls a few frames, the principle is the same.

"The goats are out" used to be the despairing call that sent the entire family scurrying to protect the orchard and pine trees and rose bushes. But if that call strikes terror into the hearts of homesteaders, "the cows are out" is ten times worse. And on three occasions already we have put the cows back before breakfast.

Our fencing isn't the best, obviously, and the charged wire running along the inside of the entire pasture was rendered useless by grass as high as my shoulders. I figured I had neither the time nor the money to build a whole new fence right now, so I reinforced the old one in the weakest spots and planned on reinforcing the rest as the steers and heifers broke through.

At the rate they're going, I'll end up with a whole new fence anyway, and it will only have taken me about six times as long as doing the job right in the first place would have.

Several people have commented on the chicken-drowning episode that got wide publicity just after the latest price freeze. Some even wondered how farmers could be so "heartless" as to destroy birds that could have fed thousands of people. Frankly, it's difficult for me to fully understand people who have such a distorted view of reality. The farmers obviously didn't kill those chicks for fun: they lost about 9¢ on each one that went into the barrels and to the rendering plant. But they would have lost over 30¢ on each one if they had fed them out. Now, it's fine to talk about the way things should be, but how many people would look at their records, see they lost $90 per thousand already, know full well they'd lose another $200 or more per thousand, and not take the same action? Don't forget some of these people raise chickens by the hundreds of thousands, and the loss on 100,000 would exceed $30,000! Even if the farmers had such high ideals that they decided to feed all the starving people, as well as the city people who can spend thousands of dollars on boats and campers and snowmobiles but who complain about paying a fair price for a chicken, it shouldn't take too much insight to realize that the moneylenders would soon own the entire farm. Do you think the bankers would bother to raise chickens, or anything else, at a loss?

Small litters of rabbits seem to be a widespread problem this summer. Does that have been kindling normal size litters come up with two or three. And no one seems to know why. That doesn't make those feed prices any easier to take.

The entire food situation is attracting a good many new homesteaders, and some of them have some pretty romantic ideas about small farming. One of my main missions these days is to preach that even though money isn't our prime concern, we still have to be realistic about our livestock operations. Yes, our eggs are often more expensive than supermarket eggs, and so is our milk, meat and even vegetables sometimes. And even though we can say we get other benefits such as quality and the satisfaction of providing our own groceries, the fact remains that we have to at least make an attempt to keep our costs in line or end up with nothing more than an expensive hobby. Chances are we won't be ruined, on the same scale as the big farmers anyway, but not many of us can afford to keep operating at a loss indefinitely even if the loss is relatively minor.

The non-economic benefits of homesteading are too precious to be destroyed by something like operating costs, especially when there's no real need for it. It is possible to break even, or better, on the homestead. But it takes good management, good methods. And showing how to use good management on the small farm is one of our major objectives.

Back to the homestead: We do have the first crop of hay in. Over 800 bales. And not a drop of rain on any of them. The oats are beginning to head out, the soybeans were looking great although the weeds are catching up with them now, the buckwheat is in blossom and alive with bees and other insects, and the wheat and corn are coming along fine. About 10 acres never got plowed at all and in fact there are still areas where the wild ducks are swimming although we haven't had a real rain for quite a while. We had about twice as much rain as normal earlier this year and I've talked to several farmers who only have about 25% of their crops planted... in July! Corn, especially, is going to be awfully scarce around here next year. We might try some emergency silage crop on those left-over acres, if they ever dry out. The pig population is down due to recent marketing, but the goat barn is full... in spite of all the people who have been here looking for goats.

Milk production dropped considerably after moving, by the way. And we still have a long way to go to fix up the milking area and mangers the way they should be.

The bunny barn is full, even if all the does don't have respectable litters, and the "bird house" is in full production. The old layers are still working in one section, the pigeons are in another, and all five decks of the brooder have been in operation with White Leghorns, Rock-Cornish, goslings, ducklings and guineas. In fact, there has even been mention of turkeys, which is something we seldom hear about in COUNTRYSIDE.

And oh yes, I never thought I'd see the day... but we have also acquired a horse. I never had much use for horses, but he's really quite a nice fellow. Just a huge goat, actually. And trained to drive, as well as for riding. We might end up being "real" homesteaders yet.

So while our life has been rather cloudy — heck, cyclonic, even — in recent weeks, there have been breaks in the storm that give a hint of brighter days ahead. We've even had time to take the goats for walks through the hay stubble, then sit on top of the hill with a vista that stretches for miles in all directions, and watch them graze and browse at the edge of the field. Add a magnificent sunset and an evening breeze off new-mown hay, and country living seems worth working for again.

Or, in the morning, on the first trip out to put the cattle back in the pasture, we stop to exclaim at the grasses whose seed heads are covered with pollen so delicate that even careful picking results in shattering the gem-like fragility. There are wild roses and morning glories with blossoms even larger than our cultivated ones, and we saw three giant herons flying over with great, swooping wings and ridiculous legs trailing behind.

And that's what life has been like here, lately, beyond the sidewalks.

15. September 1973
Homesteading and capital

This is the first of several discussions on homestead capitalization, the notion that simple living takes a lot of special tools. It's something new or prospective homesteaders don't often think about... and no doubt, after the move, I was a little awed myself at how much we had accumulated.

I'm writing this sitting on the screened-in front porch. After a day of sporadic light showers (not nearly enough to quench the thirst of the parched garden and fields) punctuated with a brilliant sun piercing through ominous black clouds, the air is fresh and sweet.

The second crop alfalfa in the field alongside the porch is ready to be cut. On the front lawn the ducks are resting under the old apple tree, preening their rapidly growing feathers. I can see the pigeons (most of ours are white) way out in the emerging sorghum shoots, picking out unsprouted seed, and every so often the alarming honk of a goose floats around the corner of the house (are they in the garden again?) and there's even the occasional crow of one of the many Countryside roosters.

If it sounds like life has improved here lately, you're right. Perfection is still a long way off... but life is great, compared with the problems we had been having.

Naturally, this doesn't mean we don't have any more problems. Today (three days after the first three paragraphs were written, which is one of my problems) the most pressing one is the hay. I cut it yesterday, and it rained last night. Again, not enough to help the dusty garden and fields, but enough to mess up the hay. The sun came out today and Dave raked the field... but it rained even before he finished. Again, not enough to show up in the rain gauge but enough to soak the alfalfa.

We're going to be short of feed anyway, so we don't need this.

Took a walk in the garden tonight after chores, and that looks pretty sad too, for the end of July. We got it in late, and we haven't had a respectable rain for over a month. To look at the bright side, it's so dry even the weeds don't grow.

All of this leads up to a topic that's been cropping up more and more outside of COUNTRYSIDE, although we don't hear nearly as much about it in the magazine as we did a few years ago. That's the idea that farm life is always serene, simple, and economical.

COUNTRYSIDE readers are actively involved in some aspect of farming, of course (you're a farmer to us even if you just have a few rabbits) so we spend more time talking about problems than about pleasures. We don't need a magazine to tell us about the joys: we're well aware of them. We *do* need a magazine to help us make those pleasurable moments a little more frequent.

But in the past few months the mass media have been running a rather astounding number of articles on the back-to-the land movement. Most of them talk about how great it is to live in the fresh air and close to Nature, so naturally, creative writers look for new angles. The most logical one is that "simple living" is a crock of baloney.

One of the most interesting ones was printed in the *New York Times* and reprinted by a number of other publications. It concerned a New York City film maker who fled to New England with the idea of living off his film royalties—and a hundred-acre wooded "farm." The article takes you through the first year of organic gardening (total disaster), a horrendous remodeling job (and a mortgage they had planned to avoid), a miserable winter fighting a wood heating system and a mile-long snowbound driveway, to a spring and mud that isolated them as completely as the snows of winter.

This homestead family concluded that they were experiencing back-country culture shock, and that they'd likely find themselves back in the dirty old crime-ridden city. "Somehow, it's getting more attractive all the time," they said.

Obviously it was the writer's aim to emphasize the bad times: not one word is said about the good times they surely had. If they don't have fun *once* in awhile, they *are* crazy to stay out there because they obviously aren't up to it.

Even aside from that, there are obvious flaws in the story and others like it that make them as misleading as those which speak only of the good times and gloss over the bad. While people who have grown up in the city or suburbs can cope with the problems they face there, when they get in the country they feel helpless. The problems are so different from any they faced before, or even expected to encounter, and they just aren't prepared.

Larry McWilliams touched on this in a note that came just this morning. He mentioned the canning they were doing and observed, "Why, just the cost of canning equipment and jars could break a guy if he had to buy it all at once! You might point out to beginners that it's best to acquire skills and equipment before they leave the city."

We've been saying that for years, on homesteading in general and on each individual aspect of it from gardening to raising livestock. "Don't *go* into it, *grow* into it" has been our watchword.

This is precisely what those people from New York did not do. Even with the proper equipment and experience, you can't expect to turn a piece of wasteland into a productive homestead in less than three to five years. I used to say that rather hesitantly, but the more experience I get the more firmly I believe it. It takes at least three years to develop any plot of ground into a good organic garden. A sensible person simply doesn't plan to feed himself entirely from the homestead garden the first year, much less make a living selling the surplus! Some city people just can't understand that, even though they're intelligent enough to know they couldn't open a grocery store or any other business without (a.) plenty of capital, not only to work with as the business grows but for living expenses until the business becomes a going concern; and (b.) one heckuvalotta experience. How can they expect to start the business of homesteading with any less? At any rate, I wish they'd stop badmouthing the total experience just because of their own ignorance.

I suspect that many city people simply assume that "living off the land" is child's play. If the uneducated pioneers could do it, they can do it. After all, they're vastly superior, aren't they?

Bull compost. A person with a degree or a whole drawer full of degrees can starve to death on a homestead if he doesn't know how to plant a garden or butcher a rabbit. It must be a blow to the pride of these sophisticated moderns to realize that the pioneers could learn their button-pushing routine much more quickly and easily than they can learn the lifestyle of the pioneers!

Country living is not always hard physical labor, deprivation, loneliness, inconvenience and misery. Neither is it always lounging on the bank of a clear stream with a fishing pole, sitting on the fence admiring the goats or petting the rabbits, or effortlessly raking in an abundance of free food in a Garden of Paradise setting.

It's a little of both. With time and the right tools (and I consider knowledge and experience to be among the most important tools) country living can attain the high point of human existence... something that can be said only for a favored few, and even then with serious reservations, about city living.

About equipment. The peak of the canning season is past, and if this is your first experience with such things I imagine your reaction is pretty much like the one expressed by Larry.

But now you have a canning kettle, jars, tongs, and other items, depending on what you put up. And more importantly, you have some experience. You know what works, what doesn't work, what recipes and methods are best for you and how to do the job a little more efficiently next year. You have a better idea of varieties and quantities to plant.

The money you shelled out on equipment wasn't spent: it was invested. Take good care of it and it will show a return on that investment for years, just like the capital investment in any other business. Amortization isn't something homesteaders usually talk about, but it's there.

If you buy all your equipment at once, of course it will break you, especially if you've just moved to the country and have other unexpected expenses too. A list of all the useful items found on the well-equipped homestead would be interesting — and probably staggering — to those who think the simple life is "simple." Everything depends on what you do, your goals and methods and even your outlook on life, so no single list would fit everybody's needs. But here's one for starters.

In the garden, the basic tools are a fork for spading, a rake, shovel and hoe. But you can't work an area as large as most homesteaders need without some sort of tiller, which is a major investment. The minor things can put you under too, when you add them all up: stakes for tomatoes (if you use them), string for laying out straight rows, trellises for climbers, boxes for starting bedding plants, a compost bin and a fork for turning compost, a cart or wheelbarrow, maybe a garden seeder for really large areas, hoses, and more.

Livestock needs feed and water utensils and cages or fencing. Goats need a manger, a milking bench, milking pail, strainer, filters and milk containers. Maybe you'll use a cheese press (and a kettle large enough to make cheese in) and cheesecloth, rennet and a dairy thermometer. Sooner or later you'll think about getting a butter churn and molds and an ice cream freezer and a cream separator. You'll want clippers and a disbudding iron and castrating equipment and special tools for hoof care and a lot more.

Then you might get involved in sticking knives, skinning knives, butcher knives, meat saws, butcher blocks, cleavers, a lard press and sausage grinder and crock for curing meat and a smokehouse.

How about crocks for pickles and sauerkraut, a mill for grinding flour, containers for storing produce and even shelf space which most modern houses don't have or a root cellar which is an even bigger investment?

If you grow grain on a small scale you'll want some form of hand seeder and a scythe with a cradle. And there are hay rakes and bee equipment and fruit trees and berry bushes and sheep shears and cider presses and gambrel hooks and woodworking tools and an axe and maybe a chain saw or a crosscut saw... and the list can go on and on.

All this, of course, is without the buildings and storage space, and the seeds and stock itself.

Nobody in their right mind could expect to do a decent job of real, all-the-way homesteading without at least the basics from this list. Yet, people do just that, every day. What's more, they don't know how to use these tools, including the livestock and garden seeds! So they end up back in the city telling everybody that homesteading is a cruel existence.

The pioneers had the knowledge because they grew up with it. They learned these things as naturally as today's youngster learns to change the channel on a tv set. The knowledge came gradually. We can't expect to do everything overnight and then call homesteading a swindle if we don't make a success of it in the first year, or the first three years.

Something else that's important: the proper attitude. Having the right frame of mind probably has to come even before the equipment and experience. *Why* are you homesteading? This colors not only what you do, but how you do it. If you just get a kick out of puttering in the soil, a garden will be all you want. If you just like to work with rabbits or goats or poultry, you can treat them like a hobby, have a good time, become an expert in your own field and probably end up with some financial benefits.

But if you approach any of these with the sole idea of saving money on groceries (or worse yet making an extra income) and especially right away, you're doomed to failure before you begin. Better find something else to do.

As you approach full-fledged homesteading, your concepts and attitudes develop and change just as surely as your experience and wisdom grow. Homesteading is a way of life that ranges far beyond the fun you have or the security you feel when looking at your well-stocked root cellar and freezer. You become more sensitive to your environment... the subtleties of weather, the soil, wildlife, natural plant growth, the individuality of animals, the laws of genetics, the realities of life and death... and the interaction of everything with everything else. You become a working crew member on Spaceship Earth rather than just another freeloading passenger. You begin to realize more fully what a tenuous thread it is that links Man to Life, and your own life has more sparkle, more vibrancy, more meaning.

This, then, is what a homesteader is. We get rather plaintive notes from folks who say "I enjoy COUNTRYSIDE but I'm not really a homesteader" because they only have a few rabbits or a goat or a garden and some chickens. They're homesteaders.

Not everybody can live on the five acres or so it would take to be as independent as possible in today's society. Not everybody would want to. And most of us homesteaders wouldn't want everybody to live like us.

And yet, that basic homestead philosophy is important for everyone, everywhere. It should be taught in schools with even more fervor than math or history, because our destiny, our very survival as a species, depends on it.

As one example, let's look at the current situation of shortages, especially of fuel and food. Hundreds of thousands of words have been written on these in the past few months, most of them by people with a technological outlook... a viewpoint that must be laid to rest if we have any concern for the future... a viewpoint that is already being replaced by the homestead philosophy.

Have government and big business "caused" the shortages by exporting feed grains, by manipulating the markets, by exercising monopolistic powers? Or are the shortages real... so real that they can only become progressively worse? Technological Man has assumed that we'd never run out of natural resources, and if we did it would be so far in the future that alternatives would be found by the very technology which caused the running out in the first place. But not only are we actually running out of many materials: others can be used only at the expense of fouling our environment, which means to any sane person that they are unusable at current levels of technology. Some technologists say we're ridiculous to sacrifice the Gross National Product for the sake of clean air and water: we say they're ridiculous to value dollars and conspicuous consumption more than Life itself.

We have long valued "The American Way of Life," and as a nation felt vaguely superior to the undeveloped nations of the world. But the plain fact is, there simply isn't enough—food, oil, and many other products— to keep the entire world on the ridiculous, wasteful level Americans have been taking for granted. Yet, those undeveloped nations are not only anxious but increasingly able to emulate the American Way of Life.

What this involves then is a total reassessment of our traditional line of thought. America may be great, but not because she plunders and produces and consumes with gluttony. There is nothing inherently good about having large homes and two cars and scores of "labor-saving" electrical appliances. The homesteader knows there is more to Life.

Changes have been coming for a long time, but the pace has quickened, if only because of economic considerations. Just a few years ago, who could have dreamed that the President of the United States would actually urge people to buy smaller cars, as President Nixon did recently? Homesteaders have a much easier time adjusting to this changing thought pattern and to the changes in lifestyle it will inevitably bring about, if only because we're on the way or already there.

One thing about living on a farm in the summer: you get plenty of company. We've been blessed with a host of city visitors in the last month. They don't bother me, as long as they pitch in with the work or stay out of my way.

I used to find it amusing when readers would write wondering if we had some sort of commune. But the other night we sat down to supper and whoever set the table had laid an extra place, just out of habit! It was rather lonesome with just the six of us Belangers here.

Many of the visitors do get involved in the work, and enjoy it. Baling hay, especially, seems to turn them on. But what most of them leave behind is more subtle than any jobs they accomplish. Their enthusiasm and envy of our way of life is even more important, because it helps perk us up when the going gets tough.

Even our kids, who would like nothing better than to spend a day in Chicago, seem to get new inspiration when a family from Chicago comes up here. Playing in the hay or the tree house becomes fun again, horseback riding becomes more exciting when kids who have never seen a horse before participate, and even drinking goat milk is an adventure. Sometimes it takes a little outside help to make you appreciate how good you have it.

Aнd of course, we have neighbors out here too. The closest ones are just across the road. George and Darlene have been painting their barn, and I gave them a hand on the peak, because I like high places and George doesn't and that's what neighbors are for. Someday I'll need some help too.

Meanwhile, back at the ranch, life goes on with the same routine Man has followed ever since he began to cultivate the Earth. The stock must be fed and watered no matter what the price of wheat or oil. The rabbits must be bred regardless of the latest news on Watergate, the price of gold or the balance of payments deficit. There are tomatoes to can, hay to put in, and we have a pig with a hernia that should be butchered.

The Earth-shaking events are still there, but they seem pretty remote when you have a supper of luscious, crisp salad, juicy sweet corn roasted on the cob and tender succulent roasted chicken, then watch a fiery sunset, and fall asleep with the smell of new-mown hay to induce pleasant dreams. When all is said and done, no matter what else is involved, that's why most of us prefer Life beyond the sidewalks.

Gardening has come a long way since 1973. A tiller is no longer essential, and there is no mention of square foot or even raised bed gardening.

As for most of the rest of it … is it really possible that so little has changed in nearly 40 years? More likely, it has changed so subtly that most people haven't noticed. Especially, no doubt, those who weren't there in 1973.

16. October 1973

First farm harvest season

Harvest season is a time of fulfillment. It's a time of change—in the weather, the appearance of the fields and gardens, and even in our way of thinking. And most of all, harvest season is a busy time. This busy-ness is reflected in my rough draft of this month's "Beyond." Set in type, it would fill about ten pages, and I'm going to have to whittle it down.

For example, on seeing the youngest of my four kids getting on the school bus, like being gobbled up by some monstrous yellow caterpillar, I was moved to write a long dissertation on the evils of formal education. It went on and on about the fantastic education a child with parents who care can get on a homestead. I expressed my guilt feelings for having sent my kids off to the city school, and sympathized with their imprisonment. (As a kid, I hated school.)

By that time the school bus was back, disgorged my crew, and I got their assessment of formal education.

They thought it was great.

I tore up my essay.

We got the oats in today and I probably have the distinction of getting the worst crop in Dodge County. The worst part was, about half of it was ragweed seed.

I had a custom combiner all lined up two weeks ago and the oats looked good. Then we got some rain and some wind. The combine never showed up. (Most likely, he took one look at that field and drove right on by.)

I finally got enough sense to go talk to a neighbor. Lorne and Edward Billings were here the next morning.

Lorne warned me beforehand that his relic of a combine only holds up for about 35 acres, but the curse of Countryside held steady: he made it through seven before a shaft broke.

We got the crop in. But the weed seeds were so green that the stuff started heating up and I had to shovel it all out of the bin again and spread it on the barn floor to dry.

We'll soon know if ragweed seed makes milk and eggs.

I had a new experience the other day. We've carried — oh, many, many pigs in our truck, and the goats have had plenty of rides, and of course we brought the sheep out here in it. But I took two runty hogs and a lamb to a custom processor (just when would I butcher, this summer?) and as we were cruising through the middle of downtown Waterloo, the lamb jumped out. We chased the darn thing for five blocks before we caught it. Sure gave a lot of city people something to smile about on a Monday morning.

Some other things I wrote about that we won't have room for: I went to Emmaus, Pennsylvania for a day to wind up a few details on the small stock book I wrote for Rodale Press. (Should be published next spring.) I visited the Organic Gardening & Farming offices and experimental farms and picked up a few ideas I wanted to share with you. Maybe later.

When I got home, we put in another 400 bales of hay, combined the oats and the wheat, and then I broke my foot.

It happened when I was thrown from a spirited stallion. That's the truth, and never mind Diane's version: would I be dumb enough to just plain "fall off a horse?"

Either way, I can't quite imagine me sitting around with a cast on for two months or so. Everybody has been doing a terrific job of taking over my share of the chores, and since the only time a farmer gets a vacation is when he's laid up, I'm trying to enjoy it. But it ain't easy!

Sasha, our No. 1 cow dog, had a little bad luck too. She got her side ripped open on a barbed wire fence.

The vet was out of town, but with two nurses here (Diane and Cathy) the decision was made to stitch her up. The suturing was done on a bed of newspapers on the lawn.

As of this date the stitches have been removed and recovery is complete. Chalk up one more for homestead ingenuity. And guts.

Everybody in this area has been complaining that the tomatoes just won't ripen. We usually start canning in July or August, but here it is September and we don't really have enough to make it worthwhile. And we have over 70 plants.

At the same time, there are people who *do* have things to can... and they can't find jars. So many people are preserving food this year that the stores are sold out.

Freezers, rotary tillers, and similar homestead tools are just as hard to get. I personally checked five dealers and found only one tiller. Every one of the dealers said they had the best year ever.

Last month I told you we had some new helpers here and that I'd introduce you to everybody when we got some pictures. We got 'em. The only one missing is Marge Davel, and the reason for that is important because it tends to emphasize that we still aren't "big business."

Marge, like almost everybody else, does her COUNTRYSIDE work at home: she hasn't been out here so we could take her picture. Marge has been with us for 2-1/2 years now, on a part-time basis. She opens mail, assigns expiration dates to subscriptions, and does a lot of other things I don't know much about because they pertain to our computerized mailing list, which I try to avoid.

Vicki Zimbric helps Marge with the mailing list, also on a part-time basis. She makes sure the computer did what we told it to do, and takes care of problems that arise when it didn't.

Vicki started just a couple of months ago—about the same time as Leona Doorenbos. Leona is supposed to be one of those jacks-of-all-trades small outfits like this find so necessary, but our Countryside Book Store has been doing such a lively business that she spends a good deal of her time just handling book orders.

You met Lynn Grosz before, when she started doing our artwork and layout and paste-up last spring. Things like that "Pick a Petal" page last month and the comfrey illustrations in this issue are hers... things we obviously couldn't do when I did the paste-up myself.

Since we didn't want to get away from being a ma & pa business, we also got Lynn's husband, Ron, to join the fun. His title is "business manager" but actually, he does pretty much the same things the editor does. Last week, for example, he built some dandy screens for the office and helped combine wheat. Right now he's setting type. We hope he can find time to sell a few new subscriptions, too.

Cathy Blaschka is the real old-timer. She's beginning her tenth year of working for us in one way or another, starting when she was in high school. Naturally, in that time she's done everything with the possible exception of milking the goats or running a printing press. Cathy is a full-time nurse and works here on her day off as chief typesetter.

Most of you know Diane, of course, who is general overseer of the circulation and advertising departments.

With all this help you might think there isn't anything left for me to do. I sort of planned it that way, but we've been so busy getting organized that I haven't noticed much change yet. I have gotten away from those 100 hour work weeks though . . . a step in the right direction.

After all, working yourself to death putting out a magazine is no way to spend a life — especially if you live beyond the sidewalks.

2014: Ron is dead. Leona is dead. Even Cathy, the youngest, is dead. So are others we've worked with over the years. Editing a memoir like this makes you miss old friends and acquaintances, especially those who are no longer with us. And it gives you a different perspective on life.

17. November-December, 1973

Thanksgiving on the farm

This harvest is an especially poignant one for me. Most significantly, it marks the end of our first season on the new homestead. A dismal one in many ways (as first seasons are apt to be in any endeavor) but in retrospect, an immensely satisfying one.

We averted total disaster in the garden mainly by the sheer size of it. We planned on having produce to sell. The plan failed, but at least we have enough for ourselves.

The carrot crop was the best ever, which I attribute to the new garden seeder we used (it spaces out the tiny seeds so I didn't waste 9/10th of them by later thinning) and to Diane's sister, Sue, who spent some of her vacation here and weeded all nine rows!

I learned to work with the idiosyncrasies of the machinery that was giving me so much trouble earlier in the year. In fact, the hay baler that couldn't make it around the field without breaking down is now one of my favorite pieces of equipment. Oh, we have minor repairs and normal maintenance to attend to, but now at least I feel I know what I'm doing.

If all's well that ends well, it was a pretty good year.

Life has been good enough that it's already exciting to think about next year. After all, planting season is only 5-6 months away!

The broken foot should come out of the cast next week. Diane says the only good thing about having a husband with a foot in a cast is that he never complains he's out of socks, or can't find two that match.

A cast is really a pain, on the farm. At first I waddled down to "help" with the chores, but when I tried to get the manure off the plaster and realized I'd have to take it to bed with me, I lost some enthusiasm. Stuffing your foot in a plastic bag and tying it up with baling twine helps, even though it's clumsy and looks ridiculous.

I ended up doing the cooking and the dishes for six weeks — the longest I've gone without milking since I got goats. And I missed it terribly!

If there were a national holiday for homesteaders, it would have to be Thanksgiving.

Who but a homesteader can appreciate what went on in the minds of the Pilgrims on that first Thanksgiving? Who but a homesteader can really and truly appreciate the meaning of a harvest festival? Who has more to be thankful for than a homesteader after the harvest?

The fields and gardens have been readied for winter. The carrots and Jerusalem artichokes have been mulched, to be dug and enjoyed crisp and fresh even after being buried in snow. Only blackened hulls under the hickory trees in the woodlot testify to the bounty that fell there... bounty shared and stored alike in the squirrels' nests and the homesteader's cellar. The vines and stalks of the garden have been shredded, and are now part of the compost heaps that steam like miniature volcanoes on frosty mornings.

The animals have been culled in preparation for the long dark months of confinement, increased labor, and the cost of stored feed. Fat and sleek, the goats rustle in new yellow straw, the rabbits take on a new sheen with their winter coats, and the Christmas goose grows fatter by the hour with the corn provided now that the grass is brown and dry.

The mow is full of fragrant hay, the grain bins are full, the root cellar is bursting at the seams. There are braided strings of onions in a dry place, boxes of potatoes in a more moist location, shelves laden with squash and pumpkins, baskets of apples, crocks of pickles and kraut.

There are shelves bending under the weight of fresh new jars of produce, gleaming like strings of jewels. The orange-red of tomatoes, the purple-red of beets and the greens of pickles and beans mingle with the sparkling hues of grape and elderberry jelly. There is rhubarb, and jars of golden honey still in the combs.

The freezer is loaded with peas and asparagus and broccoli and raspberries and strawberries and fresh pork and spring lamb and rabbit and chicken and beef... and there's more of everything in the locker plant in town.

To the countryman, this is beauty. Contentment. Security. But it's more than that, even, and certainly more than food.

All this bounty is the first fresh breeze of spring on your face as you begin the garden... preserved just as surely as the peas you planted that day. It's the arrival of the fluffy, peeping chicks and the memory of carefully lifting each one from the shipping carton, inspecting it, dipping its beak in the water fountain, then releasing it to flutter away to inspect its new environment. It's working in the garden when the soil is fresh and moist and still cool and weed-free... and it's working in the garden in the blazing heat of a midsummer afternoon when the weeds threaten to overtake everything. The larder holds not only jars of tomatoes, but the pungent smell of the vines as you picked them, the steaming afternoons canning them, the pride and satisfaction of placing the jars on the shelves.

The harvest is more than just payday for the homesteader. Your storehouse holds not only food, but memories, hopes and fulfillment of hopes, sweat, love. We may face the approaching months with some apprehension, but at least now we know where we stand. Now, after the hot and sweaty and dusty days, and before the time to thaw frozen livestock water and milk with numb fingers and fight snow piling up against the barn door, we can assess our mistakes and failures of the past season and plan for a better one next time around.

This is the Thanksgiving of the Pilgrims and the kindergarten pageants: we've made it this far, we'll make it the rest of the way, by God! This is as true and good as it is simple. Homesteaders have a much keener appreciation of the subtle changes in nature, we always say — and there's nothing subtle about the transition from summer to winter. If you have even a trio of rabbits in your barn and a dozen quarts of tomatoes on your shelf, you're more psyched up for a harvest festival than the person who trundles off to the supermarket for a frozen Thanksgiving dinner... and every other dinner... every other day of the year.

It's payday in the country: we collect the rewards of our labors. It's the opposite of April 15: we collect the taxes from the environment that depends on us for its survival. It's Independence Day, as we survey our storehouses and rejoice in our freedom from grocery bills. It's New Year's Eve... the end of one cycle, the savoring of reflections that go with it, and the beginning of a new cycle and the hopes that go with all beginnings.

Especially beyond the sidewalks, let us give thanks.

Part IV: 1974

Inflation reaches 11.3% and global recession deepens; "Lucy," 3-million-year-old skeleton, discovered in Ethiopia; Word processors resemble typewriters more than computers; Year-end Dow, 616; Average income, $13,900; Gas/gal, 55¢; Richard Nixon resigns; DST starts 4 months early and 55 mph speed limit set to save gas; World population reaches 4 billion; India becomes the 6th nation with nuclear weapons; Pocket calculators introduced.

18. January 1974

Keeping busy on the homestead

There never seems to be a slack season around here. Since we last chatted around the ol' pot bellied stove, we've butchered a hog, put up the wood burning stove in the office, cut firewood, did some fall plowing, and seem to have kept quite busy in a few dozen other ways.

Hog butchering continues to be an adventure, no matter how many we do. It does get easier, though. In the past our main problem was getting the scalding water hot enough. So this time I built a good fire under the 50 gallon drum to start with. (If you're one of those people who writes to tell me to skin the critter, as always happens when I mention scalding, forget it. I just think scalding is easier, and does a better job.)

Diane, and Lynn and Ron Grosz, all helped. It was a rainy, miserable day and we were soaked and freezing by the time we finished. But Lynn had brought one of her great homestead "meal in a pot" dinners which she had put in the oven earlier. Sitting down to a feast of chicken, potatoes, carrots and so on made the whole project seem like some kind of a party.

The next day we cut the carcass and commenced to cure the hams and bacons according to "Ann Kanable's Father's Recipe" which we printed in the last issue. Early indications are that this dry cure is going to be great... much better than the brine cure we've used in the past.

We got the stove set up a little later than we should have, and there were some pretty chilly days in the office. When Cathy started typing with mittens on, I took the hint.

I've had to add cutting and hauling wood to my routine, as well as laying a fire every morning, but so far it's been fun. Ask me about it again in March. I get a lot of help from Steve, who does a nice job of splitting. For most of his ten years he's wanted to be a hog farmer, but he changed his mind. Now he thinks he might be a woodchopper.

There might be some call for that trade again, with the energy crisis. I'd love to ramble on for a few pages about that, but since we've been talking about it here for at least three years, and now everybody is talking about it, maybe it's time for us to go on to other things.

We printed this little quip some time ago: "'May you live in interesting times' is said to be an ancient Chinese curse." That just occurred to me, because there seems to be little doubt that the coming months are going to be mighty interesting ones for Spaceship Earth.

The fuel crisis is a reality, and there is serious talk of many other shortages, including food. Depression is no longer the absurdity most people considered it just a short time ago, as many knowledgeable people admit the possibility.

Homesteaders have a lot less to worry about than most people. In fact, I think many of us would actually welcome the opportunity to homestead as a means of survival instead of a more-or-less hobby. At least I've always thought the world would be better off if there were more homesteaders.

This means we have to work harder and probably under more difficult circumstances, we have to manage better, and we have to learn more. But isn't that good, if times are interesting or not?

This page makes it sound like we've escaped the rat race not by outdistancing it, but by just taking a different direction. And so it is. It's snowing right now, but the fire is cheery and warm. It's nice to be busy, especially with something important. We work, but it's not a burden. That's what Life is all about, beyond the sidewalks.

19. February 1974

A special kind of snowfall

A snowfall like this comes about once a year. The temperature was hovering around the freezing point when I came in from evening chores and the flakes that came floating down from just above the yard light were as fluffy as goose feathers: the kind of huge flakes you see on Christmas cards.

And the next morning the whole world *was* a Christmas card. The fence posts looked like milk bottles on a doorstep with the frozen cream pushing off the caps. The wet snowflakes did a fantastic balancing act on the tree branches, and even on the fence and telephone wires. As the sun rose, the whole landscape sparkled with a lacy brilliance.

I did the chores, and even though a hundred "important" duties were waiting in the office, I grabbed the camera and headed for the woods. I know almost every rock and tree and weed there personally, but they were so transformed, so incredibly beautiful, that I saw a new picture possibility with every step. The black tree branches were thinned to mere threads against the morning sky because of the clinging snow: they looked like those delicate, fine-line etchings of the old masters, who probably got their inspiration from just such a woodland walk.

It didn't take long to run out of film, but that only made the rest of the walk more meaningful: there would be no way to relive it except in my imagination, and I sucked in every detail.

I reluctantly came back to the house, and told Diane (who had even more to do than I did) that she must walk down to the woods. There's no point in living in the country if you're just going to look out the window and say "ooh, isn't that pretty" and go about your business.

If something like this happened only once every century instead of once a year or so, poems would be written about it, it would make front page news, and children would be telling their children and their children's children about it. We take too many of the wonders of Nature for granted anyway.

I watched her go down the corn field and into the woods with the two dogs racing in circles and kicking up snow around her. When she returned there was a healthy flush in her cheeks and a fresh outdoorsy aroma about her. And we were both glad we weren't so busy making a living that we couldn't live.

Speaking of things coming every hundred years, how about that comet Kahoutek? What is it, every 80,000 years? Nothing like a little contact with Nature to tone down Man's pride. We often hear from people who moved from someplace like Los Angeles to the mountains and one of the things they exclaim about is the clear night sky. They marvel at the constellations because in the city they couldn't even see the stars. Away from the smog and lights the sky is black velvet set with millions of quivering candles. When you stop to consider that our life-giving sun is one of these candles, and one of the smallest ones besides, it gives you a sense of the magnificence of the universe. Along with the changing seasons, the changing mood of the landscape in different weather and lighting conditions, the sky becomes a marvelous teacher of the immensity of Nature, the insignificance of Man. The sky is a cathedral.

You can enhance the wonder of it all by learning something about the planets and the stars, and this time of the year provides prime viewing because the air is crisp and clear. A good book is essential. We've enjoyed *The Stars,* by H. A. Rey, published by Houghton Mifflin Company. The jacket unfolds into a large star finder, or planisphere, which is a boon to amateur astronomers. The kids got to know the constellations and we spent many a pleasant evening lying on our backs marveling at the clockwork of the skies. While it's hard to imagine how the ancients could see bears and water carriers and virgins in those pinpoints of light, we could only wonder at their mathematical and astronomical abilities that would put most modern "educated" people to shame.

The new garden and the 1974 fields are all laid out on paper, the seeds ordered, and one of these days we'll have a heat wave that will bring the temperature above freezing and me to the machine shed to start putting things in order.

The garden should be in better shape this year, and we have an ample supply of compost. The fields are something else. We'll be putting in a lot of red clover in this year's soil improvement program. Just the thought of the work ahead is exciting.

One day in early December, when the energy crisis was just building up steam, Ron walked into the office and handed me a fistful of papers. He was so darn mad about so many things connected with it that he had sat down at the typewriter to get some of it out of his system. He was particularly disturbed by many of the ads that jumped on the energy bandwagon, especially one that advised you to buy an artificial fireplace; "Beat the energy crisis: burn gas logs!"

I smiled, and handed him the sheaf of papers I had written. While neither of us knew what the other was doing, it was an impulse on both our parts, we had come up with the same idea.

After much more discussion we mapped out an article, but when we started writing it looked more like a book. Is there an energy crisis, if so why, and what implications does it have for homesteaders? That was the basis, but so many other factors are involved that it's only the beginning.

There is no doubt that all of this will have a tremendous effect on homesteading, so we decided to print all of our thoughts... and those that you contribute, of course... in kind of an on-going conversation on the real value and meaning of homesteading. If you're an aspiring homesteader, we hope the conversation will set a fire under you, and if you're experienced, we hope it will give you some new ideas and inspiration, or a chance to get something off your chest.

Too bad the people who most need this information won't see it and wouldn't believe it if they did get to read it.

Winter is a good time for things like this around here. Not that there isn't much to do, but at least there isn't as much to do as there will be when we start planting!

Besides putting out a magazine and doing the daily chores and talking about energy, the Countryside gang has taken on a major new project: a general store. It's just a start (there's an ad someplace in this issue) and we're not looking for it to be anything big, but we want to be able to provide items that are handy in the country and not too easy to find.

If you have any nominations, we'd like to hear from you. Maybe you produce something yourself and need a market or are sold on something you bought and would like others to benefit from it too. If you can provide the address of the manufacturer (not dealer) we'll try to stock it.

We're looking for things that are not necessarily good for business, but good for the Earth and good for the people who live close to it. It's going to be interesting.

In addition to new projects, we get some reading done in the winter (I just finished *The Secret Life of Plants...* a fantastic book), and we spent the weekend before New Year's moving the Grosz homestead. They now have a 20-acre place a few miles from here, which will keep them as busy as the Belangers. . . especially since they heat and cook with wood. We have a new helper, Phyllis Reynolds; the first lamb has arrived; our new book on small stock (*Homesteader's Handbook to Raising Small Livestock*) will be off the Rodale press in February; and in general, things are as exciting as ever. You don't crawl into a hole and hibernate for the winter just because you live beyond the sidewalks!

Afterword: The Countryside General Store came about after we wrote an article about hog butchering and using a bell hog scraper. Readers wanted to know where to get one. We tracked down a manufacturer, but couldn't convince anyone to advertise them. So we bought some and sold them ourselves, as a service to readers.

A decade later magazine circulation had plummeted and the store blossomed: it was bigger and more profitable than the publication. At one point UPS sent extra trucks to handle the mail

order business, (notably after we introduced Victorio strainers, and then Starplate frame connectors). We advertised on tv, and tour busses stopped at the retail store in downtown Waterloo.

But our heart was with the magazine, and when tough times arrived and we had to cut back, we closed the store instead of the magazine. It was probably one of the poorer *business* decisions I made in my life, but it wasn't surprising.

Interestingly, "tough times" for us always came when most others were prospering. When times were tough for the masses, more people were interested in homesteading. So my gloomy outlook was heartfelt, but also (and just incidentally) part of the business.

20. March, 1974

Countryside moves to a real office

L ast year was pretty mind-boggling for us. We took on so many new projects —more of them by fate rather than by choice— that by year's end my head was swimming. So my number one New Year's resolution was to get my head on straight.

I decided to set aside a specific time each week to get things organized, repaired and maintained. I took the cutting bar off the hay mower and got a new one, which hopefully will help me avoid the time loss, trouble and frustration I ran into last year when the thing kept jamming up. I took off the old plow shares, and when I went to match them up with a new set I had a hard time finding replacements: mine were so worn down they didn't look like any in the store. No wonder my plowing went so poorly last year! Ron and I cleaned out the tool shed and made it look three times bigger.

Part of this is living and learning, because frankly, having never used anything but second-hand, beat-up equipment, I didn't know what it was supposed to look like or even how it was supposed to operate if it were in good condition. Part of it was just lack of time. When the hay is ready to cut and the sun is shining, you cut hay, not practice preventive maintenance. Of course you make repairs... which means you would have been better off doing the maintenance in the first place.

Ah, but this year will be different. If I can keep up the progress I've made so far, by spring I'll have a "like new" line of equipment. (The used plow was bought for $15 and the new shares for it cost $18!) Oh sure, there will be new things to go wrong, new tricks to learn, but if I still do have a lot of trouble, there will be some satisfaction in knowing that I could have had a lot more without the time I'm spending on equipment now.

I don't know if this is breaking my resolution and taking on a new project or keeping it and getting better organized... but we're moving into an office in town. Tomorrow, as a matter of fact. If I can finish this so we can get the magazine to the printer, that is.

I'm not sure I like it, but we really don't have much choice. One of the things that has always appealed to me about "the perfect homestead" is that you can make a living without leaving home... if not by selling goats or rabbits or garden produce, then by programming computers or writing books and magazines or whatever you're good at, at the kitchen table.

But it takes nine of us to get out this magazine, and our office has been a shed that holds three people. The others work at home on their kitchen tables, which is fine, but every so often we have to get together and it's chaotic. We should be able to operate more effectively, and maybe with a little more sanity.

There is no such thing as a typical day here, but it basically revolves around the livestock. I feed and milk the goats while the boys take care of the cows and poultry. Then I start the fire in the wood stove in the office before breakfast.

I feed the sheep, goats and cows silage at noon before going out to the mailbox, which is the focal point of the day. Ron is usually going through the mail at one end of the kitchen table while John eats so he can catch the afternoon kindergarten bus. He's probably the only kid in his class whose lunch time conversation is interlaced with excited exclamations like "Hey, look at this neat letter from so-and-so!" or "Man, everybody wants a Corona grain mill!"

We work until supper time, milk right after that, and by the time we get the printing, advertising, hog, dairy, general farm, homestead and news magazines that came in the day's mail read, it's time for bed.

In-between all this we put out the magazine, run the farms and homesteads and have a little fun. Just the other morning, for example, as the kids got on the morning school bus and Diane and I were finishing up breakfast, we remarked on the particularly striking sunrise. Light was reflecting off the ice in the swampy field below the kitchen window, the trees on the hill beyond were silhouetted against a vivid pink cloud, and the rest of the sky ranged in color from black to purple to faintest light blue. So I swung my chair around, pulled Diane onto my lap, and we watched the sun rise.

John came downstairs and thought we were watching tv through the window.

Phyllis, who has sort of inherited the general store, has been taking care of the rabbits here, and she says she'll miss them when she doesn't have to come to the farm to work. But then, like the rest of us, Phyl will miss a lot of things.

She's been eating her lunch in the machine shed and tossing her orange peels to the pigs afterwards, because that's what turns her on. Last fall Ron's lunch break consisted of wandering down to the woods and stopping off in the sunflower field to gather a handful of seeds to munch on. With spring coming, we could be picnicking in the orchard again, watching the bees working and listening to the banging of the lids on the hog feeders below. Downhill, but not always downwind, although nobody ever seemed to mind.

You can be sure we'll arrange things so that these good times and simple pleasures won't be foregone entirely. Much as I love COUNTRYSIDE and all you who make it, I've lived long enough to realize that if my own lifestyle isn't what I want it to be, putting out a magazine like this is an act of hypocrisy. We may never be overly successful (like *Life* and *Saturday Evening Post!*) but by golly we'll be honest. *(2014 note: This was a joke:* Life *and* Saturday Evening Post, *both among the top magazines just a few years earlier, had recently gone out of business.)*

I'm not sure if this involves honesty, cultural bias, acclimation or just plain weirdness... but the other day I decided that a true homesteader must be someone who absolutely cannot *stand* the smell of lemon scented furniture polish, hair shampoo, detergent, and goodness knows what else... and loves the aroma of ripe billy goat! Our buck is in with the girls now, partly because of the problems of winter watering and care, and partly just to "make sure" in late January. But I don't find the buck odor at all objectionable. Matter of fact, I kinda like it.

We failed, once again, to bring a hive of bees through the winter. They were all dead (and not starved, either) by mid-January, after some -20 weather. And the price of package bees appears to have doubled since last year, which makes overwintering much more attractive. I never bothered too much about it because considering the price of bees and the value of the honey they consume during water, it was cheaper to get new bees each spring anyway.

Honey—even homestead honey—is going to be expensive this year.

One interesting effect of the current spate of shortages of everything came to light in a recent trade magazine. There is a shortage of electrical cord. So appliance manufacturers are quietly lopping off one, two, even three feet on each unit sold. *(Later note: was that true... or were cords made shorter, as some said later, to keep them out of the reach of small children?)*

I kinda enjoy watching how people are settling in and grimly accepting all these shortages. We had it so easy for so long that we were getting soft. Finding that we have to work just a teeny bit harder at living will make the whole world stronger, I believe.

And when all these shortages get down to the basic necessities, like food, more people will be ready to cope.

I like the approach COUNTRYSIDE is taking toward the energy crisis... especially when you see how some other people are handling it.

For instance, Schick is claiming that it uses 50 times as much energy to shave with a blade rather than with an electric razor. They point out that 50 million blade shavers throw away over a billion razor blades a year, millions of aerosol cans, millions of pounds of shaving cream, and billions of gallons of hot water.

This may be true, but what Schick ignores is the probable result of 50 million blade shavers switching to electrics: the enormous use of nonrenewable resources, the pollution output, the transportation and other factors involved in spare parts, accessories, and servicing.

As the Age of Waste gives way to the Age of Permanent Shortages, Schick will undoubtedly find many shavers going back to the straight razor, a cake of soap in a shaving mug, and a good old brush.

This is an academic subject for me: except for a few years in the Marines, it's been almost 20 years since I shaved on a regular basis.

While business things are a necessary part of my life, and some of them are fun and even exciting, my gaze keeps drifting out the window and up the snow-covered alfalfa field on the hill. My thoughts focus on spring.

That, after all, is what the magazine and books, our lives even, are all about. If it weren't for the thrill of heading up that hill for the first field work of the year or approaching the winter-ravaged garden with the first packet of peas, radishes and lettuce, none of the rest of this would mean anything at all.

Part of the thrill is working with Nature: of dropping tiny, "lifeless" seeds in the soil and watching them provide us with sustenance. Part of it is the challenge of raising healthier and better crops by improving the soil. And this year more than ever, part of it is the satisfaction you get from being independent, of knowing you'll eat no matter what happens to the economy and other social artifices.

With a little skill, a lot of work, and some luck, of course.

When you think about the condition of the world today, these are all important. Since we seem to have so little control over anything, including our own lives, these reasons are as good as any for enjoying life beyond the sidewalks.

21. April 1974

The big blizzard of '74

April. Or so it says on the cover of this issue.
Most of the time, it's easy to project myself ahead to the cover date and write accordingly. But for pete's sake, here it's really February, it's snowing (and the prediction is for three inches tonight) and I don't feel a bit like April.

Part of the problem is, I've really been mentally geared up for spring. Happens every February, of course: a few nice days melt the snow, the seeds that are supposed to go into the cold frame burn a hole in your pocket, a couple of lambs are born and you're psyched-up for spring. Then the sky clouds up and dumps a foot of snow on everything, and it might as well be November again.

In one way, that's a nice thing about writing for a magazine at this time of the year. I can forget about this blah period by telling myself that by the time you read this I should have my oats and clover planted, a lot of the plowing and disking done, and the new season of life will be underway.

Somehow, it isn't working tonight. Steve and I did the barn chores (as opposed to the rabbit chores, the chicken chores and the pig chores: those are all in different buildings). It was rather leisurely, which is unusual around here on weekdays. We worked together in the silo, and sang a few songs. Now that the tower is nearly empty, it's better than singing in the shower. It's always nice to feel appreciated, which may be why I love feeding silage: the cows strain at the stanchions, ready to lap up the sweet-smelling corn. You soon learn to feed those nearest the silo door first, because if you don't they'll stick out their foot-long cow tongues and upset the five-prong fork as you pass by.

On any quiet night, especially a quiet, snowy night, there's nothing quite like resting on your fork in the barn and listening to the weird sound of cows eating. The only thing I could compare it to is the sound of the ocean surf at night, but that really isn't a good description either. Cows eating have a sound all their own, which is pretty neat.

Then we turn on the water in the stock tank. (Never did get that float valve fixed to make it automatic.) The splashing water mutes the sound of the cows, but then since we're down on the goat-sheep end of the barn, the cows are fairly out of sight and mind anyway.

Our favorite ewe, Winnie the Pooh, is a Dorset. She's a wonderful mother, and in connection with what I've read and heard about Dorsets, makes me very interested in that breed in the event we expand our sheep enterprise, which is a good possibility. But she has the biggest mouth on the farm. I hear a lot from Judy Kapture and others about what blabbermouths Nubian goats are. Ours never make a sound. But

Winnie... good grief! I think I'd go nuts with a whole flock of sheep like her.

Her lamb—who somehow got named Porkchop even though we have a more or less firm policy about not naming our food—has become a really friendly little fellow, having been born during the season when all there is to do on the farm is tinker with equipment, dream about spring, and play with newborn lambs. He's spoiled, but fun. So I play with him for a while.

Then I came in the house, and here I am, "working." The fact is, I'm doing it because I want to: it seems like a good night for just sitting and thinking, and I think best at a typewriter.

Next morning, Feb. 22:
     I woke up about 5:30 as usual, and lay in bed awhile listening to the wind moaning in the pine trees on the front lawn. Visions of warm, drying March winds (well, it's almost March) set me to dreaming of spring again.

But, when I finally got up, I couldn't see out the window: it was plastered with snow. I stumbled to the bathroom in the semi-dark, flipped on the light switch, and muttered about the irksome delay in the fluorescent tube, which seemed worse than usual this morning, while I reached for my toothbrush. I turned on the water. Nothing. The realization hits with the suddenness of a frisky cow's hind leg at milking time: no electricity.

Going out to milk, I open the door and have to pause, take a deep breath, then plunge into a blinding swirl of blowing snow. Through squinted eyes I can see the driveway is blocked. No car will make it from here to the office today. Between the hen house and the milk house the drift is past my knees.

The barn door hadn't been closed tightly last night, and the horizontally driven snow blanketed half the barn floor. Not that the door made much difference: the milkhouse, which had been closed, was full of snow too. It blew through the tiniest cracks.

I milked without washing udders, and told the animals they'd have to wait awhile for a drink.

Diane was rummaging around in drawers with a flashlight, trying to find batteries for the radio. Chicago had 10 inches of snow, and Des Moines had 6 inches with 40 mile-an-hour winds. Most roads were closed.

The phone worked. We contacted the Countryside gang and told them what they already knew: don't bother trying to get to the office.

"Oh, this is fun," Lynn said. They had the wood kitchen stove going, they have a wood furnace and a hand pump and a kerosene lamp, so this real, honest-to-goodness energy crisis didn't bother them a bit.

A car trying to get through on Highway 19 got stuck on the crest of the hill a short distance from us. The driver came to ask if we had a tractor. Before we got there with the Oliver, someone else had pushed him out.

We set a couple of kettles of snow on the gas stove to wash the milking equipment and make coffee.

One of the neighbors called. The temperature in their house was down to 55. Ours was still 60. Steve stacked some wood in the old office, as we planned to stoke up the wood stove in there.

Anne-marie came in from rabbit chores with a bunny in her arms. Its outside hutch was buried in snow. Dave and I moved a cage into the milkhouse.

Diane decided to bake bread. I ground the wheat. After checking the weather again, I decided to drain the barn water pipes.

John had been after me for a long time to shave off the bottom of his bedroom door so he could close it. I had just bought a Stanley Surform, and tried it out. Worked beautifully—better than any plane I'd ever used.

What next? Well, might as well write *Beyond the Sidewalks.* The electric typewriter was useless, of course, so I dragged out the faithful old portable. The U didn't work. I fixed it. It quit again so I just substituted the 8. Never realized how important a U is in the English language.

It's 11 A.M. Looks like a long day ahead.

A fternoon:
I stoked up the woodburning stove in the office shed, although it was still comfortable in the house. It was so nice by the fire that I sat there and shelled soybeans to make soy nuts. The kids had been out playing in the snow, and appreciated the hot stove for drying out snow-caked mittens and soggy boots when they came in, ruddy-cheeked and panting.

While baking bread, Diane made a couple of pies. The kids decided to make their own mini-pies, and had a contest to see who could be most creative with fillings. To my palate, nobody won, although Anne-marie came up with an interesting roll-type thing with pie crust and butter and cinnamon. And they had fun.

Even with the young teenagers, it was relatively quiet, with no radio, phonograph or tv operating. That couldn't last, of course, and periodically throughout the day there was piano practice in the living room and trombone practice as far away as possible.

About 4 P.M. we called a couple of the neighbors to see if they needed help with milking. Lorne Billings said he had just finished his morning milking (by hand), and since the cows hadn't had water, there was no sense in starting over again! But he didn't want to put the warm milk in the bulk tank, because without the agitator, the whole lot was likely to spoil. Did we want some milk? I suggested that we run it through the cream separator and make cheese and butter.

So we dragged sleds and toboggans down the hill to their place to pick up milk. They had 300 pounds of it, in plastic jugs, in kettles and pans, in jars and the plastic garbage pails they use for sour colostrum, all sitting in snowbanks around the barn.

We got it home, did our chores, and the neighbors started arriving for a "blackout party." The kerosene lamps were going, we had candles in dark corners, and a flashlight occasionally came into play when we needed light in strategic areas.

We ran the milk through the separator, and by the time we finished (guess who got to turn the crank) the gals had one batch of butter run through the hand churn already. We put two large kettles of skim on the stove for cheese, got a little music going with the guitars and mandolin, ate fresh bread and even fresher butter. There were 18 people in our kitchen, and even though it was nearing zero outside and the furnace hadn't been running for over 12 hours, it was still 60 degrees inside. And when you're churning butter or singing, that's plenty warm.

It was near midnight when we drained the last batch of cheese for the night and turned out the lamps.

S aturday morning, Feb. 23:
Down to 45 degrees in the house. Modern houses are too open for this kind of thing. Ours isn't that modern. We could close all the kitchen doors (five of them) and the oven was able to bring it up to a habitable temperature. It looked like we'd have to find a source of water for the livestock.

But, as we pondered the alternatives and plotted our day as best we could, there was a jarring whir as the refrigerator kicked in; the lights went on; water began to gurgle in the pipes and the thermostat on the furnace came back to life.

We were, quite frankly, just a little disappointed.

Especially since I found out the water went back into the barn pipes before the heat cable had a chance to warm them, and it froze. After wrestling with that, I struggled to plow out the driveway and had equipment trouble. I started to clean the barn, got the manure spreader full, and found out it didn't work. Had to unload it by hand.

It was all a grand experience, in many ways; almost a "test run" for a self-sufficient homestead. We have a better idea of where our problems of survival lie, we know we can live with temperatures and conveniences on a much less grand scale than we had formerly thought, and perhaps most of all, it was heartwarming and encouraging to see the cooperation, the spirit, that resulted from what could have been a very rough time. Maybe this is a natural reaction to crisis, and if things get as bad as most of us have been thinking they will, a new golden age of *humanity* will arise from the ashes.

I'm firmly convinced that that's what most of us are looking for anyway, every day, crisis or blackout or not. . . and that's one of the main reasons we live beyond the sidewalks

22. May/June 1974

About the magazine

2002: Most magazine editors don't talk about their magazines (especially their problems!) in print. That's not what their readers are interested in.

COUNTRYSIDE, again, was different. Maybe it was the personal nature of the magazine, and the tremendous reader involvement. Maybe the integration of the home business with the homestead had something to do with it. Whatever the reason, many readers were interested in what was going on with the magazine itself.

This selection hints at some of the problems the growing home business was facing, along with the continuing chronology of life beyond the sidewalks.

Here's the May/June issue and since I know a lot of new readers (as well as some old ones) are asking why May/June and November/December are combined issues, I'll answer you all at once.

When *Small Stock* was strictly a rabbit magazine, and fell upon hard times, as rabbit magazines are wont to do, it was apparently decided that one way to save money was to publish only 10 issues a year. Since there are few rabbit shows in December and not many in June, ad revenue from shows was even worse than usual then. So those were the two months that were, in effect, eliminated.

We've simply kept the tradition... and I have to admit I kind of enjoy it. Not that we get a month "off"... the mail and other work keeps right on a'comin'... but you'd be surprised at how free a person can feel without a press deadline for a whole month!

And actually, although this strange schedule was due to rabbit shows and the advertising revenue they brought in in those days, it fits pretty well on the homestead. April and October may not be the busiest months, but they're close enough.

We haven't accomplished a whole lot so far this year. The COUNTRYSIDE crew spent a day working on the new hotbed in mid-March, but then we got involved in other projects and it was a couple of weeks before anyone could get back to it. And, although we used horse manure that was steaming beautifully when we put it in the hotbed, it cooled off and refused to do anything for us after that. If we *had* been far enough along to use the hotbed, we would've lost everything anyway, as the temperature got down to -10 and it was well below freezing in the frame at dawn, toward the end of March. (Today, the outside temperature reached 10 above, and the temperature in the frame was 55.)

We made the frame large enough for all of us, and with plenty of excess capacity for our market garden. We have about 60 square feet of flats, which ought to do the job... that's about 5-6 times as much as we usually use, just for the Belanger family.

One thing I've noticed already is that it's a lot more fun doing a job like this with help. Planting will be a festival, I'm sure... and I hope it keeps up through the weeding and mulching!

Chuck drove all the way to the county seat to get a soil probe so we could have the soil tested, and they were all out. No doubt, with the scarcity of fertilizer, more people than ever are testing their soil this year.

We don't use chemical fertilizers, of course, but we want to keep track of things not only so we know what types of improvements to try to make organically, but also so that in case they work we can tell you how we did it. Our biggest projects right now are in the fields that were planted to oats and wheat last year. We'll be planting clover and sorghum-sudan to plow down for green manure.

We spent a day doing the spring butchering and, as usual, picked a miserable one. It was snowing by the time we finished, and the next day when we cut the carcasses, we froze.

We still use Ann Kanable's father's recipe for curing pork but we've modified it a bit. Instead of spreading the meat out on a table and rubbing the cure in every day for a week, we merely rub it in well and pack the meat in a large stone crock. We have to pour the juice off once in awhile, and we add new cure then, but we eliminated the daily rubbing and having the meat spread out all over. Works fine.

We thought the wheat crop was something of a failure last year, but with the price at $6 a bushel now, it doesn't look quite as bad.

A note that should be of interest to all small stock breeders: air shipping of livestock, which has been difficult in the past, is apparently going to be well nigh impossible. This obviously affects people who ship stock regularly, but it affects a lot of others, too. If you're just getting started, or want to start over with some extra good stock, chances are it will have to be shipped. On a slightly different level, people who *do* ship in stock from other areas of the country sooner or later make improved bloodlines available in their own locality, creating a ripple effect that can mean better stock for everyone. So shipping is important to us all.

Among the new requirements being talked about are specific types of shipping crates, specific types of fasteners (with snaps and hasps), and the provision that no perishable food be put in the crates. Each animal will need a health certificate. These provisions would also apply to poultry and waterfowl.

Those directly affected should get the full details of the proposed changes and make their thoughts heard locally, as well as through the various national associations that are, or should be, dealing with the matter. And it would seem to make sense for anybody else who raises small stock to back them up.

I expect to hear a lot of complaining from strictly rabbit raisers in the months ahead, as we cut down on the rabbit section. (The April issue had 22 pages on rabbits, and we were flooded with complaints from people who don't raise rabbits!)

As some of you know, there's a long story behind this. We tried to make *Small Stock Magazine* go as a rabbits only magazine, and just couldn't get the support to make it worthwhile.

We don't get rabbit articles. We don't get rabbit advertising, even in the special breed issues. We don't get any response from our ads in the other rabbit publications. As I said back in September, 1971, it doesn't look as if rabbit people want, or deserve, a magazine of their own.

On the other hand, people *do* want and appreciate the countryside type of material we publish. Proof? We now have ten times as many readers as we did with the rabbits-only magazine! I'll admit that my personal preference is for the eatin' rabbits rather than the showing rabbits, but that only makes it easier and more fun to go along with the majority. No rabbit raiser can say we didn't give it a good try over the last four years.

Goat material, too, has been diminishing, and will probably diminish even more. We've had more response from goat people than from rabbit people, but not enough to keep up the quality of the old *Dairy Goat Guide.* Judy Kapture has just about written herself out, she says, and considering what she's done in the past few years, I don't blame her one bit. She not only turned out a tremendous volume, but it was all first-class material.

Of equal importance is the fact that we're tied to 64 pages for financial and mechanical reasons, and there is an increasing demand for an ever-greater variety of material in greater quantities. Something has to give.

This is not to say we won't be covering goats or rabbits: we'll just be placing less emphasis on them, and more on other aspects of homesteading. This issue is something of an experiment toward that end. Your comments are welcome, as always, but if you're going to blast us, please consider our side, which I've just explained.

The Associated Press reports that more than half a century of reflection has convinced social philosopher Lewis Mumford that the world has entered a new Dark Age.

Some of his comments:

"Economists who doubt we are heading for a depression are talking through their hats.

"People who think (the energy crisis) is a minor thing and should soon be over are living in a dreamland, really. The crisis is bound to get worse if we don't change our habits because we're consuming too much energy. Not merely are we consuming too much energy, we're consuming our capital... No economy can live on its capital. You can imagine that you're rich and flourishing if you draw on your capital. We're living on the capital accumulations of a carboniferous age when our fossil fuels were first produced. There's nothing left when they're gone."

The visiting Massachusetts Institute of Technology lecturer lists three steps he considers essential in the solution of the energy crisis:

Solar energy must be used on a vast scale, by plant growth. The second solution is to grow food wherever possible, not just where it's profitable. The third is for human beings to do more of the work now done by machines. "This doesn't mean to say that we abandon machines. We abandon our dependence on machines."

Like homesteaders do.

The nation's "outstanding young farmers" were told that the fertilizer shortage this spring will run to 15-20 percent, that means grain production will be 22.5 million tons less than farmers would normally produce, and since that's nearly twice as much grain as was involved in the notorious Russian grain deal, "predictions that consumer food prices will level off later this year could be wrong." Rep. Jerry Litton (D-Mo.) spoke to the Jaycees Outstanding Young Farmer Program assemblage in Dubuque, Iowa.

COUNTRYSIDE generally tries to be a happy magazine, even while avoiding a Pollyanna attitude toward homesteading. But recently, events that make homesteading a deadly serious business have been coming along at a fast and furious pace. I still think homesteading is the best way to live. It's fun, most of the time. But if it turns out that homesteading is the only way to survive, then our job here on the magazine is even more important than just helping you do a better job of raising livestock.

Spring, right now, is pretty much in a holding pattern. We have a lot of work planned, we can't do much of it until the weather cooperates, and you'd think we'd sit back and enjoy the last few days of "leisure." But that's not how farmers work. We're anxious to get at the planting... the fields, the garden, and the more than 2,000 trees we'll be putting in.

Meanwhile, we're working on the turkey pen, there's fencing to be done, fruit trees to prune and spray with dormant oil spray, there's still foundation waiting to be put into the beehive frames, and we must butcher a steer before warm weather arrives, as surely it will.

Work? You bet. Is it tedious, boring or demeaning? Heavens no! In fact, people who love this kind of life can't help but feel sorry for the unemployed, the bored, the super-sophisticates who feel they're too good to labor. Fresh air, exercise and a feeling of accomplishment are all reasons for living beyond the sidewalks.

2010: Since I've been comparing current prices with those of long ago, I should point out that right now, farmers are getting less than $6 a bushel for wheat... less than they got 36 years ago, when gas was 53¢ a gallon. That was leaded regular: unleaded didn't appear until 1976, and of course ethanol wasn't even on the horizon.

23. July 1974

Of horses and tractors

Sometimes I become contrary, maybe out of pure cussedness, maybe out of conviction. I'm not sure which reason applies here, but since this issue focuses heavily on horses and other equines I feel like talking about tractors.

Now if the truth be known, it wasn't too long ago when I could live quite handily without either horse or tractor. I was too used to goats to be comfortable around monsters like horses, and as far as mechanical monsters, well, I was the kind of guy who knew where the gas went in the family car and that was about it.

A lot has changed. In the first place, I learned that horses are just overgrown goats. Goats are a little easier to control physically, and they're less fearsome, but once you get to know a horse personally you can see a lot of similarities. (As an aside, I feel one reason so many people go completely nuts about goats is the intimate personal contact involved in milking. When you spend time with somebody like that, you can't help but love 'em. Rabbits probably have as much personality as goats, but I never really got to know a rabbit like I get to know goats I milk twice a day. Cows are different because they're bigger, less agile, dirtier, and again, more fearsome. They're harder to identify with.)

As I got to appreciate horses, I also got to know a few tractors.

Some years ago a reader, commenting on work horses, said he was never more proud than when driving a well-matched team, and "I'd rather work with horses than with a smelly, noisy tractor."

I defend the tractor from a practical standpoint. You don't have to feed it when it's not working, you don't have to exercise it and curry it and all those other daily things that, on many a small homestead, would add up to more hours than work time would.

While I realize that there are many impressive arguments in favor of horses (or other draft animals) on an organic homestead, I can't help but think of this every so often as I pilot my Oliver over a field. The fact is, I enjoy driving that tractor. It has a personality, like most of the machines I've had to work with, and when you get to know it there's a certain comradeship involved.

Starting out in the morning, especially if it's cool, Ollie is a little sleepy and you have to baby him. But it doesn't take long before he can really lean into an energy draining tool like the chisel plow or the forage chopper with a deep-throated roar that's as exciting as the take-off in a jet plane. Far from being a dead pile of junk. . . especially after getting to know his innards by replacing spark plugs, a generator, a flat tire and other assorted accouterments. . . Ollie is as much a friend as the horse.

Allis, the WD Allis-Chalmers, is a completely different filly. She doesn't have the guts, but is a lot more maneuverable and flighty. We have to be gentle with her on tough jobs, but on the more delicate operations she can run circles around Ollie. Personalities.

It's helped a lot to learn—out of necessity—about the rudiments of mechanics. The amount of machinery needed on even an 80-acre farm like this is astounding, and breakdowns are inevitable. We have over 50 tires on this place! My store of tools grows steadily, and with it, my store of knowledge. With both, your confidence can't help but increase too.

And confidence, whether with tractors, horses, goats, rabbits or chickens, is terribly important. It comes only with experience. Over-confidence comes from inexperience, and that's dangerous.

Ron and Lynn Grosz got so carried away as we started learning about donkeys for this issue that they ended up buying one. He's rather a nice fellow. Unfortunately, their son, Jason, is now sporting a cast on his broken wrist after sustaining a riding accident. As in my own case with the broken foot, it wasn't the animal's fault. Farms and homesteads are simply dangerous places to live, and maybe we should all just use a little more caution?

Sometimes insight comes in unexpected places. When Ron, Chuck, Phyllis, Diane and I were out in the woodlot planting seedlings, a fellow who was cutting wood on a neighbor's land came over to ask if he could cut firewood on our land. I told him we used the wood ourselves, which was okay; he didn't lose anything by asking.

But then we talked about what we were planting: 2,500 white pine, ash, black walnut, cedar and hard maple.

"Hard maple?" he roared. "Why, you'll be dead and gone before anybody gets a log off them!"

Not being very good at repartee, I mumbled something about not being as old as I looked and left it at that.

It wasn't until later that I wished I would have pointed out that the hickory he was cutting was older than he was: if we don't take care of the Earth *now*, somebody who comes after us is going to be in pretty sorry shape.

There's a story about an old, old man planting an apple tree that he couldn't possibly hope to eat fruit from, but his love of mankind was such that it pleased him to think of children yet unborn who would enjoy the apples from the tree he was planting. If we carry the analogy to air, water, soil, and substitute for our woodcutter the businessmen (and people who support them as laborers, customers, etc.) it makes a pretty poignant case for the danger we're headed for. There are too many shortsighted people in the world, like that wood chopper who never stops to think about where his livelihood really comes from.

The busiest of the busy seasons is here. We're still planting late crops... and we're already harvesting early ones, so we meet ourselves coming and going.

And while we always stress that work is play and play is work on the homestead, don't forget to make a little time to take the kids swimming or to do a little fishing. Working in the countryside is great, but that's not *all* life is about beyond the sidewalks.

2010: I'd like to go back to the old place and see what those trees look like now, 36 years later! But I'm afraid to: I'd hate to find that they aren't even there anymore. It seems that every place I've ever lived has been torn down, subdivided, the trees cut or uprooted...

No matter: I still plant trees.

24. August 1974

Everybody has to live *some*place

One of those perennial questions asked by people who are new to the concept of homesteading is, where is the best place to homestead? The way many of them put it is, where are the most COUNTRYSIDE readers, and what do they say about their locations?

Our mailing list doesn't tell us much, because we have readers in all 50 states, all provinces of Canada, and more than 45 other foreign countries. And when readers do comment on their locations, they invariably tell us what's wrong with them: too hot, too cold, too wet, too dry, soil all clay or all sand, and so on.

A few people have even asked me why I live in southern Wisconsin. My answer is probably the same one readers in New York or California would give. Through a complex series of events and circumstances, we just happened to end up here. We like it well enough, and certainly don't dislike it enough to go through the trauma of pulling up stakes and relocating just for a change of scenery.

Furthermore, having lived in a few other places, we know every area has advantages and disadvantages. The person who won't make a start until finding the perfect site is probably just dreaming anyway, and wants an excuse for avoiding having to do something.

This is not to say we don't all dream a little, or that we don't have a picture of the ideal homestead in our mind's eye, We just don't let it overwhelm us to the point where the question takes all our energies and we never get around to acting. If a live dog is more kingly than a dead lion, a second-rate working homestead is preferable to an ideal one that exists only in the mind.

A few months ago I mentioned to Larry McWilliams (in Tulsa, OK) that I wished he'd stop giving me progress reports on his garden. I was getting downright discouraged hearing about his fresh salads and early potatoes when our garden was still under snow!

His reply? Look at a map of insect concentrations. We have so many more bugs down here than you do, he said, that we need a growing season twice as long as yours just to produce the same amount of groceries! While that may be stretching it a bit, by the time you add in rainfall, tornadoes and other considerations, maybe it isn't far off the mark.

Most people who are younger, more mobile, and perhaps a little hipper (if that's still a word) than most of us seem to favor the Pacific Northwest, the Ozarks, parts of New England and almost anywhere in Canada. Their considerations are cheap land, relative isolation, and in some cases mild climates.

But there really isn't any cheap land anymore, and even the lower priced parcels are disappearing. Congestion has reached the point where parts of the Ozarks are little better than some sparsely settled suburbs and Oregon, to take one example, is actively discouraging immigration and is considering a statewide land use program.

Cheap land used to be found away from city congestion, and it was cheaper still if it was rocky or forested. Today, in many areas, "waste" land is more expensive than surrounding decent farm land as the price has been bid up by city dwellers who have been enticed by superhighways, the problems of the cities and the availability of cash to spend on spiritually or psychologically rewarding retreats, among other factors.

So where is the best place to homestead? In most cases, in your own back yard. For most people who have friends and relatives, other contacts, jobs, who know the ins and outs of local climate, real estate values, crop and livestock and market patterns, it takes a lot of guts to pack up and start over in an area that may be entirely new and strange. What's more, when the novelty wears off, they may find that the new area is no better than the old.

There are exceptions, of course, and for people who have been unhappy in their present locations for a long time, moving might not be a bad idea even if they aren't homesteading. But it's an individual decision based upon your own feelings about snow, fire ants, mildew, the changing seasons, and the host of other things that make each small area of our planet unique in its own way.

Got an interesting letter from Paul Piatt, of Santa Fe, New Mexico. He says, "I have taken *Small Stock* since about 1950 and really enjoy your magazine. I have been a rabbit raiser for over 50 years and still get some very good information from your journal. I have seven different kinds of rabbits, all pedigreed stock, and I really enjoy raising good ones and encourage others to do the same.

"Reading your journal has even gotten me interested in other livestock. I have always had a few chickens, but I have added geese, turkeys and a few goats. It is really fun to watch all the animals when they are contented."

This got us to wondering... who is our oldest reader? I know a couple of old-timers who were with us before 1950, although I couldn't say when they joined up. If you've been reading us longer than Mr. Piatt has, we'd love to hear from you.

It was a good year for strawberries and hay, here. They like water... and there's still water standing in some of the lower fields. The June 15 corn planting deadline came and went with what was to have been our major corn field still unplowed. It's becoming doubtful whether we'll get anything planted on those lands this year. The corn that did get planted is yellowing in large areas due to excess water, although sections of the real corn belt, farther south, are in a lot worse shape than we are.

The gardens here are pretty spotty too, as if germination was low. Actually, the seed companies warned about this on some crops due to poor growing conditions last year.

It hardly seems possible that summer is almost past, that the crops we planned for and dreamt of for the eternity that was last winter are nearly ready to harvest.

But already the planning goes on for next year! And, just as in every past harvest season, we tally up our successes and failures, and say, "wait 'til *next* year!" You simply must be an eternal optimist to live beyond the sidewalks.

25. December 1974
The melancholy days are come...

2002: A pattern emerges. When the economy and everything else is up, doomsayers are down. They get especially discouraged after a period when they could say "I told you so..." and then see everything return to "normal" again. That's what happened at the end of 1974, and it's probably why there were no "Beyonds" for several issues.

This long-winded December selection makes up for it, prodding further into that nagging near-yearning for a good old-fashioned depression, and a great deal more.

"The melancholy days are come, the saddest of the year, Of wailing winds and naked woods, and meadows brown and sere." — Bryant

That's how I started out *Beyond* last month, and I got so doggoned melancholy I never got the column written.

Well, that's not the truth either. I found so much to be melancholy about I wrote too much, and couldn't get it polished into something usable. The gist of it was, some of us have been having strange, almost intuitive misgivings for a good many years now, and things are getting curiouser and curiouser.

While I'm certain that a good percentage of COUNTRYSIDE readers are interested in country living for no other reason than the pleasure it affords them, there is a sizable group that regards homesteading as something much more; something spiritual; maybe even evolutionary along the lines of Teilhard de Chardin. It's hardly a secret that I class myself with the latter. For us, times are getting more and more exciting.

A certain segment of the population is actually looking forward to the coming depression, if not with eagerness at least with a certain grim smugness. It's not just a lemming instinct for self-destruction. It's more in the nature of an aching desire for a purge of the type suggested by Henry David Thoreau when he mused that it might not be a bad idea for everybody to burn their houses and all their possessions annually just to start out fresh and really taste life without getting entangled in the details. Imagine what Henry would think of us today.

Homesteaders, especially, have tasted real life. We've felt the warm sun, the stinging rain, aching muscles and the invigoration of open air exercise. We've smelled real life: warm blood and guts; moist soil in spring; dung; newly threshed oats; tomato vines; fresh milk and new-mown hay. We've seen the real world: the sun rising over mist-shrouded fields; newborn kids and lambs nursing; fragile shoots emerging from the barren soil; and 101 other scenes tv watchers will never experience no matter how artsy the writers and cameramen get.

We've lived in the real world of anticipation and despair, drought and flood, feast and famine.

We've lived in the real world... but only for fleeting moments snatched from the dream world which chains us to it with fetters of almost terrifying complexity. We need cash. We need technology. We need many of our social institutions. We need them, not to survive, but because the society we live in demands that we need them... because if we didn't need them there would be no society.

The crowning irony, of course, is that we are society!

While some people attempt to get off this merry-go-round by simply walking away from it, they don't really get very far away. Most of us don't even attempt to make the gesture.

That explains why a small group of people passively yearns for a collapse of at least a part of the society that has held them in a form of spiritual bondage. In other words, what homesteaders need to be fulfilled is a good depression.

It's interesting now to reread a letter a lady wrote to me about four years ago,

"The idea of homesteading is fun to fool around with, but how many of your so-called homestead folks are prepared to feed their chickens, rabbits and goats if the powers that be (meaning the labor unions) decide to strike the railroads and the truck lines at the same time? How are you going to preserve food if there are no jar rubbers available? Your form of so-called homesteading is still dependent on the outside world for ninety-one percent of its necessities."

Four years ago when this was written, strikes, war and civil uprisings were very real concerns among many people. We've had none of those on any grand scale... yet, canning supplies are unavailable in many areas, nails she spoke of in another part of the letter have doubled in price in three months, and as you've seen in letters from other countrysiders, we have continuing problems with just about all of our other necessities from sugar to used farm equipment to rabbit feed.

Usually, after a column like this, a reader will write to say, "We already know *why* we're homesteading: what we need from COUNTRYSIDE is the *how*." Or in another vein, "What does the energy crisis have to do with homesteading?"

Such reactions shouldn't be surprising, because some people just aren't tuned into the vibrations. But every so often that in itself surprises me.

Anybody who's been reading COUNTRYSIDE for any length of time is undoubtedly aware that they're a bit "unusual." I'm assuming here that a regular reader at least gardens and bakes bread, and that anyone who does that has run into friends and neighbors who think they're a trifle quaint and old-fashioned to do things that the mechanisms of society can do "better" and more efficiently and less expensively.

Even fringe readers can probably understand some of the jibes more serious (or more fortunate) homesteaders get: "You *drink* goat milk?" Or butcher your own hogs when you can have the job done for a "mere" $30-$40, or grind your own flour or thresh your own grain by hand?

I hadn't realized how far this line of thought had gone until last weekend, when Waterloo had its annual "Wiener and Kraut Festival." (There's a sauerkraut canning company here, and there was a meatpacking house that made wieners until a short time ago.) All the local merchants drag their goods out on the sidewalk for an open air fair sort of thing, and being local merchants, we decided to join the fun.

I brought in a goat for the city kids to pet and set up a grain mill and a Victorio strainer from the Countryside General Store.

Over the years I've become inured to just about every nasty, stupid and/or "clever" remark made about goats and goat milk. I've seen (and felt) the reaction most normal people have when it comes to butchering any class of livestock. I realize grinding grain and baking bread is a lot of hard work that is hardly justified economically today, and that not many people are interested in the other justifications. But I was hardly prepared for what happened on the sidewalk last Saturday.

I was merrily cranking away on the Victorio strainer, tossing in chunks of luscious ripe tomato and feeling really pleased at how the seeds, stems and skins ooze out at one end while the pure tomato sauce glides glacier-like into the waiting pan. Anybody who has spent hours and hours of humid August afternoons peeling scalded tomatoes in a steaming kitchen would have to be impressed.

So I was taken aback when people would come up to my sidewalk table, look at the neat little pile of refuse on one end of the strainer and the beautiful tomato sauce on the side and say, "Yuck! What's that icky stuff!"

If people know so little about where their food comes from and are so squeamish they can't stand raw tomatoes, no wonder they're so unconcerned about such things as drought or early frost, to say nothing of herbicides, pesticides, fungicides, chemical fertilizers, hormones, antibiotics, and additives and preservatives of all sorts.

One of the basic rules of journalism is "Never overestimate your reader's information nor underestimate his intelligence." There are very few really unintelligent people, but there are many who don't have the facts.

Some of the worst transgressors are the experts who are so tied up in their own little spheres of competence that they can't relate to the big picture. Plato said if you want to study something large and complex you have to find the natural seams or joints so you can move from one area to another and not be overwhelmed by the grand total. Modern man has followed this to such a degree that researchers focus on individual parts so closely that they lose sight of the total. From what we've learned of balance and ecology we know—we should know—that everything is tied to everything else. You can't blame current troubles on Arab oil, unionism, politics, monetary policy, weather in the corn belt or any other single factor.

To this end, I wistfully wish the president would have invited a couple of us to his economic summit conference. Nobody would have paid any attention to us, of course, but after hearing about some of the opinions submitted by the high-fallutin' experts, I honestly believe some of us common folk are more aware of what's happening than the professionals are.

The problem is simply that we have been treating finite resources as if they were infinite. Oil, unions, politics, our entire social order, have simply played supporting roles.

If the analysis of the problem is that simple, so is the solution: we merely have to gear our standard of living to available resources.

But that's like deciding which mouse will put the bell on the cat.

The housewife who complains about the high cost of meat gets her grocery money from some industry or service... let's say, as an example, paper manufacturing. But if she gets more money it has to come from paper, and that increases the cost of shopping bags, advertising, newspapers and magazines, feed sacks, packaging of all kinds, sales slips, cash register receipts, adding machine tapes, signs, computer forms, telephone directories, bills, envelopes, and on and on. Since everything that's sold has some bearing on everything else, you can't increase prices in one sector without affecting costs — and prices in the other sectors.

To ask a farmer to reduce the price of meat without reducing the cost of gas, feed, and all of his other business and personal expenses, is plumb crazy.

In all of these escalating prices there must be a few people who are making fortunes. Even if there is some sort of conspiracy involved (and in spite of my skepticism I sometimes have to admit a certain sympathy with that line of thought) that still doesn't get back to the basic fact.

The basic fact is, we're mining the Earth. Raping it. Taking resources that have taken millions of years to develop and won't be replenished until millions more have passed. Living off capital. And this includes not only exotic metals, but such basic resources as soil, water and air.

Industrialists say we cannot have a no-growth or even limited growth society because that would jeopardize society itself. They could be right. What they haven't explained is how society can survive on its current course of rape and plunder.

I'm writing this with a radio in the background. Gov. Reagan has just said that government spending is the culprit. George Meany blames management. Management blames labor. Earl Butz doesn't see anything wrong at all.

And as one of the poor blokes in the middle I think they're all talking through their hats.

As artificiality piles on artificiality, as transgression compounds transgression, it becomes increasingly apparent that we have to start all over on a different plane. That's what homesteaders have been aiming toward, although sometimes unwittingly. The vibrations are heavy.

One of the happy things about homesteading and farming is that you can't dwell on esoteric things for long. Somebody still has to milk and feed the animals even on wedding and funeral days, to say nothing of holidays. So while we might get worked up discussing politics or economics or whatever, before we can organize a boycott or a demonstration or anything like that, it's time to do the chores again.

And so it is here.

A few months ago we printed a question and answer about farrowing hogs without crates. I've never used farrowing crates, myself: I just can't see cooping up an animal like a hog in one of those bird cages, with no room at all to move. I've used portable pens made from field fencing. They measure 6 x 18, which still isn't large, but it's better than living in a dresser drawer. I use plenty of bedding, and losses from crushing (the number one bane of farrowing operations) have been minimal.

But this letter went on to ask about keeping sows together, which I've never done. Knowledgeable swine people weren't much help: if they're knowledgeable, they used farrowing crates. And nobody could tell me why you don't leave sows together.

So I decided to find out.

There was nothing to it, really. Our seven sows were in the finishing house, since we'd gotten out of finishing hogs when we ran out of corn a couple months earlier. Our farrowing pens had been jerry-rigged in the machine shed, so it was a simple matter to just ignore the whole works and leave the sows where they had automatic watering, ready-made fencing, and easier feeding arrangements.

The first one — a gilt — came in with a litter of five. Nothing untoward happened. The other sows didn't pay any attention to her.

A few days later one of the sows had 11 pigs. There was still no trouble from the other gals, but she crushed two of the pigs on the second day.

The next litter was 14. Two were runts. One seemed to be doing all right, but we brought the other one in the house and gave him the goat milk and TLC treatment. He was fine for three days, then died, but the other one was already dead.

The next one was my special pet . . . the kind of animal most homesteads have, and shouldn't. She's beautiful, has personality, but doesn't produce worth a darn. I have goats and rabbits just like her, and keep them around for no logical reason. She's an older sow, and only had five which is about par for her.

She still has all five, anyway.

The fifth sow came in . . . my very best one. She had 14. By the time I discovered them, 10 were dead. There still was no evidence of any violence, and I spent some time observing the situation. Everything seemed copacetic. But the other four died too. Fourteen in, 14 out.

This beat the tar out of my average, as well as my morale. It was tempered only by the prediction of all the experts that hogs marketed the rest of the year will lose money anyway, so I could consider it a blessing in disguise.

I take a certain pride in being able to beat the national average of 7.2 pigs weaned per litter. I usually do much better, even without farrowing crates, antibiotics and feed additives. I would have matched it with even half of the last litter saved . . . in spite of the non-productive pet with her record of five. An average of six isn't all that bad . . . but what happened?

I'm convinced there was no fighting or other disturbance: The orphaned mother or whatever you'd call her is nursing other pigs! Thank Heavens: I said she was my best sow—she could hardly walk with those teats full of rich sow milk. There certainly is no disease or other metabolism factor. I don't have any answers, but I'm calling off the experiment. The sows yet to farrow are being separated.

I wonder if the slide rule boys at the research stations couldn't carry this a bit further. An average of six per litter ain't all that bad. I don't have the expense of farrowing crates. There is less labor involved. The baby pigs dig right into the comfrey and goat milk at the feed troughs and they look beautiful. I spent nary a penny on medicine, vitamins, antibiotics or inoculations. With a sharp pencil, there's an outside chance even the professionals would admit I'm making more money on hogs than the normal producers.

This general idea... making a little less, but spending a lot less... has a lot of ramifications. In the area of soil improvement, a friend of mine claims that while his organically grown crops yield less than his neighbors, his costs for fertilizer, insecticides, herbicides and the labor and fuel required for their application, let him come out ahead. This could be a powerful argument in favor of organic farming. Money means more to most people than talk of sterile soil and lack of unknown life-sustaining elements in plants.

Got a letter from Maurice Telleen of *The Draft Horse Journal* suggesting that I try to get hold of old copies of the *Breeders' Gazette.* "Those old *Gazettes* have talked me into planting pumpkins, far in excess of what we can use, in my corn next year. The old time shepherds loved to feed them to sheep, and even claimed the seeds aided in worm control." Maurice says he gleans old horse info from the magazines, but has to pass up all kinds of other interesting material that would fit well in COUNTRYSIDE.

Another reader mentioned enjoying an ancient copy of *Small Stock.* We have every issue dating back to 1917. Some of them are fascinating but, as an editor, I can see undercurrents of feast and famine in what former editors had to work with, just like today. Since COUNTRYSIDE & SMALL STOCK JOURNAL includes more than two dozen magazines, some of which even went back further than 1917, a collection of everything in our past would be a veritable library!

Speaking of libraries, I always knew we cram an awful lot of information into our pages, of course. But Heather Tischbein has been indexing 1974 issues and I'm truly amazed at the wealth of data we've carried. Amazed. This index will be bound into the hard cover editions of volume 58 that will be available soon after this issue is off the press, and we'll also be making it available to readers who prefer to just keep their regular issues. If I could remember 1/10th of what I've written or edited, man, would I be smart.

John Kyl, assistant secretary of the interior, has predicted that "we'll have a crisis in materials within five years that will make the fuel crisis look like a Sunday school picnic. We've got to quit treating minerals and timber as disposable items. We've got to reclaim them again and again."

Many of the basic materials are already 100 percent imported, he pointed out.

I've never believed much in the commercial forms of insurance. I prefer to make my own. To that end I plant some corn early, some late; I raise a little beef and a little pork; I do a little farming, and a little writing, and I sell a few books, grain mills and wood stoves. And while I sincerely believe in the spiritual values of homesteading, I'd be just as content to have everything continue on its merry course and reap only the pleasurable benefits of doing things for myself.

This, in itself, is part of homesteading. When the price of supermarket food remains artificially low, as it has been, I can content myself with the knowledge that my homegrown fare is free of pesticides and other poisons, or simply that it tastes better. When the price of any given commodity goes up, I can say I'm saving money. With a flexible attitude like that, how can I lose?

But maybe, if I really had to get serious for a fleeting moment, I'd have to point to a position like that espoused by Mildred Loomis. She recently wrote:

"Not long ago I made a chair. My purpose was to provide rest and comfort, and sustain healthful posture. I adapted a design of a homestead friend with the dimensions to fit my measurements: backrest at just the right height and angle. I decided on the materials needed. I chose the right weight hammer, the proper fine-toothed saw, different textures of sandpaper. Then I put together a chair for which I alone was responsible. It is my purpose, my design, my tools, my materials and execution. Probably no one else would want it, but it suits me. I unreservedly enjoyed its making and its using.

"When a nervous friend who uses sleeping pills and seems never to be without a cold tells me he doesn't like his factory job, I nod in sympathy. His corporation is doing things he doesn't understand, for purposes he didn't choose, for people he doesn't know. I look at my loaves of bread, my shelves of applesauce, my blouse, our garden, our homestead... my chair... and I am glad."

That, my friend, is what this is all about, out here beyond the sidewalks. Be glad.

Mildred Loomis (1905-2000) was known as "the grandmother of the counter-culture," and a devoted student of Ralph Borsodi (1886-1977), "an agrarian theorist and practical experimenter interested in ways of living useful to the modern family desiring greater self-reliance" and a legendary figure in the back-to-the-

land and self-sufficiency movement. Borsodi's father wrote the introduction to Bolton's Hall's *A Little Land and a Living*, which played a large role in the back-to-the-land movement that took place during the banking panic of 1907.

Most people today have never heard of Bolton, Borsodi, Loomis — or even such stalwarts as Scott and Helen Nearing. Is that because they were "philosophers"? But then, what homesteader or organic farmer is *not* a philosopher?

Oh yes, "modern homesteading" has a long and interesting tradition, which might amaze many people who consider all this a momentary fad.

The comment about underestimating the amount of intelligence and overestimating the store of facts deserves additional comment. Today, it's easy to become overwhelmed with facts. We're drowning in facts. But there are so many we often don't have the exact ones we need. Even then, how many people know how to put them together to arrive at the right solution?

Today, the old journalism advice still holds true (although I often wonder how much intelligence is *really* available in the world), but there is another aspect to it: knowledge without *understanding* is useless.

Part V: 1975

Bill Gates and Paul Allen create Microsoft; Fed year-end interest rate, 7.25%; average income, $14,100; inflation, 9.2%; Foster Grant sunglasses, $5; gas, 44¢; NYC avoids bankruptcy with $2.3 billion loan. First disposable razor (BIC). Motorola patents first portable mobile phone.

26. January 1975
More on the depression

I didn't get as much fall plowing done as I would have liked, but a good portion of it is finished. We're using the chisel plow exclusively here now, and it's great.

Our soil is heavy clay. The moldboard plow has created a plow sole layer that was impervious to water and plant roots. Drainage on some fields has already improved with the chisel. The water can sink into the ground during a heavy rain instead of running off and taking the topsoil with it.

The chisel also is important because it mixes organic matter into the surface instead of burying it. This helps water retention as well as letting aerobic action take care of the organic matter.

The fields that have had sorghum-sudan and clover plowed down as green manure are responding nicely, too: it was a real pleasure to work them, this year. And the earthworms are coming back!

Another thing I like about the chisel is the way it handles rocks. I go bananas trying to plow some of our rocky land with the moldboard. Hit even a muskmelon-sized rock just right and the plow releases from the tractor. Better than busting the plow or tipping the tractor, but you have to back up, rehitch the plow, then play around till you get unstuck. The chisel simply flicks even small boulders right out of the ground and bounces over those it can't move.

Speaking of rocks, a city feller stopped by the other day to ask if he could have one of the boulders in the pasture to put on his front lawn. Maybe it wasn't nice, but I laughed. I've worked on some of those things even with a bulldozer and they're like icebergs. The underground part is as big as a house.

We've had some interesting comments on the new schedule and the new price. Everybody's in favor of the extra issues, and surprisingly, not much was said about the new price. I was actually hoping we'd get some complaints so I could tell this little story.

In 1972 we combined Rabbit World (32 pages, 50 cents an issue) and Dairy Goat Guide (12 pages, 50 cents an issue) and COUNTRYSIDE (20 pages, 50 cents an issue) into one 64-page magazine. People who had been getting all three had been paying $11 a year, and the price went down to $5. Many people commented, "I'm going to renew quick before you come to your senses."

It took more than two years. I never was much good at numbers. In the meantime we had a little inflation. If you think the price of feed went up, you ought to get our paper bills. (Cheerful note: postage is supposed to increase this year — again — but we'll absorb it like we did the last two.)

Our turkey experiment worked pretty well. We let them have the run of the yard, with the chickens and guineas and ducks and geese, and while they were supposed to keel over from blackhead disease, they didn't.

We lost a few young ones, though, both here and at Groszes'. Seems they were too stupid to eat. One that did eat was too stupid to get out of the way of a donkey's hoof. It's hard to think of them as stupid, now. They're friendlier than the dogs and cats, and much tamer than any of the other birds. They're as inquisitive as the goats. I was driving some nails the other day and a turkey kept pecking at the nail I was pounding. Almost beheaded her with a hammer.

I got more comments than usual about last month's column (about the next depression). Most of you agreed that the world "needs" one because that's the only way values will be rammed back into perspective. Not only financial values.

When you find a winner, stick with it, I always say. So here are some more thoughts on the same topic.

What's going to happen this year; in the next five years; the next 20 years? Nobody knows, of course, but it's possible to make some fairly educated guesses.

I know, because back in the 1950s I wrote a novel. It wasn't any good, and I especially had trouble with the ending. But that book, the ending, and the 20 years since, have taught me something about prophecy.

The book looked at the world through the eyes of a young man approaching maturity in those "good old days." The hero detected a couple of problems with that world and planned to lay out the rest of his life according to his conscience instead of according to the expectations of society. He ended up as chief rabbit keeper on a commune, which gives you one idea of what the book was getting at. (Hey, I was just a kid, then.)

The world has certainly changed in the past 20 years. No doubt some people who get nervous easily have quit reading newspapers. And yet, broad areas of today's conditions were at least hinted at in that novel. In that context, I have to say things are looking up.

This will take some explaining.

The "apathetic generation" of the '50s isn't really apathetic. Like other generations it was simply a product of its time. And the '50s were at the end of the arc of the pendulum, the point where everything stops before the pendulum begins its swing in the opposite direction.

For the most part, times were good. Watergate? Heck, during the Eisenhower years we seldom even heard about *Washington!* Only a few people knew about Lake Erie dying and that was sad rather than tragic or alarming. Los Angeles smog was a joke, at least to the rest of the country. Television was coming into its own, which made science sound very practical as well as wondrous; Korea had "proven" that there could be no more major wars; the Depression was history and safeguards insured that it would not be repeated; and high school graduating classes were told that at last the world was straightening out and all they had to do was a little minor housekeeping.

It was all as phony as the massive fins that sprouted on massive cars in those days in a burst of artificial elegance and luxury.

The only real threat was the Bomb (always singular even though there were thousands of them, and with a capital B). There was nothing anybody could do about it and in retrospect, its major impact was to make each pleasure more keen, each moment more precious, and other inconveniences more insignificant.

I probably use this quote from T. S. Eliot more than any other, but for good reason: "This is the way the world ends, not with a bang, but with a whimper."

The Bomb didn't fall. Instead we're exterminating ourselves with underarm spray deodorant. (For you who have quit reading newspapers, this refers to the possibility that the propellants in spray cans are knocking out the ozone layer in the upper atmosphere, thus exposing the planet to lethal radiation from the sun.)

Since those days of happy nothingness we've gone through Watts and Selma; Viet Nam, assassinations that until they happened were as unthinkable in the U.S. as a fuel crisis; a fuel crisis; Watergate; inflation; a deepening recession, and hundreds of little things like pressure spray cans that together add up to a problem hopelessly more massive and dangerous than The Bomb.

Yet, I say things are looking up!

Things are looking up because we're learning, and that means there's hope.

Twenty years ago we had it easy. *Too* easy. We leapt from a depression that couldn't happen again and a war that couldn't be repeated into a society so technologically advanced that we couldn't help but feel we had licked all the problems that had beset Mankind since the beginning. We didn't realize that we were living off our capital. Our wealth was as artificial as that of a person living off credit cards. No one paid any attention to the expiration date. Our faith in the future was about as solid as that of a person who spends wildly because he "knows" his ship will come in even though the ship has no rudder, no sail, and no compass.

Strange but true: nothing is ever as good as it seems, and nothing is ever as bad as it seems.

Our current troubles don't spell doom, but hope. We *could* be doomed by the mass of mistakes we've made if we ignore them and keep on compounding them. While some people are still heading in this direction (like those who say we can't afford to clean up our air because it would be too expensive or because we need *more* electricity rather than less) some people are beginning to face reality. That's where the hope lies.

The world isn't going to change as much through the efforts of politicians and scientists as it will change through the efforts of you and of me. Not you *or* me: you *and* me. We are society.

We don't have to organize any more than a herd of earthworms organizes to change a pile of organic matter into humus. We need faith in the future based on facts and understanding, and if we each live our lives according to the dictates of that logical reasoning... and if there are enough of us...we will change the world.

That large segments of society are capable of changing their views is amply demonstrated by the change in attitude toward Viet Nam in a few short years. The compulsion to change will be infinitely greater in the new crisis, because it affects our survival as a race.

Taking this approach it isn't very hard to make a forecast on an either-or basis. Either we'll heed the danger signs or we won't.

If we don't heed the signs we'll wipe ourselves out by using up nonrenewable resources or poisoning our water and air and soil or by starving due to our agricultural methods and policies or by destroying the protective ozone layer or in a thousand other ways...or by a combination of "tolerable" levels of all or several of them.

Or we'll have a shakeout. Instead of being faintly amusing, that margarine commercial that says, "It's not *nice* to fool Mother Nature" will strike terror into the heart of every living being. The vested interests will begin to admit that we can live without electricity much more easily than we can live without air. They will begin to take a broader view of nonrenewable resources of all kinds. And there will be hope.

Either way, there are rough times ahead. In one case they would constitute a temporary hardship; in the other, oblivion. I prefer to plan for the temporary inconvenience because if I'm right I'm ahead and if I'm wrong I'm extinct anyway so it doesn't make any difference.

Based on all this — including my mini-prophecies of 20 years ago that proved to be fairly accurate — what can we expect in the years ahead? There will be, as noted many times before in this column, profound changes in the American way of life. They have already begun in such areas as fuel consumption for driving and heating; food; and certain other areas. There are gripes and there will be more, but Americans are still relatively well off. People in some other countries could live off our waste and think they were dead and gone to Heaven.

There will inevitably be hunger, for the short run, because of misplaced faith in agricultural technology ("It's not nice to fool Mother Nature") as well as other short-sighted policies.

There will be changes in diets around the world. America will be largely vegetarian much sooner than most people realize, and not because of any health or moral compunctions. Junk foods and ultra-processed foods will disappear. New forms of food will be utilized, or used more widely. Sprouts and grasses may fall into this category.

There will be dramatic changes in values as the concept of Earth as a spaceship takes hold in quarters that now ignore or ridicule the concept.

Agriculture will be broken into smaller units in areas like the U.S.; and it will be decentralized and diversified within smaller areas. There will still be cities and industries, of course, but people who *want* to farm will have the opportunity. They don't, now.

Life will go on, and we may even come to look on those years in the dim future as some new "Golden Age." I have faith that enough individual humans will work together, each in his own way, to avoid the final whimper.

There is more hope now than there was 20 years ago when few people knew anything was wrong. We can rejoice in that. Prepare for the "hard times" ahead, but don't forget that happiness and even pleasure have nothing to do with the Gross National Product of any nation or of the world. It comes from within yourself.

And the best place to bring that out, right now, is on your own homestead. No matter where it is, how developed it is, make the most of it. Immerse yourself in it, enjoy it. Don't dwell on yesterday, but don't forget it, either: use it to plan for tomorrow.

Have a happy new year, but more than that, have a happy new life, beyond the sidewalks.

2014: If I changed anything here maybe I'd modernize *Viet Nam* as *Vietnam*. But I wouldn't write it today: I'm not that hopeful.

27. February 1975

Is homesteading gaining acceptance?

The concept of "homesteading" is hard to explain to people who think Wonder bread is delicious and that the world's food situation is both localized and temporary.

The state of the world must be deteriorating faster these days: homesteading — the term and the concept — is gaining acceptance.

You see it in a hundred little ways, talking with people, reading newspapers and magazines, listening to the radio or tv.

Of course, there is still a long way to go. A newspaper reporter visited us to see what was going on, and we tried to explain what COUNTRYSIDE is all about. He was confused at first, but I could tell he was getting the idea when he asked, albeit with a sympathetic smile, "And what do your neighbors think of all this?" The implication was clearly, "How do these conservative Wisconsin farmers treat you ecofreaks?"

On the other hand, the *Chicago Tribune* just ran a piece about how Kathryn Willson, 64, and her family coped with the hard times of her childhood. She ended with this thought:

"I realize that this is a much different world today, but luxury has become necessity. There have been a score or more of wasteful years —

wasting our beautiful world. Let's re-evaluate our needs, take account of our resources, and really start living again."

No doubt she, and others who think like her, don't call themselves homesteaders. But the name doesn't matter. Attitudes and actions are what count. By any name, homesteading is becoming more respectable...and more necessary for the survival of mankind.

By the way, when that reporter got back to his typewriter, the lead of his story came out like this: "The editor arrived in a pickup truck, with dirty boots and his black beard flying." The headline was, "They practice what they preach." This is about as supreme a compliment as I hope for.

In spite of the difficulty of communicating with non-homesteaders — or maybe because of the challenge — I'd love to have the chance to talk to them regularly. If nothing else, I could keep both busy and excited just addressing some of the drivel that shows up in the daily papers.

My long-time favorites include the scorn heaped on organic farming by agricultural experts who obviously don't know beans about it and the unreserved praise most economists have for the "efficiency" of our food production system.

But these days, the most often-heard Big Lie type of propaganda that makes me see red is the quote from some agricultural bigwig to the effect that "homegrown tomatoes cost about a dollar a quart by the time they're harvested and processed."

Of course! If you don't know what you're doing. With experience the statement is balderdash.

Those naive individuals who think any dumb farmer can drop a seed in the ground and grow food should consider themselves lucky to get by for even that price. Dollar a dozen eggs or $3 a pound rabbit meat is cheap, for the new homesteader or first-time farmer.

And why? Because self-sufficiency takes a heap of experience and knowledge most people just don't have, that's why.

Most people think they know how to live because they went to school and learned algebra or nuclear physics, so they're educated. But they don't know a potato from a pigweed. We know so much about complicated things that we assume we know everything about simple things, but it just doesn't follow. Technological man is an arrogant creature.

Those dollar a dozen eggs are payment for an education not learned at school and rarely at home. The person who thinks he has nothing to learn will soon prove the expert is right when he says it's cheaper to buy groceries. But the humble, and truly smart person, who learns from the experience and sticks with it, will eventually make a fool out of the expert.

That's why we've been saying for years, start out slowly, learn by making *small* mistakes which are not nearly as expensive or discouraging as big ones, and you'll do all right.

It always frightens me to see people quit good jobs in the city and move to the boondocks with no experience whatsoever. I feel sorry for them...and I dread the setback they give all of homesteading when they go back to the city, broke and bitter.

Another story that's becoming more common with the growing acceptance of homesteading: *everybody* can't go back to the land.

True enough...even though if all the land in the U.S. were divided equally each family would have something like 22 acres, some good enough to farm. If all the cropland were divided, each family would get nine acres, which is certainly sufficient.

But nobody is saying *everybody* should or would want to, go back to the land!

If we were to do away with wasteful industrial production (planned obsolescence and that sort of thing) and our wasteful methods of farming (putting more energy in than we take out) there would be a lot of people standing around...until they got back to the small farms. They want to be there now but there's no place for them because the current system runs on nonrenewable resources, not labor.

Even aside from all this, it seems a bit silly to imply that since everybody can't homestead, nobody should.

Some of these things get me pretty riled up, but I'm no crusader. These are just thoughts I think while I'm feeding the hogs or plowing, things I discuss with friends around the potbelly stove in person or through the mail and the magazine.

On the other hand, these thoughts are the reason I work on COUNTRYSIDE rather than retiring to a hidden valley somewhere and tending strictly to my own homestead.

We lost a couple of duck dinners the other night. The flock wandered onto the highway, which hadn't happened before. Won't happen again, either, at least for four of them. There wasn't even anything left to pluck.

During the summer, one of my favorite pastimes is taking the goats for a walk. They don't go much for that in the winter so I usually have to go alone. But I led them up the hill the other day and it was surprising to see how they relished the dried, frozen weeds, and it was certainly refreshing to be part of the herd again.

I'm sure it would get boring, but if I could do anything I wanted to for a living, I'd like to be a goatherd.

Life is a compromise, so I'm sure not going to complain about not being able to spend all my time sitting on a mountain with the goats. But it is nice, once in a while, to dream about what Heaven on Earth would be like.

When I set priorities, the list is topped by having the finest garden possible and raising the best stock I know how... all, of course, in the interests of having a happy, healthy family that would be able to enjoy all the best things in life. (It goes without saying that my list of the "best things" would be considerably different from the average American dream.)

The city worker wants no more, and no less. He just goes about it differently. I think I have a better chance of success than he does, if only because his success depends in large part on bosses and stockholders and the gross national product and the government's monetary policies. Mine depends mostly on me: my skills, my ambition, my labor, my ingenuity in cooperating with Nature. If I fail it's my own fault.

This makes my life more vibrant, more real. If I can't explain that to newspaper reporters, I suppose there are some COUNTRYSIDE readers who are a little puzzled by the concept too. I can only feel sorry for them... and I can only feel chagrin at my own ineptitude at putting the concept into words.

One problem is that our points of reference are a world apart: they think we can go on living off our bank account of nonrenewable resources forever. I know better.

Then too, how do you describe a sunset, or the taste of a snowflake?

I'll keep on trying, but you really have to experience it for yourself. Naturally, beyond the sidewalks.

28. March 1975

The office expands again

This column alludes to the "new office." In 1975 we moved from the small space we rented from a local insurance agency, into what had been a downtown meat market. We were on a roll.

"Work" is a funny word, with funny connotations. Not funny ha-ha, funny strange. If I'm sitting in an easy chair smoking my pipe and reading a book, am I working or playing? If I'm shoveling dung, or stripped to the waist glistening with sweat hoeing the beans, am I working or playing? Like so many other things, it all depends on the circumstances. And considering the circumstances, homesteading is mostly play.

In our society sitting and reading is usually considered relaxation, and sweating certainly indicates working. But maybe we're as mixed up there as we are in a lot of other areas.

For a migrant laborer hoeing is definitely work, and reading, pleasure. But for a writer or professor or businessman who has to keep up with his profession, reading is the work and hoeing is definitely a form of relaxation and exercise.

That's one of the attractions of homesteading.

Most of us speak in glowing terms of self sufficiency and all that, but our neighbors and relatives who see us exhausting ourselves planting and cultivating and harvesting and preserving can sit back and tell us we're crazy for spending so much energy providing what we could get with a few minutes' work at something more "productive" and "efficient." But if we spend our days driving a truck, teaching, selling shoes or insurance, or welding auto bodies, doggone it, it feels good to squat down to milk a goat, to immerse ourselves in the contented clucking of the hens as we gather eggs, or to strain unused muscles a bit as we toil in the garden. Then we're playing, by definition.

Most Americans play by spending money for golf clubs, snowmobiles, bowling, or a six-pack in front of the color tv. Our play is just as diversionary, probably more healthful...and if we handle it right, a whale of a lot cheaper even if the homestead *isn't* in the black.

All this is one aspect of homesteading that is grossly neglected. Sure, if we do it right we can live much more cheaply by producing our own food. Of course our food is free from poisons, contains more nutrition (we believe that despite what the lab technicians tell us) and tastes a whole lot better.

Of course our skills will be much more valuable when the price of food reaches its proper and just level, and they might mean survival if worst comes to worst. But doggone it, we might not live that long. Let's pay more attention to right now, today!

I've known all this in a subliminal sort of way for years, but it struck home the other night as I guided the pickup into its parking space next to the silo. I'd spent the day at the new COUNTRYSIDE office, tearing out old wiring from the former meat market that is now our new base of operations. We've put up paneling and walls, poured concrete, laid carpet, built shelves, painted, and did a host of other jobs.

And the sense of peace and well being as I drove into our yard was overwhelming.

After dinner we went out to do chores. Anne-marie headed for the chickens and rabbits, Dave leaned into the goats, Steve saw to the needs of the cow and I checked the pigs, fed and watered the bucks, sheep and dry goats, and threw down hay for everybody. Tomasina Turkey was perched on her fence and submitted to my petting. I squatted awhile to watch the week-old lambs try to get into their mothers' grain, and picked one up to feel the peculiar coarseness of its baby wool. In the buck barn, I had to give Oscar a stern talking to to keep him from spooking Caesar and Daniel away from the grain. The seven cats formed a circle around the bowl of warm frothy milk and I had to sidestep around them as I carried a bale of alfalfa to the Jersey. I had to laugh when I found the cow actually licking a tiny lamb that had wandered away from its mother, who was too busy with the grain to notice the prodigal.

When I checked the chickens they gathered around me to peck at the snow on my boots, and when I looked in on the 22 feeder pigs they ignored the snow and chewed on the boots themselves. Pigs like to chew on boots.

Anne-marie was washing eggs and the boys were straining milk and skimming cream when I went down to the basement to rub the hams and bacons curing there. Sasha the collie and her puppies watched with some kind of reserved anticipation as I rubbed the sugar cure into all corners and crevices and returned the pungent golden meat to the crock we use for curing. They live in the basement.

Then it was time to turn the cheeses, and Dave was churning butter while Anne-marie and Steve did dishes.

With the chores done, the kids got at their homework or read (the radio was blaring, of course), while Diane and I went over some of the dozens of newspapers and magazines we get for the sake of the magazine and the letters and other material we'd brought home with us.

When the kids were in bed, we changed the radio to softer music and I turned to a science fiction novel while Diane took up some sewing.

After all these years, it's hard for me to imagine what a "normal" life is like. Could I really sit in front of the tv with a can of beer? Would I really enjoy Saturdays more on the golf course than I do when we're grinding wheat and baking bread or cleaning the barn? Do I really "work" 18 hours a day?

Maybe COUNTRYSIDE magazine is nothing great or special, but if I can help just a few people realize their potential and enjoy life the way I do, it has to be worth all the trauma involved in publishing a magazine.

But more than that, the way I feel about these goings-on dramatizes the value of homesteading, per se. I really don't much care, myself, if homesteading ever becomes economical, or necessary. For me, it's the only way to live a vibrant, meaningful life. And in today's world, that could be worth a heap more than all the groceries we collect off the homestead.

When I was a kid my dad told me the way to get a vacation from a routine and boring job was to do it backwards. I tried it. I started my paper route with the last customer and finished with the first. It worked. I saw houses and street signs from new angles, I had to think of what house came next instead of tossing the paper almost by reflex, and it was a totally new experience.

I've used this technique on nearly all of the jobs I've held since then and it's always worked. But it has never worked as well anywhere as it has on homesteading, which by its very nature is diversified.

Today's farmer growing corn or raising hogs needs a lot of skills, but not nearly as many as the homesteader. We're vet, carpenter, tanner, agronomist, cheesemaker, dairyman, butcher, orchardman, cook, sausage maker, poultryman, herbalist, and dozens of others, all in the space of 24 hours. Sure, we're not terrific at many (or even any) of them. Most people will agree that in today's boring specialized social structure most intelligent humans aren't so great at their specialties, either, if you look at the quality of present day goods. But we're learning, we have control, we're in charge. There's satisfaction, and a lot more diversification than running your paper route backwards.

Lynn Grosz brought it up. "Chore" is a dumb word for a homesteader, because most of our chores aren't drudgery at all. Our language just doesn't have a word that describes what we do for fun. And moreover, what we do for fun is still regarded by many in our culture as harsh, unnecessary, even foolish labor.

Those who laugh at us now may starve someday. But that's beside the point. I live for today, not some dim and distant future. And if today were the last day of my life, I'd want to do my chores, same as always.

This is one of many concepts that is changing in 1975's culture. Work is only getting paid to do something when you'd really rather be doing something else. On the homestead, work is play, and play is work.

Let the rest of the world seek their plastic and neon transient pleasure. Let the city people scorn my home-cured hams and smoked rabbit and tomatoes won from the Earth by sweat and toil after a normal work week at my desk. I feel I'm more human, more alive and aware, by marching to the beat of my own drummer, beyond the sidewalks.

29. April 1975

Finding the optimum size... of anything

" Bigger" and "better" are almost synonymous in America. Bigger cars, tv and movie screens, busts or buildings, are just assumed to be "better."

But according to the pendulum theory, we tend to overreact. And these days "smaller is better" seems to be gaining as the national philosophy.

I would submit that neither extreme is true. There are no blacks or whites in anything, but only shades of gray. Of course, for people to whom thinking is a painful and unfamiliar process, it's always easier to judge things by classes rather than by individual analysis and evaluation.

Instead of saying bigger or smaller is better, we should be saying "This has an optimum size of so-and-so for this particular application."

One of the most interesting examples of this kind of thinking is coming from the agricultural colleges, strangely enough. For years their goal has been more per acre: more corn, more hay, more of everything and bigger was better. The reasoning was if you spent a dollar on fertilizer and made anything more than a dollar extra, you were making money.

This basic idea hasn't changed, but there's a not-so-subtle shift in the wording of the bulletins from the ag colleges. Now they say point-blank, "Don't aim for the highest *yield* per acre."

The reason is simply that with the high cost of input, maximum yields no longer mean maximum profit. You can settle for something less than maximum yields by using a little less fuel, fertilizer, herbicide, etc., but still make more money.

This is certainly a step in the right direction, and one that will definitely help organic farming as well as homesteading. There are other examples, of course. Smaller cars. Smaller families. Somebody wants to split up General Motors and AT&T and I guess you'd even have to wonder about the interest in Pygmy goats and Dexter cows in this context.

All of this is very encouraging for the small farm, small business, and for many aspects of our humanity.

But as I said, we tend to overreact. The trend is too new to detect any mass migration in this direction yet, but I'd be very surprised if it didn't happen. There is an *optimum* size for everything, and we ought to be smart enough to figure out what that is.

I've worked small patches of hay and grain with a scythe, and I don't see any particular merit to it. Neither do I see any special efficiency in a self-propelled combine that costs more than most of us make in several years of labor and requires enough land to support a homestead just to turn around on. The cost of capital, materials and other factors negate the efficiency.

Perhaps the best example of the inefficiencies of bigness, to me at least, involves magazine publishing. *Life, Look, Saturday Evening Post* and some of the other household names in the publishing industry disappeared primarily because they were too big. Oh sure, there were other factors such as postage rates and the effects of tv, but in the main, they couldn't survive simply because they became too big to make effective use of the economies of scale.

On the other hand, as already noted, smaller isn't necessarily better, either. And I have personal experience to back up that conviction, too.

While doing some business-type figuring the other day, I was surprised to learn that, in spite of the ravages of inflation, in spite of a doubling in the price of paper and many other ingredients of printing, in spite of three postage hikes and increases in the minimum wage and social security and other taxes, you are now getting twice as much COUNTRYSIDE for your dollar as you were five years ago! Five years ago you got 120 pages a year for $3; today you pay three times as much, but you get *more than six times as much.*

In other words, if we were still very small we wouldn't be serving you as well...and if we pass our optimum size, we won't be serving you as well either. The same has to be true of farms, telephone and steel companies, government...everything.

Let's hope we've learned this lesson and can use that knowledge intelligently.

I recently received the following interesting letter:
"I will not be renewing my subscription. We had a disastrous 1974, having been feeder cattle raisers.

"We have not saved money as a result of your magazine. We raise cows, not goats...never rabbits and few chickens. We operate large machinery. Your magazine is interesting and quaint, but we must save somewhere."

Since we've been claiming lately that you can save the subscription price — and probably a lot more — by reading COUNTRYSIDE, does that mean we're lying? Not at all. Read that letter again: "We were feeder cattle raisers... no goats... never rabbits... few chickens... large machinery... disastrous."

It becomes very clear that *reading* a magazine is no better than wishing. The reason these people didn't save money with COUNTRYSIDE is that they didn't use it. Big farmers can save money on food as well as suburbanites and city people, but they have to follow homestead principles to do it. These are needed now, more than ever. Read COUNTRYSIDE, yes. But use the ideas and information, too.

Ever wonder why our civilization begins the new year in January? There's nothing "new" about January 1 except according to a calendar that really is about as meaningless as a clock set on Daylight Saving Time or the value of a dollar.

For homesteaders who live simple, meaningful lives according to the sun and the seasons, the New Year begins with the vernal equinox, the first day of spring.

There is as much mystery, legend and romance associated with spring as there is with the First of January, but at least it has some basis in biology as well as tradition. In spring there are new lambs and chicks. There is new green in the fields and forests, and here in Waterloo, even the Maunesha River has "new" water since the scum and algae don't show up until later.

Spring is the season of hope, because a young man's fancy turns to love... and because an old man stoops to plant tiny seeds in the moist and fertile soil without even bothering to wonder whether he'll be the one to reap the harvest. In spring, it doesn't really matter.

If all men are created equal and spring is the season of re-creation, then all men are especially equal during this season. The newest gardener has no more weeds than the oldest professional, and at this point they have equal chances for bountiful harvests. The disappointments and failures of past seasons are dimmed or forgotten, and there is only determination, hope, and joy.

Happy New Year. Happy Spring. Beyond the sidewalks.

30. May 1975

(Sounds like this editor needs a hug!)

The first part of this one amuses me: I've lost count of how many times I've written something similar, or some version of the fable where the man takes the advice of every passerby and ends up carrying the donkey on his back. It's bad enough for a magazine: I wonder how a politician can run a country based on opinion polls!

Despite the many advantages, there are also drawbacks to listening too closely to readers (or voters). All too often those with the loudest voices have the least amount of information... and the ability to process it.

One of the most interesting parts of an editor's job is reading letters from readers. You find out what people are thinking, how they react to what other people write about, and hopefully, you find out what to put in the magazine that will please and help the most people.

But sometimes it's just plain confusing, especially when it comes time to write *Beyond the Sidewalks*.

For example, if I talk about what we did on the COUNTRYSIDE homestead last week somebody will tell me it's narrow and egotistical. But if I write about the effect of labor-intensive homesteads on industrial pollution and the reserves of fossil fuels, I'm a self-proclaimed expert with no qualifications trying to foist my personal hang-ups on readers. If I talk about how nice it is to live beyond the sidewalks, I write Pollyanna pap; if I tell what a tough time we had keeping the cows in the pasture or setting up the wood stove, I can't do anything right.

If I talk about pigs, some readers are shocked to learn that I eat pork when the Bible (or Koran) clearly admonishes against it. If I mention the puppies some readers are shocked that our purebred collie isn't spayed. If I talk about the tractor I should have a horse that doesn't pollute and use fossil fuels and if I talk about the horses I'm nothing but a hobby farmer.

If we advertise COUNTRYSIDE in other magazines we should cut it out and lower our price instead; if we don't advertise (and even when we do) people say, "I've been looking for you for years! Why on Earth don't you advertise?"

Each month some people write to tell me how naive and sophomoric my column is while others compliment the same column for being perceptive and clear-headed.

No wonder so many editors are manic-depressive, and in their old age become cynics.

Ah yes, but I'm only a part-time editor. My real life is spent on the homestead.

I used to be a real writer. I spent so much time in airports and hotels, all the cities I went to started to look the same. When I decided life was too short to waste like that, I became a homesteader.

This morning I woke up without an alarm clock before dawn and went out to do chores. I was milking the goats when the sun started oozing over the horizon, firing everything it touched with a ruddy gild.

The goats were glad to see me. They didn't care about how I was dressed or how I looked, they didn't care about my income or education or race or whether I had ever been convicted of a felony.

No wonder some people like goats better than they like people.

This is one reason there will always be homesteaders. When you begin your day full of peace and joy the pressures and petty frustrations that come later seem easier to take. Homesteaders produce something more, and more important than food. They create their own islands of sanity, beyond the sidewalks.

31. June 1975
The war is over

Any nation, like any individual, can be expected to defend itself. If our food supply were cut off by an enemy we wouldn't starve in silence: we'd mobilize. If any of our valuable natural resources were being confiscated we'd fight to protect them. And if the lives of our friends and families were endangered by the weapons of an enemy, we wouldn't cower like cornered lambs: we'd rush to get in the first blow.

We were doing chores last night while the barn radio brought us up-to-date on the last hours of American "involvement" in Viet Nam. Our favorite radio station being rather creative, the news was followed by a selection of war protest songs from the past ten years. So it was hard not to think about war, even in the peaceful atmosphere of hay-munching livestock.

The waste, sad in any war, somehow seems even sadder in Viet Nam. But then, I had considerable personal interest in this one since I was in the Marines during the early stages of it. I was also involved in anti-war activities a decade ago, and watched with fascination as people who were worked up to a patriotic frenzy in those days lost interest in what they had believed was a just and honorable cause.

All this is interesting because it applies to the new war, which hasn't even begun in earnest. I mean the *real* war. The American involvement in *America*.

Our country is being threatened in ways that make the threat Viet Nam posed no more dangerous than the shadow of a cloud on a summer afternoon. There are bombs hanging over our heads by slender wires, our national resources are being pillaged, our food supply is being threatened just as seriously as if we were an island nation facing a blockade.

But almost no one seems to care. What's more, some of the people who consider themselves the most patriotic Americans are actually aiding and abetting the enemy, which in more sane times is called sabotage.

Why, if even a cornered rat will defend itself, are so few Americans prepared to face the grave danger? Because, as Pogo so wisely said, "We have met the enemy, and he is us."

Specifically, so few face up to the dangers because they refuse to believe they exist.

Our food supply is threatened? No doubt about it. There are many reasons, but the most important one to me, as a farmer, is the fact that virtually all of our soil is *dead*. It's only a matter of time until it produces nothing at all. Those who believe in chemicals laugh at this, but those of us who have worked with real, living, organic soil... and then have had to deal with a piece of lifeless and sterile ground... not only believe it earnestly: we're scared to death. Agribusiness, in all its aspects from monoculture to concentration of food production in the hands of a few — and those few being more interested in profit than in health and other social factors — is a greater threat to this country than any outside enemy could hope to be.

Our natural resources are being gutted by that same enemy. You name it, they're taking it, by stealth, and under a thousand guises.

Oil is being siphoned off, not by embargoes and the sabotage of pipelines and refineries, but by wanton destruction of an irreplaceable resource through mass waste of oil-derived products ranging from phonograph records and panty hose to snowmobiles and dead-heading trucks running empty due to federal regulations. The brigands — us— are plundering not only gold and silver, but coal and oil, tin and magnesium, copper and molybdenum... and even our water, soil and air. These treasures are being swept away not by pillaging Vikings, but by our own greed and hedonism. To our descendants (if any) the results will be the same.

The lives of our citizens are threatened by that same enemy. There are nuclear power plants, supposedly safe enough to make some people claim there's only a chance in thousands that a disaster could occur. That's not good enough. Not when you consider the results of even one minor accident when you're dealing with a force like that. Is the air conditioning or the electric garage door opener or can opener really worth the risk? There were more than 600 tornadoes in the U.S. last year. When the more-power proponents can guarantee that none will ever strike a nuclear power plant, white blackbirds will fly backwards.

And what about all that nuclear waste?

There are additional lethal weapons in the form of air pollution, water pollution, food pollution (both in junk foods with no nutritive value and in food additives with no long-term proven safety) and the list doesn't end there by any means.

Why, if a nation can become hysterical about killing Japanese or Nazis or Cong in defense of its valued principles and cherished freedoms, can that same nation be so oblivious to even greater dangers?

Mob psychology is fascinating. Would there be as many wars if they were declared only by mothers of 18-year-old boys instead of by pompous politicians? And if speeches and flags and national anthems can arouse such fierce emotionalism toward outside enemies, isn't there some force that could mobilize the patriots against the enemy within?

Chores finished, I switch off the light and pause for a moment in the dark, savoring the sweet barn smells and the music of Joan Baez against a background of rustling straw and animals settling down for the night. I flip off the radio and walk back to the house with gravel crunching beneath my boots and stars shimmering overhead.

The war is *not* over.

32. July 1975

Random thoughts while driving a tractor

Driving a tractor can get mighty boring. I've spent an awful lot of time on the Oliver lately, and it sure gives you time to think... about all sorts of things, silly and otherwise. You think about the redwing blackbirds that flit dangerously close to the tractor's wheels and the pigeons who follow the grain drill at a respectful distance. You think about the tenacity of life (weeds and field mice) and the fragility of life (the baby pigs born dead this morning and the pepper plants chewed off by the rabbits during the night). You think about earthworms and clouds, and dozens of irrelevant things and important things. You even find yourself thinking about what other farmers think about as they navigate fields a hundred times bigger than yours!

This month's offering is a collection of random thoughts while fulfilling the more boring aspects of spring fieldwork.

***

There's an old saying that the only time a farmer is rich is after he's dead. Everything he owns is tied up in land, machinery, and livestock, and he doesn't have much to spend on the things city people seem to crave.

But a person isn't rich by the amount of money he has: he's rich according to the way he spends his time. That's why most farmers would rather be "poor" in the country than "rich" in the city.

***

One man's meat is another man's poison. I can't cut hay, inhaling the delicious aroma so symbolic of country living, without recalling the story of the GI in France during World War II who passed the word that the Germans were using some new form of poison gas. When a country-bred officer investigated, he discovered the aroma of new-mown hay.

***

Modern man thinks he's so smart. He has plastic and elastic, lasers and masers, paper clips and zippers, all at his beck and call. But, can any individual refine gasoline from crude oil, make a tv picture tube or fashion a light bulb? Our technology is a nebulous and fragile thing, and no one person can begin to understand all of it..

The peasant from the Middle Ages would be more adaptable to our times than most of us would be to his. He'd soon learn to push buttons...but how many of us could shear sheep, spin wool, weave cloth and make clothes? Or butcher hogs and cure hams and smoke bacons...or milk cows and goats and make cheese and butter?

The thought behind this is undoubtedly one of the driving forces that will keep homesteading alive no matter how advanced our technology becomes. Even when self-sufficiency isn't necessary in an economic sense, it's necessary for some people for psychological reasons.

***

Mention "jack-of-all-trades" and the "master of none" is a natural sequel. This is one of the erroneous assumptions of our specialized society, because all of us are masters of *something*... and if we can dabble well at others, we're more complete human beings.

If nothing else, being a jack-of-all-trades makes us more appreciative of the skills and abilities of those who are masters... skills too often taken for granted by those content to be experts in their microcosmic ivory towers.

***

Relative to the above, I've never really decided what I want to be when I grow up. I'll probably never be a great writer or an expert farmer, and there's an even smaller chance that I'll be an expert printer, welder, cook, mandolin player, carpenter, or any of the other things I dabble in.

If I had stayed with cooking (one of my first occupations), I'd probably be pretty good by now. While I don't condone mediocrity, isn't there something to be said for being at least passably competent in several fields as opposed to being truly expert in only one?

***

"From each according to his abilities to each according to his needs" is a favorite axiom of those who are socialistically inclined. What they fail to heed is that as their beliefs are put into action, the needs of the incapable increase and the talents of those who don't need much are decreased.

***

"Democracy is a very poor form of government, but it's the best we have." This is true. But too many Americans today remember the last part of that quote and forget or ignore the first part.

***

Some day, even the staunchest opponents of the doomsayers will have to agree, the world will be down to its last gallon of gas. Ever wonder what will be done with it? Will it be pumped to a hotrodder or snowmobiler, will it be used to carry goods from a factory to a store, will it be burned in a tractor tilling land to produce food, or will it be enshrined in some museum?

Whatever the disposition of the last gallon, you can be sure that most people will recall the waste of gasoline in our generation with a certain amount of bitterness...and with amazement at our short-sightedness.

1995 note: A more likely probability would be some development that would make it unnecessary to extract and refine that last gallon, putting gas in a class with buggy whips. But if so, we've made amazingly little progress in the past 20 years.

***

I was describing the vibrant organic soil of our former homestead to a visitor (contrasting it with the concrete that passes for soil where we live now) and really played up the worms, the nematodes and microbes and all the other soil life that made it positively vibrant. "My goodness," she exclaimed, "it must have tickled your feet to walk on it!"

***

How many people realize the role that petroleum plays in agriculture? Present productivity would be just about impossible without oil, not only for motive power on the farm, but as feedstock in the synthesis of chemical fertilizers and pesticides as well as the processing and distribution aspects of the food chain. As the cost of oil increases, the cost of food can hardly do otherwise.

***

While farmers use more and more mechanical energy to replace human energy, that mechanical energy becomes more expensive and more scarce. At the same time, 9% of the human work force is unemployed. Too bad nobody's smart enough to put two and two together. (Or smart enough to invent a new kind of economics.)

***

Speed is a hallmark of American life. We have instant printing, one-hour dry cleaning, sudden hamburgers. But nature can't be hurried. It takes almost four months to produce a pig, five for a goat or sheep, nine for a human or a cow... and all you can do is wait.

***

The secret of success in farming (or one of them) is to never buy anything you can't fix yourself.

33. August 1975

What is truth?

Truth is an absolute, right? I mean, if something is true, it's true and that's all there is to it.

However, that doesn't always seem to be the case.

How can it be that one goat raiser will tell you not to breed a doeling until she's at least a year old, while another will say she should be bred at seven months? How can one rabbit raiser tell you rabbits must be raised on wire floored cages, while another will claim the floor must be wood? How can one homesteader say comfrey makes excellent feed, and the next say his livestock won't eat it?

No doubt truth IS truth, but the truth changes according to even minute changes in the situation. Let me explain:

If you've been reading COUNTRYSIDE you know there is a great deal of controversy regarding the rubber band method of dehorning goats. It involves putting very strong, tight rubber bands around the base of the horn. Circulation is restricted, and in about a month the horn falls off.

Some readers have written to say it works fine, but others tell horror stories and swear they'll never subject a goat to that kind of torture again. They can't both be right... can they?

Several of my goats are horned. I personally like the looks of horns even though the official COUNTRYSIDE position is to discourage them. But I do *not* like gashed udders and bellies horned goats can inflict, nor do I appreciate the nuisance of horns around my keyhole mangers. We decided to remove the few remaining horns in our herd with rubber bands.

I had used this method before with no problems except for the rubber bands breaking. One doe who had had the treatment about three years ago had broken the bands and I hadn't replaced them. There was a groove in the horn, however, and by now it was several inches from her skull. I put bands on this doe again (close to the skull), as well as on several younger does.

The younger animals' horns came off beautifully, most without even bleeding. Some, who lost theirs through butting, had a bit rougher time of it but still nothing serious. It was certainly less traumatic for them (and me!) than sawing them off.

But the old doe retained hers. All right, so she's older and the horns are thicker. No sweat.

Until one evening when we found her, one horn missing, her white Saanen face and neck crimson with blood and a little geyser of blood shooting up from the center of the horn root.

Blood stopping powder didn't seem to do a thing. We tried to apply pressure to the artery, but she obviously wasn't too thrilled about that idea. We finally heated up the disbudding iron to cauterize the artery, and eventually the spurting stopped.

We spiked some water with molasses to get her to drink as much as possible, and watched her carefully for any signs of shock. Naturally, she was confined to a box stall of her own. And although she still has one horn, everything turned out all right.

So who's right: those who say dehorning with rubber bands is a snap, or those who say it stretches the limits of humanitarian treatment? Maybe both of them. Or in another sense, neither.

It could just be that the method works fine, particularly on younger animals, and if the animal is confined alone and watched carefully, particularly in the latter stages. You can scrape your knee, wait until the scab dries, and flick it off with no problems, but if you try to peel it off before it's really ready you're asking for trouble.

Maybe it's true that truth is an absolute and that what's right is right, but how often do we have all the facts, all the tiny, seemingly insignificant details, that will make one situation exactly the same as another?

One point that emerges from this is that it's *so* much easier to disbud kids! Some people will still maintain that horns shouldn't be removed at all, of course, but give them time: eventually they'll encounter a ripped udder, and will change their minds.

And then there are those who think the entire question is misdirected. They think we should breed goats without horns by finding out what's really behind this problem of hermaphroditism when polled goats are mated. (The offspring of two naturally hornless goats are commonly hermaphrodites—neither male nor female.)

What this boils down to is this:

First, we very often lack the basic information we need to make a proper decision. That lack of information can be due to our own ignorance or the fact that *nobody* knows what will happen in a given situation.

Second, even when some knowledge is available, we don't always properly assess all the factors involved in the problem, because they seem so insignificant or for some other reason.

And third, instead of trying to solve the immediate problem, maybe we should work harder at preventing it from ever occurring.

Most homesteaders see their tiny portion of the Universe as a microcosm of the Universe: the atoms in a speck on your finger are composed of stars and planets...just as the Milky Way is composed of nuclei and protons whirling around each other. And they will try to apply lessons learned on the homestead, to the cosmos.

Is nuclear generation of power good or bad? Are agricultural chemicals good or bad? Is dehorning a goat with rubber bands good or bad? In all three cases you'll find people who honestly believe the answer is either good, or bad.

But you'll also find those who will tell you that none of these things are *all* good or *all* bad. With enough knowledge, experience and care, any of them can be used wisely. (But note that if you don't have enough knowledge to dehorn a goat, you might end up with a dead goat. If you don't have enough knowledge to mess around with the balance of Nature on a planet...)

And there are also idealistic and creative people who say that the whole question is wrong. It doesn't matter if these things are good or bad if they're not necessary! Would it be necessary to talk about nuclear power if we had sensible energy policies or if we made good use of such resources as the sun and the wind? Would it be necessary to even consider using agricultural chemicals if we worked closely enough with nature so that we had an agriculture that didn't *require* chemical fertilizers, pesticides, herbicides, fungicides, hormones and antibiotics?

It obviously wouldn't be necessary to talk about dehorning goats if the kids were disbudded, or better yet, born hornless.

* * *

Homesteaders like to talk about the simple life, even though most will admit it's hard to see where the simplicity lies at the current stage of the art. But homesteading today is not the end of a road. It *is* the road. It's a realigning of priorities that will enable us, little by little, to achieve real simplicity. Certainly it would be simpler to have polled kids than to discuss and experiment with dehorning. Sure, it would be simpler to make direct use of the sun's energy than to go through the agonizing process of developing reliable, proven safe nuclear energy. It would definitely be simpler to farm with natural agricultural methods than to work within a maze of chemical effects on ecosystems.

But getting there... That's not so simple. If we work on current problems wearing blinders so we don't see the possibilities of eliminating those problems together, we aren't progressing.

* * *

Heard a story the other day from a neighboring farmer who was visited by a little city girl who thought milk came in plastic cartons. She watched the milking process with some interest, but when one cow saw fit to answer nature's call right there in the barn the little visitor was appalled.

"I'll never drink milk again," she solemnly swore.

* * *

That's the American mentality, of course. I delight in the episode from "All in the Family" where Edith Bunker tries to serve up some beef tongue to Archie. "I ain't gonna eat nuthin' out of a cow's mouth!" he fumes. "Fry me an egg!"

Our neighbors across the road asked if we'd "mind" if they'd spread the manure from their horses on our land.

Mind? I helped them!

* * *

Dr. Walter B. Shelley of the University of Pennsylvania's Dept. of Dermatology knows that the average population of germs in one square centimeter of underarm is an incredible 2.4 million. He knows that the equivalent square centimeter on the scalp harbors an average of 1.5 million; the forehead, 200,000; and that even the "cleanest" part of the human anatomy, the back, averages 300 germs per square centimeter. But even though he knows all that, Dr. Shelley puts nothing on his skin or hair and uses no medicated soaps. "If I am in a good stage of health my skin will take care of itself," he asserts. Most of the germs are harmless, and some are beneficial.

Even after a good shower, which washes away millions of germs, it only takes about four hours before you're covered again as densely as any like area of soil.

Would Nature go to all that trouble—would Man have survived as long as he has—if there weren't some symbiosis, some mutual benefits which we don't fully understand?

If something is natural it's in balance. Messing around with it will be useless at best, or at worst will cause damage the manipulator never dreamed of... in water, air and soil, as well as on the human skin.

* * *

John Denver's song "Thank God I'm a Country Boy" has reached the unchallenged number one spot on the Belanger hit parade.

The only time I can't stand the song is when the manure spreader breaks down or some other problem arises, I'm up to my elbows in grease or worse, and Diane waltzes by singing "Thank God I'm a Country Boy."

* * *

I'm often torn between mounting a soapbox and declaiming to the world about the follies of our way of life as I see them, and giving up altogether to concentrate on just living my own life. But just about then the chicken house needs cleaning and there's another magazine deadline and I never get to jump either all the way in or all the way out of the fray.

* * *

How can anything as cute, as delicate, as fluffy as a newly hatched chick, grow up to be a beady-eyed pugnacious rooster?

* * *

Through a series of misfortunes that can only happen to homesteaders, we have three Rouen drakes, and only one hen. The drakes are so old and tough now that nobody's too keen on butchering them, so they just sort of hang around.

The other morning when I went out to do chores I had to count twice to confirm that there were, indeed, five ducks instead of our usual four. The fifth wandered in from who-knows-where, and... you guessed it. It's a drake.

* * *

A friend of mine (who also happens to edit a magazine similar in content to COUNTRYSIDE) agrees that the traditional American way of life is dead. But he doesn't think homesteading, on a family basis, is the answer. When the hordes from the cities begin to starve, he reasons, they'll pillage the countryside as they've done before in history, and the family unit will be defenseless. What we need, he says, are communities based on homesteading principles.

He may be right. But if he isn't, the family unit has a greater capacity for changing the system, not by revolutionary means but through evolutionary means. And if he is, competent homesteader families should be pretty welcome on those communes.

A spects of homesteading that will never be captured on tv, or in a book or magazine:

The incredible lightness, the contented chirping, and the fresh aroma of baby chicks.

A goat being milked who takes time out from her grain to turn her head back and nuzzle your ear.

A cow's careless tail swatting you in the face while you're milking. The scruffy feel of a hog's back, or the surprisingly coarse texture of a newborn lamb's coat. The sun rising in the mist over a silent (except for the birds) countryside.

34. September 1975

The canning lid shortage

The canning jar lid crisis has hit the Belanger homestead — in spite of all the reassuring things we've been saying. Diane reports going to a store which apparently had so many inquiries they put a sign on the door: "No canning lids."

Of course, we still have options. We, and most other people, still have freezers, and while I don't have a great deal of confidence in them for the long run, I doubt if they'll go into a state of melt in the next year or so. There is drying... and we intend to do quite a bit of that this year if only for the experience. (We need it. Our past experience with this ages-old method of food preservation has been less than satisfactory.)

But the most promising option we had was the Ives-Way Can Sealer, which uses plain old-fashioned tin cans. And we just put up a batch of beans with the outfit.

It has several drawbacks. There is extra labor involved, but not that much. The green beans we canned had to be heated to 170 degrees in the pot, then put into the cans and reheated again.

But the biggest problem, as I see it, is the cost. The cans cost almost a quarter apiece, which means they're worth more than the produce. (Sound familiar, all you who are familiar with the farm-retail spread?) And the can sealer costs $89.95, which would buy quite a few groceries, even at today's prices. The cans and the sealer, incidentally are available from the Countryside General Store, which is why we got to test them.

The process seemed to work all right, but I'm disturbed by the cost and the tin that will be dumped. I've heard of a gadget that allows you to cut the rim from old tin cans and thus reuse them, but all the leads we've followed up on this have been dead ends. We have also been told that you simply have to cut the can in a can opener sideways to take off the rim and they'd be reusable, but we tried that and it didn't work. The new cover simply wouldn't seal, maybe because the can wasn't beveled like the original ones are.

At any rate, I'm more interested than ever in drying. Yes, there will undoubtedly be lids available next winter, and probably next canning season. I, for one, don't think the present shortage is a conspiracy any more than I think the oil crisis is a conspiracy. I think the world is simply outrunning itself. Which makes me leery of freezers and future dependence on canning lids and lots of other things.

But we have a root cellar, which will be stocked with carrots, beets, squash, potatoes, pumpkins, onions and other staples. We'll have plenty of dry beans, open-pollinated corn for corn meal mush, muffins, bread and so on. We'll have Jerusalem artichokes and turnips and some carrots under mulch in the garden, witloof chicory for winter salads and dried herbs for condiments. And of course, we'll have fresh milk (goat and cow), which also means cheese, yogurt, butter and ice cream; fresh eggs and plenty of salt pork, to say nothing of our other grains.

I can see where the canning lid crisis will have a terrific effect on people who have sweated and struggled over the summer with their gardens, only to see it all go for naught. But at the same time, I consider this an object lesson, a portent of things to come.

And we'd better be ready. It'll be much easier in this year of transition than it will be a few years down the pike, when it's too late to learn the basics of survival.

I just read a book about bio-dynamic farming, which, if I read it right, is organic farming but a little more scientific. One of the rules the author proposes is that you should have another crop planted within *three hours* after you take the main crop off.

I tried it. Finished combining the winter wheat about five, got the load in the bin by 5:30, ate supper, chopped the straw (three hours isn't long enough to let it dry, rake and bale it!), did the evening chores, and chisel plowed until 10 P.M. I was up at five the next morning to finish the plowing and the boys helped with the disking and dragging. I got buckwheat in the ground that afternoon.

Total time elapsed: about 20 hours. And that was only a small field. So much for textbook theories.

I took a walk out to the back 40 to check the crop progress today and took a shortcut back through the woods. It took a long time...as I got waylaid picking mulberries, blackcaps and gooseberries. The hickory nut crop looks like it will be a good one, too.

One of the most interesting neighbors I ever had was a fellow by the name of Hamre. I was in my 20's, he was in his 80's, and whether because I had time to listen to him or because I was keenly interested in what he had to pass on I don't know, but we did a lot of talking.

I recall vividly that I was just getting into organic gardening and farming at the time, and although he wasn't familiar with the term and wasn't too interested in new-fangled things anyway, he was organic without even knowing it. Many of the tales he told of his experiences of eight decades of farming and gardening, including his father's work breaking virgin Wisconsin land, backed up many of the "new" ideas I was experimenting with. He scorned the modern combine and hay baler, because the quality of threshed grain and loose hay was much better, he believed... but he also practiced electroculture, again without knowing the term. He just knew that he had always done it, and it worked.

But actually that's another story. What made me think of Hamre today was the discussion we had, sitting on his front porch after an afternoon's work in our gardens, about technological advances he had seen.

I remember being amazed at the time about the resiliency of the human psyche: here was a guy (and only one of many I knew) who was born into a world that was little changed from that of George Washington, or for that matter, Charlemagne. Horses provided power and most people (even in the industrial U.S.) lived close to the land.

When he was growing up, things began to change. He would tell—with a poignancy that history books can never convey to today's young people—what it was like to see his first automobile or tractor or use his first crystal set. The first airplane he ever saw was at a county fair where a daredevil pilot thrilled the audience with fearless feats of flight.

It seemed fantastic that a person could witness such tremendous changes in one lifetime and adapt so readily. He went from horse-powered agricultural life to one of color tv, farm machines that could do in minutes work that once took him days to accomplish, man in space, cars that not only had radios and air conditioning but which didn't have tool kits! He used an automatic washing machine, a rotary tiller and a freezer. He flew on jet planes. And still the advances came faster and faster, until they were almost expected on a regular basis.

These technical things have held our attention for some time now. They've been held up to us as progress to be proud of, as signs of our great culture and our wealth and power and of things to come. And maybe that's why people like Hamre could cope, even though somebody like George Washington, were he dropped into our time period and thus encountered the approximate same culture shock, would go bananas in short order.

But wait a minute. Have we *really* been unaffected? Are the technical advances made within the lifetimes of most people living today *really* being taken in stride...or are there hidden complications?

Maybe we're accepting the nuclear bombs, the direct distance dialed telephone calls and potato chips that stack, but what are these and other things doing to the way we *think*?

If you consider this unimportant, think for a moment about the effects of other seemingly insignificant things on the human psyche and ultimately the world. The types of toys a child plays with, his environment, the attitudes of others towards him, the type of education, state of health and countless other factors all play a role in shaping the human personality.

I submit that changes in the way we think because of technology have even more subtle effects on the world than the "things" themselves. What's more, our thinking is being manipulated not only more and more rapidly, but we're being kept off balance constantly, which is a brainwashing technique for driving people insane.

Example: middle-aged and older people of today grew up being told that a large car was a sign of success and substance. But suddenly, anyone who drives a luxurious car is stupid.

Automatic central heating became a part of life, replacing the wood box or coal bin with the touch of a dial. Today we should dial down and get out the shawls that were put away with the kindling and the ash bucket.

Formerly, large families were applauded. Literally, as recently as on the Ed Sullivan Show, when he would regularly introduce mothers with 20 children. Today any couple with more than two children (preferable adopted) is suspect; a woman with a litter would be stoned.

We're told we need catalytic converters on our cars to sop up harmful exhaust emissions...but a month later the experts tell us the converters themselves give off dangerous fumes of a different kind.

Is it Cape Canaveral or Cape Kennedy...or Cape Canaveral again?

Who are the good guys and who are the bad guys? Are we in a recession or not? Are eggs one of the best basic foods available, or will they kill you? Are suntans really healthy, as we always heard, or is a tan setting you up for cancer?

According to those little articles in the newspapers, coffee is bad for you one day, and the next day somebody else says it isn't; good old milk ("Nature's most perfect food") can cause cancer...and so can bacon, burnt toast and about a zillion other things. Vitamin C cures colds...or maybe it doesn't.

Put it all together and you come up with a program that couldn't do a better job of driving an entire world berserk if it were designed to do that job!

The product of this is a form of technological man, for all practical purposes designed, or selected, to cope with rapid change, confusion and flip-flops. No one can know everything in such a system and what you believe depends on which experts you rely on and how you interpret them. The easy way out is to skim the surface, take everything at face value and go along with the crowd.

That's the easy way... but is it the right way? Have we become so overwhelmed by masses of data and contradictions that we just give up and don't even attempt to think for ourselves any more?

"Modern" people who have the latest of everything, who are accustomed to having others not only grow their food and do their butchering, but even baking their bread and peeling their potatoes and cooking entire meals, no doubt find it easy to let others do their thinking, too.

All of this is one reason I don't spend much time condemning technology, much as I dislike certain aspects of it. Our philosophy is much more important than our technology and homesteading is, after all, largely a state of mind: a philosophy.

Modern man could very well become a race of robots. But one group, living close to the basic facts of life, making their own decisions out of necessity, seeing for themselves what's right and what's wrong because they *do* things rather than rely on the system to provide everything... that group will maintain its humanness, beyond the sidewalks.

35. October 1975
Random thoughts just keep a'coming

I can tell I'm getting older. My gardening credo used to be, if you can't eat it, I don't plant it. But this year I put in some flowers, including a couple of old-fashioned varieties of roses. And I like them.

There's a certain beauty in a tomato plant or a stalk of corn, but the beauty in a flower has a different quality... maybe because it *is* useless. I guess you just have to have a certain outlook (in my case, an outlook that came only with age) to appreciate that practicality isn't everything.

Our Jersey cow just freshened, and the addition of a calf to the barnyard menagerie has added a new dimension to the Belanger homestead. And the cow is adding a lot of butter and cream to the Belanger table. (We still drink goat milk.)

Diane and I met Ralph Engelkens, who is perhaps the nation's most visible organic farmer, last night. He farms 700 acres near Greeley, Iowa. His low-key approach is refreshing in comparison with the professors who say we'll all starve to death if we give up our chemicals. Ralph's attitude is, I don't really give a hang what you do, but if you're interested here are the documented results of how my farming has improved in the 18 years I've been organic.

His yields are *not* lower than his neighbors'. Since he has all his feed tested (he raises something like 800 beef cattle) he knows the nutriment level of his feed is higher than any of his neighbors', which means he pays less for supplements. His lower input costs also translate into dollars and cents, of course. And after all that, he can still point with quiet pride to the observation that while his neighbors' land is getting poorer, his is getting better; while they're marketing empty, synthetic food, he's feeding people real food with real nutrition. (One of his demonstrations of this is two ears of corn, one chemical the other organic, in two glass jars. The chemical one turned to mold and mush in a matter of months. The organic one is still sound. And they were both picked in 1963!) According to laboratory tests, his corn *stalks* have more protein than the average hay!

His clinching theme: I don't care if you go organic or not... but I'm convinced that you will, or someone else will be farming your land. There is just no way the toxic method of farming can sustain itself much longer.

When I left the Acres, USA conference on natural farming in Kansas City on August 1, the headline in the morning paper said that area had the driest July on record. And when I arrived back in Madison, Wisconsin, the evening paper there said we had the *wettest* July in 25 years. There's a drought, all right, but not all over.

According to the oscillation theory of cosmology, the universe is between 16 and 20,000 million years into the expanding phase of an 80,000 million year expansion-contraction cycle. The number of previous cycles, if any, is not determinable, but scientists do know the universe is 13.7 billion years old.

The banded louse and the parasitic wasp *Caraphractus cinctus* each weigh 1/567,000 of an ounce, and their eggs weigh 1/14,175,000th of an ounce.

Why, then, should I be concerned about the policies of the Federal Reserve, the prospect of increased postal rates, or the fact that nobody has gotten around to putting up a toilet paper holder in the new bathroom at the COUNTRYSIDE office?

There are two kinds of mistakes to make in this regard. One is to reflect on Man's place in the Universe, to the exclusion of everything else. Such a person could end up sitting in the mud, naked and hungry, but oblivious to his plight because he's lost in the ecstasy of his mental explorations.

The other end of the scale is more common, at least in our society. Too many people worry too much about the insignificant details, and get so wrapped up in them they never notice that there might be more to human existence than the daily grind. They spend so much time wiping a speck off the eyepiece of the telescope that it never even occurs to them to look *through* it to see the stars.

Most of us try to follow a middle road. We work to eat and live, but we also are alert enough to make the puzzling observation that Man is...*different* from other animals.

Modern, technological, artificial living seems to take us closer to the materialistic end of this scale. Homesteading, with its emphasis on first-causes, is a little to the other side of the center.

This is just one more reason homesteaders are the people of the future, the faltering first step in the evolutionary direction envisioned by Teilhard de Chardin.

I have to set something straight. I am not a prophet, a witch, an astrologer, or anything of the sort.

I have to set this straight because I've been getting a lot of mail lately from people who say something like, "I thought some of the things you said a couple of years ago were pretty silly, but I recently reread some of those old issues... and it's uncanny."

Honest, folks, I'm just a simple country boy, with a typewriter and printing press. And it's been a puzzle to me that more people couldn't see the signs that have been plain as a buck goat in season.

Well anyway, the next thing these folks want to know is, what's next? Like I had some inside line to a crystal ball or something.

I don't but I can tell you anyway because it's still as plain as any postmark (which means you only have to know how to decode it and then you still can't be real sure).

The people who tell you that the "recession" is over are full of what we have out on the floor of the bull pen... *unless* they mean the recession is over and now we're setting the stage for the real depression. The people who are still worried about high prices for food and oil still have their heads in the sand, because we ain't seen nothin' yet. Those who speak of the basic resourcefulness and resiliency of the American spirit probably have something to talk about... but they darn well better temper it with the basic greed, stupidity and short-sightedness which is also a part of our American heritage.

My long-range observations and predictions haven't changed any more in the last couple of decades than has that old oak tree in the center of our woodlot. Stronger, a little more moss on it, more detail in its branch structure and a more firmly rooted foundation, but it's the same tree. Our nation and our civilization are in an inexorable downturn because we've mistaken the means for the ends. We have gained space travel and lasers and masers and transistors, but we have lost our humanity. Our souls. We have escaped from the scrounging for physical survival that has marked the history of mankind, only to become entrapped in the scrounging for spiritual life, which is really what distinguished man from the beasts. We have sold our descendants into slavery so we could drive 70 miles an hour down a freeway to nowhere.

It hasn't really been a freeway. We're coming to the tollgate.

Now, there are certainly COUNTRYSIDE readers who homestead because they can't afford groceries at the supermarket, or who just get a great deal of satisfaction from being somewhat self-sufficient, or even who just like fuzzy bunnies and cute goat kids. They can skip over *Beyond* and some of my favorite parts of the magazine the way I skip over the sports pages in the daily papers, and still get their money's worth. But I've come to realize that there are also a great many readers who have progressed beyond that, who are interested in the basics of living for far more serious reasons. And for them, I print this advice.

Our homesteading is, and will be, ineffectual from a practical standpoint. Most of us are not good enough managers or serious enough to make or save a great deal of cash on our efforts under current conditions.

What's more, we won't be a great deal better off in the harsh days ahead. The economic and social system just has too great a stranglehold on every resident of the kingdom, no matter what his location or lifestyle. Rural water and air are just as polluted as city water and air, to take one very basic example, and God knows the tax collectors are everywhere too.

No, the values of homesteading are something else. We learn things about Life...about untold eons behind us and before us...by watching and caring for our animals, our soil, our plants. There are no answers that can be written in magazines, books, or newspapers. They're only in the Earth and the stars, and no Man can convey them to any other. We can help direct each other's attention to them, to encourage our brothers' concern with the eternal truths and whatever, but that's about it.

The happenings of the next few months and years really have little bearing on eternity...and as any observant homesteader knows, there *is* an eternity. And as I just mentioned, there really is little or nothing we can do about it, individually or collectively. But here's what I see happening. (No timetable included.)

After a period of somewhat uneasy stasis, the real world depression will hit. Not, as we've mentioned before, like the crash of '29. That was a mere bruise, compared with the concussion to come. It doesn't take much imagination to consider the implications and results of something like that.

Either as a result or because of concurrent threads running through contemporary history, there will be chaos of other forms. Nuclear holocaust is inevitable, in the long run. Whether it's because of an earthquake or tornado hitting a "peaceful" atomic power station, an ego trip by some third-rate power, or a plot by terrorists who even today could easily carry an atomic device into Manhattan, is hardly worth debating. The Bible tends to indicate, according to many people who read the book, that it will happen in the Mideast, and soon. I'd be willing to put my crop on their wagon.

Armageddon.

You really have to be a science fiction fan to even get the idea of events from then on. We're not talking about selling apples and Hoovervilles and soup lines. We're talking about back to the caves, gang.

While I haven't one iota of proof, I can say with great confidence that this has happened before... and often. Point to Atlantis if you want to. Immaterial. It will serve as an example. There's no proof that Atlantis ever existed, but the organic gardener who has observed the rapid decay of paper and metal under natural conditions knows full well that a few million years would obliterate every vestige of even our civilization, which some people consider the epitome of human existence.

Moreover, cycles are a normal part of Nature.

We may have reached, and surpassed, this point many times. Nature "quickly" (time is relative) recovers from the transgressions against her. So what could make it different this time around?

Homesteading. Yes, the knowledge of goat milking, rabbit butchering, grain grinding and all that will stand the homesteader in good stead while cities are burning. But, when the starving mobs from the cities sweep across the countryside, not even the most remote homestead will be safe from pillaging and destruction.

However, some will survive. They will have the means for survival, physically. And certain of them will carry the seed for survival of the species of Man as a higher being, because of the innate qualities of the person who is attracted, not to rabbit raising or country living, but to true homesteading.

There are only a few of us. But we have a destiny that elevates us above the manure and sweat to the stars that the astronauts will never visit.

Back to the present, and basics.

Modern society cannot survive because it's based on false values...not only spiritually, but physically. That includes economically, of course. We require a new respect for the Earth and for Nature that is virtually impossible among our people, who in the U.S. think food is manufactured in the back room of the A&P and who in the "poor" regions of the world, think comfortable survival is a prerogative of the rich. There is just no way to change all of this at this point in the present cycle. Religion won't do, politics won't do, economics surely won't do it. It's a lost cause, because it's too late to redirect basic human motivations that should have been properly channeled at the beginning of the Industrial Revolution, or earlier.

This means, you're lost. I'm lost. If we're talking about maintaining our bank accounts, our homes (and mortgages), our cars and tv sets and dishwashers and automatic washing machines. We're even lost if we only value our 40-hour working weeks, our free-time, the clothes we wear. Dialing down and slowing down look ridiculous in the face of what's to come. It's freeze, and halt.

There is no safe place to put your savings. There is nothing you can say to your children, or grandchildren. All you can do is to sharpen your skills and hone your senses that can be passed on by example.

Some of you may be astute enough to note that this *Beyond* is a rash departure from the almost Pollyanna pap I've been spouting. There's a reason. In fact, there are several.

One is that such establishment sources as Econometrics are now saying that the BIG crash is coming in 1978. Good grief, Charlie Brown, even Merrill Lynch is bearish about America! Their recent report entitled "The Economic Outlook Has Changed", predicts that the economy will decline again in 1976. They cite all sorts of esoteric high-fallutin' facts and figures, but what's new, *Beyond* readers? Takes some of the fun out of being a radical doomsayer when even the nation's largest stock broker agrees with you.

What am I doing about all this? Not a darn thing. I'm living my life as I've always lived it. Honestly, simply, to the hilt. Sure, we have a food supply. We've always had a food supply, because we live simply, and directly, without reliance on anything or anyone else. There are no special investment secrets, because there are no "safe" investments—except one.

Our only investment... our only security... is in ourselves. Our skills, experience, and philosophy. Let the others hoard food and gold, thus hastening the process we speak of. Homesteaders can do better.

I'll continue to milk my goats and till my fields and garden. And I'll continue to publish COUNTRYSIDE, until conditions make it impossible, which will surely be in my lifetime. Because not only are there no viable alternatives: what I have to say might affect the next cycle!

There couldn't possibly be a stronger motive for any human activity.

Okay, end of sermon. Let's get on with the chores. Lots of wood to cut this month.

Was this really as far off-base as it might sound to some readers?

Not, if you compare the important factors we're talking about, then and now. The evolution has been so gradual, most people don't even notice anything happened (and of course, about half the people alive today weren't even born, then. Median age today is

just over 30 years — and the world population has doubled.) The notes for each year in this book tell the story.

But also, today's mainstream economists really do refer to the '70s as "the disastrous decade," and not only because of inflation.

36. November 1975
Living in interesting times

((These are mighty interesting times we live in" is a line that isn't likely to draw many protests from anybody, these days. But like many other flat statements, it has two faces.

The most obvious to most people is the one shown daily in the news media. Threats on the life of the President of the United States tripled last month: over 300. There is evidence that the White House was involved in conniving to kill off newspaper reporters. Dockworkers are refusing to work—out of sheer consideration for their fellow Americans—unless those fellow Americans happen to be grain farmers. Lots of interesting things, and new ones every day.

But there's another side to the coin. "These are interesting times we live in" can have another meaning, for people who are attuned to other possibilities.

Like homesteaders.

Here are some interesting things that happened to me recently.

I woke up with a start. None of this drowsy, climbing out of the depths of slumber stuff. Wide awake, and rarin' to go. Light streamed in the bedroom window.

I had fieldwork on my mind so I didn't even think of lying in bed. I pulled on my jeans and went to the kitchen before I even looked at my watch.

It was 3 A.M. In this latitude in October the sun doesn't rise until after 7. The harvest moon, directly over the barn, shone so brilliantly I could easily see the Rouen ducks waddling down the driveway as if they were as confused as I was about what time of day it was. The white geese were even more noticeable: they lit up against the dusky lawn like diamonds in a new engagement ring.

I got a lot of reading done before chore time.

It was Sunday afternoon. I haven't spent much time with my family lately, so when I finished the field I was plowing I invited John, our youngest, for a walk.

We inspected the winter wheat, poking a slender seedling out of the earth to examine the shriveling wheat berry and the probing, developing root. We stalked a flock of pigeons feasting in the field that had grown

Canada field peas. We marveled at a filmy cocoon, with the caterpillar still visible inside. We watched a blue heron glide overhead on its way to the marsh and noted the similarity of its grotesque profile to that of a pterodactyl.

We turned our tour toward the woodlot where we discovered that the hickory nuts had started to drop. That led to almost an hour of gathering nuts, accompanied by discussions of Indians whose nut-gathering was akin to our garden and field harvesting; biennial cycles of production; and of course, squirrels. (John is seven years old.)

The sun was sinking fast when we returned to the house with our bounty, weary from stooping and chilled from the gathering damp evening air, but content with the comradeship found only between a father and son who have spent the afternoon in the woods. The newspaper headlines are very far away tonight. Here on the homestead, we have interesting things of our own to ponder.

M onday morning I noticed two goats in heat, the first of the new breeding season. These were two of our better does, scheduled to be bred to two specific bucks. (We have five).

But I was late for work at the office, and had much to do there. Breeding could wait until evening.

At evening chores, the first thing I noticed was that two bucks were missing. I knew at once where to look for them. There they were, in with the does, with wide grins on their faces. The two wrong bucks, of course.

First experimental breedings of the year.

I 'm a firm believer in chisel plowing. But my old plow, rusty with age and bent from rocks and beat-up from use, not only travels with several teeth merely skimming the ground: during a night session of plowing a depth gauge broke off and in the dawn's early light was nowhere to be found. It was time to invest in a "new" used plow.

I paid more than I thought I should have. But the first time I used it, its value doubled, in my mind. It dug in smoothly, churned the soil efficiently, saved me half the gas and half the time and three-fourths of the frustration... and made me wonder just a bit more about the "economy" of the older, less efficient, much cheaper implement. Interesting implications there.

T he mailman stopped in yesterday. "Do you know you need a new mailbox?" No, I didn't. Somebody had gone along Highway 19 clipping off mailboxes, and ours was one of them.

Interesting what some people do for kicks. Is it because there isn't enough *meaningful* activity in their lives?

Or maybe they just need better ways of keeping busy.

142

We have had two Collies for many years. Sasha is a farm dog. She has a natural instinct for herding, and it's a real pleasure to watch her work pigs that have broken through the gate that separates their pen from the garden. Mellow was less businesslike, and therefore, on most occasions at least, more fun. Sasha was the undisputed boss and had Mellow positively cowed.

Mellow died, giving birth.

Now Sasha is an entirely different dog. She's friendly and responsive, but moody. Lonesome, perhaps. In view of their relationship, the change is interesting.

Diane sent Dave, our oldest son, out to the grain bin to replenish the kitchen wheat and she told him to grind some for Saturday-morning bread baking. He did. The bread was delicious... the first from the new-crop wheat... but there was something odd about it.

It wasn't until later that we found the guy who had grown up with animals and grains and home-ground flour for home-made bread had brought in not wheat, but rye. (And once Steve, craving some fresh horseradish, ground some roots he found in the cellar, but it didn't have any bite. He had ground the witloof chicory that was supposed to become Belgian endive.) City kids don't get educations like that.

Judy Kapture was here and suggested that we go for a Sunday morning horseback ride. I haven't ridden much since breaking my foot falling off a horse a couple of years ago, but she insisted.

She took Colonel, the gentle gelding, and I took Shoofly, a mare that hasn't been worked much lately. We were out in the back forty when Shoofly decided to head for home in the manner of Ruffian...with me in the role of Ruffian's final condition. I managed to calm her down after a riotous ride through low hanging tree branches and other exciting obstacles, but willingly traded mounts with Judy. Even then I walked Colonel most of the way due to my shaking knees.

Judy did just fine, but agreed that Shoofly needed a lot of work.

When we got back to the house, Dave and Steve took our places and made Shoofly back up, do figure-eights, and all but stand on her head. Smart aleck kids.

The fall plowing is done. The garden is put to rest under a bed of mulch. The mows are stacked high with hay and straw, the grain bins are fuller than they've ever been since we moved here, the freezer and shelves and root cellar are stocked for another year. If a homesteader with assets like these didn't read newspapers or magazines, didn't listen to the radio or watch tv...how could he say there was anything wrong with the world?

Personally, I don't care any more about Jimmy Hoffa's whereabouts than I care about Judge Crater's. Personally, I don't care for people taking pot shots at the president but it's not a major factor in my daily life. Personally, I'm getting just a little tired of reading about George Meany, Earl Butz, inflation, unemployment, energy, bussing, massage parlors and gay liberation. None of these are as vital, as meaningful, or as interesting as the everyday happenings here on the homestead. These are interesting times we live in, right here, beyond the sidewalks.

2014: Horse racing was quite popular in 1975, and Ruffian was a superstar. She died after suffering a compound fracture in a match race with Foolish Pleasure.

37. December 1975

A homesteader by any other name...

What is a homesteader?

It might sound funny, but I've spent so much time and effort being one, and writing about *how* to be one, that I really haven't thought too much about *what* a homesteader is. I'm sure I'm not alone. Over the years we've received many letters starting with "I'm not really a homesteader, because I only have five acres, 12 chickens, two goats and a garden..."Zounds! If that's not a homesteader, what is?

Consider these two extremes. Let's call one "city life" and the other "country life."

The city is in a terrible state. The streets are filthy (and so is the air and the water) and they are threatening. There is crime, violence, corruption and general unrest. Even with a high rate of unemployment, inflation continues to soar. The largest city in the nation is on the verge of bankruptcy, and there is dissent on abortion, women's rights, and malpractice insurance for doctors. There is concern over energy, pollution, traffic, drugs, taxes, and education. And that's only part of it.

Country living is in sharp contrast. In the countryside the grass is green, the sky clear blue, the winds soft. The white, vine-covered cottage is the epitome of peace and tranquility. A clucking hen and her brood, scratching in the dooryard, are the only sign of vigorous activity. A gentle, doe-eyed Jersey cow lies in the white-fenced pasture contentedly chewing her cud; a fat hog lies lazing in the warm sun; even the flies are lethargic. The long rows of garden produce, luxuriant green against the weedless rich black earth, hold forth the promise of taste delights unmatched by even the finest restaurants. The garden, in combination with daily gathering of eggs clean and warm from aromatic straw nests and the pails of rich foaming milk, symbolizes security in a manner that a credit card can't begin to approach.

Okay, okay, city life isn't really all that bad and country life isn't really all that good. When we face reality and admit that there is some good and some bad in each, we begin to get an inkling of what true homesteading is. But there's more. The city person steps into a high powered car in an attached, heated garage, pushes the button on the automatic garage door opener, and drives down to the local supermarket to buy a loaf of bread.

The homesteader bundles up against a chill wind, takes a container out to the grain bin, fills it with plump kernels of wheat that were grown with much sweat and strain, and stored with care, and lugs it back to the house. There the grain is laboriously ground into flour with a hand mill, mixed with other ingredients from the homestead, and baked into golden brown loaves of fresh bread.

This city version is certainly true, in many cases. The country version is also true in many cases. But they aren't the only alternatives. Just as every city person doesn't *have* to put bread on his table that way, every homesteader doesn't necessarily follow that pattern either.

What happens, for example, if a city person doesn't like the taste of gooey bread, wants to save some money, wants to provide more healthful food, or simply wants to get *involved*? He or she could buy white flour, sugar, yeast and a little salt and oil, and bake bread at home. Or they might go a step further and buy whole wheat flour. They might use other natural ingredients, and they might even buy whole grain and grind their own flour, right in the city.

Most rural people don't grow their own grain, for all kinds of very good reasons, so in regards to bread there is apt to be a great deal of slopping over from one lifestyle to the other. If the country person buys bread and the city person bakes it from scratch, which one is the homesteader?

That's bread. We can also look at vegetables. The person who buys everything canned and frozen is at the opposite end of the scale from one who provides every single morsel for the table. If the "homesteader" sneaks out and buys a pizza, does he lose his homesteader's membership card? And if the city person plants a row of lettuce, isn't he... just a little bit... becoming a homesteader?

Homesteaders provide more than food for themselves, right? They build their own homes, furniture, tools, provide their own clothing, entertainment, and so on. Ideally, that is. But that's an ideal that's as far-fetched as the cow that never goes dry and the sky that's always blue. Most homesteaders, again for some very good reasons, are far from self-sufficient in these areas.

Meanwhile, look at the people in the cities who remodel their homes; build furniture and grandfather clocks and kitchen gizmos, knit, sew, and even spin and weave! If a lady in town does all the sewing for her family, I would submit to you that she is more of a "homesteader" than the gal in the country with mud on her cheek and manure on her boots who doesn't sew at all...at least so far as a particular aspect of life is concerned.

We could go on and on, through every sphere of human activity. It makes no difference where you live: if you are entertained by playing a musical instrument or home-made games, you're more self-sufficient— more of a homesteader—than the person whose only entertainment is passive and centers on personal non-involvement, such as spectator sports or tv viewing. If we display all of these activities on a scale we can see they range from "high personal involvement" to "low personal involvement," and to a somewhat lesser degree, from "high technology" to "low technology."

Furthermore, we can see that few people are bunched up on either one end of the scale or the other. One person might be very close to the low-involvement end in bread, but have high involvement in clothing, or the other way around. The point is, "homesteading," from this viewpoint, is on a sliding scale. The plain fact is that even people like me, with land and livestock and homesteading tools and experience, are not 100% on the high personal involvement end of the scale...and even most apartment dwellers aren't completely on the low involvement end.

It's true that we have moved, as a nation and a world, very much closer to the low personal involvement end of the scale in relatively recent times. It's also true that the super-technologists I'm always taking issue with see an even more rapid movement in that direction. In many cases we've come frighteningly close to the science fiction ideas of meals in a pill, throwaway everything (the ultimate in noninvolvement) and even impersonal orgasm. Maybe even impersonal reproduction—test tube babies.

No one can say whether we'll ever go all the way. I doubt it, personally. The interest in homesteading, in all its forms, seems to back up that belief.

The main reason is that we are human beings, individuals. We rebel at efficiency that destroys our humanity, because without that we have no reason for living. Up to now what we've seen, on the surface at least, is mainly a squaring off of the rapidly burgeoning technological society with our basic human emotions. Most of us just aren't aware enough, or sure enough, or facile enough to put it into words. So instead of seeing Man as an entity which has much to gain from both ends of the scale, we overstate one end (and understate the opposite) to make things clearer in our own minds, to give ourselves, as individuals, a clearer sense of identity and purpose. While this does help make others more aware of our position, it also tends to create a rift between "city" and "country", or between "technology" and old-fashioned methods and ideas. The rift is artificial.

We rhapsodize about country living and country things, because that's as far as we can get from those mysterious lines on grocery products (UPC codes?), a society which recognizes us not as people but as numbers in computers, and test tube babies. It's over-reaction. And of course there is a great deal of over-reaction in the opposite direction, too.

I'm not too interested in grinding seeds between two stones and baking my bread in a mud oven. The idea of wearing animals' skins doesn't especially appeal to me. I'm not even going to be adamant about providing all of my own food, if it means that in so doing I have to sacrifice some other aspect of my life that makes me human.

Neither do I want to be a number in a computer, a cog in a machine. I don't want to have everything done for me (or to me). I have animals on my farm in that position, and I think I'm higher than they are. I think I'm *capable* of complete self-sufficiency, but it would be a 24-hour a day job...and there would be no time or energy for the things that make me human. I enjoy good music, reading, occasional travel, a certain amount of comfort and ease, and time for insight and reflection.

I'm a human being. A homesteader. My own man. And with that attitude, I could be a homesteader even in a town or city.

It's a lot more clear-cut, a lot easier, and much more fun... beyond the sidewalks.

Part VI: 1976

U.S. annual inflation rate, 5.75%; Federal Reserve interest rate, year-end, 6.25%; Gas/gal: 59¢; Polaroid camera: $28; Ink jet printer invented; gas, 59¢; year-end Dow, 1004; average income, $16,000; Steve Jobs and Steve Wozniak start Apple Computer Company.

38. January 1976

Winter on the homestead

What do homesteaders do during the winter?

Spring, summer, and fall are the busy seasons, when there is always planting or weeding or harvesting and preserving; baby goats and lambs and chicks to care for; fences to fix and roofs to repair. Winter, with its feeding and watering and cleaning and other everyday chores, might appear like a salt mine to some modern people but to the homesteader it's a vacation.

So what do homesteaders do during the winter?

Winter is the time when farmers traditionally make repairs. Goodness knows that could take up all my spare time, but since my machine shop is the open air variety and the open air has been 10 below (with the chill factor not included) I pass on that traditional activity.

It would be pleasant and profitable to spend the long winter evenings in the woodworking shop, building birdhouses for the yard and orchard, extra cheese presses, or a new milking stand. I don't have much of a knack for that. Then there's spinning and weaving, which I find fascinating but which I'm sure I'll never get around to trying; macramé and knitting and sewing, all of which I've done but which don't appeal to me as hobbies; and many other things that just don't grab me.

My winter hobbies are reading the kinds of books I don't get to read during the rest of the year, and on weekends... cooking.

Cooking is one of my favorite things to do any time of the year but it becomes a special challenge on the homestead during the winter. The homesteader has less to work with then. During the gardening season, *anybody* should be able to concoct a scrumptious meal in the country. In late winter it's more of a challenge.

Turnips have been one of our staples on this place, mostly because we have a terrible time growing potatoes. There isn't a whole lot you can do with turnips. After you've tried them boiled and baked the cookbooks desert you, and there's a limit on how many boiled turnips you can eat in normal times.

Carrots have been a bumper crop here for several years, ever since we discovered those garden seeders that space the seeds for you. So we eat a lot of carrots, in many different ways.

I always feel compelled to select the meats that Diane passes over when she looks for dinner in the freezer: hearts, tongues, neck bones, things like that. City people think that because we do our own butchering we have steak every day, forgetting or not realizing that meat animals have other parts, too. Those other parts present great opportunities for creativity!

The usual homestead vegetables—green beans, peas, broccoli, and so forth—can be something entirely new and different under the aegis of a great chef. I'm partial to sauces, myself. Cream sauces and cheese sauces and sweet and sour sauces are only the beginning.

A refrigerator full of milk can keep me happily occupied for hours. Diane usually makes the butter and yogurt and we don't use much ice cream during the winter, but I have a ball making cheese. Considering the opportunities for experimenting with cheesemaking, this alone could be a full-time hobby.

And then there are the grains. I get turned on by grains the way football addicts get turned on by bowl games. Since we grow wheat, rye, barley, buckwheat, soybeans, corn, oats, amaranth, and millet, there's never any lack of material to work with. I can spend hours grinding them into flour; poaching and cracking them for cereals; soaking and cooking and roasting them for snacks and more.

Last Sunday was fairly typical. I planned a nice supper of tongue casserole in curry sauce with baked carrots, turnips au gratin, and green beans in white sauce.

Then I skimmed milk and used the skim to start a batch of cheese. I toasted some wheat and coarsely ground it, providing a couple of days' worth of hot cereal makin's for breakfast. We had extra eggs so I pickled a couple dozen using two different recipes. I kept some out as an afterthought and added deviled eggs to the supper menu. Then I parched some of the new open pollinated corn for after-school snacks.

I had a great time and felt like I was really getting into the nitty-gritty of homesteading. After the planting and harvesting, the feeding and milking, this is where homesteading converges. The moment of truth is in the kitchen.

There was one thing wrong. Everybody in the family hated my cooking. The farina smelled burned, the parched corn was too hard to chew, the cheese was too salty, and who on earth would eat a dead pig's tongue unless they were absolutely starving!

And what, turnips again!?!

Just wait, I tell them. Someday you'll be hungry and then you'll be glad you have good food like this.

Well, at least I had fun, and I thought supper was delicious. Diane is muttering something about a mess in her kitchen and that she's glad Sunday only comes once a week. I sneak the bag of parched corn into my dungaree jacket pocket and go out to do chores.

When the work is done I sit on a bale of straw and have a talk with my favorite goat. While we're talking I munch a handful of parched corn. It's pretty hard. I offer some to Calpurnia.

She tries to chew it for awhile, then spits it out and takes a mouthful of straw, as if to try to kill the taste.

I wonder, am I too old to learn how to spin or build birdhouses?

39. February 1976

The dying age

"We are living at a time when one age is dying and the new age is not yet born." —Rollo May

I'm sure psychiatrist Rollo May neither knows nor cares that COUNTRYSIDE has been saying the American way of life is dead for more than six years now. I said it privately even before then, and yet I find his refinement tremendously exciting. Our statement is simple, blunt, and without hope. May's phrase echoes ours, explains the utter confusion of the times we live in (how can there be a sense of destiny or purpose between ages?), and goes on to light a candle for the future. Bless him.

This is the core of modern homesteading. That might confuse those who think homesteading is living in the country with a garden and a goat, and it might even puzzle those who have a slightly broader outlook. Homesteading in a physical sense can actually encompass a great deal less than making cheese and picking your own tomatoes, as we've pointed out many times before. But regardless of the amount of land you care for, regardless of the number of animals you're charged with or your degree of self-sufficiency, homesteading encompasses a great deal *more* than the sweat and blood and manure of the physical aspects.

To put it another way, homesteaders are not homesteading because they like playful goat kids or fuzzy bunnies or vine-ripened tomatoes. They are not reading COUNTRYSIDE for those reasons, or because they're trying to save money or because they don't like to eat the chemicals that are served up in supermarkets. Homesteading is a school of thought, and the physical act of homesteading is simply a commitment to that philosophy.

The homesteader who grows his own vegetables is not telling agribusiness "I like to putter in the garden." He's saying, "I don't want to be told what to eat." Not only does that mean he doesn't want to eat chemicals; it means he doesn't approve of the destruction of soil and soil life by industrial farming; he refuses to pay homage to a marketing system that professes to be the epitome of efficiency but which is in reality a boondoggle on a grand scale; he refuses to place his very sustenance in the hands of a system that places profits, gross national product, international relations and other factors ahead of his personal well-being, and much more besides.

This is one small example, and the list is endless. I see it every day in letters from readers, and I doubt if all of them are themselves aware of the full import of their commitment.

It might be appropriate to address this in terms of freedom, in this bicentennial year when the patriots of the dying age are out waving flags with gusto. Oh yes, many of them see the problems, or some of the problems. But they insist that we've overcome problems before, and we'll do it again, as they use the old solutions on brand new problems. They insist that their technology will cure everything, so they treat a case of terminal cancer with aspirin and a band-aid.

Some things are unspeakable, even among friends. Homesteaders talk about the values of homesteading in terms of the dying age: the satisfaction of doing things for yourself; the taste of homegrown products; money saved; fresh air and exercise; distance from city smog and crime and bustle; the higher quality of their food. They're fooling everybody, sometimes even themselves. They're making a statement even if they don't care about making statements. What they really mean is that the established system is flawed, and must be replaced. By working to replace it, they are midwives at the birth of the new age.

*   *   *

How many of the freedoms which the patriots of 1776 are so lavishly praised for winning are actually still with us? If industry poisons the water you drink or the air you breathe or the food you eat, you're not free. If a vast and bungling bureaucratic government taxes you and uses the money for projects that are in conflict with your ideals and principles, are you free?

While there are a myriad of subchapters under each of these, government just has to take the spotlight. The disgust of Americans with government boondoggles has reached gargantuan proportions. How long will it be before a Boston Tea Party demonstrates its disgust with the food stamp program abuses, unemployment benefit ripoffs, the growth of bureaucracy, public service pay rates, the farcical social security system, OSHA, zoning regulations, compulsory education, foreign aid, wasteful grants, interest on the public debt, the high-handed tactics of so-called public servants, and a host of other outrages against freedom?

Stepping back from the dreams of the past and the nostalgia that accompanies those dreams today, and the mass confusion that is an inevitable part of this time between ages, we get a much clearer picture of the future. There can be little question about its being a new age. Homesteaders—in the broad sense of the term—*are* the midwives!

At this point I must interject that recent events have had a profound effect on me, personally. Sure, I'm a homesteader, and if that were the extent of my commitment, I'd be sitting back grimly preparing for the next convulsing of the uterus delivering the new age. Sure, I'm an editor, and I do my best to divine where the world is going so I can head it off at the pass and have a more relevant publication. But I'm writing this as a human being.

The original draft of this column was much, much too long to print. It involved little things like the nagging thoughts that plagued me when several homesteading friends butchered their last rabbits and sold their last goats, and the insights I received when Diane and I spent a long weekend in North Carolina chatting with John and Jane Shuttleworth of *The Mother Earth News*, and the feedback I get from you at the other end of the mail route. It involves my personal year-end assessment of my own homestead and my own life. It got enmeshed with the opinions of our managing editor, Heather, and other people around COUNTRYSIDE. If no man is an island, then no man's thoughts can even begin to approach insularity. And that's why, of all the reams of material I have to work with when I write this column, I chose Rollo May's quote to expand on. That way I'm not claiming, but rather *agreeing*, that we are truly between ages and that, as a society, we have neither purpose nor goal.

At the same time, my commitment to homesteading tells me there is hope. Doesn't the midwife always see hope in the midst of anguish?

That's the tack I'll be taking as a human being in 1976. Because this magazine is a very personal and honest part of me, that's the tack the magazine will take in 1976 too, no doubt.

We're living in exciting times. To fully explain the implications of everything touched on in these few pages would take volumes, but few people would read them, even fewer would understand them or agree with their premises, and those who would most agree wouldn't need them anyway.

Let me add also that this is being written on New Year's Eve, which always has a sort of mystical quality for me even though I consider the vernal equinox a much more logical beginning of a new year. And I'm at the office, not at home where I usually peck out *Beyond*.

The office is dark and quiet except for the roar of the Modine units that feebly blow lukewarm air and dust around the place. I'll soon be getting in the truck and driving home to a warm and bright house vibrant with the activities of the people I love most. We'll eat, and while revelers are gathering in Times Square and watering holes all over the world, I'll be going out to the barn. I'll go up in the mow of sweet-smelling hay and limber up a few muscles tossing down bales. I'll water the cow and the calf while Dave and Steve milk and feed the goats and cow. We'll take care of the chickens, the rabbits, the horses, talk to the turkey who sits on the gate and the guineas who perch on the 220 volt cable running from the silo unloader to my welder and look in on the automated hog facilities.

And do you know what? For a short while I won't really care about the world's problems. I won't care about new ages or old ages because I'm at the center of the universe and in an age of my own. And it's good, because that's where life is. Not in the past, not in the future, but in this very moment.

It's important to clean out the fingernails of homesteading and get down to the cuticle once in awhile. It's important to see the relationship between the old dying age and the age that isn't born yet. But it's also important to recognize that we are human beings who might not be here tomorrow.

That's why homesteading just has to be the only recourse for thinking, sensitive people in these times. Come to think of it, hasn't a simple life, close to nature and truth and reality, always been the answer? You can have your economists and politicians and high-fallutin' experts. I'll be doing just fine, thank you, with a little space to do my own thing beyond the sidewalks.

40. April 1976

If you have to ask the price, you can't afford it

We had hoped to have a report on our readership survey (which was included with the January issue) ready by now, but we didn't quite make it. Not only did we have thousands to deal with, but they're still coming in.

Your comments and cooperation are of tremendous help to us, and we want to thank everyone who took part. Hopefully by next month we'll have a report on what a fairly sizeable cross-section of COUNTRYSIDE readers are thinking and doing. Believe me, it'll make an interesting article.

We're also giving many of your ideas and suggestions serious consideration, and it looks like we'll be making some rather startling improvements in the near future. Of course, one person's improvement is another's poison, so we don't expect unanimous approval. However, the improvements will be more in the line of additions rather than changes in our present content, because the survey showed that you overwhelmingly think COUNTRYSIDE is doing all right.

Perhaps the best proof of this is the frequent comment that COUNTRYSIDE is "fine the way it is, but it should come out twice as often!" Believe me, that's one suggestion we're not looking into! Most of us are wondering if we're going to get our gardens in even with our *monthly* schedule!

This falls into the category of unfinished business, too. The first new turnip recipe to come in as a result of my March column was from Diane Ford, of Hollydale, California. (And it arrived in February, which indicates the postal service is zipping those magazines out a little better than they have been.) She suggests cooking the turnips until they're soft, dicing them, and adding them to sautéed bacon and onion. Then she adds molasses and pepper and cooks until done.

And Jan Wilt, of Wiltshire Nubians in Florissant, Colorado, sent her recipe for raw turnip salad, which also arrived in February.

Turnip Lover's/Hater's Salad
Four cups shredded pared white turnips
Two red apples, cored and diced
Two tablespoons finely chopped fresh parsley

Two tablespoons finely chopped fresh onion
Toss with a mixture of:
One-half cup sour cream
One tablespoon cider vinegar
One tablespoon sugar (I use honey)
One teaspoon salt
Ground pepper to taste

She claims turnip lovers love this, but best of all, turnip haters rave about her "crispy cole slaw!" Reminds me of the time Diane took fried rabbit to a potluck and everybody commented that it was the best chicken they ever tasted. (No need to mention Rocky Mountain oysters.)

Jan also added, "At 8,400 ft. elevation, our summer nights are too cool for successful growing of corn and tomatoes, but conditions are just right for superb root crop harvests. Colorado potatoes are the best in the country... a flavor different from potatoes grown anywhere else... and they are not mealy. Carrots are divine! Each year we left most of the giant ones which had pushed out of the ground pretty far for the deer, and they finished them off with gusto."

Turnips don't seem to be very popular, you don't hear much about them... and I have to admit I never gave them much thought. But now that I think of it, they have a lot going for them.

I plant mine in July, either where some early crop has been taken off or in a garden section where a green manure crop has been plowed under. (My garden green manure is more commonly called "weeds.") The labor benefits of this off-season planting are obvious, but there is also less of a problem with weeds in such late planted crops. I use the Esmay seeder, so there's no thinning.

Turnips can stand some frost, and we usually have quite a bit of decent growing weather after the first frost. Only frost-hardy crops are around to enjoy it, of course. And turnips are simple to harvest. Hardly any real *digging* is involved. Forget about canning, freezing, drying or any other preservation that requires work. Toss 'em in the root cellar. In March we're finding a soft one now and then, but most of ours are still in fine shape. And while Jan doesn't mention if she's tried it, I'm sure she'd find that her Nubians would enjoy the extra turnips as much as the deer. Our pigs, cows, and chickens eat them too.

All in all, a very noble—but neglected—vegetable.

And by now, the ground is thawing enough to permit us to dig Jerusalem artichokes and parsnips!

This next item is a mixture of old and new business, or perhaps we could call it an update. From an issue of COUNTRYSIDE in 1970:
"The Navy has discovered a 60 percent reduction in numbers of living organisms in the soil beneath antenna cables of the first phase of Project

Sanguine. The huge, underground radio antenna proposed for northern Wisconsin operates on extremely low-frequency radio waves, which supporters said would not destroy wildlife.

"The scientists who conducted the soil test took samples at the antenna site both before construction and a year later. The second sample showed far fewer members of each of more than 20 different species of insects, worms and other forms of animal life normally found in the area," the report said.

"This brings up something else that has long intrigued me. It has been known since 1937 that man has an 'electrical system.' And these Project Sanguine tests show even low-frequency waves affect lower forms of life. My just-wondering sort of question: Does anybody know if all the radio and tv and other man-made waves bouncing around us have any affect on man?"

From an Environmental Protection Agency news release dated Feb. 2, 1976: "A specially built radiation monitoring van will check the intensity of broadcast radiation from UHF and VHF television and FM radio transmitters in major cities of the United States within the next two years...

"Radio waves (electromagnetic radiation) are present everywhere in the environment in small amounts. In cooperation with an inter-agency working group chaired by the President's Office of Telecommunications Policy, EPA has begun the study to determine how much electromagnetic radiation there is in different parts of the nation and to find out what health effects, if any, the radiation can have on humans...

"The survey will be combined with health effects research data, which are concurrently being developed by EPA's research activity. The combined data will be used to determine whether environmental criteria are required to control these nonionizing radiating sources."

This seems to me to have a number of implications, including the gentle, snowflake methods of nature compared with the bulldozer atom bomb approach of Man: How long will it be before somebody "discovers" that the things we organic farmers and gardeners have been saying about soil life and chemicals are true?

Of course, this particular study is looking for "health effects" and today that probably means cancer or something. They won't find what they're not looking for, so I don't think they'll find much of anything. The effects are probably far too subtle for most modern scientists. If the effect of the radiation was the mass insanity which seems to be affecting much of the world today they wouldn't discover it because they wouldn't agree that most people are insane.

But this makes me think of something else, too.

If we know that electromagnetic radiation is present in small amounts in the environment, and we know that Man has an electrical system (as do other living things), and we know that astronomers can detect minute amounts of electromagnetic radiation from space...why can't they all be connected? In other words, if we would have sensitive enough equipment and if we were looking for the right connections, maybe we could prove that living things are somehow affected by the radiations from space. This would make astrology scientific, and therefore respectable.

In this case, peace wouldn't reign because the moon is in the seventh house and Jupiter aligns with Mars, but because the stellar configuration would result in electromagnetic radiation that would affect life in certain predictable patterns.

One reason I mention this is that, over the years, we've run many articles on doing things by the signs. We invariably get three reactions.

One group of readers ridicules our choice of material because "there is no scientific proof." A second group adds its affirmative comments, because "it works." A third group quotes various religious writings that claim widespread belief in such black magic is one of the harbingers of the Second Coming. (Others could quote religious texts that say just the opposite.)

But somehow, I can't help but think of all those old dudes who were ridiculed or burned at the stake for such heresies as saying the sun does not revolve around the Earth, and the world is not flat, or that disease is caused by teeny little things called germs. And it can be applied to such homestead lore as cider vinegar, comfrey, and many others.

It's interesting...and alarming...to reflect on how many activities we engage in with the bulldozer approach: economics, education, agriculture, you name it. Maybe we've been overly impressed with Nature's floods, hurricanes and tornados and too condescending to microscopic soil life and gentle snowflakes. Since Nature seems to have done better without us than with us, I for one am rather inclined to take a closer look at her methods.

Kidding note: of our first six does to freshen, three had twins, three had triplets... and they were all bred by the same fence-jumping buck on one brief afternoon! Such virility has *got* to be impressive! (No, they were not all bucks. They ran 50-50.)

One of the questions we've been asking each other around here as we sit among boxes of readership surveys, is why people do the strange things homesteaders do. I'm probably a pretty fair example myself, but I doubt whether I could put it into words that made any sense...except in a story like this:

It was a rather normal day at the office, as magazine offices go. There was lots of activity. Writing, conferences, decisions, phone calls...in brief, a broad spectrum of office life. There are always details to be attended to, thought about, discussed, pondered, and acted upon. It's an exhausting way to make a living.

I went out to do chores after supper, and Katie was starting to kid. I finished milking and she was contentedly eating with...with a kid's head sticking out her rear. The kid was blinking and looking around and altogether natural looking.

I washed up in a bucket of hot, soapy water, and went in to investigate. It was a simple problem. The kid's front feet were tucked back under its belly. I was able to maneuver the legs around under the chin where they belonged, and the next time the doe strained I pulled the kid out.

Nothing else happened. I went in again, found another kid swimming an arm's length from the outside world, and tried to draw it out. Hind legs. I got them out, lost my grip in the slime and they were sucked back in. Another try (the pelvic bones contracting against my arm, the uterine slime warm and cobwebby) and I got the legs out again. With a good grasp this time, and the doe helping, the limp, squished baby goat came out into the world with a gush. I cleaned the mucus from the mouth, nose, and eyes, got it breathing, and handed it to Diane who had clean towels waiting.

The third one was born without assistance.

I washed up, gave Katie a bucket of hot water, left her to rest and came in to the typewriter. *Beyond* is due tomorrow.

I mention this mostly for new homesteaders, or those in the planning stage, but unfortunately, they are perhaps the ones least able to grasp it. If they wonder what the birth of some goats has to do with why people work at full-time jobs, then go home to work some more, I can only muse over the story of the fellow who was admiring the millionaire's yacht. He wondered how much it cost. "If you have to ask the price," the millionaire said, "you can't afford it."

Homesteaders, and hopeful homesteaders, don't have to "ask the price." That's just the way it is, beyond the sidewalks.

41. May, 1976

Pet rocks and inflation

Some time ago, market researchers discovered that the kinds of pets people have tend to be related to the kinds of people they are and the kinds of relationships they seek and can tolerate.

For example, the time and emotional demands of "caring" for a goldfish are usually less than those involved in caring for a dog and are some indication of the degree of involvement people want or can stand. The time and emotional demands of caring for goats are greater than those of caring for most dogs, which would seem to mean goat raisers are a little different from the rest of society.

But on the other end of the scale, what about all the people today who can cope with nothing more than a pet rock?

John Kishler, president of the company that conducted research on the fad, suggests that the pet rocks and trained sticks that are proliferating today might be some indication of the extent of the depersonalization of people and relationships in our society.

With this pet rock thing getting into such areas as pedigrees and even cemeteries (how can you tell when your pet rock is dead?) COUNTRYSIDE & SMALL STOCK really should be giving them more help. After all, we *are* the world's leading small stock journal, and in our 60-year history we've been in and out of many types of small stock including skunks, nutria and others that were faddish. Of course we would have to set size and weight standards, and we wouldn't deal with anyone who kept rocks on a commercial scale. But no doubt we could perform a great service for homesteaders who wanted to use their rocks for utilitarian purposes as well as pets.

How *do* you tell when a rock is dead? We could show how to skin a rock, make stone soup and perhaps how to train rocks for such jobs as paper weights and doorstops.

But on second thought, perhaps we should leave the job to *Rolling Stone*, or better yet to some journal that deals with people who actually enjoy being impersonal and dehumanized.

Maybe you saw another item in the papers recently which is almost as silly as pet rocks and trained sticks and even more ominous in its implications.

A presidential commission is going to try to learn the cause of inflation by investigating the "middleman."

We had hoped that the economists and other experts were just playing dumb until they figured out what to do or whom to blame, but sometimes you have to wonder.

Any homesteader could tell any economist that if you have a farmer plant potatoes, have a trucker haul them to a warehouse, pay storage costs and brokerage fees and more truckers or railroaders, ship them to a factory where more high-priced help with expensive machinery makes them into French fries which are then packaged in fancy containers and frozen using expensive energy and then stored and shipped and stored again, with more expenses for salesmen, advertising, transportation, fuel, rents and interest and taxes at every step and then pay for all these services and many more we haven't even mentioned, it obviously should cost a little more than planting your own potatoes and making your own French fries. The fact that in many cases, with certain food products, it is *not* cheaper to grow your own, demonstrates not the "efficiency" of such a ponderous and wasteful system, but our lousy accounting methods which set artificial prices on many ingredients of this system.

This inefficiency is both fueled by, and in turn fuels, inflation. Everybody involved in the handling and processing... telephone operators and printers, advertising executives and bankers... millions of people who never even come close to actually providing food or shelter or any other basic necessities... not only play an integral role in "production" under this system: they demand, and in some cases require, an ever greater share of the ultimate cost of the production. Which of course becomes a vicious circle.

Middleman is Everyman—each one of us. And if all the experts with their high level committees and erudite theories and complicated solutions really can't see that, they aren't fooling anybody but themselves.

They probably *can* see it, but they also know that no one wants to bell the cat. No one wants to be the first to even slow down the spiral. So we mouth opposition to inflation and tsk-tsk about its effects and go on *creating* it with a thousand times more vigor than we fight it. Even a relatively painless measure such as a wage and price freeze is heralded by great public outcries of "unfair!" and "discrimination!"

Even without inflation we think we need more money this year than last year, because we're more experienced or have more seniority or because somebody else gets more. This contributes to inflation, of course (we are all middleman), and with inflation we add even more to our demands and expectations.

And while we mill around in confusion, trying to decide who is to bell the cat, we blame the middleman, big business, labor, government, farmers... and politicians create committees to investigate something that needs no investigating at all. Investigations that cannot prove anything, because the answer has been in front of us all along and no one wants to admit it or face it.

The answer does not lie in printing more money, playing with the prime rate or the GNP or the balance of payments or in passing laws. It lies in human nature, which cannot be controlled or legislated. The answer lies in individuals, or, if they refuse to accept the responsibility, in the natural course of events which means a collapse of artificial economics and a return to a basic and stable foundation of plain old survival.

The experts, even if they see the logical answers, are not likely to suggest them. Can you imagine the professional life expectancy of a politician who would dare to suggest letting some air out of the bubble in order to put life on a more stable foundation? He would be so clobbered by business, labor and consumers (to say nothing of the normal politicians who tell people what they want to hear) that he wouldn't know what hit him. This lack of leadership (and the intelligent citizenry to back it up) is disastrous, because inflation causes a great deal more trauma than that experienced between the paycheck and the checkout counter.

Higher prices are only one visible effect of inflation and its causes. For many of us, the drive for ever-increasing efficiency is an even more important one. "Efficiency" is desirable to hold prices down, and food prices in particular. The reason, of course, is that people can only eat so much. Therefore, a constantly growing GNP, a constantly expanding industrial base requires that people consume a great deal more than just food. Constant economic growth requires that people use many more products than could remotely be considered basic necessities, and in order for people to be able to purchase these, the cost of the necessities such as food and shelter must be kept low.

So, not only has the price of food been kept artificially low in order to fuel the rest of the industrial economy, the drive for "efficiency" and low prices in the food sector has driven us to the use of chemical agriculture without regard for the long-term consequences to either the Earth or the living creatures that depend on the soil for nourishment and survival. The drive for efficiency has resulted in monoculture, in huge operations and huge machinery that result in a great portion of our food dollars going to moneylenders and speculators. It has resulted in the generally sad state of affairs surrounding the ecology and environment of our self-contained spaceship, Earth.

And, it has resulted in the dehumanization of so many of the four billion passengers on that spaceship.

With constant growth, the bubble must sooner or later burst. The alternative is to let the air out slowly, and to tie it off securely at some point before it completely collapses. Which, of course, is not very likely.

But that is exactly what homesteading attempts to do, consciously or unconsciously. Homesteading is a very private, and admittedly small measure for deflating the bubble when compared with the forces that are still working at *in*flating it. But by engaging in home food production, by making a chair or a bookshelf or a cabinet, by sewing a dress or a shirt or in any way doing without high-tech products or services, homesteaders are making a significant beginning. They are getting back to the point where the Earth provides everything... as it does even now... but where the loving care and patient skill of the individual transforms those natural gifts into useable goods that support life and make it meaningful.

Such activities help to stem inflation by circumventing the artificial "efficiencies" and support systems that cause it, the dehumanizing and self-destructive greed which is at the core of it all.

Whether the bubble bursts with a bang or the air is released slowly, homesteading, in one form or another, is the only possible life-style of the future. It might not involve livestock; it might not even involve the countryside. But the way will certainly be clearer and easier, it will certainly begin, beyond the sidewalks.

42. June 1976

Workaholics, loonies, and homesteaders

One big difference between the modern farmer or homesteader and the peasant of a hundred or a thousand years ago is that the modern tiller of the soil has a lot more to think about while performing some humble and routine task.

I was planting oats and had a lot of time to reflect on a casual comment Dave had made at lunch. (Unlike barn cleaning and certain other jobs, there isn't much opportunity for father-son discussions while planting oats.) He was reading the newspaper while waiting for me to finish my soup and sandwich, and he remarked on an item about workers in some company enjoying working 12-hour days — three days a week. Dave mused that that sounded pretty good to him, too, since we were working 14 hours a day, seven days a week!

My first reaction was that farming was like that, and that as the planting season wore on it would get worse before it got better. It was only later, while droning along in a 20-acre field with the wheezy old Allis, that I had time to reflect on it.

Could it be, I wondered, that many of our current problems have something to do with our rather quaint notions of leisure? Could these notions be as contrived and as phony as some people thought the oil crisis was? Why is "leisure" so much more desirable than "work"?

If I'm working as I write this, I've run well over the 100-hour mark for the week already and it's only Friday. Or am I playing? Was I working or playing when I was planting those oats? I honestly can't tell the difference, and I can say with a great deal of conviction that I've never worked a day in my life. Well, almost never.

The idea that work is play and play is work is an integral part of the homestead philosophy, of course. The possibility that we are all workaholics, or nuts, has crossed my mind. But there's more to it than that, it seems to me.

I find it as difficult to grasp what all those people who only work 40 hours a week do with their extra time as some of them find it hard to see how I manage to farm 170 acres, run a magazine and write a book a year, as well as provide the bulk of my family's food in homestead fashion.

Certainly there are many worthwhile leisure-time activities. But just as surely, the bulk of the time of the vast majority of people is simply wasted.

Why, then, do so many people feel so overworked, so rushed? And why is leisure held in such esteem?

The more I thought about it the more convinced I became that it's all a crock. Leisure is one more disastrous side effect of the industrial revolution and ought to be done away with.

What would an industrial society do with all those people who'd be sitting around with nothing to do because of all the efficiency technology has brought? You gotta keep 'em happy, so you make them think their enforced idleness is desirable. It's not difficult to glamorize a bad habit. Look what they did with smoking.

Unlike smoking, which benefits a relatively small segment of the populace, leisure benefits the entire technological economy. It not only creates a market for snowmobiles and bowling balls and golf clubs: it also creates a new marketing strategy for almost everything else. Because we think leisure is so desirable, we believe we can't live without ready-to-eat foods, ready-to-wear clothes, and labor-saving devices and gadgets of every description. Ever wonder why people work only 40 hours a week and still complain that they don't have time for the things they *want* to do? Maybe all that efficiency, all those labor-saving devices, really aren't doing what we've been led to believe they do.

What better way to keep up the gross national product than to pay grown men $1 million to kick a ball, to beat on each other or to leap across a canyon on a motorcycle? Imagine the effect on the economy of all the goods ostensibly designed to make life easier and therefore to increase leisure. All these things not only create jobs: because we are led to believe that we need them, we end up working more, not less, just to get them.

So many of the things that bug us homesteaders are really part of this edification of leisure. Leisure is put on a pedestal because the industrial state doesn't know what else to do with us and of course, it also does a great deal for the entire economic system.

I doubt very much if leisure, at least past a certain point, does a thing for us in terms of human values. More likely the opposite is true.

In the process, "work" becomes debasing. It's not fun, because fun is something that's not work. And of course many jobs are *not* fun because as the process ground on, we came up with many tasks that are so far removed from basic life needs that many workers can see the results of their efforts only in terms of a paycheck...and that's the *real* debasement of work.

Homesteaders know better. They know that work can be fun and that fun can be work.

Many people laugh at us for working so hard to produce food and other items that we could easily purchase. But they miss the point, for the fact that we do meaningful work to produce these items is one of the rewards in itself. The other rewards — freshness, chemical-free foods, and the rest — are almost secondary, in many cases.

Maybe what we need is a campaign along the lines of the anti-smoking effort, which is attacking a long-revered thought pattern with remarkable success. We need to be told that leisure — as portrayed by advertising and the media — is not as great as we've been led to believe, that it might be damaging to our mental and physical well-being, that it could actually be harmful to our social and economic health.

We don't need more fuel-guzzling monsters and chemicals on our land. We need people who are collecting unemployment checks or who are dissatisfied with their assembly line jobs to work the land more intensively to produce food. We don't need more highways and vacation areas and tv programs: we need to dignify gardening, and livestock raising, and various home crafts. We don't need more golf courses and bowling lanes and physical fitness programs: we need to be told that it is *not* demeaning to use our bodies for practical, meaningful labor.

Pushing a button to open a garage door electrically and riding around a golf course in an electric cart have been glamorized to a dangerous level. It's time we straightened out our priorities. Let's make it glamorous and desirable to spade a garden, chop wood and shovel manure.

The sensible homesteader will recognize that this doesn't mean a peasant existence where you have to break your back just to eke out a living. Surely there can be some kind of balance between that kind of inhuman drudgery and the bread-and-circus syndrome. If there is, no one comes as close to practicing it as we homesteaders.

A recent issue of *Newsweek* reported that Teng Hsaio-ping has apparently been exiled to a commune and "assigned to the ignominious task of collecting manure." A reader echoed my sentiments exactly when he commented, "Manure shoveling happens to be a large part of my daily routine, but I had been unaware of its ignominiousness."

He went on to say that he has long admired the Chinese policy of periodically reacquainting bureaucrats, professionals, and politicians with the basic, mundane labors of the masses. "No better place than behind a cow to ruminate that rhetoric isn't, after all, the sustenance of the body politic."

By knocking leisure off its pedestal and doing away with the ignominiousness of honest labor, we'd go a long way toward eliminating a host of problems ranging from juvenile delinquency to ecology.

Some of us are already there, for there's no lack of meaningful, practical, invigorating work-play, beyond the sidewalks.

Some people might not understand the 38-year-old reference to Evel Knievel and his motorcycle. Most ball players now get way more than a piddly million bucks a year. But the comments about people sitting around with nothing to do are even more up-to-date in 2014 than they were in 1976.

However, this could do a much better job of defining leisure and what it *should* consist of. But that's a whole 'nother topic.

43. July 1976

The naming of Pheasant Field

Agriculture is "the noblest profession." People involved in real dirt farming on any level — a couple of rabbits and a garden, or hundreds of acres — know this intuitively. And one of the noblest traits of any farmer or gardener is the keen respect for nature that results from close association with it.

The sun was lost in the dazzle of the bright blue June sky as I guided the little Allis into the alfalfa field with the sicklebar mower trailing behind. It was a new stand, lush and thick, and as I walked through it to lower the mower blade it reached my knees.

The first swaths released the fresh, sweet aroma of new-mown hay which, combined with the blue sky, warm sun and gentle breeze, made this truly a "noble profession." It became somewhat less noble, of course. The lush growth and an improper setting resulted in frequent jamming of the cutter bar, making it necessary to get off the tractor and unjam the mass of juicy stems and make some adjustments. After several circuits of the field the pitman stick picked up a string of mown hay and spun it into a rope that would have done any spinner proud. More unjamming.

But then, cutting a clean swath on the downside of the hill, I noticed a rustle through the grass just ahead of the chugging tractor.

On the next round I kept my left foot poised over the clutch as I neared that point, but nothing happened. On the following pass, without warning, a young pheasant burst into the air and out of the way as the mower kept on chewing its way through the hay.

The following pass was again uneventful, even though all my senses were alert.

With each swath the standing hay area grew smaller by seven feet, making the birds' refuge less secure. Another round with nerves tensed, eyes straining, clutch foot poised. Not a ripple.

On the next, two birds scurried out of the way as the clutch slammed in to give them clearance.

Little by little the cover of standing hay grew smaller. With only a few passes to go, three pheasants — a hen and two youngsters — took to the air. After a brief but furious fluttering of short wings, they glided over the already wilting alfalfa into the winter wheat on the other side.

Once more around the track. Yet another pass and two more pheasants joined the others. A frantic explosion of wings slapping air just ahead of the voracious mower blade, then that long, smooth glide into the wheat and a parting of the stems as the birds continued to flee on foot into the security of the standing grass.

Then I hit a stone and broke a tooth on the mower and went back to the shop to remove the broken piece and rivet a new one into place. Surely any remaining pheasants would have escaped to safety by joining the others by now.

But there was still a sense of caution when approaching that section of field. Nothing happened. There wasn't even a rustle ahead of the chomping mower blade.

Finally, the last pass, less than seven feet wide. Difficult to cut because I not only had to keep the grass on the tractor side of the mower from getting tangled up in the machine, but the far side of the blade was also picking up mown hay that was lying in the wrong direction, getting jammed.

The parting of the grass ahead of the blade told me that there was still a bird that refused to yield to progress, to the might and power of man and machine. As I stomped on the foot clutch to give the bird room, the idling blades clattered away like some live monster that was hungry for material to chew up.

I eased up on the clutch, moving the rig forward. Easily. Cautiously. Another young pheasant blasted out from the remaining stand and glided into the wheat.

The mower clattered on through while I watched for jam-ups, mechanical problems, and tell-tale partings of the grass.

Suddenly there was a flash of brown feathers at the blade. I slammed down both feet, on the clutch and the brake, but the floundering bird was behind the mower in the cut hay.

I slipped the gears into neutral, secured the brakes, and jumped off the tractor.

The bird fluttered away from me, but got tangled up in a strip of uncut alfalfa and was easy to catch. One leg had been chopped off.

It wasn't bleeding. I left the tractor and took the bird down to the house. Diane put it in a box where she puts all the sick pigs, goats, chicks, goslings, ducklings and everything else that needs nursing on our place. I went back and finished up the field.

After evening chores, and burying the pheasant in the compost pile, I walked up to the hill to the mown hayfield. The alfalfa was wilted in the blazing sun that steamed the moisture from it and the searing southwest wind. Perfect haying weather.

There was no sign of life except for a pair of redwing blackbirds exploring a section of mown hay. No pheasants.

I knew they were there, of course. I also knew that their number, diminished by one, was part of a natural cycle. If it hadn't been for my mower, the bird would have died because of foxes or other natural causes.

And yet, there was a sort of funereal sobriety over that field. Something had died there that day and its death diminished me.

A silly thought for one who routinely slaughters rabbits, chickens, goats, lambs, pigs and calves to feed his family.

Silly, and yet...

Life has varicolored meaning, beyond the sidewalks.

44. August 1976

Cows can't tell time
(but they sure know what time it is)

We moderns brag of "controlling" nature. We think we can control even time, the very stuff life is made of. The Concorde can beat the sun and arrive in New York before it left London; we press a switch and turn night into day, summer into winter (or winter into summer). We can eat fresh strawberries in December.

Ah, but again we fool ourselves, and those who live in the countryside are keenly aware of the deception, because in the countryside, time, like everything else, is concrete and real. The quality of sunlight is different at dawn than it is at dusk, and different in January and August. The smells, the feel of the air, the sights, the job routine, are all different from day to day and year to year and no two moments are ever alike. Time is truly "a measurable period during which a process continues."

Y ou can tell it's 5 A.M., and August, by the color and the angle of the light striking the bedroom wall. The sun is not yet over the horizon, but its impending arrival is fittingly heralded just to the north of neighbor Wilkie's skyscraping new silo.

There is a certain feel to the air, a kind of dryness underneath the morning mugginess that says it's going to be a hot, Wisconsin August day.

The cattle and goats are still resting in that prenatal position of theirs with their heads flung back over their flanks, but the sheep are out munching the drying grass. The roosters are crowing, of course, but they've been crowing sporadically most of the night. The cats, too, never seem to sleep and they appear as if by magic out of nowhere at the clatter of my milk buckets. The dog rouses herself from the garage and comes along, tail a'wagging, and then stops to stretch and yawn.

The birds sound as birds sound only in the morning (and with calls far different than in spring) and the cackles and squawks and cries of the barnyard fowl are augmented at this time of the year by the spring hatch: more numerous than at other times of the year, old enough to sound mature, but not quite ready for market or the freezer.

The pigs, of course, lie piled up in their pig piles, snoring. Pigs are only human, and see no need to wake up until moved by hunger or a nature call.

The light streams in the east barn windows like fluid gold, highlighting the dust. Milk hisses into pails, water tinkles into stock tanks and animals jostle one another vigorously in their eagerness to break their fast. And even before chores are done, the heavy low-angled sun has become more watery and the orb itself less noticeable.

E ven the grain bins tell the countrysider what time of year it is: the barley is almost gone; the oats are only ankle-deep; the corn and other grains running low; and all of them have a late-summer dryness and deadness to them.

After breakfast...and an August breakfast is likely to include cantaloupe, or fresh pears, and fried eggplant, as well as the year-round staples...preparations for combining get underway.

The combine itself has been checked out, the 75 zerk fittings greased, belts and canvases checked. This morning the remaining barley is shoveled into sacks and stored outside the bin and the entire bin is swept down and out in a cloud of choking dust that hangs on the morning air. The grain auger is heaved into place, and tested.

Seems strange how a job is always finished just about the time the first batch of cookies comes out of the oven. It's already too hot for coffee, but too early for iced tea or lemonade. Cold goat milk washes down the crumbs very nicely.

I like to use the Allis WD tractor with the combine (an Allis 60), partly because of the hand clutch, but perhaps more so because it's easy to jump off of... and I seem to do a lot of jumping on and off the tractor when I combine. The 60 has a crazy trailer hitch ball on it rather than the more common and simpler pin hitch, so it takes a wrench to get the thing hooked up. And then I have to crawl under the combine to tighten up the drive belt. Two other levers put tension on the main canvas. I check the gas and oil in the tractor, ease on the PTO to check out the combine, then head out to the field.

The sun is high by now, and even my slow but bouncing progress down the farm road raises clouds of August dust behind. This ride is always pleasant, as it takes me past the long and narrow garden, where I can assay the condition of the tomatoes and beans from the tractor seat; past the Jerusalem artichokes and the comfrey on the one side and the wheat on the other. The road rises abruptly where a finger of the woodlot juts out and that, in combination with a hard left turn (the cumbersome combine jostling behind) demands slowing down and concentrating on driving. With the combine offset way to the left, I'm forced to drive the tractor into the oats a ways, but even so, there are half-ripe choke cherries festooned over the scour-kleen as I skirt the woods.

Then, the barley field.

I love barley. I consider it the best pig food there is, I love the way it waves in the early summer breezes, I enjoy the beer that's made from it, I like the smell of it. And I get better yields from barley under my organic program than I get from anything else. It also fits in very nicely with my journalist-farmer lifestyle. And this is the moment of truth, the culmination of the year of planning and labor and investment that every farmer has in virtually every crop on his land.

I turn the Allis into the field, engage the PTO, and the cutter bar begins to clatter. Slowly, ponderously, the canvases begin to move, the cylinder begins to whirr, gears mesh smoothly and belts warm to their task. As I ease up on the clutch the entire train moves out, the paddles sweeping golden stalks of grain into the mechanism.

I don't really enjoy machines. Internal combustion engines are infernal engines, to me. But a combine is a wondrously complex, wonderfully simple machine. Of course, I know mine inside and out, having been inside and out more times than I can recall. But at least it's *logical.* I like it.

We — my machines and I, which are really one machine — move down the field. The little tractor is roaring, the combine is roaring, and I lean back, tense, watching for problems and straining to ascertain the proper speeds and settings.

The paddles spank the rustling stalks into the clacking knives, they are swept up the canvas in swishing waves, sucked into the cylinder in a whooshing vacuum and the golden grain is whirred from the stalks. As the straw is bounced out of one side of the machine in a dusty fluffy windrow, the grain is carried up the elevator to fall hissing into the tank. It's beautiful, poetry in motion, and I can never combine without thinking of all those thousands of tons of grain that have been cut and threshed by hand since the beginning of agriculture.

But we're talking about time.

Farmers in this area know that combining doesn't go well until 11 A.M. It takes that long for the August sun to beat the moisture from the grain, and the dew-logged stalks tend to jam up the cylinder. Knowing that from painful experience, I take it easy, but still manage to get a few masses of stalks up the canvas that the cylinder just can't handle. The slip clutch on the combine complains noisily as the entire machine slows down, and then it's off the tractor, up on the combine, unjam the mess, down off the combine and back up on the tractor. And I think of my father, who said that if he was working running his paper-making machine the company was losing money. When everything runs smoothly there isn't much to do.

The tank holds 18 bushels, and when it's full one of the boys is there with the truck. The combine is pulled up to the pickup, the auger is lowered, the auger clutch engaged and the grain rains down into the truck bed and in a cone of aromatic edible gold.

Another round. I glance at my watch to make sure the old wives' tale about 11 o'clock is really true.

It is, and things go so swimmingly I hate to break off for lunch. But the belly knows what time it is too.

Lunch tells as much about the time of year as the other events of the day: it's dominated by tomatoes, which we've been eagerly awaiting since last spring, and are now on the verge of getting sick of.

The afternoon drones on, the little tractor roaring, the combine singing a cacophony of gears and belts and pulleys, the grain sss-ing into the tank and then into the truck.

Again by one of those strange coincidences, the field is finished just about suppertime. The truck is full, so I haul the last combine load back to the farmstead in the combine.

We eat, and do chores, again in a very different atmosphere. The animals are — different — at evening chores. Those who were awake 12 hours ago seem a little haggard now, and those who were sleepy this morning have a little more bounce. The chickens are beginning to roost, but the pigs act hungry. And the boys are beginning to poop out. In fact, they disappear when the truck is unloaded, and I empty the last combine tank in the bin myself. It takes an extension cord and light before I'm finished, and the eerie shadows cast by the artificial light are another indication of the time.

The combine is backed into the shed, the tension taken off the belts, and I walk up the hill around the barn in the dark. The goats are still rustling in the manger and the pigs are banging their feeder lids with gusto, but the birds are quiet. The air is quiet, but in a different way than it was 18 hours ago. I'm tired, but I feel good.

And I don't have to look at my watch to know it's time for bed, beyond the sidewalks.

45. September, 1976

The shadow of Sasha

There's something about a family dog. And, like so many other aspects of human existence, we often don't fully appreciate them until we lose them.

We've had many dogs. Some stayed just a short while, and others became an integral part of the family.

I can vividly recall Midnight, Diane's Cocker Spaniel who I thought was a little pest when we were dating (Diane and I, not Midnight) back in our high school days. I never really got to know "Middie" and I didn't care for her, although Diane had loved her for years. Maybe in some subconscious way I even felt I was competing with the little black beast for Diane's affection.

I thought it was just a dog. It was several years later, after I'd been through the Marine Corps and joined Diane on the University of Wisconsin campus as a student, that I fully realized that Middie was more than just a dog.

I had picked Diane up at her dorm and had noticed immediately that she was out of sorts. We were walking along Lake Mendota when she told me that she had received a letter. Middie was dead.

She must have been close to a hundred years old, in dog time, and had some form of cancer. She was put to sleep.

It was the first time I can remember seeing Diane cry.

*   *   *

My own children had Smokey, a striking replica of Midnight, and his demise was particularly traumatic. He never left the yard. But when the kids crossed the road to ice skate on the mill pond, Smokey went along for the frolic. He was several paces behind, as dogs often are, and was hit by a car. The car never stopped, and I'll never forget the looks on those little faces as the kids came running back home. The dog was bleeding profusely from the mouth when I reached him, acted vicious when I tried to move him, and was dead by the time I got him home.

It's tough digging a grave when there's ice on the skating pond.
It's tough digging a grave anytime.

Smokey's replacement was Roxie, a Collie-type pup who soon put memories to rest. And she whelped, producing one of the dogs I've felt most akin to. He was more German Shepherd than Collie, and was named Bortan after a science fiction story I was reading at the time about the last dog in the world. There was nothing special about him, really: we just seemed to hit it off together. He was affectionate. He was intelligent. He was fierce and he was big. He was a man's dog, and we got along fine.

And one bitter cold New Year's Day, Bortan and Roxie both disappeared. We never learned what happened to them.

*   *   *

Grandpa thought kids should have a dog, and certainly kids who had goats, rabbits, geese and everything else that our kids had, needed a dog. He picked up Sasha at a farmers' market. She was a friendly Collie pup, and very soon exhibited an astounding herding instinct.

When we lived on the homestead, Sasha would run the fenceline, barking at the neighbor's cows on the other side. But it wasn't until we moved to a farm of our own that we began to appreciate her talents.

When our heifers broke out of their pasture, it was Sasha who alerted us to the escape and who got the most pleasure from the roundup, nipping at flanks and heels and driving the stupid beasts back through the break in the fence. She was just as good with hogs.

Of course, Sasha also felt it her duty to exercise her authority by barking at the horses standing innocently by the gate at three in the morning, rousing us from bed to see what on Earth was going on out there.

She lost my sympathy several years ago by drawing blood from an escaped goat who was innocently munching silage in the barn, and on those occasions when she would drag a goose or a duck up to the back porch. She had the instinct, but lacked training. And I lacked patience. Sasha and I were not the best of friends, on several occasions.

But she took it so badly that I bent over backwards to make it up to her. It took years. Only recently did she become a real farm dog, trotting out to the fields with the tractor, leaping into the pickup on the first invitation, as well as keeping a constant eye on the livestock.

*   *   *

The other night, the kids were swinging on the thick rope strung from the old elm tree behind the house, and Sasha, in her usual playful mood, was nipping at their heels. And accidentally got clipped in the chops. She was subdued, but we couldn't find anything wrong with her and didn't think much of it. She was awfully quiet today, but it was a rainy, dreary day and the entire household was out of sorts. Nobody paid much attention to the dog, under the circumstances.

And when I checked on her after evening chores, she was dead.

I lifted her to the back of the pickup she had so eagerly leaped on so recently, and drove her out to the back 40.

It had been raining, but the ground was still dry beyond a shovel's depth. It was hard going. The grave is a shallow one.

I took off her collar, and the bright green Dodge County dog tag she had acquired only a few days ago.

Good-bye, Sasha.

*   *   *

You can't live in the country without a dog. This is being written in June, and by the time you read it in September we'll undoubtedly have another piddling pup slopping goat milk all over the garage floor. Sasha will blend in with the Midnights, the Smokies, the Bortans of years past.

And yet, it's experiences like this, memories like this, that make living beyond the sidewalks so intense and personal.

Rest in peace, old friend.

*   *   *

Postscript: It's eerie, but when I walk to the barn in the morning with my milk pail I sense a shadow behind me, and turn, expecting to see Sasha. It's the shadow of the honey locust along the drive.

I hear a rustle, and expect it to be Sasha. It's a chicken, or the wind.

I wake up in the middle of the night wondering if the sheep we just put on pasture are all right and if Sasha is on the job, and then I remember...

These are the moments that hone to keenness the edge of living beyond the sidewalks.

46. October 1976
A walk under the stars

It was one of those days when nothing went right. You know what I mean: you've had them yourself. Doing the evening chores is usually therapeutic, but even that didn't help. One of the calves was scouring, the Toggenburg buck (who I'm positive can walk up walls like a fly when no one is watching) was in with the Nubian does, and the stock tank overflowed to make a dandy mudhole in the barnyard.

Back at the house, things were no better. Nothing interested me, and the tv was blaring in the living room, along with the radio in the kitchen and another (on a different station, of course) from one of the bedrooms. I decided to go for a walk.

The night was pitch black after the glare of the lights in the house and I gingerly picked my way up the hill from memory and touch rather than sight. But after a while the house lights were only dim yellow squares behind me, my eyes began to adjust to the darkness, and I could make out the familiar features of the path in the dim starlight.

I intended to "just walk," to let the cool night air sweep away the cobwebs and litter in my brain so that hopefully, with a good night's rest, tomorrow could be a fresh start. Then I looked up.

Directly above me and stretching from the northeast to the southwest horizons the Milky Way exploded in a display of stardust. In the crisp still air of that country night portions of the sky were white with stars too numerous to even be distinguishable. And even against that dusty background, the brighter stars were as uncountable as leaves on a tree.

The sight was breathtaking, and I was filled with a sense of awe, not because I never look at the stars or because they are seldom as numerous and as bright as they were that night, but because they were so unexpected. Their majesty conflicted so jarringly with my mood. I gazed up until I got a crick in my neck, and then laid on my back in the damp and cold grass.

Years ago, when I had more time — or more sense — I studied the stars. Tonight I learned I had forgotten what little I had known even about the constellations, but the disappointment that brought was negligible under the majesty of that canopy. And I remembered enough to know something about their sizes, their distances. I can never look at the stars without realizing, in awe, that the light of some of them I see has been traveling for thousands, even millions of years: some of them may actually have exploded or died unknown ages ago, but the sight of that death still hasn't reached us!

Then, staring at one small portion of the universe, a strange sensation overcame me. I was not looking up at the stars, I was looking *down* on them! They, or anybody out there, were looking up at me!

As the feeling of being part of the universe swept over me, anything smaller than a star system faded into insignificance, and I forcibly felt my own insignificance.

In the universe, the death of a star is a relatively common occurrence. If the disappearance of a star even many times larger than our sun is of so little concern, how much more unimportant must a planet like ours be in the scheme of things? And how downright laughable our fervor and expenditure of energies and talents on mere human affairs! Our politics, our economics, our wars and social problems, all fade into the insignificance of one flyspeck in a thousand-head feedlot. What difference does any of it make, among the stars?

And if it makes no difference who the president of the United States is, or even *if* the United States is, if the universe doesn't even bother to take note of our accomplishments or our failures, how would it react to the thousands of truly tiny things we self-centered humans think are so important? When we look at the stars, where can we see any importance attached to a teenager with acne and without a date; to a businessman whose shares of stock are taking a beating; to a farmer trying to cope with a piece of junk machinery?

Strangely enough, even as these thoughts pass through your mind as you lay under the stars, there is a certain indescribable feeling that counters the feeling of insignificance. It's almost as if projecting yourself to the stars makes you part of the universe; you don't care about the small things because they don't matter. You are a part of something much bigger, much more important.

About that time the new thoughts that have shoved the troublesome thoughts into the background threaten to create a headache as painful as the one they were supposed to eliminate. Besides, the grass is downright wet, and cold. So I come back down off my hill. Back to Earth. Back to reality.

The path is reversed. The lights in the windows of the house become brighter as I approach, the stars dim and recede. In the living room, the lights are painfully glaring.

I still have my problems. But they no longer control my actions, my life, because they have been put in the proper perspective. I'm a human being, and "troubles" are normal. But I'm also something more than a human being.

The stars shine everywhere. They carry the same message to everyone. It may or may not be true that the message makes a lot more sense to those who live and work in the countryside, but I do know one thing: the stars are certainly brighter, away from the city lights, beyond the sidewalks.

47. November 1976

A Thanksgiving celebration

There is something special about a holiday on the farm, and there's something extra-special about Thanksgiving on the homestead. The day is more leisurely than usual, but that can be deceptive...because I can often relive the exertions of the entire year over again in the space of a single day.

Chores are a regular part of life on a place with animals, holiday or not. But on Thanksgiving, we set up the festive mood by catching 40 extra winks. Even then, there is none of the hurry usually present at that time of the day when people have to catch the school bus, get to the office or attend to fieldwork. Without the hurry, the chores are actually fun. While we're feeding, milking, cleaning and bedding, I can imagine the rest of the nation gathering around their tv sets, ready for a day of parades and football games, and I'm glad to be in my barn.

Diane started working on the turkey when I left the house, and by the time I get back the kitchen already is beginning to look and smell like Thanksgiving. She's well-organized, and asks only that I bring some potatoes and squash from the root cellar. This task, too, is leisurely, and especially so because to my way of thinking the root cellar is the focal point for Thanksgiving.

I find myself stopping to admire the bags of onions, the crates of potatoes, the jars of beets and beans and the tins of honey. It seems like only yesterday that I was plowing the garden, and planting it in spring air heavy with the aroma of apple blossom and fresh compost. Somehow, in the same instant, I can also find myself reliving the rest of the growing season: the cold spring rains; the hours of sweat and exertion in choking heat and dust; the reward of the first tomato. The rototilling, the composting, the mulching, the harvesting, all are embodied right here in the sights and smells of the root cellar.

How different it must be, I think, to work only for a paycheck! Where do the factory workers and farmers who do not have root cellars go to appreciate Thanksgiving, to savor the rewards of their labors? There is no beauty or satisfaction in their check stubs or bank accounts, which may be why they are all in front of the tv screen.

Leaving the cellar, I sense that the harvest closed the door on one season and opened another, to the snow and chill winds of winter.

I peel the new, still thin-skinned potatoes, and hack open an iron hulled Hubbard squash while Diane seemingly works on a dozen dishes at once. From time to time we pop into the living room to glance at one televised parade or another, to join the younger set in their oohs and aahs over some particularly striking float or balloon. But when we've gone as far as we can with the meal preparations, I head for another leisure activity: hiking over my fields.

This is a regular job, of course, and always a pleasant one. But on Thanksgiving it is more so. The primary purpose is to get some exercise and fresh air... and to get away from the stomach-kneading aromas beginning to arise in the kitchen! But I can never walk my fields without thinking one way or another of soil improvement or future cropping plans. And this, too, has a Thanksgiving aspect. Because I have no specific purpose, because I'm in no hurry, I recall the days spent in each field. This one is where I lost my wallet disking. Here is where we planted when a sudden shower came up and by the time we finished, clay was clinging to the metal rim of the grain drill wheels like mud pies on a stick. Here's a length of tangled, rotting baling twine, indicating the spot where the knotter gave me so much trouble I had to go back to the house for the operator's manual.

But now all is quiet, waiting. It almost seems as if it has reverted to nature and I no longer have anything to do with any of it. This too is part of my Thanksgiving, for it tells me how insignificant I am in the scheme of things, how transient, and how thankful I should be for even being allowed to intrude upon the scene momentarily.

The wind is brisk and I'm inadequately dressed, with blood still thinned by the heat of summer, so I go back to the house.

The kitchen aromas of Thanksgiving are overpowering now, especially after the walk and the minutes until dinner drag on like hours.

Finally, the feast.

There is none of your truck-transported impersonal fare here: everything but the cranberries came from our own soil, our own efforts. We watched over this turkey since he was a day-old, stupid poult; we planted the potatoes and the squash; grew the wheat for the biscuits and ground it into flour with our own muscles. The butter is from our own cow and churn, the milk from our goats, the carrots from our own garden and the honey sauce oozing over them from our own beehives. And again, I wonder how those eating from cans and boxes and frozen packages can possibly relate to the real meaning of the harvest festival.

Again there is no hurry at evening chore time, and again there is food for thought: the harvest, the thanksgiving, is neither the beginning nor the end, but part of a continuing process. The animals not only need to be fed and milked again, but they are bred, harboring within their bodies the fetuses that will be involved in future harvests. The winter-sown grains, too, represent the next season, even though the dust has barely settled from the last harvest. Then there are the plump seeds that will be planted next spring, cleaned, bagged, and safely stored — and of course the life in the soil goes on.

Tomorrow will be another workday, more hectic, more intense than today. But the reflections of the harvest festival will carry over to affect even the most mundane task.

Who else can be as close to the source and beauty of life as he who produces his own food? Who else can so clearly see the real meaning, and necessity, for giving thanks? To everything else I add a prayer of thanks for being able to live and work beyond the sidewalks.

48. December 1976

Maybe leisure isn't *all* bad...

*W*inter...

As winter settles over the north country, I can't help but reflect on what a truly amazing season this is.

I'm amazed, for instance (and I always have been) that seemingly fragile birds and animals can survive such an inhospitable environment. When the temperature drops far below zero, when the northerly winds whip crystalline snow against tree bark like sandpaper on a pine board, when the lakes are frozen solidly enough to support the trucks of ice fishermen and any possible source of food (it would seem) is buried under drifts of snow, isn't it amazing that the deer and the chickadee, the pheasant and the field mouse, can carry on?

When humans "freeze to death" scurrying from their automobiles to their doorways, other creatures of nature manage to spend the entire winter without so much as a hot bath or a cup of tea.

Isn't it amazing that the flies and mosquitoes, which disappear with the first chill of fall, can be lurking in nooks and crannies, oblivious even to blizzards that paralyze cities by closing airports and stalling snowplows and closing schools, only to return in numbers as great as ever the next summer?

I find it rather marvelous that the alfalfa, the winter wheat and the rye...and the dandelions and pigweed and burdock and thistle...can be hibernating under that blanket of snow, only to burst forth when the warm rains of spring fall again. I can't help but reflect that if for some reason winter were to last for a couple of years instead of a couple of months, it's likely that we humans would perish...but the dandelions would be as robust as ever when it was finally over.

To me it's amazing that, while the rest of nature tastes winter — really tastes it — we humans try to turn it into summer and then complain every step of the way. We complain about heating bills, about shoveling snow, about stalled cars, while the more stupid beasts accept winter for what it is. Maybe if we weren't so smart we'd wear warmer clothing (to make up for the animal's thicker winter fur) and adapt to cooler temperatures, we'd learn that winter is no time to go anyplace that requires shoveling snow or starting a car.

As you might have guessed, I happen to like winter. These aren't just words of a simple country hick who doesn't know any better, because I've spent winters in southern California and on the beaches of Hawaii, and in the past I've joined the throngs of northerners who journey to Florida and Mexico with snow melting on the trunks of their cars. Winter, like all of nature, has its place in the scheme of things.

Most of us, and I'm afraid that includes me, botch it. We botch winter by acting as if it were summer, but only colder and with more inconveniences. And I know how I'd like winter to be.

I'd like winter to be what it is for the rest of the natural world: a time of rest and recuperation. It's not really the season of death, as so many think and as I've written before myself: life is an ongoing process, death is an ongoing process ("We are all dying, with a little patience") and winter has no monopoly on either.

To me, the ideal winter would include the time to follow the time-honored country tradition of repairing, maintaining, and sharpening tools. I can hardly imagine the thrill it would be to spend whole days going over the mower, the combine, the rake and the baler, replacing worn bearings and gears.

Then, too, winter should be a time for sitting before a crackling fire with a good book.

My ideal winter would include frequent walks down to the woodlot, and over to the marsh, to marvel at the ice patterns and the tracks of birds and animals whose presence is only attested to by the marks in the snow.

There is time for physical activity, of course: winter, I think, is the best time for cutting and splitting wood, because you can work up a sweat doing that even on a fairly frigid day. The biting crispness of the air, the pleasant burning sensation in your lungs and on your cheeks, is as much a vacation to the countrysider as a trip to warmer climes, because a vacation is only doing something different. And being outdoors in winter is different.

I love to milk by hand in winter, my forehead pressing into the warm flank of a cow or goat, warm milk steaming into a pre-chilled bucket. No flies, either.

Dropping bales of hay from the top mow in winter brings back memories of blistering summer days. Now I'm comfortable in stocking cap, mittens, long underwear, thick socks and heavy jacket: when the hay went in I was stripped to the waist and drenched with sweat that the chaff clung to like feathers to tar.

When I feed the pigs, they rise from their pig-pile, their flanks steaming, and knowing about things like wind-chill factors and the shock of climbing out of a warm bed or hot shower, I think they must be uncomfortable. They don't seem to mind.

Horses are different. When they approach the water buckets on a snowy evening, their coats glisten in the light coming through the barn windows with a frosted luminescence reflected from the ice on their coats. I'm momentarily amazed at their seeming comfort, until I reflect on how I know I look with snow or frost in my beard...which is entirely bearable until I get in the warm house and notice it.

I feel sorry for the chickens in the winter, though. Their feet look so cold. But after filling themselves at the feeder, and scratching around in the ground corncob litter for dessert, they hop back up to their roosts and encase their feet in a fluffy featherbed of Rhode Island Red down, so they're all right too.

For the countryman who has planned ahead, there is always a crackling fire to return to. It's true, the dinner fare often lacks the variety and flavor of summer, but that isn't a necessary adjunct to winter. Without the pressures of garden and fieldwork, there is more time for food preparation, for experimenting. Corn meal pancakes or muffins can never taste as good as they do when the meal is freshly ground and cooked over a wood fire while a blizzard rages outside. During the winter, there is more time for the busy homesteader to play with sprouts, with cheeses, and the heat generated by bread-baking is much more welcome in winter. Winter may be the season for sauerkraut and vinegar pie, but it's also a time for thick rich stews and long-simmered baked beans.

The problem with winter, of course, is that most of us fight it. We try to make winter into summer. We want our homes to be as cozy as Bermuda, in every corner, instead of hotter than Hades next to the stove and as frigid as the North Pole in the corners away from it. We want to eat June peas and strawberries and asparagus instead of salt pork and baked beans and dried apple pie. We want to make our roads and driveways and sidewalks clear and passable as they were in July, so we can go goodness-knows-where for goodness-knows-why.

Maybe, someday, we'll come to our senses. We'll recognize that winter, even here in the north (and maybe especially here in the north) is a very special time of the year with a very special message. We'll learn to live with it, instead of letting it pass by our windows while we dream of the tropics.

In a way, maybe winter is one more golden nugget of life that technology has snitched away from us.

I'm fully aware of the COUNTRYSIDE readers in more hospitable climes, who either don't appreciate what I'm talking about, or who have fled south to escape the rigors of "the season of death." But personally, I feel sorry for both of them. They're missing something special.

And the way we're handling winter in the north nowadays, so are we all. Even beyond the sidewalks.

Part VII: 1977

Inflation: 6.5%; Federal Reserve interest rate at year-end: 7.75%; Gas/gal: 65¢; Average annual income: $15,000; July 13 25-hour NYC blackout results in looting and disorder; Jimmy Carter elected president, warns that Americans need to make profound changes in oil consumption; GPS inaugurated by U.S. Dept. of Defense; First MRI scanner tested; First Apple II computers on sale

49. January 1977

New year: Looking back, planning ahead

January seems like a good month to check over the successes and failures of the past year, but even better, to gloat over the unspoiled 12 months that lie ahead. In January, the new year always looks like a fresh canvas must look to a painter, a new ream of paper to a writer, or an unplowed field to a farmer: we can move in, and make of it what we want to.

Maybe this sounds too poetic, but what else is January good for?

The analogy of an unplowed field or a fresh stack of paper is an apt one for me. I'll never forget the first time I turned my new (to me) tractor into a seven-acre field when all I had been used to was a 1/3-acre garden. It was immense. Awesome. I felt like an ant accidentally dropped in the center of the basketball court. For the moment, my vision of a field of waving grain, the dream of the grain bin filled to overflowing, faltered, and I was certain I'd never get all that plowed...much less planted and harvested!

Or the stack of paper. Even now, after writing four books and many other pieces, it amazes me to realize that every sentence, every word, *every single letter*, is put down on paper one at a time. Just think of it: you press one key on a typewriter, then another, then another...and before you know it you've written a book. Or you plow one strip, then another, and another, until the whole field is done.

Or you live through one day, then another and another, until a whole year has passed. And a lifetime.

It's depressing.

In January a whole year stretches out and we should be delighted in the thought that we can make of it what we will. But if we're realistic, we remember that there have been other Januaries...other years...other blank canvases and unplowed fields. And the reality somehow never quite matched the dream.

That's no excuse to stop dreaming, however. For without that vision of the bulging grain bin, would we even bother to start plowing? And if we didn't, the dream would obviously never even come close to being realized. Mankind survives on dreams...of filled grain bins, of books that stir minds and hearts...dreams of smooth roads and grand cities and clean and just government. Teachers dream of the upstanding citizens and scholars they are helping to form, architects dream of the comfort and beauty their work will provide others, honest politicians dream of a better life for everyone. Poets just dream...but there is a little of the poet in us all. A job that cannot involve a dream is drudgery. A life that cannot hold a dream is a waste.

And at the beginning of a new year all but the most crass and insensitive are dreamers, if just for a little while.

Everyone's most cherished dreams are private and individual, shaped by who-knows-what. By a minor childhood experience, by the offhand remark of a teacher, by a book or even a passage read somewhere in the long ago? Dreams are made of smoky stuff, and often we don't realize where they came from... or where they are swept away to.

My own are surely different from yours and they're different from mine last January if only in degree. Time and experience changes us, softens us, and often even impairs our ability to dream. But I hope I never lose mine.

It doesn't matter that I dream of a small country place, a little white cottage and rose bushes and goats that never get out to destroy them. I may never have the spotlessly clean, sweet smelling, light and airy barn I dream of, with a few goats of the highest quality and the sweetest disposition. I'd like a few sows, that always farrow on time with nine in a litter and never lay on any of them; a dozen Rhode Island Reds that lay regularly and never scratch in the garden or flower beds; a small flock of sheep that always twin and geese whose eggs hatch. I dream of a garden with long, clean, green rows, of a pasture whose green luxuriance contrasts with the white fence and blue sky. I dream of luscious strawberries, blemish-free apples and pears, and bushels of firm tomatoes. I dream of a life unfettered by worries about money, health, children's problems, machinery breakdowns, taxes, and the energy supply.

Am I wrong to dream? Are you? Of course not.

Our dreams may never come true, but they serve two important purposes. They give us a goal to work toward, something that makes life meaningful and worthwhile.

And they make the real world more bearable.

I have no idea of what people dream of in the cities. But we have goals to spare, dreams yet undreamt, in the countryside. We share the dreams of poets, beyond the sidewalks.

50. February 1977
In a holding pattern

I was particularly struck by one idea in Maurice Telleen's new book, *The Draft Horse Primer*, which was reviewed in COUNTRYSIDE last month: how horses were forced off the farm. You'll recall that he pointed out that back in the early days of tractors, if you wanted to buy a new team of horses you generally looked to a neighbor, and paid cash. But if you wanted a tractor, not only could you get credit: the dealer would take your old team in trade. And more often than not, that team would wind up as dog food, which seems like just about the slickest way to deal with the competition that anyone could imagine!

(A similar ploy was used in the 1930s when General Motors bought streetcar companies, then trashed them, to sell more cars.)

If we dig into this just a little we can easily see that there was a lot more to it, of course. While plenty of farmers held onto old Dobbin until the last possible minute (and even then most were sorry to see him go), there were many more who enjoyed the convenience of the tractor.

But the thing that fascinates me is how it all came about, and even more importantly, what the change did to all of agriculture.

Mankind is basically lazy. It's not too surprising that tractors would appeal to many horse-farmers who could see not only the advantage of using less physical labor to get their field work done, but also the very real advantage of not having to care for horses 365 days a year.

But what they could not see — perhaps what no one at that time could see, certainly not as clearly as we can today — was that this was the real beginning of agribusiness, and the end of farming.

With horses, the farm was largely self-sufficient. But once he purchased a tractor, the farmer was at the mercy of industry (including the finance industry). The machinery became more complicated so that he, or the local blacksmith, wasn't qualified to maintain it. Machined parts were required, and of course there were new requirements for gas and oil.

The oats and hay that had gone to the horses could be replaced with other crops that could be sold to pay the interest on the tractor and the costs of maintaining and operating it. And of course, since the farmer could do more with a tractor that didn't get tired and was more powerful to begin with, because he didn't have to spend time hauling horse manure or currying or polishing harnesses, the advantages of the tractor loomed even larger. So he worked more land to make more money to meet all the extra expenses.

The significant factor here is that this was helping to create an *industrial* base for agriculture. Once the manufacturing plants, the dealerships and salesmen and mechanics and others were all set up, they had a vested interest in agriculture. Their concern wasn't just to make life easier for the farmer. Their concern was to make a profit. And to make a profit, even just to stay in business, they had to keep pushing. Unlike the horse dealer who sold a team and then forgot about it, the industries with plants and payroll and investments and vested interests had to keep the farmers coming back for more.

It's not fair just to blame industry, of course: the farmers themselves had a great deal to do with it. Hesitantly at first, then with more and more gusto, they embraced the industrialization of agriculture. It was almost as if industry had found a way to skin farmers alive and make them think it felt good.

We suspect that even this might not have had too much effect without certain other conditions that grew out of the same phenomena. Most of them revolved around the power the factory laborer soon acquired.

In the beginning their pay was magnanimous, at least compared with what they could earn on the farm. Although their work was strenuous (even for children) and living conditions were often terrible, both were often better than rural conditions of the time. For a wide variety of reasons, workers flocked to the cities and factories.

But as their production continued to make it possible for farmers to feed ever-increasing numbers and therefore "freed" even more farmers from the land (enabling them to become enslaved in the factories), it became necessary to find still more ways of producing income from industry; many of these affected the spending patterns of industrial workers as well as farm workers, and because of the fact that industrial workers were easier to organize, they *did* organize and exercise their power.

The upshot was that their earning power kept pace with "the cost of living," much more easily than the farmers'. This put even more economic pressure on farmers, a greater need for even more technology, and the whole system became like a dog chasing its own tail.

When industry both figuratively and literally killed off the horses, it locked farmers into the industrialized system, first by making them think they enjoyed the dry plucking they were getting, and then by hanging them by the thumbs so there was no escape even for those who knew what was really happening. And industry has been "killing off the horses" in one way or another ever since.

Look at capital costs: land, the machinery and equipment a "normal" farm is considered to require today; the use of fertilizers, herbicides, pesticides and other chemicals; the buildings and tools and other aspects of farming that *depend* on industry. Who are all of these benefitting? The people who work the land and care for the livestock, or the industrial sector of society?

There is no arguing with those who are even now pointing out that life is easier today because of the industrialization of farming, or that more food is produced or that many other benefits and conveniences have followed in its path. I'm certainly not saying the mistake was getting rid of the horses. What I am saying is that we made the mistake of throwing out the *farmers* with the horses, an exaggerated case of throwing out the baby with the bath water. We became so thrilled with the system of industry and technology that we completely lost sight of what it was supposed to accomplish. The means have become the end. We have to go back to where we started to stray off the main path and determine where we went wrong, which is different from saying we have to go back to the good old days.

Most COUNTRYSIDE readers know all of this, of course. What's more, most of us could be quite content just quietly going our way, working things out for ourselves, without regard for the rest of the world, industry and agribusiness included. But it's not that simple. Industry and the society it has forged have such a stranglehold on everything and everyone that they really can't allow us misfits to rock their boat, even just a little.

COUNTRYSIDE readers know that *something* will come along to smash the rose-colored glasses agribusiness and industry in general is wearing. It might be connected with the supply or cost of energy; the ultimate realization of the deadly effects of any of thousands of chemicals; changing weather conditions that could make agribusiness farming methods ineffectual; an economic upheaval that would destroy the agricultural system based, not on small, privately owned and operated family farms, but on house-of-cards financing for land and equipment. Inflation alone will have its effects, as would the problems of the cities, unemployment, and any of dozens of others. Any single one of these could send the system toppling and there are so many possibilities that the chances of just one of them occurring is a virtual certainty.

While there are many opportunities for real farmers to move into position to fill the breach, there aren't many clear-cut answers yet. We're still in the planning stage, we're in a holding pattern. Most of us realize that we don't want to make a 180-degree turn and go back on our own tracks, but we can't be sure what direction to angle off at, either. But more and more people are thinking about it, and the time will come.

In the meantime, we'll wait, and we'll learn while we're waiting.

2010: This sounds almost tiresome, today, especially since it looks like nothing much has happened in all the years since this was written. At least you have to give this guy credit for persistence.

51. March 1977

Evening chores, and it's 22° below zero

When I sloshed the buckets of hot water into the stock tank the layer of ice on the bottom cracked like gunfire, and the frozen snow squeaked under the horses' hooves as they left the shelter of their shed to come and drink.

It was 22° below, with a chill factor of minus 56... and it was even colder in the silo, where the northwest winds funnel down.

I watched the horses drink, making certain that they had enough but not wanting to haul more than necessary only to have it freeze in the tank. They didn't seem to notice the cold at all. Neither did I, actually, having just arrived from a warm house and a hot dinner, and wearing layers of heavy clothing. If I was uncomfortable at all, it was from thinking about the warmth that was only yards away.

Thinking, you know, sets Man apart from the other creatures and causes most of our problems and unhappiness. Of course, it also brings our greatest happiness and rewards... but that wasn't what I was thinking about.

I went into the haymow, leaning into the door with all my weight to force it through the snow that had drifted up alongside it. I flicked on the dim light and climbed the ladder to the upper mow with the icy wind howling through the partially open door.

And as I started to toss down bales of alfalfa, I thought. I thought about why I was out here on such a night when I could have been reading a good book, or doing almost anything else, for that matter. I thought about the challenges of the coming year: the drought, the hog market prospects, the equipment repairs I had intended to make during the winter until the temperature never got above zero for five straight weeks and I decided I wasn't all that crazy after all.

I thought about business challenges: marveling at the people who claim they don't like our color covers (as if they'd applaud God for making a black-and-white sunset); puzzling over those who say we're too organic or not organic enough; wondering about the readers who write to warn us that the few pages we devote to "big" farming are ruining COUNTRYSIDE.

I thought about the 120 tons of lime piled on my fields, lime that was supposed to have been spread last fall. I thought about the young father who called to see if we had any goat milk for his infant daughter who couldn't tolerate cow milk; about the paper cutter that needed some welding that I knew was beyond my meager capabilities; about what to get my son Steve for his birthday.

And then, worn out more from the thinking than from heaving bales of hay, I stood on the foot-square beam, high above the mow floor, leaned back against the hefty cross-member, and with steaming breath, trying not to think, rested.

A buck rabbit (who had escaped from his cage last summer and who had taken up residence in the haymow) hopped out from his burrow in the straw on the mow floor and nibbled at the spilled oats outside the bin under the north mow.

Lucky rabbit, I thought. He doesn't have to think. He just does what he must. Like the horses, who work when they're made to work, but who have all their food and water brought to them, their waste carried away, who stand expectantly for petting and brushing and kind words...Who is the master, and who the slave? If there were a king in this small homestead world, would it be the dumb animals, or the dumb homesteader?

The simple truth is, we each do what we must, according to some vast cosmic plan we can't begin to understand. An apple tree will never bear potatoes, a buck goat will never sire a poodle. And I am what I am.

The pigeons roosting on the hay fork track above me rustle, their beady orange eyes becoming accustomed to the dim light. Lucky pigeons. They don't have to think. They coo, and fight, and flutter, but they don't even know they're pigeons.

But I know I'm a Man. I crawl back down the ladder and the buck rabbit scurries back into his burrow.

I open the hay chute door and can hear Steve and John going about their duties in the barn below. Sheba, the German Shepherd puppy, looks up at me inquisitively, and when I push the first bale over the edge she flees with her tail between her legs. She'll learn, even without thinking.

In the barn, the boys have the radio blaring. They've fed grain, milked the cow, and bedded the calf. I milk the goats. What does a goat think about when it's being milked? What do boys think about when they do chores?

I turn off the radio. The only sound is that of animals rustling in clean barley straw and chewing hay. I don't think I'd like to sleep in a barn when it's 22 below. But the animals don't think about it.

Is that the answer? Instead of worrying about what magazine readers want, about the horrendous amount of work to be done, about anything, wouldn't it be better to just do what has to be done at the moment, like the rabbit in the haymow?

Maybe. But somehow, that doesn't seem right. It's true that we each do what we must, but we humans somehow have acquired additional responsibilities. That entails both rewards and punishments. It entails thinking. Making decisions.

The solution, I think as I turn off the lights and heave the door shut, must be balance. Some things are to be taken seriously, others not so seriously. As St. Francis said, Lord, let me change what can be changed, let me accept what cannot be changed, and give me the good sense to know the difference, or something like that.

There were no stars. As I trudged back to the house, the wind picked up a handful of snow and showered it down my back. It felt like it would be a lot colder by morning.

52. April 1977

Why buy the cow if the milk is free?

2010: I must have been in an awfully down mood when I wrote this. At the very least, farming was losing its appeal. And yet, there is a kernel of truth here.

The casual reader might think that the discussion on food prices in this issue doesn't have much to do with homesteading, or providing your own food. Actually, it has a lot to do with it.

Ever since I've been homesteading I've been troubled when friends and relatives belittled my efforts at providing for my own family, for working so hard to produce something that I could have bought in any grocery store for a fraction of the price and effort. At times, especially in the early days, I was bothered by the uneasy feeling that they were correct, even when I knew in my heart they weren't *right*.

This has had a great deal of influence on the more than 5,000 pages that have been printed under my editorship, as well as the books and articles I've written. I'm convinced that one of the main reasons homegrown food costs as much as it does, for most people, is that they don't know enough about producing it, and just about everything I've done journalistically has been an attempt to help remedy this.

But I've also pointed out more than a few times that one of the reasons it's tough to homestead profitably is because food is artificially low-priced, it's highly subsidized. Why buy the cow if you can get the milk for free, or nearly free?

Agribusiness, being more business than agri-, takes the apologetic and defensive approach. They like to point out that Americans spend a great deal less on food than most other people, and that only about one-fifth of the average person's income is spent on food. But instead of being good, as business would have us believe, it's bad. It's bad not only for farmers and homesteaders, but for everyone.

Food is subsidized by the farmers themselves. In fact, I often wonder how long it will be until some enterprising journalist takes a look at the average farm operation of today with the same critical appraisal given factory work at the beginning of the century. While it may be true that most farmers aren't really bad off, it's also true that everything is relative, and in a relative sense most farmers are no better off than those unorganized and exploited factory workers of another era. While union members and others are pleading for hourly wages that seem astronomical to farmers, for working hours that border on the ridiculous, with paid vacations and other fringe benefits that can't possibly have any relationship to the actual worth of what they do...while urban workers get all this and still clamor for more, the average farmer puts in 12 and 15 and 18 hour days, most work 365 days a year, and they are only going deeper into debt. What's more, these farmers are joined by their wives, their sons and daughters, which effectively lowers their actual hourly rate of pay even further.

And then they have to listen to people who buy gas for their boats and campers and snowmobiles without a quiver complain about the "high" cost of food. Saying "nobody farms to get rich anyway" is too absurd to warrant comment. As a farmer, I'll give away the rewards of my labor when somebody is ready to give me the clothing, machinery, and other things *I* need.

Do the occupants of those cars and campers that pass by our hayfield where the whole family is working on a steamy Saturday and smile and wave as they pass think we're out there sweating just for *fun?* Do those city pheasant hunters, who park on my alfalfa, throw beer cans on my fields, then nod and smile when they see me picking corn, actually think I should spend my weekends gathering food for my hogs while they play and then *give* them the pork... as well as picking up their litter?

The vacant gazes and fixed smiles tell it all. Those people haven't the slightest idea of what farmers do, or how or why or where their food comes from. And that, I fear, is at the heart of many of our major problems today.

Homesteaders overcome this, to a degree, by at least gaining a keener awareness. They can *understand* the physical, mental and financial contribution of the farmer, even if they're personally involved on a different level of commitment.

However, there are even more significant food subsidies: we are robbing future generations, and perhaps even our own, for the dubious privilege of eating cheap food now. We are doing this by our over-reliance on nonrenewable natural resources such as petroleum, and even more seriously, by mining soil fertility for the sake of cheap food.

Cheap food is politically expedient, which has been amply demonstrated in recent years. It's highly unlikely that food prices will rise on any rational basis, that is, to provide a fair return to the family farmer and to enable the nation to live off the current productivity of the soil rather than its capital by allowing farmers to farm *properly*. But if it doesn't happen on a rational basis, it's almost a certainty that it will happen *despite* the "consumer advocates" and the politicians. And sooner than most people think.

Then there will be no need to discuss the relative prices of organic and chemically-grown food. There will be no need for homesteaders to rationalize their activities as a hobby.

There is no such thing as a free lunch.

53. May 1977

Springtime on the farm... and more work

The lull before the storm: as of today, March 11, our farm here in southern Wisconsin is poised on the brink of spring. The countryside is holding its breath, and like anyone who holds his breath, becoming more impatient by the moment.

All of our livestock (except the dairy cow) overwinter on deep litter. I feel the system has a lot going for it, including the savings in labor and bedding, as well as more comfort and cleanliness for the stock and better retention of valuable manure.

By this time of the year some well-bedded pens have their floors raised so high it would seem that the animals would be in danger of falling out. There *are* a lot more goats in the aisle by March, and not long ago a Jersey bull was feeding at the corn crib. He had merely stepped over his fence... which later was built up to the ceiling.

And those ceilings! Fortunately, with the mild weather, my stocking cap is riding high, serving as an early warning system and forestalling any serious concussions. But there are still a few lumps and some crude words every now and then.

One problem is that the pens can't be cleaned when the fields are too wet to drive the tractor and spreader on them, and yet, when the pens (and fields) thaw out, more bedding is required to keep the stock dry, and the problems increase. So we wait, impatiently.

Mucking out such a treasure of organic fertility is both a joy and a heck of a job. The matted down, steaming, sinus-wrenching richness has bent some of my best pitchforks and always gives my aching back fair warning of what's to come in the weeks ahead on the farm and homestead. Tackled on that scale, it's "dumb work," the kind most people finish high school or college to avoid. But coming as it does on the heels of months of inactivity and impatience, it serves as a spring tonic. It feels good, physically, it feels good mentally to know the value of that already partially composted organic matter, and the monotony of the chore gives me time to ponder the other tasks that lie ahead.

In years past, I've done part of the job by tearing out all of the barn partitions and putting the front-end loader to work. Since I just sold the loader, I can look forward to a great deal more exercise to get me in shape for spring planting.

Actually, one of my most serious problems during this period is a peculiar occupational hazard: after a few days of unaccustomed clenching of a pitchfork, my hands bind up like claws and typing is like playing the piano wearing mittens. You wouldn't think that would bother a two-finger typist like me, but I always make sure I have all my deadlines met *before* barn-cleaning time.

We did get a sneak preview of spring last weekend by planting red clover in the winter wheat and rye, and by reseeding the main permanent pasture.

Over the years, we've acquired a couple of Horn and Cyclone hand seeders, and we also picked up a brand-new Cyclone at the Countryside

General Store just to test it out. For anyone who might not be familiar with these tools, the only way I can describe the Horn (also available from the store) is as a canvas bag with a shoulder strap, and a long metal tube protruding from a cul-de-sac at one corner. The operator merely fills the bag with seed, sets the opening of the tube to the desired gap for the seed being used, and walks down the field waving the tube back and forth. I can never use this tool without thinking of its description in a book written during the last homestead revival, back in the '40s, by a college professor of mine. He recounted that a neighbor showed him how to use the Horn and described the procedure as, "Jus' walk down the field waving th' tube like you was pissin'."

The Cyclone is more refined. It has a crank which turns a square propeller which scatters the seed as it falls through a slot which can be set with infinite adjustment. The seed is spread much more evenly with the Cyclone, and over a wider span, which might make the added cost worthwhile to anyone who is going to use it seriously. There is virtually no difference between the old models we have and the one sold now, except that the spreader propeller is made of plastic, naturally. But it's sturdy plastic, and the metal on the old ones is bent and rusted, so perhaps it evens out in the long run.

I didn't keep track of the time, but two of the boys and I did three acres of pasture so quickly that Diane said if I hadn't been along she would have sent the boys out to do it again: she wouldn't have believed they had done a proper job. So we took her along to seed clover in the wheat and rye. Since she's the one who sells the things, she ought to know what they can do, right?

We covered 10 acres — over 100 pounds of clover seed — in less than an hour. Sometimes it takes me that long to get the grain drill out of the machine shed, seeing how it's parked behind the baler which has to be jockeyed out first. Diane said sometimes it takes me that long to get the tractor started.

It was decidedly pleasant work. With the Horn, there was a metallic tinkling as the tiny seeds go coursing through the tube to meet their rendezvous with destiny, and a deep whooshing sound if you swing the tube with enough gusto. But that's all. The Cyclone makes a bit more of a mechanical sound, since it has gears, but it could hardly be called noisy and the only fumes came from my labored breathing as I slipped and stumbled over half-frozen clods.

So help me, this is the truth: ever since last July, when Roger Williams said in COUNTRYSIDE that he prefers working with his horses rather than his tractor because with the horses he can hear the first flocks of geese go over, I've been impressed with the idea. And last weekend, as I was planting clover with a hand implement, I heard the cries of the first flock of geese of the year, long before they hovered into view. The Cyclone seeder has earned its place on our farm.

One point that might interest some readers who are either new to farming or who live in more hospitable climates: Clover, which we plant with all small grains as a soil improvement measure, can't be sown with fall planted grains because the grains are planted later than the clover should be. But if the clover is sown in early spring, right on top of the ground, the alternative thawing and freezing serves to cover it sufficiently for good germination. Oats and other small grains can be sown the same way, which is one of the small ways homesteaders can get the jump on agribusiness farmers who must wait until soil conditions are right to be able to drive tractors and grain drills onto fields.

The barn is full of kids again, and milking has become a major chore. As usual, our bootleg milk customers who were filtered out during the dry period have lost interest, and it will be a major project to find replacements. Meanwhile, we make cheese. That means whey, which has always gone to the pigs. But we have no pigs.

We've always had a pig, even when we lived in town. Here on our farm we have a beautiful setup for pigs, and they are our primary enterprise. And worst of all, my new book on raising pigs was the March *Organic Gardening and Farming* book-of-the-month club selection. And I don't have a pig to my name.

The problem is water. No, not drought: we put in a respectable harvest of grain last year despite the dry weather here. But our underground water pipes to the barn, the henhouse, and the pig shed, all froze early last December. In years prior, I hauled water to as many as a hundred hogs in milk cans, up over the hill around the barn and down to the pig shed, but this year I decided I could better serve humanity by writing about soil fertility, the cost of organic foods, and other problems of major importance. Besides, mankind obviously wasn't much interested in pork anyway: the last batch I sold grossed just one-half the price of a similar group sold exactly one year earlier, even while all of my input costs have increased.

The frost went down seven feet. Our pipes are four-feet deep. They still haven't thawed out. I think it was a good time to take a vacation. Hauling water from the house for sheep, chickens, goats and horses provides all the exercise I need, or can tolerate.

So the whey goes to the chickens. That, along with the longer days, has sent egg production soaring.

Diane even bought a few dozen eggs for awhile, which, with the pig episode, was embarrassing as the dickens to one who believes in practicing what he preaches. But when the whey was added to their diet the fool chickens went berserk. One day we got more eggs than we have hens, which either means we can't count or that even the roosters got inspired.

I'm running germination tests on the oats and spring wheat, and one of these days before the last-minute rush starts, I'll be taking seed down to Bob Tooley's mill for cleaning. The lettuce is up in the cold frame, and the early tomatoes were planted just the other day. The garden seeds have arrived, the organic fertilizer has been ordered, this year's seedlings for the woodlot and fencerows should be delivered soon, and work is underway on preparing equipment for the hectic days and long hours to come. We're still trying to decide what breed of chicks to order...my beloved Rhode Island Reds are due for replacement by something more exotic...and we'll have to let Rick Abendroth at the local hatchery know how many goslings and turkey poults we'll be wanting pretty soon. Our ducks and guineas will be self-propagating.

My idea of spring was aptly worded by Longfellow (we don't hear much about him anymore) who said, "If spring came but once a century, instead of once a year, or burst forth with the sound of an earthquake, and not in silence, what wonder and expectation there would be in all hearts to behold the miraculous change! But now the silent succession suggests nothing but necessity. To most men, only the cessation of the miracle would be miraculous and the perpetual exercise of God's power seems less wonderful than its withdrawal would be."

My spirit aches for the show of the perpetual exercise of God's power. And that, my friends, is why I live beyond the sidewalks.

54. June 1977

Farming: just a business, or a way of life?

The USDA and the rest of agribusiness try to tell us that farming is no longer a way of life. Farming, they say, is no more than just another business.

Some of us know how wrong they are.

Our youngest son, John, is just starting to take a serious interest in farming. Until recently he was a typical ball-playing bike-riding tv-watching nine-year-old who hated to get up in the morning. When the school bus loomed up suddenly as out of nowhere (as it does occasionally in the country) John was sure to be the one who couldn't find his jacket, or his books, or his other shoe.

But when we got a new truckload of feeder pigs, John was put in charge of them. It changed his life. He was suddenly able to get up in the morning, he could miraculously lift buckets of feed and water that were "too heavy" just days before, and instead of heading for the tv set after supper, he headed for the barn.

Now, I obviously don't expect John to do a man's job...but I can't help but believe that the job is helping to make a man out of the boy. And that's not business. That's life.

One of the first introductions our kids have gotten to field work has always been drilling grain. They obviously aren't allowed to ride on tractors, and watching plowing and disking is pretty boring. (Come to think of it, plowing and disking are pretty boring!) But when we're sowing small grains, they can ride on the platform behind the drill. If they fall off it's no worse than falling off a bicycle. They can "help" by occasionally inspecting the seed hopper and telling Dad when it's time to refill. And when Dad is lugging 100-pound sacks of seed, they have someone to talk to.

It was during one of these refill sessions that John was sitting on the fertilizer hopper of the old metal wheeled John Deere Van Brunt, running his hands through the seed oats like King Midas in his vaults of gold coins, and he noticed that they looked just like the oats that had come off the combine last summer.

Of course they did. They were the same oats.

But if we combined them last year, what was the sense of putting them back in the ground again? Why didn't we just feed *these* oats to the animals and go fishing?

That got us into a discussion of how and why seeds, and plants and animals, increase. It gave both of us something to think about on subsequent trips across the field, and gave rise to an extracurricular project, too.

John knew that one seed planted produced a head or a stalk with many seeds. Due to the lack of heads of small grain at this time of the year, we chose corn, and counted the seeds on a single ear. There were 774.

We run two farms. The second is about half a mile down the back road from the home farm. When planting, we have to do some juggling to get both a tractor and drill, and a truck with seed, down to the other place. The other day the juggling involved driving the tractor over, then walking back to get the truck.

We took a shortcut, through the fields. It was a pleasant day. Sheba, the German Shepherd, was ranging ahead of us, and John had his shirt off for the first time this year.

On that brief hike we saw deer tracks, learned to identify several species of trees and noticed their early spring buds, and heard a trio of blue jays without even catching a glimpse of them. And the USDA was trying to tell me I was engaging in business, nothing more.

Ranging back over the years, there were countless other episodes of a similar nature, with all of the family. There were cold winter nights when throwing down hay from the mow developed into sprees of rope-swinging, hide-and-seek among the fortresses our kids have always built in the haymow, or impromptu wrestling matches on the mow floor. There were sweltering summer days when we'd take turns on the hay wagon to see who could stack the bales most skillfully and thus claim the largest load. There were emotional learning experiences when animals were bred, born, castrated or died.

My own father worked in a paper mill and I never knew what he did until I worked there too, during summer vacations when I was in college. Paper mills aren't exactly a way of life. But farming? Is farming only a business?

Well... maybe it is. But it's not a business of dollars and bushels as the USDA would have us believe. It's the most important business in the world... the business of making not only money, but men.

We make both livings, and lives, beyond the sidewalks.

55. July 1977

These little piggies go to market

July is the middle age of the year. The Earth grows productive and wealthy and fat, but its life is half gone, and it knows it.

The midpoint of the year, July combines both beginnings and ends. We cut and bale hay, combining winter wheat and rye starts later in the month in our region, and we gather honey and garden produce, but along with these early harvests comes planting buckwheat and the fall vegetable garden. In some ways, the carrots and cabbages and turnips and bok choy planted now and harvested after frost are the most appreciated produce of the garden... the children of tired loins.

When the corn is cultivated and the early cuttings of hay are in the mow, life on the farm slows down, if ever so imperceptibly. The hot days and muggy nights (when you can stand at the edge of a field and hear the corn grow) produce a lethargy that isn't conducive to looking for extra work. I really intended to repair the steps on the front porch when the field and garden work slackened, to realign the tilting clothesline posts and putty some windows in the henhouse, but somehow it doesn't really seem important any more. Not in July.

When I was younger, full of impatience and enthusiasm and dumb energy, July was a wasted month. Maybe it was just too pregnant and it made me nervous. But now, being a little older and tireder — and wiser? — I welcome the respite. I don't fight it, but take advantage of it.

The sun rises yellowish in the northeast, glinting off dew-studded leaves of waist-high corn. The morning radio announcers will declare it "another perfect day" and so will the golfers and boaters and vacationers, but the farmers will stoop and poke their fingers into the widening cracks in the soil and pray silently for rain.

I do the morning chores and even at this time of day, when it's relatively cool, the sound of crystal water splashing into the stock tank reminds me of something I once read about the use of fountains in desert oases for their psychologically cooling effect.

In this kind of weather I put the house milk in the freezer to cool it down rapidly, then go back to finish up feeding and cleaning. Eggs are gathered several times a day to keep them from poaching, too. Even after the most routine, least exerting activity, I'm drenched with sweat. It's a heck of a day for livestock, especially hogs (who can't sweat), but the main task on the day's agenda is shipping hogs. A hog that's ready for market is ready for market, and that's that.

With our breakfast plates cleaned and the sun still fairly low in the sky, we back the truck up to the hog pen door and put the ramp and gates in place. Then the fun begins. With panels, skill borne of experience, a great deal of teamwork and coordination and patience... and a few well-placed cuss words... we manage to get a uniform lot of the pig-headed beasts on the truck. As I stand on the tailgate and slam the back gates of the stock rack into place I'm panting, drenched with sweat, and I know that the hog smell I smell is not from the hogs, but from my boots, pants, and hands.

The old truck is willing but hesitant about taking its shifting live cargo of almost a ton up the hill and around the barn, but I coax it gently and, lacking the intelligence of a pig, it responds. The pigs seem oblivious of the movement, and busy themselves rooting and snorting in the bedding.

Hauling pigs to market is one of the most nerve-wracking things I do. I am always convinced that one of the 220-pound behemoths is going to stand up on the rack and crash through it to land sprawling on the highway only to be struck by some city attorney in a Cadillac, who will sue me for every penny I have and could ever hope to make. It almost happened once with a lamb, which we chased through backyards in Waterloo in what turned out to be as merry a spectacle for on-lookers as the day the goats followed the children to school when we still lived in the village.

But 25 miles later (with only a few rough moments, mostly at stop signs) we make it. I back up to the ramp at Jones Dairy Farms (yes, that's a hog-processing plant) and we're home free. Well, almost.

Why are pigs as hard to get off a truck as they are to get on?

They move down the meticulously clean aisle, sniffing and snuffling every inch of the way. Steve opens gates ahead of them, I close gates behind them. We have to wait for a load of Chester Whites ahead of us, moving up as they move up, but it's a relaxing wait.

When we reach the marking chute, I know the hogs are out of my hands. With the strictures of the press gate and the experienced (almost bored with experience) prod of the elderly gent manning the tattoo marker, the pigs move through to the last good-bye for their former caretaker and master; onto the Fairbanks-Morse scale.

When you raise a pig and butcher it yourself, there's a certain spiritual link between man and beast. Here, the link is broken when the pigs march onto the platform scale (still sniffling the ground ahead of them) and the yardman closes the gate behind them with a resounding clang. They are no longer my pigs. Others are moving up the aisle behind us, and there is no way I could shout "Wait!! These animals are my friends! I raised them from babyhood and I won't let you murder them!"

I don't look back, but open the gate to the buyer's office, step through the footbath, take a long swig from the drinking fountain, and busy myself looking at the cartoons and other clippings on the bulletin board. The teletype clattering reminds me of my newspaper days, and I idly wonder how they keep the thing so busy chugging out market reports and hog belly futures.

The buyer fiddles efficiently with the scale, stamps the weigh ticket, and motions to the yardman, who moves what were formerly my pigs out to the holding pens. Another group of squawking snuffling hogs enters the scale as the buyer writes out my check.

I can't help but think what a crazy system this is. I bring my pigs in and say, "Here, take them," and never even bother to ask "What will you give me for them?" When I sell COUNTRYSIDE magazine I figure the cost of gathering material, editing, typesetting, pasteup, printing, postage and all the rest and say, "Sir or madam, it's going to cost you $9 if you want to get this magazine." I know what these pigs cost me, I know what it cost for grain and overhead, but I bring them in without any idea of what I'm going to get for them. And then they try to tell us farming is a "business."

I always expect the worst. And I try to act nonchalant. The buyer hands me the check, I say "thank you" without even looking at it, and I stop for another drink on the way out. Only outside do I dare to look at the check.

The pigs were a little heavier than I had thought, and the price was a little better than I had anticipated. That doesn't mean we made a whole bunch of money: adding everything up at the end of the year I'll still find out I'm making one heck of a lot less than minimum wage... but it's better than I had *hoped* for, and that gives me a psychological boost. In addition, since I don't believe in credit, the check improves my liquidity tremendously.

And besides, I don't have a truckload of snorting, lunging pigs behind me on the drive home. I feel good.

We roll into the driveway, climb out, and stagger into the house.

"Yeugg, you smell like a pig," Diane says. I wave the check under her nose. She closes her eyes and smiles. "I don't smell a thing," she says.

John has the worms dug, and after a light lunch, we load the fishing poles on the truck and take off for the Maunesha River, just down the road. Lounging on the bank with my red and white bobber being gently nudged by the current of the stream, I detect the faint aroma of the hog barn. I think I should have changed clothes.

56. August 1977

Wind song

As we tramped over the fields of our prospective dream homestead, the Realtor waved deprecatingly at the overgrown fencerows saying, "Of course, you'll want to bulldoze that brush out." A swift glance at Diane told me she knew the fencerows would remain, and the knowing smile that passed between us said "why bother arguing with him?"

We are staunch supporters of fencerows.

Modern farmers — or farmers who consider themselves modern even though they're somewhat behind the times — don't care much for fencerows. In their view, those ribbons of trees and shrubs aren't "productive," they take up valuable space, and they rob moisture from nearby crops. So they grub them out, pile up huge heaps of limbs and roots, and torch them. Two fields become one, and sometimes four, five, or six become one, as farmers plow fencerow-to-fencerow and then tear out the fencerows.

A generation ago progressive farmers took a different view. Encouraged by government programs, dust bowl conditions and their own sense of stewardship of the land, they *planted* fencerows throughout much of the country. Today, even fencerows that were planted out of need and foresight are being destroyed.

How soon we forget. Millions of acres are again subject to blowing, and they *are* blowing.

Criminal as that might be, I must confess that I have some more personal attachments to these geometric strips of wilderness "wasteland." I recall pleasant summers on my uncle's farm when in my boyhood imagination, the fencerows were every bit as exciting as the work horses, the haymow, and other facets of small farm life in those days. To a young boy, the area between the dusty road and the field of rustling corn or hay stubble was as vast as the territory explored by Daniel Boone. There were raspberries and blackcaps and wild apples to eat, birds and rabbits to add interest and excitement, and the privacy of "a special place" where grownups and the older kids never ventured.

Perhaps some of the same values still appeal to this somewhat older kid. But if age and experience dim some attractions, they enhance others.

The difference in the numbers and variety of wildlife on the fencerow farm and a nearby farm without fencerows is startling. That alone has tremendous implications for organic farmers. And who can put a price on the value of such wildlife to the farm family, especially one that has a deep love for nature but spends much of its time in more urban areas at such unnatural occupations as publishing magazines? If the fencerows slow down the wind and soil erosion, they must also reduce wind damage to crops and undue evaporation.

Quite immodestly, I will say that our fencerow is one of the finest I've seen. A fencerow landscape architect, if there were such a profession (and perhaps there should be) couldn't have done better. There are raspberries, strawberries, gooseberries, chokecherries and juicy sweet wild plums. There is an apple tree that, far from bearing the small and bitter wormy fruit we usually associate with wild apples, produces the tastiest apples I've found. There are hickory trees, black walnuts, and the only butternuts I've seen in a long time.

On the section along the road, we don't race the squirrels for the nuts, but the city folks who stop to gather them. We've had wool dyers harvest our sumac, and others seeking the same plant to make tea. In one particularly favored section there are several clumps of osage orange, a rare tree this far north.

Someone obviously cut down trees in our fencerow in the past. Clumps of maples with 15 and 20 trunks are scattered throughout. One of my most looked-forward-to projects is "timber stand improvement" in my fencerow, taking out some of this competitive growth so that in addition to everything else, the rows will provide firewood on a sustained basis.

Some people might thrill to setting a plow into the earth, taking a compass reading, and heading off on a day-long furrow toward the horizon. Not me. I much prefer to be in the back 40, or even the back 20 of the front 40, and not be able to see the house. The expense of the few rows of somewhat stunted crops along the trees is more than recovered by the pailsful of sunwarmed berries we gather, the sight of the rabbits and foxes and deer that seldom stray far from the shelter of the rows, or even the flash of a scarlet tanager amidst the foliage.

Bulldoze my fencerows? I would just as soon part with my two typing fingers.

I thought of that farm salesman again last spring. There were a couple of thin spots, and the fencerow needed a few hazelnuts and pines, and I wondered what he would have said if he could have seen me, not bulldozing, but planting more trees in the fencerow.

57. September 1977

Like fat toads in a garden...

Life, most people will tell you, is good. Oh, there are occasional rumors of famine and pestilence and other forms of human misery, but on the whole, most people today have enough to wear and a place to sleep and the proportion of those who don't is as low as it's ever been. We have more knowledge, more education than any other people in history, we have conveniences un-dreamed of by the most pampered empresses, pleasures enough to numb a caliph. Although few are certain where it will end — or even what it means, now — we are satisfied.

Like fat toads in a garden.

Life in the last half of the 20th century is a never-never land of science fiction and dreams; fiction becomes fact and dreams come true, we smugly tell ourselves. At the same time, it becomes increasingly difficult to separate fact from fiction, and people find themselves wondering if they're dreaming, or if they're only dreaming that they're dreaming.

Life is good, we say to each other so often that we find ourselves believing it. There are times, however, times that seem to become more and more rare as we become more "civilized," when we find ourselves nagged by subtle doubts.

Times like the early hours of the day when we lie in the predawn darkness, thinking. Moments like those spent on a wild secluded hill watching a hawk soar on updrafts in the distance. Moments beside a gurgling shining brook trickling through a green-canopied valley.

In those rare moments of doubt we find ourselves, not saying life is good, but rather asking, "What's life all about?"

Because such moments require the proper setting and the proper frame of mind, because (like the rainbow) they appear spontaneously under a specific set of circumstances, they are as rare as any other perfect gem. Undoubtedly they often pass by many who aren't able to recognize them, to grasp them and suck from them the nectar that makes man something more than the other animals.

Homesteaders are nourished by those moments.

Of course life is good. Of course our pleasures and conveniences and knowledge are desirable. But is that all there is?

Homesteaders do not work outdoors in searing heat and bitter cold simply because they think there's anything inherently wrong with central heating or air conditioning. They do not butcher animals for their meat or grind wheat for their bread only because they don't appreciate the convenience of store-bought.

Homesteaders live simply — and perhaps a little more harshly than their means would allow — because at one point or another they have seen that there is more to life than appears on the surface.

Many people are toads too satisfied to search for more satisfaction of a different nature. But somehow, it's difficult to be a human toad when you live beyond the sidewalks.

58. October 1977

Eating naturally... with the seasons

We planted an acre of sweet corn this year, and by mid-August the kids rebelled against eating fresh, butter-drenched corn on the cob every day. To make matters worse, that's when the main crop came in and they had to help with the canning, drying and freezing in addition to eating it.

It was hard to remember that only a few months earlier nothing would have tasted better than a fresh ear of corn.

I suspect that most people, those who buy their groceries in cans and boxes, have no concept of seasonal eating patterns. On the homestead, it's as natural as the progression of the seasons.

Consider the type of diet our ancestors, with extremely limited means of preserving food, might have lived on.

In the spring the basis would be such overwintered root crops as parsnips and Jerusalem artichokes — at least in my part of the country, which is a long way from the Garden of Eden. The first shoots of green, the lettuce and radishes and onions planted in the cold frame in the waning days of winter, would be welcome indeed, and the dandelion greens and lamb's-quarters to follow would be eagerly sought out.

The milk flow increases in the spring, with goats freshening and cows on pasture again, and that means an abundance of yogurt and cheese and milk for drinking and cooking. Egg production increases too.

Little by little other garden produce becomes available, and then abundant. String beans, beets, mustard and other greens, all provide both nutrition and a happy respite from the fare of winter.

At the peak of the growing season the homestead faces a veritable embarrassment of riches. There are salad makin's galore, vegetables without end, new crop honey, and fruit so fresh it still retains the sun's warmth. There are new potatoes, marble-sized thin-skinned delicacies that are seldom found in supermarkets and expensive at farmers' markets because they're almost as perishable as dreams. Spring lambs are fat, and both chicken and rabbit fryers are at their prime.

In autumn the diet becomes more coarse again. The late summer heat has withered the succulents and we depend more heavily on the squash and pumpkins, the turnips and cabbages.

With the onset of winter we enjoy fresh pork, as the summer-fed hog has been butchered. The best cuts are eaten first, the rest cured and smoked or stored in brine to provide meat for winter. For a short period there may be a meal of Chinese cabbage or kale or other frost-hardy vegetable, but the abundance and variety of summer is past.

Winter belongs to the root cellar, and we dine on potatoes and cabbages that we had no need for earlier, and which store longer than others. Egg production is down, milk production decreases, and fare is simple and homely.

Later on in winter, the dried peas and beans come into their own along with the grains. The fresh meat is gone. The brined vegetables are at their most appreciated. The potatoes and other roots in the root cellar become shriveled, perhaps scarce. There is nothing even resembling green stuff. Hen's eggs are as scarce as hen's teeth. Any fruits and berries that may have been preserved are long gone and vinegar pie becomes a great treat for dessert.

And then, just as it seems all hope is lost, the first shoots appear in the cold frame, the parsnips become diggable and the first dandelion greens appear on sheltered southern hillsides. The cycle begins anew.

We modern homesteaders, with glass jars and pressure canners and freezers...and in a real pinch a visit to the A & P or a pizza joint...don't have to follow this regimen. We don't *have* to. But I wonder if that's really the blessing we take it for.

All animals, including us, follow certain biological patterns. We need a certain amount of sleep and we're affected by other more-or-less regular cycles. Most animals also *eat* according to the seasons, except where the grain scoop of man interferes.

Mankind has existed for thousands of years, eating according to the seasons. Preserving food by canning has been practiced only in the last hundred and fifty of those years, and widely only in this century. Freezers were a rare luxury only a generation ago and the rapid transportation of fresh products from subtropical climates to snowbound areas is also a very recent development.

I wonder if, in spite of this abundance, we aren't missing something.

Nutritionists, don't bother to correct me with data on the body's chemical requirements. Historians, you don't have to remind me how tough things were before we learned how to serve the same menu in Southern California in June and Sault Ste. Marie in January. If that's all you can come up with you don't understand what I'm getting at.

It's a challenge and a special delight to preserve the most perishable products of the homestead to assuage the miserable depths of winter. But I really wonder if nature intended for us to go as far as we have. Maybe our dietary requirements are not only chemical.

If nothing else, we have a greater appreciation of our food. The fresh corn is gone now, but the tomatoes and carrots are coming on strong. The kids are complaining already.

Have I got a surprise for them! Coming up next: cabbage and turnips.

59. November 1977

No pretty pictures, but some graphic thoughts...

Butchering is not a particularly pleasant topic. It doesn't make for pretty pictures. And while writers may extol the golden smoky flavor of a ham fresh out of the smokehouse or the succulence of a thick-cut pork chop from a home-fed pig, it's not particularly easy to write about, either.

Butchering animals that we've raised from birth (and before birth, actually) separates the homesteaders from the "gentlemen farmers."

Butchering isn't the kind of thing you'd want to read about (or we'd want to write about) every month. But it's a fact of homestead life.

It's a fact of life in the sense that, except for milk and eggs, it's the *reason* for raising livestock. Without butchering, the animals are only pets, an expensive and time-consuming hobby that most of us could ill afford.

It's a fact of life in the sense that most of us eat meat in one form or another, and if we shirk the responsibility of transforming surplus buck kids or rabbits or chickens into fare for the table, and then have someone else do the job (which is what happens when we eat at McDonald's, or any other restaurant or if we purchase meat to prepare at home), then we're adding just one more facet of artificiality to our lives. We're removing ourselves another step from reality.

No one enjoys watching butchering, I'm sure... at least no one with normal emotions and sensitivities. And yet, like so many other things that we discuss here that aren't "enjoyable" in the traditional sense of the word, there's a lot to be said for it.

Doing our own butchering increases our sense of independence. It creates a deeper feeling for the interrelationship of man and animal. Odd as it may sound to the uninitiated, killing gives us a greater respect for life.

At one point or another early in any homestead career everyone, I'm sure, gives serious thought to the tenets of vegetarianism. Not only have we been conditioned by our society to recoil from killing, from blood and guts and the primal stench of raw bleeding meat, but it almost seems at times as if there are deeper and more remote inhibitions which lend credence to the vegetarian thesis.

And yet at the same time, there is something proper about it all. All living creatures bear a kinship to one another, we are all interdependent, and we all support one another through the biotic pyramid.

It's hard not to have the mystical aspects of butchering cross our minds now and then, even if we don't dwell on them. The economic realities are even more persuasive. If we want hens for eggs, we must face the biological fact that 50 percent of all chickens hatched are cockerels. If we want goats or cows for milk, what do we do with the 50 percent of the newborn that are bucks or bulls? And then there are spent layers and cull cows.

And if we were to suddenly stop eating meat, what would become of the pigs, the sheep, the geese? Would we let them proliferate and overrun us, or would we simply exterminate them without making use of them?

No, the balance is weighted, the course is clear.

We must care well for the animals while they depend on us, both for economic and deeper reasons. When they reach their prime state for our purpose, we must dispatch them with skill, with compassion, with reverence.

Then, when we draw our chairs up to a table bearing such provender, we are not inclined to gluttony, to mere sensual satiation. We are, rather, participants in a feast of life.

My first experience with small stock was when I was a pre-teenager. I raised pigeons. We had chickens and rabbits too, but I loved my pigeons, and that love set a pattern that through devious and unplanned events and circumstances made me what I am today. I could never butcher a pigeon. But my flock increased beyond all reasonable limits and my financial capacity to properly care for them. I couldn't butcher a squab, but my father could. They were delicious.

We had chicken and rabbit on the table when I was a pup, but the first time I had to butcher a rabbit on my own was an experience that momentarily erased all memories of such dining pleasure — and thoughts of such pleasure in the future.

It was winter, and fresh snow covered the ground and the table where the ritual was to take place. The warm blood turned the snow into precariously stacked crimson crystals, and I gagged. It was not the neatest butchering job I've done. The first time at anything is never easy.

Butchering, like most other aspects of homesteading, is a skill. Proficiency comes with experience. Today a chicken, tomorrow a rabbit, then on to sheep and pigs and cows.

With experience and proficiency, the blood is lessened, the trauma decreased, and roasts and chops and steaks more recognizable. But it never gets "easy."

I've been a cook, and in that (as well as in other professions I've perused) I've been maddened by the finicky eating habits of so many people. They have no *respect* for food, be it a tomato or a once glorious Hereford steer. And that is one of the spiritual benefits of homesteading.

We could discuss the economics of meat-eating, or of doing the work ourselves. We could talk about the niceties of preparing a crown roast or a spicy dry sausage. We could go on at length about how home-grown and home-butchered can and should be on a completely different plane than mass-produced and slaughtered meat. And in this issue we do.

But to me, one of the most remarkable aspects of home butchering is the heightened awareness and appreciation it entails. If you have yet to slaughter your first lamb, read the instructions. Then, tuck in your resolve and act swiftly and firmly... and with reverence.

I can't help but feel that the flavor of our food is due to more than chemical properties, and that it nourishes more than our bodies, beyond the sidewalks.

60. December 1977
"Living with less" and loving it

I don't know when I first wanted to be a homesteader, but I remember *deciding* to be a homesteader in the mid-1950's.

My idea of homesteading at that time was building a cozy little cabin in the woods and living a simple life. We chose the wilds of western Ontario. It didn't last very long.

Life progressed on an erratic path, but the dream persisted. Working as a migrant laborer, I looked to the day when the crops I handled would be my own. Grinding grain scavenged from an empty boxcar on the siding behind our house, it was because we were poor, not because we were homesteading. I rolled out dough with an empty beer bottle because we didn't have a rolling pin, and didn't even see it as appropriate technology. When I needed to go a mile, or a hundred miles, I rode my single-speed balloon tire bicycle, not to conserve resources, but because it seemed right. And I didn't have a car.

Life has continued to progress. Only recently did it strike me that I was as much a homesteader then as I am now, and in some ways *more* of a homesteader.

It's true, we finally made it to the country, and we have rabbits and chickens and goats. But there's been some backsliding, too. The bicycle (same one) doesn't get used much, now that I have a truck. We broke our vow never to have a tv set when a relative gave us a used B&W one (on the day Kennedy was assassinated, if you can image). We even have a real rolling pin.

Chickens and homesteaders and goats don't make a homesteader. Land doesn't make a homesteader. Attitudes make a homesteader.

This may be of some comfort for those readers who are, now, where we were 25 years ago. It may help explain my frequent exasperation with those who say, "I have a few goats and chickens and a large garden, but I'm not really a homesteader, because I live in town and have a full-time job."

Not a homesteader? Horsefeathers!

One of the major problems is the term itself: "homesteader" just hasn't been able to shake its original meaning, even though it's been used in the modern sense for at least 30 years. (I first ran across it in an article in *Readers Digest* in the mid-1940s.) In more recent years, we've been having a heck of a time getting new subscribers when we talk about homesteading. Nobody wants to read a homesteading magazine when they aren't homesteaders... and if they only want a few animals and a little independence and a little simplicity in their lives, they don't consider themselves homesteaders.

However, in the past few months another term has come into widespread use, a term many people can identify with. It's Voluntary Simplicity, or VS.

To my way of thinking, voluntary simplicity is homesteading, and homesteading is voluntary simplicity. True, homesteading has a rural connotation, but I agree with Boston photographer Jock Gill who was quoted in Geof Hewitt's book, *Working for Yourself,* as saying, "I equate homesteading with economic independence, and though it may be a lot easier to be independent in this way where the cost of living is lower and the materialistic temptations fewer, the idea that one must go up-country to lead a simpler, more basic life is ridiculous. It can be done in the city as well.

"After all, freedom is what homesteading is all about, isn't it? You can find freedom anywhere. The limiting notion that freedom is spelled c-o-u-n-t-r-y is unimaginative, dull, and in the end, irrelevant."

Another angle on this is offered by Robin Clarke in his new book, *Building for Self-Sufficiency.* He proposes that the divorce between the head and the hands in modern culture "turns us all, in the end, into less than half a person. And anyone who learns to use them together again will, I guarantee, experience a rejuvenation not normally associated with the mundane tasks of laying drains and learning to make a ridge ladder. It is all something to do with bringing your life back under your own control and of spending your time at a number of highly different jobs. The human being, surely, was never intended to do the same thing for hours on end for most of his waking life. There is more to living."

Sound familiar?

Ask the average person what he thinks about homesteading, and he'll say he thought all the free land was gone. But ask about voluntary simplicity, and you'll get quite a different reaction.

A Roper poll published in May, 1976, indicated that 51 percent of Americans believe that the nation "must cut way back" on production and consumption to conserve resources and keep the economy strong. Only 45 percent felt that traditional lifestyles could continue unchanged.

A year later, pollster Louis Harris reported that the American people had begun to show "a deep skepticism about the nation's capacity for unlimited economic growth, and are wary of the benefits that growth is supposed to bring." Seventy-nine percent said they'd place greater emphasis on "teaching people how to live more with basic essentials" than on "reaching higher standards of living." And 63 percent said they felt that the country should emphasize "learning to appreciate human values" rather than finding ways to create more jobs for producing more goods.

If homesteading/VS is not animals and gardening, what is it?

It's a complex attitude comprised of a wide range of more specific attitudes. Love of goats or rabbits or poultry may be one of them, but not necessarily. However, people who do live in the country and grow crops and raise livestock have a tremendous advantage. They, or many of them, can much more easily understand ecology. Not just the relationship of DDT to brown pelicans or of deforestation to flooding, but the complete range of interrelationships and interdependencies. They know the complete truth about the source of our most important fuel, food. They know, even if they don't always understand, the total interdependence of every life form in the biosphere. They know that man can never conquer nature, because man is part of nature.

Immersed in an urban environment, it's too easy to get into the habit of thinking mankind is somehow superior to nature and can control it. In the countryside there are too many reminders to the contrary to be duped by that fallacy.

That fallacy, of course, is widespread. It's the basis for materialism, which leads to greed, the mining of the planet's resources (including soil fertility and air and water quality), the struggle for bigger and better everything, the belief in the need for constant growth. This has been the norm, the basis for the American Way of Life.

As we've said many times in this magazine, that way of life is dead. The surveys cited offer dramatic proof that we who say that are now in the majority.

I F that's the case, what's next? In the past, we've said that homesteading was the only alternative. We still say it... but let's make that more acceptable by calling homesteading VS.

The Futurist devoted its entire August 1977 issue to "learning to live with less." If anyone isn't sure what homesteading, or VS or COUNTRYSIDE, for that matter, is all about, they can get a crash course from this issue.

In an article titled "Get Poor Now — Avoid the Rush Later" environmentalist, architect and energy expert Tom Bender wrote, "There is no longer any doubt that our age of affluence based on depletion of our planet's non-renewable energy and material resources is at an end and that *major* changes must be made in every aspect of our lives."

The first change must be made in attitude, for without that we're changing only form, not substance.

Examples are everywhere. "Natural" has become an in-word, a selling word, so the food processing giants market "natural" foods grown with fertilizers that mine soil fertility and devitalize the product itself, foods that undergo all the transporting and handling and packaging and advertising and marketing inherent in the old system. "Natural" has become such a potent marketing concept it's even employed in selling cigarettes and Scotch whiskey.

We've changed the form, but not the substance.

Many universities and agribusiness firms are getting in on the organic boom. They "discover" that plowdown alfalfa improves the growth of the subsequent crop, so they begin to isolate and synthesize the factor responsible; they "discover" that foliar feeding works, so they feed synthetics; they discover that plowing causes soil erosion, so they develop no-till planting which uses herbicides without regard for the broad meaning of the webs of ecology.

Many people, of course, haven't even changed the form. You've seen examples: county agents, nutritionists, business-people, who say "Organic foods are no different than any other foods" without the foggiest notion of what organic methods are really about; or "The nation can't *afford* to have clean water and air, or to try to farm without poisons, or to delay building nuclear power plants" and on and on.

One good recent example was a column in the Sept. 19, 1977 *Newsweek* headed "The Future Doesn't Work." Written by Bernard Sloan, it starts off with "It seems to be the fashion these days to equate a lower standard of living with a better way of life." You can imagine the rest.

One of our readers who sent me a copy of this article, Jill Livingston of Horse Creek, California, said, "I can't believe that this guy is serious, much less that he was paid to write it. This is an example of what we're up against."

The gist of the piece was that the author doesn't want to reduce energy consumption because it makes him uncomfortable. "Having just lived with foods that went stale, mildewed and rancid moments after opening, I'd like to put in a word for preservatives." And again "Our family has just relived the joys of homogenized milk. And one sound I never want to hear again is 'Yuccky!' expressed by a child at the sight of globs of cream curdling at the top of the milk."

Was the Sloan family roughing it in the backwoods, milking the horrid cow that produced that nasty cream, growing and storing their own grain and vegetables? Not at all. They lived for two years in metropolitan Sydney, Australia. (Our Australian readers might want to comment on the harsh and primitive conditions Mr. Sloan seems to have found in their country.)

Yes, Mr. Sloan, it *is* the fashion today to equate a lower standard of living with a better way of life. Some of us, for whom the fashion is decades old, can more clearly see the inescapable truth of that, for we've seen the bones of the simple statement fleshed out as the years have passed. The age of affluence... the high material standard of living... was based upon depletion of our planet's non-renewable resources. That age is past, whether the Sloans of the world like it or not. In fact, with their attitude, they are actually hastening its passing.

Mr. Sloan is enjoying a lower standard of living, even materially, already, although he apparently hasn't noticed it yet. He is paying more for fuel, for food, and nearly everything else. His food is of poorer quality, certainly than that of a self-sufficient homesteader living in VS. The physical world around him is polluted, blighted, diminished. But he and all his kind fiddle while not just Rome, but the planet, burns.

His simplicity is forced, and forced simplicity equates with poverty.

If the past 10 years have wrought such remarkable changes, what will the next 10 bring? Some of us know very well what the future holds, and that adds a grim satisfaction to the joys of living in voluntary simplicity, especially beyond the sidewalks.

Afterword 2010: Again, my first reaction is, "hasn't anything changed, in all that time?" Those references to surveys and quotes about the need for voluntary simplicity are amazing: how come nothing ever came of them? In some ways, it seems like we might have even gone backwards.

On the other hand, these kinds of ideas must have helped beef up the morale of the doomsayers, who had been running out of support.

2014: On the third hand, maybe this simply means that evolution, especially the kind we're talking about, is a jerky process, not a smooth transition. Then too (as any animal breeder knows), as a species evolves, not all individuals are equal participants in the transformation: except for sudden mutations, it requires many generations. (See p. 424ff.)

Part VIII: 1978

Inflation: 7.62%; Federal Reserve interest rate: 11.75%; Gas/gal: 63¢; DJIA, year-end: 805; Eggs, 48¢/dozen; New York strip steak, $2.39/lb.

61. January 1978

Where life is...

Every year about this time (meaning the beginning of a new year) I find myself looking back over the year just ended, and over all of my years. Every year it takes longer... and gets more interesting. That's been especially true this year, because I've just spent several evenings going over back issues of COUNTRYSIDE.

I've been involved in more than a hundred issues of this magazine. I've left just a little bit of myself in each one...and of course, I've gained a little from each one too. Editing a magazine just has to be one of the most educational jobs anywhere, with the possible exception of teaching. At any rate, I seldom look at back issues except for their reference value, which I find to be considerable, and lazily poring over those dozens and dozens of long outdated magazines was, for me, very much like turning the pages of a family photo album.

There's a letter from Mrs. Casey, who used to write regularly, and who now seems like an old friend (although I never met her face to face). Here's a letter from Bob Bennett, long before he became our rabbit editor. And in this issue is a piece Judy Kapture did on the giant guinea pigs she met while in the Peace Corps — capybaras.

There were "Beyonds" when owning my own farm and a real tractor was only a dream, when all of my energy and attention went to making not 170 acres, but a single acre, fertile and productive. Reading again about our single pig, or how I built a henhouse out of waste slabs from a local lumber mill, or how successful our first experiments with narrow row planting were, a powerful wave of nostalgia swept over me.

It seems like a long, long time ago.

I don't print the magazine any more. I don't set the type. I don't even write all of it. And I suspect — no, I *know* — that if I had continued to do all of that for these past hundred issues, working hundred-hour weeks, the magazine wouldn't be here today and neither would I.

And yet, looking at where we are today, I sort of hanker for those long-past times. I guess I agree with the advertiser who claims that getting there is half the fun.

COUNTRYSIDE is "successful." No, we don't have a large circulation, or a lot of advertising, and we don't make a lot of money. But it's comfortable and as stable a little business as any small-town weekly newspaper or hardware store... and that kind of business is all I ever wanted. Only when I got what I wanted, I found it wasn't what I wanted.

The other night (and magazine deadlines being what they are, this means late autumn) all of this was weighing pretty heavily on me. I was sitting at my home typewriter trying to compose an office memo — I guess I still do work 100 hours a week — but it all seemed so futile. The older boys had gone rabbit hunting, our daughter was gone, Diane was busy in the kitchen, and John, our youngest son, was bored and listless. He suggested that we go for a walk.

It was a very pleasant night, and as we started out the farm road which skirts the base of the hill hay field, the moon was just beginning to rise. It was so dramatic we paused to watch it, a giant glowing orb that turned the clouds to a golden red. As the two of us stood there, I knew it was going to be a worthwhile evening.

We continued to the "quarter mile mark," the fenceline dividing the front 40 from the back 40, and our pylon for foot races, jogging, horse races and other events requiring a point of reference. The road makes a sharp right turn, then climbs a steep hill, and runs into a town road.

We followed the blacktopped town road past the neighbors whose car-chasing dogs seemed somewhat unsure of themselves when confronted by two people on foot. I spoke to them and they returned to the house, keeping a confused but wary eye on us.

We reached our other parcel of land half a mile from the home farm, where we're building a new home to escape the highway widening project which is destroying our present homestead, and to have a more ecological and countryside-type house. Topping the glacial drumlin, we could see the new construction clearly in the moonlight. And that, too, filled me with mixed emotions. We had planned the "ideal homestead" more than a dozen years ago. Now our children are almost grown and will be with us for only a short time, and it seemed like a case of too little, too late.

But John is young, and we still have much to share. (That was him on the cover of the October issue.) We descend to the building site, and scratch our collective JB in the still-wet concrete that had been poured that day.

We take the ridge home, a long narrow glacial deposit of remote hay fields, scattered forest on the steeper slopes, and a few small contoured corn fields. The moon is high now, and seems to have lost some of its brilliance. From this height, we can see the sky glow of distant towns, the throbbing red pinpoints of their radio station towers, and the thin line of roads marked by the headlights of silent vehicles. It's a world apart, the ridge is, and yet, the rest of the world is so close you feel you can reach out and touch it.

And on nights like this, you feel you *must* reach out and touch it... but you're afraid.

The ridge descends, quite suddenly, and we're back on our farm. We wade through knee-deep plowdown clover, stumble across a fall-plowed field, and end up back at the quarter-mile mark.

We've walked a mile and a half at a brisk pace, but I propose that we jog the last quarter-mile. It's something I learned a long time ago — on the high school track squad, in the Marine Corps, I don't know. Builds character, or something. Always push yourself near the finish line.

With the aroma of clover and fresh-plowed earth still in our nostrils, the house smelled like boiled turnips. John goes to bed. Diane is in the living room, reading. I go back to the typewriter, and think about what to say about a new year.

As I roll a fresh sheet of paper into the machine, I decide that whatever I say, however I say it, the message should be this:

Don't dwell on last year, or become preoccupied with next year. Make this day, this hour, count, because that's where life is... whether or not you live beyond the sidewalks.

62. February 1978

The real crisis behind the "crisis"

I ducked into one of those little down-a-half-flight coffee shops for a quick bite to eat between seminar sessions, just to get out of the Manhattan hotel... and its out-of-town crowd and atrocious prices. The lady took my order and then, in a display of human friendliness I'd never experienced in New York before, said "My gosh, what happened to your thumb! "Following her gaze of loathing, I looked at it.

I had just taken the bandage off, and the green and purple and black swelling from the knuckle to the tip was sensitive even to the air: the weight of the eyeballs that were on it now made it positively throb. The nail, black and misshapen, hadn't fallen off, yet, but it was loose and I knew it would, soon.

"Oh, you wouldn't believe it anyway," I said sheepishly. "You wouldn't know what I was talking about." She squared herself before the counter in front of me, put her hands on either side of the ketchup bottle and napkin holder, and leaned towards me, and looking me straight in the eye, defiantly said, "Try me."

"I smashed it under a hydraulic cylinder on a combine," I said.

Her eyes clouded, her brow furrowed, she said, "You win," and walked away. But her curiosity was piqued, and when she returned with my hamburger she kept up the conversation. I had to explain that a combine was used for harvesting grain: I was a farmer.

"Oh," she said, brightening, "you're from Pennsylvania." From her tone I got the distinct impression that anyone who ventured beyond Pennsylvania would fall off the edge of the Earth, as if following one of those medieval maps that near the perimeter warns, "Here be dragons."

"No," I said. "Wisconsin."

From her reaction, I couldn't be sure she had ever heard of the place or had any idea where it was. She was obviously sorry she had ever started the conversation, and dropped it.

I am a member of a minority, a group whose numbers are diminishing daily. In many cases, there are no outward signs to stigmatize us. In others, you might be clued in by a creamy-white forehead above a sun and wind-reddened leathery face, or a friendly self-assured handshake from a huge calloused paw. We don't ordinarily dress, or act, differently from most other people, if only because two-thirds of us earn more money from jobs other than the occupation which makes us a minority, and we therefore *are* "other people."

We are farmers.

We don't farm for the money — although many of us would like to at least be able to make a modest living, farming. We obviously don't do it for the gratitude of the masses we feed, because there ain't no gratitude. When you come right down to it, we probably farm only to please ourselves. We *like* farming, we enjoy the work, the challenges, the satisfaction and what it represents.

This undoubtedly is one reason farmer's strikes and protests have never worked. Farm leaders have been telling us that farming is no longer a way of life, but merely a "business." Yet, what business would continue to operate at a loss? What ordinary worker would persist even through the devastating experience of salary decreases and the erosion of savings? How many people, today, would work the hours farmers work, under the conditions farmers work under, for even minimum wage, to say nothing of far less than minimum wage?

So we continue. And when we give up there are others eager, or at least willing (depending on the times) to take our place.

For America (and indeed, most of the world) this has meant a steady and abundant supply of food. In fact, it has meant such a steady food supply that most people, in New York and elsewhere, have no idea where it even comes from. What's more, they couldn't care less.

It's sad, and it's not right. It's not fair to the farmers, whose compensation falls far below that of those with less training, experience, responsibility, investment, dedication and ambition. But worse, it isn't fair to those who "assume" that their tables will always be laden, that the supermarkets will always be amply supplied. Their assumption is wrong, and they haven't the ability or interest to question it.

The assumption is wrong because the intense economic pressure on farmers causes them to "mine" the soil in ways that are as unfathomable and as undramatic to the city-dwellers as... well, as the workings and purposes of a hydraulic ram on a combine. They can't relate to, and have no interest in, soil erosion due to excessive row cropping, loss of soil fertility and tilth, and dozens, maybe hundreds, of other effects of mismanagement brought about by economic pressure. The adage to "Get big or get out" is simply an admonition to "Get yours while you can."

Future generations will pay. Some of us feel *we* will pay... next year, or the year after or the year after that, but soon.

Farmers can't do much about it. Not as long as non-farmers have no knowledge of, or interest in, their food supply. Not as long as the "Get yours while you can" companies — and some farmers, admittedly, although they don't deserve the title — are whitewashing the facts and lulling the populace into complacency.

Everyone wants cheap food, even at the expense of a minority of workers, even at the expense of future generations. No one wants to be troubled learning about something as basic and natural and omnipresent as food. And that is the real crisis in "the farm crisis." No one is in control. No one cares. Everyone will pay.

63. March 1978

Some clear thoughts in the fog

The road was covered with a viscous slush and the fog was so thick I could see only a few yards ahead of the pickup's hood. I parked, got out of the truck with my axe, and the slamming door echoed back from the wall of damp air. Trying to peer through the fog, I had the same sensation of claustrophobia I get wearing a bee veil.

I couldn't see the first fencerow, much less the small patch of woods beyond, which was my goal. Walking was difficult in the wet, heavy snow that reached the tops of my boots, and I stopped to rest when I reached the fencerow.

Sitting there, catching my breath, I noticed a bunch of box elders that were not only crowding out some young hickories and wild cherries, but were also encroaching on the hayfield. I hacked down a couple of dozen of the slender saplings, then continued across the field.

The patch of woods — about three acres, according to my estimate — is a long, narrow strip. I'd never done any work back there: no firewood cutting, no thinning, no planting. It was too remote from the barn to have been used for pasture by any of the previous owners, but it's as far from being a virgin forest as an eroded cornfield is from being a virgin prairie. It needs a lot of work, and in my schedule of priorities, its time has come.

There are a few magnificent old elms in the patch — magnificent even in the aftermath of Dutch elm disease. There are also several crowded stands of popple as well as scattered hickories, wild cherry, and other assorted species.

I file it all in my mind as I pass among the trees: which of them are to stay, which should be removed because they detract from the health and vigor of the entire stand, which areas need reforesting. There are windfalls, which interest me as firewood, but at this time of year I'm even more interested in cull trees. Culls take light and moisture from crop trees and if I can cut them in the dead of winter, they'll make better firewood.

Besides, when else would I have time to cut trees?

Near the end of the strip, I crossed over it and began to work my way back along the outer edge. But it was time for another break. I sat on the bole of a fallen tree, and lit my pipe.

I still couldn't see more than a few yards, but as I sat there, I heard a car pass along the road to the east. It was a good quarter of a mile away, but it sounded as if it were bearing down on me, and to tell the truth I glanced over my shoulder in some concern.

My neighbor to the south was out with his manure spreader. The chugging of the tractor, the clatter of the beaters as the PTO was engaged, the shifting of gears when the load was emptied... I saw it all as a blind man sees, for my eyes saw nothing but hanging grey mist.

And then, just a little to the east, there came the roar of a chainsaw. Not a buzz as of a distant sawyer, but a roar, as if a trespasser-thief were cutting down my own trees a few rods from where I sat. It was, of course, another neighbor, who was a step ahead of me in his timber stand improvement, or TSI as we would-be foresters call it.

Then there was the sound of children shouting, again, sounding as if they were going to come plummeting down the hill on their sleds and sweep past where I sat smoking my pipe. Then Roger, who rents the grey house (the original farmhouse here), came out to fetch some wood for his stove. I heard him speak to the dogs, and could imagine them cavorting at his heels. It was easy to imagine, because I've seen them before from near this spot, when I was driving a noisy tractor. But now I sat unseeing and unseen, but even more aware.

I was at the center of the world. There was activity all around me, and in my mind's eye it was all very clear. My sense of awareness was not limited by sight: it was not hampered by trees or the sweep of a hill or the hulk of a barn. It was not stretched by the view of a tractor piloted by some unknown farmer crawling over a far-off ridge, or by a mile-high airplane peopled by strangers riding a contrail into the distance. It was a close, tight circle. It was comfortable and friendly. I was a very private individual, with my silent private activity, and yet there were friends and neighbors within earshot, within the circle of my life.

If they had bothered to pause and listen, I would have been on the edge of their circles... circles which would have taken in people and activities I couldn't have been aware of, in the fog. And those circles would have touched on still other circles, until the whole world was encased in an interlinking coat of protective mail.

My TSI didn't take a giant leap forward. But maybe, just maybe, I improved more than the woodlot did. And after all, which is more important? I am a link in the chain mail coat of humanity. But logs grow on trees.

As I grow chilly, stand, and head back to the truck, I idly wonder if it's possible to get such weird thoughts if you don't live beyond the sidewalks.

64. April 1978

Passing to a New Age

E verything has an age. Everything develops in stages. The Earth itself measures ages in awesome spans: the Age of Reptiles, the Ice Age. Mankind measures ages on a less grand scale: the Stone Age, the Golden Age, the Dark Ages. A tiny insect may be born, mature, procreate and die, all within a span of hours, and a rainbow often lasts for only moments. And they all interact. Modern homesteading today is in a fairly early stage, but there are growing indications that its time has come, and it's showing signs of maturing.

I was thinking of this in particular, and age in general, while reflecting on a couple of new homestead publications which came to my attention, and my own birthday coming up in Aries. *Homestead Harmony* reminds me very much of my own first issues of COUNTRYSIDE. It's 12 pages, typewritten, and the first issue is interesting and fun to read. It has a certain pristine innocence and charm that clearly speaks of youth. Thoughtful youth.

In rather vivid contrast, I also received a copy of *In Defence* (sic) *of Nature,* subtitled "The Revolutionary Hippie Publication." The four-letter words, the chip-on-the-shoulder attitude, the almost frantic attempt to be "revolutionary" and the general straining to be taken seriously, all of these speak of youth, too, but with a far different effect on the reader.

M eanwhile, as I said, I was also thinking of my own "ages." When you're 16, you can do anything because you're young and healthy and intelligent and strong... but you can do nothing because you lack education, experience, independence and power.

When I was 16 my two major interests were farming, and writing. But farmers were going out of business in droves, those who remained required more capital and experience than ever, and I had neither. So I raised rabbits and pigeons, did farm work when I could, and wrote.

No one listens to a 16-year-old writer. Naturally I tried to write as if I didn't have acne and a lot more hope than experience, but not much of what I wrote was published.

When I was 21, I was in college, studying journalism. English, or literature, would have bored me to death. That wasn't my kind of writing: I wanted to be where the action was. Not at the fires, in the courts or the legislative halls. I wanted to write about everyday people, everyday happenings. It seemed to me that individuals, "little people," if you will, have had more of an effect on history than kings and presidents. All the unknowns who made "drop-outs" and "funky" and "hangup" and "bummer" a part of the English language had as much of an effect on the language as Shakespeare; the people who practice equality have more of an effect than the supreme court; the people who buy natural foods and practice organic living have a greater effect than the FDA or USDA.

No one listens to a 21-year-old student, of course.

The times had somewhat caught up with me when I reached 30. "Back to nature" and simplicity had gained a certain toehold... but so had the "never trust anyone over 30" syndrome. I was caught in the awkward position of not being able to write what I really wanted to write, either for the under-30s, who didn't trust me, or for the older folks who still weren't attuned to that "hippy" stuff. So I lived my own life and wrote about rabbits and goats.

Then, I faced 40.

You anticipate it, of course, but it still hits with the thud of a bale of hay falling from the top of an overloaded wagon and landing on the nape of your neck. Forty years old! Your life is surely more than half over, but your most private dreams and goals are as far away as ever, or farther.

Suddenly you realize that the editors who thought you were too young and inexperienced at 16 and 21 are now younger than you. You can't run as far or as fast as you used to be able to, you can't work as long or as hard as you once did, and the novelty of finding an occasional gray hair has worn off.

You *change*, between 16 and 40, even if your basic ideas and ideals stay the same. With experience comes insight, you know what works and what doesn't, you know what's important and what isn't. And perhaps most importantly, you not only know what you know but you know what you *don't* know.

And yet, even as you change, so does the rest of humanity. The world has changed far more rapidly and significantly than I have in the past 24 years. I'm still a small farmer, a writer, and I still have the same beard I had then. I have the same beliefs about ecology and appropriate technology and energy (fortified, of course, with experience and new developments). But today, all of these are commonplace. In fact, very many of the ideas and ideals of the flower children and the beatniks before them are now firmly established in the popular culture.

And why not? The beatniks and the flower children now *are* those straight, middle-class middle-aged people. Stu Brand and John Shuttleworth and Jerry Belanger are now 40 years old, and their magazines have practically become part of the establishment.

Thus, it's not surprising that new 16 and 21 and 30-year-olds are going through their stages, or that new magazines must spring up to meet changing tastes and ideas. Because of the interplay of ages of mankind, of the Earth, and everything else in nature, no two people and no two moments can ever be exactly the same.

This diversity in humanity, and in homesteading, can only be a strength, as important in human affairs as it is in ecology, lending vigor, stability, and permanence.

For my part, the world has made great strides in catching up with the main ideals of my youth, and all that remains for me is the detail work. While in no way would I want to be 16, or 21, or even 30 again, I'm very happy for those who are.

But in so many ways, 40 is a much better age for homesteading: youth is a time for changing the world; middle age is a time for knowing what cannot be changed, and living with it...and that's much more attuned to the whole concept of homesteading.

In fact, I have a strong hunch that life really does begin at 40, especially beyond the sidewalks! Instead of trying to change the world, I'm content with the daily drama of raising goats and rabbits.

65. May 1978

Something's coming...

According to the rules of magazine writing, I should be talking about May, when you're reading this: about plum blossoms and newly hatched chicks and goslings and the aroma of fresh-turned earth.

But actually, it's an overcast day in March. There are still sizeable patches of dirty snow on the ground, especially where the Blizzard of '78 piled up drifts, but the temperature is above freezing. If it rains (and it looks like it might) the last remnants of snow will disappear fast.

From my window I can see the sap buckets on the maple trees behind the house, the pigeons on the barn roof cooing and billing, and the roosters and drakes likewise going about their spring domestic duties. And while you won't believe I'm not making this up, a flock of

Canadian geese just passed directly over the view from my window, a sure sign of early spring.

I t's awfully hard to think about May, on a day like this.
The first seeds of the bedding plants were planted in flats just the other day: tomatoes, peppers, cauliflower and other members of the cabbage family. The ground is still frozen and we have yet to taste the first Jerusalem artichoke or the sweet parsnips of spring. How can I get enthusiastic about the blossoming of flowers not yet sprouted or the parade of chicks and ducklings newly hatched from eggs not yet laid? I'd rather savor this moment, here and now.

Besides, for me, the future is in doubt today.

For one thing, I'm very much in sympathy with the farmers' strike and I really have no clear idea of what I'm going to be doing in the way of farming. I'm one of those who would actually be money ahead if I didn't spend the thousands of dollars it takes for fuel, machinery repairs and maintenance, seed, and all the rest. And being an organic farmer, the idea of having the entire farm in green manure for a year has a certain appeal to me, too.

Even the homestead is in doubt. Our new home, on the back 80, which has been under construction since last summer, still isn't finished and I don't even know where we'll be living in May!

And then there are a bunch of other, even more personal things. Our oldest daughter graduates from high school in May and has told us she intends to leave the nest. Things like that.

Maybe I don't want to write about May because I don't want it to come. Not yet. I'm not ready. In so many ways, it seems as if the month ahead of me is a forked road with neither fork marked: it might even be a dead end.

But there's more. It might be because of my personal situation and outlook, but I also see disturbing events on a much wider scale as a part of this spring. Events that will make all my work of the past 10 years suddenly take on new light and meaning. Events that will make whatever I write now, to be read in May, utterly irrelevant.

It could be, of course, that I follow the news more closely than a sensible homesteader should. Maybe I read too much into the farm strike, the coal strike, the value of the dollar and unemployment and inflation in general. Maybe in May, when you and I both read this in print, I'll feel foolish and you'll be only too willing to agree.

Uncertainty. Maybe that's all it is. All the normal patterns are disrupted, and the future is even more clouded than usual.

There's a point to all of this.

The reason I'm boring you with my personal doubts and problems is that I know you have them too. If you're a farmer, you face the same production costs I do, and with markets more uncertain than ever (even on top of the certain uncertainty of the weather) you can't help but be uneasy.

If you're in business or work for business, you know as well as I do and perhaps better than I do that my fears are based on facts. The prices of nearly everything we sell in the Countryside General Store have jumped, and jumped again. Our suppliers, just as we, face higher social security and other taxes, higher postage, and higher salaries, which oddly enough, are necessary to keep up with other rising costs. The steel settlement has triggered price increases, the coal strike will certainly trigger price increases, and the postage increase on magazines in April will hit that aspect of our business... and yours, whatever it may be.

In brief, even though life itself is uncertain, we probably live with more fear and doubt today than at any other time in our lives.

Except when we're homesteading.

On the homestead, I *know*, within certain limits, what May will be like, with almost as much assurance as I have that the sun will rise in the east tomorrow. The homestead is governed not by the laws of economics, not by politicians or scientists, but by far greater natural laws.

The homestead is governed by the laws that decree that the days of spring shall grow longer and warmer; that the sap shall rise in the maples and the grass turn green; that an egg shall hatch in 21 days and that a seed shall germinate and grow according to its kind.

In business — any business, including farming — the struggle to hold down costs, increase revenues, and in general to survive among constantly shifting social and economic patterns, is a treadmill. It may be exciting and challenging to some people, it may be necessary to civilization, but it's no less insane for that.

So once again — and perhaps now, more than ever — the homestead is an island of sanity in an insane world. The sun, the wind, the rain, the birth of animals and the growth of plants... these are all certainties in an uncertain world, and therefore they are great comforts.

And here's something else you may find hard to believe unless you give me more credit for writing fiction than I deserve: In the time it has taken me to write this, the clouds have thinned and the sun is shining brightly.

No, of course that couldn't mean anything... could it?

66. June 1978

Another new beginning

Each spring is a new beginning. Each dawn is a new beginning. At sunrise in April they reinforce each other to present both the senses and the spirit with an overwhelming feeling of freshness.

I finished disking the first field yesterday, and after a long day in the sun and wind, I was ready for bed at an early hour. Accordingly, by 3:30 A.M. I was slept out, anxious to get at the planting. Of course, you don't plant at 3:30 in the morning... not around here, anyway. So I ended up here at the typewriter thinking about spring, and dawn, and new beginnings.

The fourth quarter moon is high in the sky and almost due south, and the swelling buds of the maple trees outside my window are silhouetted against its mottled surface. The sky is clear but even now, in the dim pre-dawn of half-light, there are no stars.

The roosters are crowing from their roosts, but the first homestead critters to parade past my window are the ducks, the hens gabbling furiously and the drakes conversing in their quiet whispers. They act as if they know exactly where they're going and are in a hurry to get there even though their destination — a mudhole in the lower field — is only a vestige of its former ducky glory. As I count the dark shapes waddling past the milkhouse I see another hen missing and make a mental note to search out the nest and if necessary give it some protection.

The chickens are out now, scratching in the barn driveway. One of the hens ventures over to the dog's dish, outside her house, and pecks at whatever crumbs are left from last night's supper. The dog, only her nose poking out of her door, blinks disinterestedly.

High in the branches of the maple a pair of grackles is going through a mating ritual, the male preening and puffing, the female feigning disinterest. And on the ground below them, a white Leghorn hen races by on roadrunner feet, hotly pursued by a red and white rooster with his tail fanned out, his hackles raised and his wings drooping in undisguised lust.

My window faces south, and it's a long time before the first direct rays of the sun strike the north side of the barn in front of me. The extreme angle of the shadows makes the entire barn appear like a different picture of familiar surroundings.

I wander over to the kitchen window, which faces east, for a better view of the dawn. The sky is cloudless. The sun, momentarily hidden behind the neighbor's silo, washes the eastern sky with a pale yellow.

220

"Red in the morning..." Good day for planting. Even as I watch, the sun bursts forth from the right edge of the silo, and blinds me.

As I sit down at the typewriter again I hear a rooster pheasant call from the garden and the guineas, scratching in the drive, look up in alarm, but without answering the call. And here comes Turkey, who has become something of a family pet in the last five years. There is no sign of the cow, the horse, the goats or anyone else, and the dog remains asleep even with the sun in her eyes. Morning, as some of my children are quick to point out, is for the birds.

Once it breaks over the horizon, the sun moves rapidly, and while it's still "dawn" (and certainly very early in the morning) some of the magic of sunrise has already been lost. The rest fades quickly. You have to get up early and look sharply to discern new beginnings. You have to anticipate them, even. Even then, there are surprises: as a chicken struts out of the shadow of the barn, it's startling to see that its shadow is six feet long!

The sparrows and pigeons are building nests, picking up bits of straw and twigs and feathers from the drive. The barn swallows, which returned only the day before yesterday, are resting briefly on the power lines to the barn.

With morning chores, and breakfast, the beginning of the smaller cycle, the daily cycle, is complete. Tomorrow will still be spring, but that beginning too wears on. And if, as I suspect, there is yet some greater cycle than the daily and annual ones that are so plain to see, that too is unfolding, whether we notice it or not.

How can anyone help but notice cycles, you ask? It's simple.

It's 5:30 in the morning. Look what most people have missed already...just by not being awake.

67. July 1978

How a farmer/editor "relaxes"...

Ah, it feels good to sit down! I mean on a chair, instead of a hard, bouncing tractor seat with the dust in your eyes and mouth and a roaring engine that tires you out just listening to it all day and the sun and the wind that dries out your skin and burns it and puts a perpetual squint in your eyes. Everything is done on the July issue of COUNTRYSIDE except for my column, I spent a good day in the fields, and now I can rest.

Yes, it feels good to just sit here with my boots off without having to think of farming or the magazine.

Speaking of the magazine, maybe I should rewrite that editorial on anti-organic propaganda while there's still time. It's an important topic, but I didn't develop it nearly well enough, and I certainly didn't write it with anything like the skill and care it deserves. I know I can do better...

Oh, for Pete's sake, Belanger, let it alone. COUNTRYSIDE readers know as much about it as you do, nobody else will even see it, and if they did they wouldn't believe it. Forget it. You're supposed to be relaxing, remember?

All right. I'll just browse through the Madison newspaper, here.

Hmm. Here's an article by a young farm wife who says she was a former fan of Ralph Nader's. It seems she heard him speak to a farm group, and now she's disillusioned. Guess I can agree with her on some points. But she says Nader claims it's possible to farm without pesticides, and that makes her mad, because she knows it is NOT possible. Nader isn't a farmer, so what does he know, anyway? He says there's proof, but she complains that he doesn't offer even one example.

Well, I guess I could offer her a few examples, including a few dozen we've written about in COUNTRYSIDE, as well as my own farm. But what the heck, I've already written too many letters to that newspaper (where I once worked as a reporter) without getting any printed. No point in wasting my time. Goodness knows I've got other things to do.

Like the garden. There are always things to do in a good garden, and it's still light enough to see. Maybe I should go out for a few more minutes... after all, that's relaxation.

One reason, I think, is that our garden is now on virgin land. The soil is dark and crumbly, it holds water like a sponge, it doesn't cake over after a rain, and it's loaded with worms.

Sure is different from that field I was working today... or any other field that's been plowed and fertilized and sprayed for years. The disk reduced the big clods to smaller clods, but they're still clods. The soil is so thin it's anemic. The soil test indicates that it's low in everything but magnesium and clay, and any pioneer farmer would have declared it "wore out." It needs subsoiling, calcium, N, P and K, and most of the trace elements, to say nothing of organic matter. There are no worms, and probably very little other soil life, because there's nothing for such life to live on.

The field is worn out, but a very short time ago as history goes it must have been as fertile and as full of life as my garden is now. What happened to it? Why the difference? How much time and study and thought and effort and money will it take to restore it to its former, natural state? What can I learn from that experience to at least prevent the garden from going the same route?

The worst part is, I know for a fact that the field is "normal" as far as agribusiness is concerned. It's the same kind of field the world is depending on for survival, not just for this year but for all generations to come. What bothers me is how some people, and in particular farm

222

people, can see such things and still fail to heed the signs. I think of the editorial again, and the young farm wife...

Oh, come off it, Belanger. It can't be all that bad. You ain't so smart, and there are plenty of people who don't see anything wrong. Maybe they're right and you're wrong.

I'll read something else and get my mind off the topic.

Here's a commentary from CAST (Council for Agricultural Science and Technology) on an article in *The Washington Post.* I recall the article. It was pretty good. But CAST seems to disagree. They say, "Nowadays, most people accept agricultural abundance as a matter of course, along with better health care and other advances in technology." (What's health care got to do with it? Why not along with more cancer and heart disease or automobile accidents?) "But a few people object to modern farming, complaining that new varieties do not taste good or have other faults. Machines are opposed as dehumanizing, and chemicals are claimed to be unnecessary and to cause more problems than they solve. This is the theme of an article about pesticides by Daniel Zwerdling that appeared in *The Washington Post* on March 5."

CAST comments on Zwerdling's assertion that pesticides create superstrains of weeds and insects, that the chemical industry persuaded farmers to begin using pesticides, and that farmers are "hooked" on chemicals. "There are numerous flaws in these arguments, not the least of which is Mr. Zwerdling's low opinion of the mental capacity of farmers. He asks us to believe that farmers are foolish enough to adopt, and make standard practice, expensive products and procedures that are not only ineffective but usually caused them harm. We are asked to believe that farmers are unable to understand so simple an economic proposition and instead become enamored of chemicals as a kind of contagious 'habit' that they cannot break."

Hey, wait a minute. That's not the way I read it. He was talking about fields like mine, where nothing grows without chemicals because chemicals have damaged its God-given ability to renew itself. Most farmers are hooked on chemicals because the time and expense of restoring the natural balance is just too great, given farm prices and the competition from the flagrant abusers of those chemicals. It's not that farmers can't understand simple economic propositions, but just the opposite. The problem is the difference between short-run economic propositions and long-term prosperity, or even survival. Maybe CAST never heard the story of the goose that laid the golden eggs.

Aw shucks, what do I care about CAST. I know facts that have a bearing on what they say but which they never mention. I know what I've learned, and I know what works for me, but most of all I have an ideal I'm shooting for: I want my 170 acres of cropland to be just like my garden.

But I was going to forget about all of that and just take it easy for a few minutes.

Ah, here's something that should interest me without getting into farming. It's headed "Journalism and Science." It says, "Are responsible journalism and sound science incompatible? Is it necessary for a writer to sensationalize science stories to get space? Must we use polarized language on critical national issues like environment and public health?" No, I certainly wouldn't think so.

Oh, I see. He doesn't like headlines like "Pesticides feared upsetting ecology badly." It's strange, but except for that *Post* article, most seem to take the other side, the chemical side. This guy seems to be saying, be fair to both sides but be more fair to my side. Let's see... this was written by James H. Lake. Uh-huh, he's the president of Elanco Products Company, the outfit that makes farm chemicals.

I'm supposed to be relaxing, away from it all. Put aside the magazines and newspapers and think of something else.

Say, that sure was pleasant yesterday evening when the neighbors dropped in to chat, even though it was tempered somewhat by the news that their farm had been sold. Milking 70 cows got to be just too much, and they're looking for a smaller place where they can run a few head of beef and keep a couple of hogs and enjoy life a little.

It's funny, though. We got to talking about farming, naturally, and farm economics and whatnot, and the subject of bigness and machinery and chemicals came up. Machines are opposed by some as dehumanizing, CAST says (oops, we weren't going to talk about that any more) but CAST is made up of ag engineers and scientists. Here was the neighbor, a guy with two barn cleaners and 80-foot silos with unloaders and all the rest, talking about the dehumanizing aspects of his machinery. Should I believe the scientists, whose only real concern in the matter is their science, or the guy who feeds and milks the cows according to their specifications and sees something wrong with it all? He's a darn good farmer, but not only is he concerned about his use of machinery and chemicals: he says he refuses to drink milk from the store, and when his cows are gone can he get raw milk from me?

Why sure, we have plenty of milk. In fact, I don't know why I keep on milking, to say nothing of the other homestead things I do, when I've got my hands full with a business and a farm. Maybe I'm one of those who is too foolish to understand simple economic propositions.

Or maybe it's a different kind of economics. Maybe instead of killing the goose in an attempt to get all the golden eggs at once, I'm willing to tend the goose and let her lay at her own rate.

Or maybe it isn't economics at all.

No, of course it isn't. Making a living and security are important, all right, but there are different ways of making a living, and different kinds of security. I don't understand the anti-organic people, and they don't understand me, not because either of us have the facts muddled, but because we don't have the same goals, the same outlook on life. That reminds me of...

Oh my goodness, here it is time for bed already, and it seems like I've hardly got farming out of my mind at all. But then, some people get bored with their jobs and their lives and need mindless diversions. Not me. Not most homesteaders. We're working, and thinking, and living... and enjoying every minute of it... beyond the sidewalks.

68. August 1978

Hard...and soft...

I savor the aroma of freshly turned earth, of new-mown hay, of growing tomato plants. I love my animals. I appreciate the home-produced food I eat, and I get great pleasure from the birds singing in my fencerows, from a gentle rain, and from the wind on my face.

But none of these are my real reason for living beyond the sidewalks.

The real reason is a special feeling and a special way of thinking that I, at least, can find only in the countryside. The animals, the views, the special sounds and the special silences are all a part of it, but they're really only the wrapping on the package.

The package itself is something that's all but impossible to describe to those who don't experience it for themselves. It's a sixth sense that is fertilized by a peculiar type of homestead awareness and drowned out in a mechanized, impersonal setting.

This picture *(of a huge, rough, ancient glacial boulder, with a fragile fern growing out of a crevice)* has been used many times before, because to me, it carries a special message — about homesteading. There are no cows in it, no fences, not even a cultivated plant. Just a rock, and a fern.

But the rock is very old, it's very hard, it's durable. It will probably be in the same location where it has lain for thousands of years, thousands of years in the future, perhaps even after all traces of humanity have vanished from the Earth.

The fern, on the other hand, is very young and very fragile. The tender fronds will not last more than a few months.

And yet, the lasting rock and the fleeting fern go together. Their dissimilarity is not jarring, but harmonious. They are "nature," both are important, and the two together are more than either one alone.

Modern, mechanized, mercenary man would say that because the stone is substantial it "counts," while the fragile, ephemeral fern is easily destroyed and has little value, and there is no connection between the two. A sixth sense that could be developed by an awareness of such contrasts is dulled by too many human artifacts and perhaps even by too much human contact.

Although some people who have known me well would disagree, I consider myself a very sensitive fellow. I can cut the throat of a 200-pound hog or a half-ton steer without much hesitation... but not without deep feelings. And with the stench of blood and guts barely washed away, I can cup a fluffy little chick in my hands and delight in its life and its weightlessness with the same kind of sensitivity.

It's not easy to be sensitive in an impersonal society or a mechanized world. Psychiatrists are making a lot of money from those who try and fail, they're probably making even more from those who don't even dare to try, but they're making the most from those who are sensitive about the wrong things and in the wrong way.

This is one part of homesteading that is so difficult to talk about because so few "normal" people can appreciate or understand what it really means. How, the coarsest among them say, can you bear to take an animal you've raised from birth out behind the barn and clunk it in the head? How can the same person who delights in the fluffy weightlessness of a chick or the helplessness of a newborn lamb or the squeaky-clean innocence of a pink piglet nonchalantly butcher it a few months later?

Or, more subtly, they can't understand how a grizzled old tiller of the soil can shield his leathery face with a gnarled hand to observe a sunset and actually feel a flame of poetry rise up in his breast.

The strange thing is, when you begin to understand, it becomes even more subtle. How, you ask yourself, can you get as much satisfaction from the sweat, the muscular strain, the scratches and the dust and the heat encountered in baling hay, as you do from pausing on the hill behind the house that evening listening to the night songs of the birds and the chorus of the frogs as night envelops the land?

Ah, but there's the answer.
It's an awareness. Sensitivity to things unsensed by less finely tuned individuals. Almost a sixth sense that has been lost by those who live in the world of plastic and neon and automation.

Nature is full of opposites that are all part of the same mystery. Nature is hard, and soft; immense and miniscule. There are thunderstorms and tornadoes and the crashing waves of the sea... and there is goose down and spider webs and butterfly's wings. There are entire galaxies beyond the range of our telescopes, and bacteria that live only in the guts of tiny insects.

And there are such unexplained natural forces as electricity, which can be a jarring thunderbolt or a mere trickle from a distant star. And love.

People who are closely tied to things mechanical, to impersonal relationships (and that includes food and sustenance as well as people) find this hard to figure. They just can't see how a thing can be hard, yet soft. True farmers can't explain it... but they don't have to. Most city people are too insensitive to notice any of it.

But the homesteader, the Earth-child, neither farmer nor city-dweller yet both farmer and city-dweller... the homesteader knows. The homesteader can carry this sensitivity far from the fields and paddocks that spawn it, to the offices and factories and computer rooms, to the shops and classrooms, wherever it is that homesteaders spend their hours at bread labor. Thus, unobtrusively, homesteaders continue to change the world for the better.

We aren't out here just for the fresh milk and meat and eggs and vegetables. We earn rewards most people don't even know exist, unless, like us, they're beyond the sidewalks.

69. September 1978

Just wait 'til NEXT year!

September is the season of maturity, in the countryside. The fields and gardens are ripening, over the hill, nearing the end. But more than that, it's the time of the year the countrysider can see his mistakes, knowing it's too late to do anything about them, but resolving to improve next time.

It's funny, but no matter how old we get, how experienced we become — no matter how many mistakes we make and vow never to make again — we can always wish we'd done things a little bit differently.

When you're dealing with a human lifetime, all of this can be pretty gruesome, but when you're dealing with the annual cycle of the countryside, hope springs eternal. We can always say, with both enthusiasm and conviction, "Just wait 'till *next* year."

My kids caught on to that at an early age. I vividly recall them, even as preschoolers, hearing me say "Just wait until *next* year," and saying, "Aw Dad, you said that last year."

Yes I did. I say it every year. And every year, I mean it. It's one of the neatest things about being a countrysider. Maybe nothing is ever perfect, but there's always hope.

To tell the truth, I didn't make very many mistakes this year. That's because the only people who don't make very many mistakes are those who don't do anything, and I didn't do much of anything.

Oh, it wasn't my fault, of course. People who don't do anything always have excuses. I have some dandies.

With the weather the way it was last fall, I didn't get any of the winter grains that are so important in my overall farm plan planted. That meant I had more than usual to do this spring. But then we had a very late spring, and since my main crops are spring small grains... and I should have planted more than usual because of the bare ground where the winter grains should have been planted... I got hopelessly behind.

Then I fell and hurt my back. Hefting tons of organic fertilizers and 50-pound bags of seed and jostling along on a tractor didn't make it any better, and I didn't put in the 20-hour days farmers ought to put in when they're behind.

And then it rained. And it rained and it rained. The boys cultivated one field of corn, but too late, and under less than ideal conditions. The weeds grew as fast as the corn. First crop hay was cut, and rained on, and rained on again, and the second crop grew right up through it so that raking the black stems was something like combing bubble gum out of your beard. And of course, the nutritional value was about the same as feeding animals damaged copies of COUNTRYSIDE, staples and all.

So then, when my midsummer crops of buckwheat and sudan grass were supposed to be planted, I was behind fitting the fields for those, too. And with all the rain, the weeds in the barley made combining a nightmare, and the green weed seeds made the barley heat up in the bin. So I said the heck with it, instead of running to catch up. I'll just skip ahead and do my fall plowing early.

So while 1978 was a disaster, now I'm right back on schedule, and I can say with firm conviction, "Just wait 'til next year."

I've always felt that my diversification helped me. We've always had pigs, we usually have a few cows around, and until very recently (when the market went up) we've had sheep. (I seem to have the knack for getting into things a few years before the time is ripe and giving up at the time I should be getting in.) I raise winter wheat and rye to feed the hogs in case the corn is hit by blight or drought or an early frost, and I grow a little corn in case the winter wheat winterkills. This last year, none of that helped much.

But it was a fantastic year for homesteading.

The gardens grew lush and prolific. The fencerow foraging produced as much as growing domestic berries and fruits would have. When it was too wet to do field work, I could pay more attention to the more intensively farmed homestead. Our root cellar and cupboards will be full.

So even though the farming operation was a disaster, we won't starve, and we won't have to eat store-bought junk. We'll have a hog fattened on comfrey and goat milk, and beef, and plenty of potatoes and beans and tomatoes and carrots, and so far as I'm concerned, if you can have bacon for breakfast and beans for lunch and potatoes for dinner what can you complain about?

I'd love to be a farmer. And I still think I might make it, if the price of oil goes high enough that my kind of farming begins to make economic sense and when the vulture of chemical farming comes home to roost and if my back holds out.

But homesteading is something else altogether. You have more control, even in adverse weather, and it has more meaning, and with mounting inflation it only becomes more profitable.

Trying to balance both of them is a challenge, I admit, but I love it. And the best part is, while I love it now, I can always say just wait 'til next year, when it'll be even better.

Beyond the sidewalks, of course.

70. October 1978

When the new and different is old and familiar

We've moved, finally, and I could fill pages and pages with "news and views from the Countryside homestead." Everything is new and different.

It's true that we're less than half a mile down the road from the old place, on land we've owned and worked for several years... and the new barn is twice as old and four times as rickety as the old barn... but you know what I mean. A different frame for the sunrise. Different shadows. Different birds and weeds and smells and sounds. Moving half a mile is little different from moving a thousand miles.

Much of what's new belongs in the hard and practical part of this magazine, but alas, nothing is finished enough to report on. The tower for the wind electric converter is up, but the blades are in the garage and the generator and synchronous inverter still aren't here, even though they were ordered a full year ago. The root cellar isn't finished either, nor the summer kitchen or the greenhouse. In fact, the geodesic dome home itself is still a long way from completion.

Of course, life goes on, whether plans are put into action or not, whether dreams are fulfilled or only frustrated.

Our horse had been confined to a barren, paved barnyard ever since the pasture fence became hopeless. He was ridden to the new place, and turned onto a lovely, lush pasture.

The minute we left him alone, he jumped the fence and ran back to the concrete where he stood, waiting to get in.

How human of him, to become so accustomed to purgatory that heaven becomes hell.

Maybe he was just lonesome. He was the first animal to be brought over. We left him in the barnyard and moved the goats, and then the cow. None of them will stay in the pasture either.

But there really isn't anything for them to destroy, at this point. They don't wander far, so I've been letting them have the run of the place. They're living in "temporary" quarters that seem to be the mark of every normal homestead, no matter how long we've had to make the temporary permanent, and they spend most of their time lying in that shed.

But when the goats go out to browse, the cow follows. She obviously thinks she's one of them.

The pigs were confined to the barn. When they broke out, they headed for the garden as quickly as if they'd been provided with road maps. If I don't have time to repair an entire pasture fence, at least I made sure those hogs stay in the barn.

I used to take walks around the farm with the dog. Now, we're accompanied by the goats and the cow. As I check the progress of the corn and the buckwheat, the hickory nuts and the wild plums, the animals trot along, sometimes ahead of me, sometimes behind. When I stop, they stop, and grab mouthsful of grass.

But the part that seems most important to me is when I take a long break at one of the mulberry trees to fill up on the juicy black fruit, getting my fingers stained purple. Somehow, it seems significant that when the small herd of goats is stripping leaves from the box elder and nipping the heads off Johnson grass, the goatherder is browsing the mulberry tree. It's one of those things, one of the simple things, that could be held under a magnifying glass to give us a glimpse of much larger events and more complex processes.

Whether events and surroundings are new and different, or old and familiar, there is always occasion for such moments of pleasure, beyond the sidewalks.

71. November 1978

Moving off the homestead, fiddling on the roof

I used to wonder what it would be like when I no longer worked the old homestead.

It was easy to imagine future generations honoring me for the wholesome fresh fruit they enjoyed, thanks to my foresight and industry. Surely someone, someday, would appreciate the mellow soil I left as a legacy — fertile, full of life, and eager to produce.

My moldering carcass would be forgotten, but at least no one would curse my bones for leaving behind a barren desert, depleted by over-cropping and sterilized by biocides.

When we bought the homestead, it had been a farm, plowed right up to the doorstep, the old apple trees ripped out, the hillside pastures plowed and planted to king corn. We shoved the fields back from the doorstep like the pioneers shoved back the wilderness. We made a garden. We limed, and spread compost. We planted shade trees and fruit trees and nuts, and even a windbreak. We planted bramble fruits and rhubarb and horseradish and asparagus, we set up crop rotations, and reforested the woodlot. We used green manure as if it were our major crop... and it was.

And the Earth responded.

The earthworms came back, unfettered by biocides, and well-fed by tillage practices and organic fertilization. The tilth improved. The soil came alive again.

Then we moved down the road to the "back 80" and the old homestead had outlived its usefulness. And, through one of those crazy quirks you never can plan on, without a realtor, without even advertising, without even intending to, we sold the place.

There was a lot to think about as I packed up my belongings, just as there's a lot to think about when cleaning the hog pen. But this wasn't so much cleaning the Aegean stables as it was cleaning a cosmic attic.

There was COUNTRYSIDE'S old office, in the shed behind the barn, with boxes of letters and artifacts that had lain untouched for years. A fat possum was asleep under one of the boxes, in fact.

There was the "bunny barn," with the now empty cages and feeders and nest boxes piled up along one wall. As I loaded them onto the pickup, I could see Anne-marie scooping feed to the rabbits, scolding the naughty ones who spilled it as fast as she dished it out, and I couldn't help but wonder what she thought of her homestead experience, in her city job and apartment a thousand miles away.

As I stowed away the feeder and nests from the henhouse, I fondly recalled when Dave was in charge of the chickens and could barely handle a full waterer. Today he's, I don't know, about 6'6" and 190 lbs., and could care less about chickens, or anything else on the homestead.

There was an old milking machine in the lower shed. We never used it, because Steve did all the milking by hand, faithfully, and with dedication, for years. I thought he might want to get into dairying on a small scale, so when I got a chance to pick up the machine for a song, I grabbed it.

Steve, also taller and heavier and stronger than I am, hasn't milked for years except when the old man is out of town, and he doesn't seem to miss it.

I gathered up the farrowing crates, and John, the youngest, came to mind. I remember him as a baby in the goat shed, for some unfathomable reason, calling the goats "horsies." No, he was told, those are goats. "Horsie gopes," he said, and that was a family name for the goats for years afterward. But John never really came of age on the homestead, or the farm, until he discovered he could take care of the young pigs.

While I was moving out, the new owner was moving in.

He seemed interested in my organic methods, but he didn't really want my comfrey, my Jerusalem artichokes, my horseradish or my berries. And he thought fruit trees were a waste of time because you had to spray them too often and he could buy apples and pears and cherries and plums more cheaply than he could produce them. In fact, as it turned out, I could dig out what I wanted, because he intended to plow up to the doorstep, again.

It didn't really hit me until I was down in the machine shed loading up the fanning mill, the hammermill, the horse harness and plow and other assorted equipment. The big tractor roared behind the barn above me. I tried to tune it out, although I knew what was happening. Just from the sounds, the voices, I could see the logging chain wrapped around the tree, the powerful John Deere diesel take up the slack...

And then the wrenching sound of the tree being torn out by its roots touched my soul. In that instant I could see the soil being assaulted with acidulated fertilizers, sprayed with biocides, plowed to the doorstep. I slammed up the tailgate and drove out the back way.

As I calmed down, I felt like fiddling on the roof.

Then, as I unloaded my possessions at the new homestead, I couldn't keep my gaze from wandering up to that barren spot on the hill...

That's where I'm going to plant new fruit trees, and asparagus, and comfrey, beyond the sidewalks.

72. December 1978

Fall plowing

On crisp, clear evenings of autumn when the harvest moon hangs red in the sky like a Chinese lantern, I rush through chores and sometimes foist them off on the rest of the family entirely. When the geese fly south and the dry corn leaves rustle in the moonlight like palm fronds along a tropical beach, there's magic in the air. I'm powerless to resist. It's time for fall plowing.

As I haul my desk-bound bones up to the tractor seat and turn the key, the engine roars to life and the fatigue of a full day's work in an office falls away like the cocoon of a butterfly in spring. I'm a new man, ready to attack my second career with as much ambition and excitement as I approached the first, 12 hours ago.

This isn't homesteading, of course. Homesteading is milking goats and gathering the eggs, feeding the hog and the sheep and the rabbits and the steer, digging potatoes and churning butter and splitting firewood. Going out to plow when the moon is rising is a farming ritual. And yet the experiences and the emotions are homestead ones.

The air is already chilly, and I jerk the hood of my sweatshirt over my head. I pull on the leather gloves, activate the hydraulic ram to raise the plow, ease the tractor into gear, and move out to the field.

The first few rounds demand attention... watching gauges, setting a course, letting the engine warm up, getting the feel of the machine again. But then it falls into a routine, and becomes almost boring. I get time to think.

M aybe that's one reason I love night plowing.
You get time to think, without interruptions, and while still performing a useful service even beyond the thinking. Better yet, your thoughts are focused. Your whole universe is delineated by the glare of tractor lights a few rods before and behind you, and the rest of the dark world doesn't even exist.

But it's more than that. It's... maybe it's the solitude. That's a commodity that's far too rare for most of us, and often confused with loneliness. People who are parents, or who work with other people, or worse yet who work with the public, have a great, often unrecognized need for solitude. Night plowing provides that. I can't be interrupted by a phone call or a problem or even by what might be happening beyond the constricted beam of my headlights.

The field of vision may be narrow, but it's constantly changing as the tractor toils through the field. Occasionally the plow hits a rock, striking sparks and leaping from the soil, and that creates a little excitement and flow of adrenaline. Sometimes it plugs up with trash, forcing me off the tractor to shove the massed sod and stalks out of the way. Then comes the end of the field, where raising the plow, turning, finding the return path, and lowering the plow to the proper depth at just the right place are always enough to keep you awake.

But my attention is certainly focused on a very narrow track, and that keeps my mind from wandering and being distracted.

Oh yeah, I can't help but think of the indignant letters I get about "plowing" from people who've read "Plowman's Folly" but who've never turned a furrow... or who never read Faulkner's sequel... or don't know a chisel plow from a drill press. But about that time my headlights pick up the eyes of a small herd of deer, that stands transfixed until I approach too uncomfortably close. Then they act confused and mill about, and finally at the last moment bound away into the darkness.

When the field is finished (I prefer small fields) I pull back the hydraulic lever to raise the plow, throttle down, throw in the clutch, and shove the tractor into high gear. The temperature gauge is high, the fuel gauge is low, the fiercely twinkling stars seem to be raining down chill on the land, and I'm tired. My leather gloved hand eases the throttle forward as my left foot eases up on the clutch, and as the tractor takes off in high gear, a spray of fresh earth catapults from the tires.

As I drive back to the house, chill and fatigue set in. I'll get up in the morning, milk the goats and do the other homestead chores, and show up at the office for another day of downtown problems and frustrations.

But one of the reasons I'll be able to muddle through is, I've found a few hours of solitude, beyond the sidewalks.

Part IX: 1979

Inflation: 11.2%; Year-end DJIA: 838; Federal Reserve interest rate: 15.25%; Average annual income: $17,500; Gas/gal: 86¢; Three Mile Island nuclear accident; Sony Walkman introduced ($200); Snowboard invented

73. January 1979

Planning the New Year on the homestead

January is one of my favorite months. That's when I'm most successful at farming and homesteading.

The goats may be dry, the hens not laying very well, and the frozen water in the barn becoming wearisome, but none of that matters. January is the month for planning. Since no one plans for anything less than perfection, in January the place is as perfect as it's ever going to be.

My desk is cluttered with the tools for planning. There are seed catalogs, chick catalogs, soil test results, maps of the farm, plans for crop rotations, reams of scribbled notes and lists of things to be done "when the weather breaks."

I feel like a first-time homesteader all over again. While I groan at the price of fencing, in my mind's eye I can see the pasture enclosed by straight, tight fences, the sheep grazing contently in belly-high grass without even trying to break out. As I make a list of machinery repairs to take care of, I'm convinced that a new bolt here and a little welding there will keep everything rolling smoothly through the season, with no downtime. As I make up the garden seed order, I'm not buying packets of seeds: I'm buying rows of lush vegetables, in bountiful variety, with neither too much nor too little of anything.

Don't tell me it's all a dream. Reality will return soon enough. Let me enjoy this vision of perfection while I can.

Planning is not only a great deal of fun. It's perhaps one of the most important things we homesteaders do.

One very important part of planning is setting goals. Not only do I want to know where I'm going, but *why*.

In January, I have the time and the inclination to lay this yardstick alongside everything I do or intend to do. It's a way of trying everything on paper (or in my head) before wasting time and money and energy on something that could be done better... or perhaps shouldn't be done at all. It often involves inspecting not only the methods, but the goals themselves.

One of my primary goals is soil improvement. To this end, crop rotations are essential. Hay is crucial in the crop rotation. But hogs, which have been my main enterprise, don't require much hay. Selling hay isn't in accord with my goal of soil improvement. Therefore I need more cows, or sheep, or goats, to make use of the hay. The options are worked out, mulled over, rearranged, and inspected again from yet another angle. What are the market possibilities for each, how can I make the best use of my resources (including facilities and experience), what fits in best with my lifestyle and personal inclinations?

Everything is examined in the same way. Should I plant corn as a feed grain, or should I plant barley? Do I really want to devote that much of the garden to potatoes? What's the sense of keeping so many goats? Why do I bother with the homestead at all... or why do I insist on being a farmer?

I'm the only one who can make those decisions. Not only does no one else have quite the same goals, experiences, resources and inclinations as I do: I'm the one who has to make the investment in time and labor and cash. I'm the recipient of whatever losses or rewards result. A county agent or farm magazine might assume I should plant corn, because there's more money in corn than in other crops in this area. Most farmers choose corn over, say, barley.

But I don't want to use commercial fertilizers or pesticides — my soil improvement goal again — and barley does better without these than corn does. I can sow clover with the barley, and give soil improvement another boost. Since barley is planted and harvested before corn, I can spread out my workload and manage to farm and still publish a magazine. The result is a very personal decision, stemming from a great deal of thought and consideration.

Or, one homesteader might tell me homesteading is merely a means of beating inflation. Another maintains that it's spiritually uplifting and good exercise and fun, but doesn't really pay. Yet another might advise me that the way the world is going to pot, homesteading is a matter of survival. My approach to the homestead might well depend on which line of thinking I follow. But more likely, I have to decide not which line to believe — there's a kernel of truth in nearly everything and even a stopped clock is right twice a day — but I have to decide which facets are most important to me, based on my personal experience and convictions. And to make certain they truly are important, I have to know *why.*

Homesteaders and small farmers are a wondrously diverse lot. We range from hobbyists to money-grubbers; some of us go after stark practicality, others pursue only lofty ideals; some of us are only playing, while others of us are deadly serious.

Most of us are in more than one category. For us, there are no hard and fast rules, because we're operating in uncharted, untamed, lawless wilderness. As a result, planning — thinking — is far more important than it would be if we had some simple goal, such as maximum financial gain, or maximum enjoyment from gardening or livestock production. Not only is it easier to plan the simple goals, but there are plenty of precedents, and we could profit from the experiences of others.

Homestead planning is harder. There are few guidelines, limited sources of specific help, no pat formulas.

Perhaps, as so many of the things that have concerned homesteaders for the past decade or so come to crisis points — things like the environment, the food supply, energy and the economy — the task will become more clear-cut and more help will become available. In some ways this is already happening.

But for now we're on our own, battling a wilderness that's just as much a frontier as the one encountered by the early homesteaders from whom we take our name.

And frankly, for those (like me) who feel there's something unsettling about womb to tomb programmed living such as so many seem bent on achieving today, all of this is one of the key satisfactions of living beyond the sidewalks.

74. February, 1979

Belangers get a vacation

Vacations are supposed to relax you, get your mind off your troubles, and let you go back to the routine of daily living refreshed and enthusiastic. Everyone needs a vacation once in a while. But there are different kinds of vacations.

I'm not much on travel: rather, like Thoreau, I prefer to travel in my own backyard. So when Diane suggested that we spend a few weeks with our daughter in Florida, I told her to give me a call when she got there.

The first few days she and John were gone were relatively normal. In addition to doing the regular chores and the regular office work, I did the household tasks that are usually the others' responsibilities: bringing in firewood, feeding the cats and dogs, and all the rest. I'd been looking forward to spending some time alone, but it looked like I wouldn't get time to do anything I'd planned on doing.

But then, late in the afternoon a vicious wind kicked up from the east, the kind that makes even our airtight wood burning stove roar.

While I was doing chores I foolishly left a walk-through barn door open and a gust of wind caught it and slammed it closed with such force that the window broke. It also wedged it farther into the frame than it was supposed to go, and I couldn't open it. I had a moment of claustrophobia when I realized that all the other exits were secured from the outside. But when I gave up struggling with the door and started thinking, I found a board, and using it as a lever, pried the door open.

It wasn't snowing hard, but what there was stung my face like icy needles. Once back at the house, I spent a pleasant evening in front of the fire.

The next morning the east-west section of the driveway was swept almost clear, but the north-south part was piled high with drifted snow. After chores, I got out the tractor with the snow blade, and went to work.

The snow was too deep for casual scraping. I had to raise the blade, back into the drift, and haul it off bit by bit. Progress was slow. And then I lost a pin from the three-point hitch and the blade came off and I had to mess around with repair work. And when I finally did get the drive cleared, the township plow still hadn't been down our road. So I did office work at home.

Later in the afternoon it started snowing again. When I went to do chores that night the wind had stopped, but huge, fluffy flakes of snow were falling. In the dark, I couldn't see them, but they tickled my face.

I must tell you something about how I do chores. When I found the water line to the barn was broken, I contacted a plumber to replace it. He didn't make it before the ground froze. So I haul water, two buckets at a time, for 12 goats, a horse, 20 sheep, one cow, and seven very thirsty hogs. The few chickens we have seem to fend for themselves, and thank goodness we're temporarily out of rabbits.

Given that situation, I usually don't have time to just sit in the barn and enjoy the animals, the aroma of fresh barley straw, or the sound of hay being munched. I observe the animals, of course: that's one of the most important factors in livestock management — to see who's in heat or who isn't eating or who just isn't acting quite right. But I don't usually have time to *enjoy* them.

But with nothing else to do, nowhere to go, not even anyone to talk to, I sat in the barn, a black cat rubbing against my leg, the dog lying patiently at my feet. Then I strolled to each stall and pen, usually being nuzzled by one creature or another. When I scratched the most spoiled sow behind the ears, she closed her eyes and grunted with pleasure, and when I moved away she protested indignantly and reached her head up to my hand again.

After awhile, enough is enough. I turned off the lights, closed the door, and trudged back up to the dark and empty house through thickly falling snow.

I had never noticed that the house had a presence, almost a personality. But that night it seemed unusually quiet and empty and, somehow, lonely. I turned on the radio to dispel some of the gloom. The weather forecaster called the storm "a biggie."

I ran through the storm checklist as routinely as I touch my pocket to make certain my Buck knife is still there. The woodbox was full, the lamp filled with kerosene and the wick trimmed. Groceries are never a problem: I could eat well for months without leaving the house. If the need arose, I could get water from the old well with a bucket on a rope.

I spent another pleasant, quiet evening, reading things I usually "don't have time for," making plans and dreaming dreams that on other evenings get set aside in the face of more urgent matters.

B y morning, the snow had stopped. But something was different. As I went through the livestock routine again, I found myself thinking about different topics than usual, and in a subtly different way. It was as if all the petty day-to-day problems that usually hang over me were muffled by the snow, like the carrots under the mulch in the garden. It was as if the aloneness — as distinguished from loneliness — had scraped down to the core of life, peeling back the rough bark of petty detail and revealing what is truly timeless and beautiful.

The feeling of refreshment and rejuvenation took me by surprise. I seldom find it when I purposely seek it — Sunday afternoon walks, in escapist reading or other relaxation, or on vacations. But now, it had found me.

The forecast called for another foot of snow to come and a temperature of 20 below, so there was no point in even trying to plow the driveway again. There was no place to go anyway, and that pleased

238

me. I went back to the typewriter with more enthusiasm than I had been able to muster in months.

It was a renewing experience. A great vacation. And I learned, once again, that we don't have to search for whatever it is the human spirit longs for by looking to other places or even other people. We can usually find what we need in our own backyards, in ourselves, beyond the sidewalks.

75. March 1979

Let the politicians and scientists debate: Homesteaders learn the truth by living it.

I could feel it on the way down to the barn after supper. Tonight was the night to write *Beyond the Sidewalks.*

This monthly chore doesn't show up on my calendar. It's not part of any rigid schedule. Whenever I try that, I end up tossing out what I write.

I have to feel it. I have to know when it's time, like the old farmer who knows when it's time to plant corn, or butcher the hog, or pluck the geese.

There's nothing magical about any of it. It's when a set number of factors fall into place to put everything together and give the signal. Maybe neither I nor the old farmer really know what those factors are, or how they fit together, but we never miss the signal.

As I toss bales of hay from the mow to the barn floor below, I wonder what to write about. While the signals are unmistakable, they never lay out the details. They never do the work for you, or make it easy. The usual topics — plowing a field or butchering a pig... or throwing down hay — don't seem sufficient, tonight. There must be something else.

I drop through the hay chute and pick up the bales for the last time. I remember planting this alfalfa, and mowing it and raking it. It was hauled off the baler onto the wagon, hefted from the wagon into the mow, tossed from the mow to the barn floor, and now finally from the floor into the mangers, where it will be turned into meat, wool, and milk.

If I have the urge to write *Beyond,* there must be something there to share: it hasn't failed me in well over a hundred months. But what is it?

Even when *Beyond* is about burying a dead dog, it says a lot more, at least for those who have ears to hear. The complexity of what I feel... of what I'm compelled to share... is too much to lay out in stark, rational terms. Only a poet could put those emotions into words, and I don't have the skill, so I can only speak of what I know best.

My thoughts as I check the sheep jostling for position at the hay manger tonight are obviously influenced by what concerns me during the day. But what concerns me during the day is influenced by what I think of as I watch the sheep... and by what I've been thinking about all my life. And tonight, I can't tell if I've reached another cusp, or if the world has reached another cusp and I'm being swept along with it.

I suspect the latter. And I'm not resisting, because I've been waiting for it, for a long, long time.

The chores done, I hunker down in the goat pen. Natasha, the old lady of the herd, comes to rub against me, and we ruminate together, each in our own way.

She was on the cover of the old *Dairy Goat Guide* once, before its reincarnation, so you know she's been around awhile. I suddenly recall that that's her being born in the pictures in *Homesteaders' Handbook to Raising Small Livestock,* and that dates her too. It seems like I wrote that book ages ago.

It's hard to think of Natasha as being old. It's hard to think of me as getting old, too.

What's it all about? What have I learned, or really shared? Have my "between the lines" kind of communications really done any good, or should I have devoted my time to my own homestead instead? Should I have taken the advantages when I had them to push for a mass circulation magazine so I could at least touch the minds and spirits of millions of others?

Natasha turns to butt a young doe away from a wisp of alfalfa, mouths it, and spits it out. Then she goes to a corner and lies down.

Does any of it really matter?

I know who, and what, and where I am. I know where the politicians and economists and journalists are coming from. I know what it's like to be a farmer and live in a world apart from all of them.

And I know it doesn't do any good to write about it, straight out. A star athlete or a sex idol could change more minds than I could, speaking honestly.

But even so, I decide as I clamber over the fence, I can't just quit. I can't just settle back and concern myself with my own homestead, knowing I'm right and few others care. I refuse to deal only with the mechanics of homesteading. Maybe I can't just come out and say what homesteading really means to me, but I can try to convey what I feel in more simple terms.

I can speak of my dead dog, or what goes on in my mind when I plow in the glare of a harvest moon and the tractor headlights, and the love Natasha shares with me. While it won't attract the masses, or maybe even change anyone's mind, it's the best I can do. It's also the least I can do.

240

The animals are settling down as I make my way to the barn door. I give them one more glance, and switch off the lights. I close the door, and my footsteps crunch loudly in the snow as I make my way back up to the house, the dogs at my heels.

I know it's time to go from the dark and cold outside, into the warm and light of the house, and write my column. But what do I say? How do I put into words what it means to me to live beyond the sidewalks?

76. April 1979

Some things are more important than others...

When I turn into the first field to be seeded to oats, I really don't have much time to think about the things most journalists consider important. There is too much to do. Farmers only pay attention to important things, I tell myself.

No matter how you tune an old grain drill in anticipation of the first decent day for planting, there are always field adjustments. I had checked it over, cleaned it, greased it, replaced a worn roller chain, and calibrated it by "planting" a few handsful of seed in the driveway.

But once in the field it didn't take long to discover that one fertilizer hopper wasn't emptying. It took awhile to locate the problem and correct it, and then a seed tube on the grass seeder attachment, which was planting my green manure clover, fell off and got smashed under a coulter. With some luck, I found it and managed to bend it back into more or less serviceable shape.

And then, after a few trips across the field, there was the transfer of seed and fertilizer from the pickup to the drill. I don't like hurrying, usually, but it doesn't pay to turn off a hot tractor for such a brief spell and I don't want to waste fuel with the tractor idling. So I hurry.

Then, as the morning wears on and the tracks of the drill begin to give the field an appearance of satisfying progress... and I make a few trips across the field with nothing going wrong... I begin to relax. There's something about being on a small tractor in a fresh spring field, with a south breeze on your face and the warm sun falling on your winter-pale arms, and the field mice and moles scurrying safely out of the way and the returning redwing blackbirds hovering about the rig like gulls around a garbage scow.

Even then I don't think about unimportant things. Maybe the bouncing shakes it out of me. Maybe I'm seduced by the spring air, or perhaps the greening buds of the trees in the fencerow are too soothing. Whatever the reason, not once do I think of Jimmy Carter, or China or the Middle East.

What's important?

Thoughts of old friends, journalists I have known, cross my mind. Dave is an executive editor on a big city newspaper. I recall he won some award for his political reporting not long ago. Important stuff.

Sue, according to the alumni newspaper, is working out of London with a wire service now.

Al and I worked on a newspaper and several magazines together over the years, and now he has an important position in Washington, D.C.

Me? I'm planting oats.

What's important? What, according to the definition, is "marked by significant worth or consequence?"

It occurs to me that maybe I'm just not very ambitious. I never really thought of working for a wire service, or a metropolitan daily, or a big magazine. I only went to college because I figured I couldn't get a start in farming, and my second choice was being editor of a small-town weekly newspaper. While it doesn't seem like a very important goal, I never even got that far. After working on big newspapers and big magazines, I decided it would be just as easy to break into farming as it would be to have my own weekly newspaper, so why settle for second choice?

Eventually the truck is too far away from my work for efficiency, so I turn off the tractor engine, walk back to get the truck, and move it down the field. When I park, the absence of mechanical sounds leaves me quivering in withdrawal: it's time to take a break.

There are little droplets of moisture in the plastic bag of homemade cookies Diane handed me as I left the house, and which I left on the seat of the truck. The water in the canteen isn't as cold as when it came from the well. I sit on the tailgate and wriggle my back to make a beanbag chair of oats, and get attuned to the sound of spring while I munch cookies.

What's important? One of my old buddies wanted to be a sports writer. Made it, too.

Whenever I think of what's truly marked by significant worth or consequence, I think of that vision of Spaceship Earth hanging in the void.

Maybe some people see that picture and try to discern political or religious boundaries, or economic factors, or maybe even world championships in athletics. Or maybe a science writer or an ag journalist sees the challenge of feeding four billion-plus people with those finite resources.

I share some of those concerns, of course, because I'm a crew member of that spaceship, and I've spent all of my working life as a journalist, as well as being a homesteader and a farmer. But from where I sit, none of it seems to be of primary importance. On the contrary, all of these seem to spring from something else... something more primal.

As I get back up on the tractor, I sense what it is. As I course back and forth across the field, intent on neither leaving gaps between rows or overlapping, I feel what's important.

I'm attuned, as I'm sure none of my successful old friends could be, to the thunderous proclamation of Life in the gossamer disguise of Spring. I can see, if only for a fleeting moment, that what's truly important has something to do with Life, and the interrelationships of Life, and the Source of that Life which encompasses all living creatures.

Some of those old friends, who are now in big-time ag journalism, tell me that organic farming is too full of mysticism to suit them. They want scientific proof and dollars-and-cents facts.

I can give them some — after all, I am a journalist, still. But not with a great deal of journalistic fervor. It seems too much like casting pearls before the swine. I don't have the time to waste.

I have more important things to do. Goats to milk. A garden to tend. Sheep and hogs to care for. Oats to plant, beyond the sidewalks.

77. May 1979

Letting the world catch up...

As I lock the office door and head for the pickup, the daylight is startling. Just a short while ago, it seems, it was dark at quitting time.

The air is balmy and the Wincharger atop the COUNTRYSIDE roof is spinning lazily. After spending so many hours poring over the stack of letters from readers and immersing myself in their visions of the future, I feel I've been in some august hall listening to ringing rhetoric and debate. The fresh air and the greening prairie grasses and the blossoming fruit trees outside the office seem like another world.

I've become totally engrossed in how all those readers — people I feel I know as friends — regard the future. But after all, it *is* one of my favorite topics, the reason I got into COUNTRYSIDE in the first place and certainly one of the main reasons I stay with it.

If I turn right out of the parking lot, it's 3.0 miles home. If I turn left, it's 3.1 miles. Both roads trail through the marsh, which is especially soothing this time of the year. I turn right.

I've been in business for myself for 18 years. When I started, a first class stamp was 3¢. Sometimes it seems like everything else has changed as much as the cost of postage. The very fabric of the world itself has changed. Dramatically.

That doesn't disturb me at all. On the contrary, I've been anticipating it. I've often wondered why it was taking so long. I'm ready not only to accept it, but to welcome it with a sense of relief.

I knew, 18 years ago as an editor, and longer ago than that as a person, that the old order was changing and *should* change. I figured I had the insight and abilities and training to be a journalistic midwife at the birth of the new age. It seemed like a worthy goal. I wasn't that sure of myself all the time, especially when I was put down as being naive or a "pop philosopher." I've never been inclined to be very aggressive anyway, and it made sense to stay cool, attract what audience I could by talking about rabbits and goats and pigs, and slip in the important ideas whenever it wasn't too jarring.

For 18 years I've made an honest living, which was more than I could have done had I said what was really on my mind. But I always felt unfulfilled.

No more. As if the daily news reports weren't enough, now I've found that at least a few people in the world can see the same things I see, and it's a great feeling.

The battered old pickup casts a long shadow as it rolls through the marsh. The water is still high, although it no longer covers the road as it did earlier in the spring. I love the marsh, its inaccessibility, its timelessness. The truck crosses the Maunesha River, passes through the marsh, climbs out of the valley, and I turn it south along the ridge. Now the marsh is spread out between me and the setting sun.

Where do I go from here? I wonder as I slow down and swerve to miss a cock pheasant standing in the middle of the narrow road. It flees, road-runner-like, without rising.

In the past, my premonitions and convictions led me to sell woodburning stoves, long before an "energy crisis" and wood's meteoric rise in popularity. When everybody else started selling them, I quit. It was no longer a service to my kind of people. Others were selling the stoves, and I could move on.

It was the same when just about every other publication in the nation started treating solar energy and wind power seriously. I'd already done it, they were doing much more than I had and they were doing it better, and it was time for me to move on.

I'm still rather proud of being the one who popularized the Victorio strainer for processing tomatoes, and I'll admit I made a lot of money while doing it, but again, when everybody from the local hardware store to Sears started selling them, I found other things to do. The important thing wasn't selling tomato machines. The important thing was that more people could quickly and easily process their homegrown produce.

Today, low-level radiation, underground housing, and many other topics we used to talk about in COUNTRYSIDE are no longer absurd. The mass magazines, and even the newspapers, have picked them up. By leaving them behind like a snake sheds its skin, I'm getting closer and closer to my real ambition.

Those physical trappings never were my primary interest, I remind myself as I slow the truck alongside one of my fall-plowed lowland fields. Even small stock, which I *did* build a reputation on and did extensive outside writing on, was never a primary interest. Sure, I've always loved animals, but there was something deeper behind it. My real interests, the reason I got involved in all of those other things in the first place, is just now coming into its own.

Maybe I am, too.

I stop the truck, get out, and walk to the field. It's drying nicely, and if the weather stays like this it should be ready for disking and planting in another day or two. I stoop to pick up a handful of earth and crumble it, and squatting, I squint into the sun just above the marsh grasses at the other end of the field.

My interest has been life itself.

That's too broad a topic to tackle head-on. Few readers would be interested, and no publisher or agent I ever dealt with would touch it with a ten-foot pole. Much better to write about rabbits and goats and windmills, and work in the truth when it seemed to fit.

But the general view of life has changed... just as the views of solar power and wood heat and all the rest have changed. I don't expect any publisher to call me tomorrow and say he's changed his mind, and wants to see a rough draft of the ultimate *Beyond the sidewalks*. They'll wait until it's a sure thing... just as they did with solar and wind, and homesteading itself.

But this time, when the time comes, I'm not stepping aside. For me, this is what it was all about. I'm heartened by the one-ness I feel with my fellow countrysiders, and if I'm lost in the shuffle on this one it won't be by choice. If my voice isn't heard then, then maybe I can consider myself a failure.

Or will I? I feel myself grinning as I stand, glance over the field, and anticipate planting it to corn. Shouldn't it be satisfaction and reward enough to know I was on the right track all along, that I wasn't really crazy after all?

I let the soil sift through my fingers. If nothing else, I ought to get a heck of a lot of credit for perseverance.

As I head back to the truck a red-tail hawk swoops low in front of me and wheels upward. The sky is still light. Maybe there's still time to do a little work in the garden.

78. June 1979

Are homesteaders elitists?
This one is, and he's proud of it!

T he right front gang of the wheel disk had broken at a weld and had been jammed back so that one of the disk blades sliced into a tire. It's not easy to find used 8:50-15 tires, to say nothing of tubes.

While I was scrounging for replacements, I had time to think about a few things that had nothing to do with tires, or fieldwork. One of the thoughts I dwelt on was the comment I've heard from a number of people recently, that we countrysiders are somehow "elitist." If I were an editor sitting in an office, I could think of half a dozen ways to answer such an accusation. Since "elite" means a socially superior group, I could say, yer durn tootin' we homesteaders are an elite, because people who live within the laws of nature just *have* to be socially superior to those who try to bend nature to their own wills. Moreover, homesteaders know what's happening in the world: doesn't that make them socially superior to those who merely insist on producing more nuclear power, or more agricultural chemicals, or more pollution?

Of course, an elite can also be defined as a powerful minority group. At first, that might seem a little ridiculous to apply to homesteaders. Us, powerful? As of today our influence in Washington, our economic clout, and our numbers, make us about as powerful as a newborn lamb.

And yet, we seem to have a power that comes from beyond us... the kind of power Victor Hugo was referring to when he said, "Greater than the tread of mighty armies is an idea whose time has come." One can resist the invasion of armies, but not the invasion of ideas. The ideas that constitute homesteading — how we regard energy, the food supply, organic agriculture, personal economics, nature — these and many others are ideas whose time has come, and it's from them that we derive our power. If that makes us elitist, so what's wrong with it?

By the time I locate a suitable tire and tube, it's raining. And by the time I get the tire changed, the disk jerry-rigged enough to drag it back to the shop to be welded, I'm soaking wet and caked with mud. And when I start the tractor, the wheels just spin, throwing up gobs of clay.

I climb down from the seat, and as I bend to unhook the hydraulic ram the diesel exhaust from the underslung muffler on the John Deere is blowing in my face. The warmth feels good on my cold, wet skin, but the fumes are noxious.

The hitch pin is buried in the mud now, and by the time I scrape away the oozing soil, locate the safety pin, pull it, and manage to knock out the hitch pin, I'm covered with slime from my toes to my neck.

I clamber back into the tractor seat once again, almost losing my footing with all of the muddy lubrication, and as I sit down I quickly learn how wet I really am. My hands are muddy, and something inside me recoils at having to get the steering wheel all crudded up. Dumb. Like not wanting to hit the rabbit you're butchering too hard, lest you hurt it.

I shove in the clutch, put the tractor in gear, lock the differential... and spin my way out of the slimey rut. Mud sprays as I hightail it out of there.

I heave a sigh of relief. If there's one thing I don't need, it's a tractor buried up to its axle in the mud.

I put the tractor in the shed and douse the engine, and stiffly move toward the house. I have the feeling Diane won't let me in.

I'm wet, and I'm cold, and tired... but I still have to do the milking, feed the sheep and hogs, and a few other chores besides. Somehow I sure don't feel very elite.

But then as my boots squish with every step and raindrops drip off the end of my nose I recall being "elite" under similar conditions before. It was constantly drilled into us marines how "elite" we were...

A rivulet of rain slides down my face, and as I absent-mindedly wipe at it with the back of my hand, I can feel the cold muddy smear get painted across my cheek.

Yes, I decide, I *am* part of an elite corps. I'm a farmer, and a homesteader, and they're both something special. If some people can't handle that, if it bothers them to think of all the poor souls who *aren't* special in the way homesteaders are, that's just too bad. I happen to be proud of it.

That's a crass attitude, I decide as I reach the house, take off my boots, and pour the water out of them. Maybe I could refine it somewhat... if I were just a little warmer, a little drier, a little less tired.

But why bother? For the moment, I like being as cruddy and exhausted as I am, and I like being special: part of an elite, if you will.

I chuckle as I wring out my socks and find myself actually feeling sorry for those who don't live beyond the sidewalks.

79. July 1979

You don't need oil for a quality life

One of the things that amazes and puzzles me as I read about the energy situation is that people invariably assume that the problem is "not enough." We have to find *more* oil, build *more* nuclear reactors, relax air quality standards and burn more coal. Why? Would life really be so bad if we cut our energy consumption, say, in half? Such an idea would be met with derision, of course, but I don't think it's that ridiculous. That's because when I was growing up, per person energy consumption in the U.S. was just half what it is today.

Power Lawn Mowers and Quality of Life

Politicians and industrialists tell us we'll all suffer if we have less energy, but I don't buy that. The simple chore of cutting the grass provides a good example.

We used a reel-type hand mower, because there wasn't any other kind. I can still hear the clickety-clack of the lawn mowers in our small town neighborhood... a far cry from the drag-strip atmosphere of lawn mowing today. They were sharpened occasionally, and oiled periodically, but that was the extent of their maintenance. Contrast that with the rope-pulling and fiddling and cussing that accompanies most lawn mowing sessions today. Gas and oil and sparkplugs add to the quality of life? You'd have a hard time proving it to me.

Unless you happened to get really dirty, Saturday was bath night. You didn't just turn on a faucet and have a tub full of hot water.

The teakettle of water boiling on the stove was poured into a shallow tub of cold water from the tap... which is why many people of my generation still take baths in two inches of water and have children who can't comprehend why there's something disturbing about taking a 20 minute hot shower every day of the week.

We didn't particularly stink, either — and that was even without the deodorants today's tv ads make us think are so crucial to our social acceptance. At least people smelled like people, and not like French whores.

The Iceman Cometh

We didn't have a refrigerator. We had an icebox. A kid who never had an iceman's horse-drawn wagon come clomping up the street on a hot July day is missing out on some of the quality of life, the way I measure it.

We would stop our games and watch the taciturn iceman as his lethal-looking pick flashed in the hot sun and split the huge block of crystal into the size ordered by the orange and black sign in the window. We could feel the icy cold even from a distance, and the sun suddenly felt hotter.

Then he'd hoist the block to his shoulder with his wicked looking tongs, and pulling the heavy quilted tarp back over the cargo on the wagon, give us a stern look which we took to mean we'd better stay away from his ice.

But as soon as he rounded the corner, our sunburned bodies couldn't stand the temptation. Cautiously at first, then more boldly, there was a scramble to find the largest slivers of clear, cold ice.

Who needed tv violence for excitement when you knew that the iceman could reappear at any moment with his long pick in his belt holster and swinging his heavy tongs? Who needed an ice-cream wagon?

Washday

Washday was wash *day*. *All* day. My mother got up early and shoveled coal into the water heater, or boiled water in a large kettle on the basement stove. (Some clothes were actually boiled in that copper kettle, stirred with a stick the size of a broom handle.) She did have an electric wringer-washer. Heavy baskets of laundry were carried up the stairs to be hung in the sun to dry. This is one area where efficiency could have been increased and labor eliminated... a solar water heater would have been appreciated, and a ground level laundry room... but it had its good points, too.

One of the first thrills of accomplishment I can remember was when I grew tall enough to take down the clothesline. Until then, that had been my father's domain, so I knew I was approaching manhood. An even greater accomplishment was being able to put *up* the clothesline, because it had to be tight enough to support the dead weight of wet clothes.

Naturally I griped about it as time wore on, but doing things you don't like to do is educational and character-building too. It's hard to see a child of today getting the same kind of experience by taking clothes out of an electric dryer.

There was no tv, of course, and the radio was something you listened to Judy Canova on after the Saturday night bath and maybe The Shadow on Sunday afternoons when you weren't visiting relatives... not something that was blaring raucous noise from every direction, 24 hours a day. I enjoy music as much as anybody, but there's something about seeing somebody with a transistor radio plastered to his ear as he walks down the street or the blare of tinny sound at a public beach that makes me quite certain that eliminating such pollution would add considerably to the quality of life.

There were no plastics in those days, few synthetics, no anhydrous ammonia fertilizer, no myriad of other products that are taken for granted today, and made from oil. But I never once had the feeling something was wrong with the quality of my life just because I didn't have access to enough fossil fuel.

We didn't have a car, but then, few others did, either. We walked to school, to church, to do the shopping. Today, high school teachers sometimes have trouble finding parking spaces at work: the students have them all, even if they could walk, even if bus service is provided. And the parking lots are larger, too.

Wisconsin alone goes through a million gallons of gas on a "good" weekend... in snowmobiles. People think nothing of using a 300 horsepower car to drive two blocks to pick up a pack of cigarettes.

What is "quality of life," anyway? Does it require hair dryers and every manner of electric kitchen appliance and electric toothbrushes and knife sharpeners and openers for tin cans and garage doors? Do we really need every corner of every room to be hot in winter and cold in summer? Is quality life denoted by motorized everything — from hedge clippers to tv antennae?

Quality in Human Terms

Once, when I was younger, an elderly but vigorous relative and I cut down a huge and ancient maple tree. We used a two-man crosscut saw. I learned how to use the saw and how to sharpen it. It took a long time — it was a very large tree — but as we worked, and as we rested, he regaled me with marvelous stories of the days when he as a boy, worked in the lumber camps of northern Wisconsin.

It was, as I said, a very large tree. But that's not why I remember it so vividly. I remember the stories, and the old man treating me as an equal.

Today, such a tree would be toppled in a fraction of the time with a chainsaw, with the kids more than likely watching so-called exciting or educational things on tv, having been warned to stay far away from the *real* excitement and education.

Let's not confuse quality with sybaritic pleasure. They aren't the same — even if you don't live beyond the sidewalks.

2014: Today, this makes me think of all our Amish neighbors and acquaintances, most of whom would chuckle over it.

80. August 1979

Back to the sidewalks — for a while

Some days it seems like half the people who write to us know all there is to know about publishing a magazine. Unfortunately, publishers aren't that knowledgeable, and we have to take time off periodically to exchange views and techniques. Most of these confabs take place in New York City.

It should come as no surprise to learn that New York is not one of my favorite places. In fact, leaving the homestead to go *anywhere* for more than a few days is a little like dying. I approach it with sadness tinged with dread, but accept it as inevitable.

Perhaps some of that is due to the extensive travelling I did just before we began homesteading in earnest: I tired of it. More likely, it's that I have no desire to pay superficial visits to other places when I'm keenly aware that I don't know half of what there is to learn from my own homestead. Or maybe it's simply a case of different strokes for different folks.

In any event, with a mid-afternoon flight, I figured I had several hours to "say goodbye to the homestead." I planned to just relax and enjoy myself for that period.

It got off to a poor start, though, when, shortly after dawn, I heard unusual noises outside the bedroom window... not unusual in that I couldn't recognize them immediately, but in that it had been a long time since the sheep had gotten out of the pasture.

My shout woke Diane. I pulled on my pants and boots fireman-style and rushed out the door. It was with as much shock as satisfaction that I watched the sheep, the goats and the cow plunge through the broken fence as I shouted some ancient animal herder's cries, and go racing back to the barn.

The fence in this particular pasture was a single strand of smooth wire. I turned off the fencer, and began to search for the break... but I couldn't find the fence at all! Every insulator from every rod post had been pulled off.

Eventually, after skirting the entire pasture, we found the wire: all tangled up in the middle of the field. It was like sorting out a quarter-mile long tangle of steel yarn.

It took a long time to straighten out, and even then we had to cut and splice several sections that were hopelessly messed up. Fortunately, we had extra insulators.

As we worked, we speculated on what possibly could have caused such havoc. Our conclusion was that the deer, which had been trampling the southern edge of the winter wheat, blundered into it.

It took an hour and a half to restring the whole thing, and by then New York was starting to look a little better to me.

Milking is always a special event when I know I'm going to be away for awhile. It's not just a chore, but a farewell, and farewells are always poignant. Similarly, the other chores take on added significance. I notice details that usually go unnoticed in the normal rush; I dawdle; I soak up every detail of the experience to carry with me back to the sidewalks, as if gripped by some mortal fear that I might never return.

Then, it's time. I put on my suit and tie, board the plane, and within a matter of hours I'm on the sidewalks of New York.

The days pass quickly. It's good — maybe it's even necessary — to meet with other people in the magazine business periodically. After all, while the information on homesteading in COUNTRYSIDE is its reason for existing, it's the paper and printing and postage and other details that make it possible. New ideas and inspirations that have nothing to do with homesteading, but which will help me publish a better homestead magazine, are found in every corner.

But when the work sessions are over and the conferees break up into smaller knots in the restaurants and cocktail lounges, the talk turns to the merits of Jaguar XKE's and Gucci shoes and the best little restaurant in Rome... and I wander out to find something familiar in a strange land. I find a horse whose life's work is pulling a buggy through Central Park, and pet it on the nose.

And very quickly, it's all over. I'm home again, and it almost seems as if I'd never been gone. And yet...

My outlook on life has been broadened again. As the hog manure oozes over the toes of my boots, I find myself thinking of Gucci shoes and the people who wear them. Surely those people would be as uncomfortable here in my barn as I was in their city.

I think of their Jaguars as I put a tin can over the rusty muffler of the old Allis-Chalmers when I've finished hauling manure. I think of their restaurants as I sit down to a salad that, only minutes before, was growing in the rich soil of our garden.

Certainly, not everyone would enjoy living the way I do, and I don't even try to sell anyone on the idea. But there are those of us who, with our eyes wide open, have made our choices. We know that for us, the only way to live, the only place to be, is beyond the sidewalks.

81. September 1979

Capture a sunbeam: make hay

I like hay. There's something about it that says "countryside." Something simple, yet joyful. Hay is hard work and snug security and basic.

I cut the last of the second crop today, which should give us about 2,000 bales altogether: plenty for our sheep, goats, cow and horse. If we do happen to get a third crop, which is chancey, since I always seem to get the first two in later than most other people and hay doesn't cure as well in the short days of autumn, our barn will be full.

It's been said that more young men have left farming because of haying than for any other single reason. That may be true, and yet...

As the mower clicks easily through the tender young alfalfa, all I have to do is guide the tractor and stay alert in case anything jams up or goes haywire. (Interesting cliché, that.) I glance at the sky now and then and wonder what the weather will be like for the next three days. I could end up with some wonderful, fragrant, leafy, nutritious alfalfa... or a mess of blackened leafless stems good only for mulch. There's nothing I can do to insure success: it's up to fate, and nature... which may be one reason farmers are so doggone philosophical. And I think of the hard work ahead of me.

My sons have town jobs, and haying is basically a one-man operation here again. Did they lose interest in the farm because of the hard work of haying, or was it something else?

We don't put up enough hay — being primarily a hog farm — to warrant a bale thrower or other automated goodies. I cut it, rake it, and if I can find someone to drive the tractor while I load the wagon from the baler, fine. If not, I let the bales drop on the ground, and come back to pick them up later. It's not economical or efficient, but I don't mind. It feels good to use my body, and it's a pleasure to work with the basic feed of my flocks on a one-on-one basis.

And yet, I can't help but think of when the boys were young...

Every one of them got their first experience driving a tractor during haying, and what a thrilling challenge that was! It was a big help to me, having someone drive and operate the baler while I stacked the wagon, and being right behind, I could monitor the fledgling drivers. When they set off on some tractor-driving farm job on their own, I was confident of their abilities.

And, as each of them grew up, it became a measure of manhood to be able to lift bales. The first job was to hook them off the baler and slide them across the wagon to me, or an older brother, who did the stacking. The guy in that position took a lot of ribbing from his siblings whenever it looked like the bale was in charge of the balee.

But eventually, about the age of 10 or 11 I think (time goes so fast I can't recall exactly) the young man weighed more than the bale of hay, and could hoist it up on the wagon stack.

With the pride I've seen in such an accomplishment, it's hard to figure out why farm boys consider haying such hard work...

But they keep on growing, and their interest and goals and challenges change. And Dad is left to put up hay, alone.

But I like hay. I like working with it so much that, once in awhile, I get out the old push-type hay loader dating from the 1890's, and put up a few wagonloads loose.

The ideal would be to have a team of horses to pull the wagon and loader, while I stacked and called out commands (even though the horses would know full well what to do.) Lacking that, I can sometimes find someone to drive the tractor.

The loose hay cascades down from the loader, and I spread and stack it on the wagon. With gusto, at first... but it quickly becomes a true chore. The cloud of dust is choking, and my arms begin to ache as the sweat pours off my body, but dagnabit, it feels good. If I were a serious commercial farmer, I'd probably say I couldn't afford it. It'd be like setting type by hand for COUNTRYSIDE. Quaint, and fun, but highly impractical.

But why does anything have to be practical if you enjoy doing it?

I *am* a farmer, and a practical person. Yet, as this month's *Question* shows, most homesteaders find relaxation by doing things on their own homestead. For me loading hay with my working antique is recreation. I don't sweat any more than those people jogging, I don't get any more sore than those who play tennis for fun. And when I'm *really* relaxing... when there isn't much else to do, or I'm not really in a mood for fun and games, I cut hay with a scythe. Just to prove I can do it... and that I could do it on a serious basis if I had to.

Sometimes, I wish I had to. It might take a few days to get in shape, but the swish-swish of the scythe is relaxing, rhythmic, quite unlike the clatter of the mower powered by the rumbling tractor. The scythe uses no fossil fuels, has no gears or chains or lube points, and is really an extension of myself.

I rake the hay with the wooden hay rake, and load it with a pitchfork. It's the best hay I ever put in the barn.

As the last bale goes into the mow, I'll stand back with the glow of satisfaction usually associated with a gleaming row of jars full of pickles in the root cellar. A barn full of hay represents security for a barn full of animals; it encapsulates summer sun, and sweat, and a lifetime of memories as well as any locket of hair in a scrapbook.

A few months from now, the hayfield will be covered with snow and the wind will be swirling drifts around the barn door. I'll climb into the mow, and as I throw down hay to the livestock the aroma of this August day will soften the chill of winter.

Maybe it's true that to young men, haying represents low pay, backbreaking work, and drudgery. But young men inevitably become old men. The arms become weaker, the back more stooped, maybe the mind even becomes a trifle fuzzy at times... but the simple, more basic things in life take on new dimensions. They're full of meaning and memories.

And I ask you, where else can you make hay, besides beyond the sidewalks?

82. October 1979

Even sleepless nights are different beyond the sidewalks

Our bedroom in our "sort of" underground house is about four feet below grade, and the windows are at ground level. It was no trouble at all for the cat to wander under the outward opening glass and claw his way up the screen.

The combination of the tearing sound of claws on the screen and the raucous meowing woke me as abruptly as if the bull had bashed down the bedroom door.

I got the fool cat's claws disentangled from the screen and shooed it away, looked at the clock — it was 1 A.M. — and lay back down. Diane had stirred only slightly and was sound asleep again.

I was wide-awake.

I listened to the sounds of the night. The horse snorting in the pasture, the frogs in the marsh, the little screech owl in the black walnut tree on the other side of the garden.

Black walnuts... gardens. They don't mix, black walnuts being toxic to tomatoes and related plants. I can't move the garden, heaven knows, but I hate to cut down a tree like that.

But it *is* beginning to die out, and it *would* make excellent firewood...

Firewood. We have plenty, even though I'm a bit behind in harvesting it. It takes about five acres of woodland to support a homestead on a sustained yield basis around here, and we have all of that. And since I've been doing timber stand improvement, there's a lot of oak and hickory and wild cherry and black walnut around here that's going to keep somebody warm in the future. It probably won't be me. Most of those trees will see more of the future than I will. (Yes, yes, I'm well aware that back walnut makes excellent, and very valuable, lumber. That's another story.)

But then, isn't this whole farm geared to the future? My crop rotations, my care in building up the soil, my refusal to use herbicides and chemical fertilizers... are they really doing me any good, or do I follow those practices just because I believe there's going to be a tomorrow even if I'm not around to witness it?

Just as I begin to feel noble, a dog barks in the distance, and I can hear our own dog rise from her curling place at the front door. In my mind's eye I can see her peering out into the darkness across the valley, ears alert, and I forget the nonsense about being noble. Her collar rattles as she shakes herself and settles down again.

The future. Nobility. Principles. Ha! I'm just as selfish as the farmers who over-fertilize and spray biocides and over-crop just to make money.

They can rest easy at night knowing they're good businessmen, and I can rest easy knowing I'm a good crewmember of Spaceship Earth. And that someday soon, when the chemical fertilizers and sprays and other industrial agriculture inputs are out of reach in terms of cost, as well as unpalatable in view of the new knowledge we're gaining about the world, my kind of farm will be on top of things.

Just as the train of ideas begins to smooth out and it seems that blissful sleep might knock all of this idealistic speculation out of my brain, I'm startled by the sudden clamor of the geese, honking and squawking at some unseen danger (something totally harmless, or a fox?). Suddenly it's quiet again, but I know very well I won't get back to sleep soon.

So I get up, slip into my boots and trousers, pull on a shirt, and walk outside. The dog follows as if a 3 A.M. stroll were an everyday occurrence.

The night is still, the sky clear, and the Pleiades make it spectacular. I always thrill to shooting stars, and the entire canopy of the heavens, not because they make me feel insignificant and humble, but because they make me feel like part of something much bigger than the daytime world. I'm not going to conquer anything, nor are the heavens a threat to me. We're part of the same, wondrous universe.

Out here, the hassles of the daytime world seem even less significant than the buzzing of unseen mosquitoes. If the six o'clock news or tomorrow's headlines and editorials were presented out here, tonight, my dog and I would pay less attention to them than we pay to the springtails and actinomycetes at the edge of the compost heap.

Important? You bet. Relevant to who and what and where we are right now? Hardly.

The dog and I wander down through the wheat stubble, along the fencerow, and back again. The chill, damp air seeps through my clothes and I know it's headed for my bones. I begin to feel drowsy.

I go back to bed. Diane's warmth as I cuddle against her tells me I was colder than I thought I was. It's good to be back in the real world.

The light streaming in the east window hurts my eyes. I open them, slowly and painfully, and through a blur see Diane in front of the mirror, combing her hair.

"Are you going to sleep all day?" she asking, twisting toward me while still pulling the comb through her hair.

I close my eyes and flop back on the bed. I can hear the sheep baa-ing as they trot out to the pasture.

With the pillow over my head, I realize why it's so difficult to explain the feelings I feel, the experiences I experience, the thoughts I think, to people I meet and deal with during the day.

No one I talk to during the day was ever inside my skull in the middle of the night, walking in the wet grass. We can talk with words, but not with feelings, because we hide them, even from ourselves, when the sun comes up.

There is more than one world on our planet... and we are all natives and aliens at the same time. There is the bright, harsh, noisy world outside my window right now, and the softer, less complicated world I visited in the middle of the night.

I know that somehow, therein lies the real reason I've chosen to spend my life beyond the sidewalks.

2014: Any references to the future of the farm, in any of these essays, is melancholy, considering how this story plays out.

83. November 1979

A Thanksgiving heritage

It has happened to me, so I'm sure it's happened to you, too.
Casual acquaintances hear that we make butter and cheese, butcher our own meat animals, and even (Heavens!) milk dairy goats. Their reaction is a mixture of shock and amusement. People just don't do those kinds of things any more. There's no need for it. Those who are, are "going backward."

We're not going backward at all. We're merely going forward in a different direction.

Thanksgiving is a good time to pause and consider just why we *do* homestead. It's traditional to give thanks after the harvest, and to reflect on our blessings...

But if our homestead harvest wasn't up to par... if the potatoes should run out or sprout before spring, if the hams should sour, even if all the jars of canned produce would happen to come unsealed in the middle of winter for inexplicable reasons... we *could* go to a grocery store, couldn't we? And if the potato crop is poor here, we'll get potatoes from some other region, or even some other country, won't we? We don't *have* to homestead to eat — and very few people homestead at all.

So why do we do it?

Some of us would rather be gardening or raising chickens than playing tennis or golf, but is that all there is to it?

When I take the time to walk through the fields on Thanksgiving, the dogs ranging ahead and the chill wind rustling the dry leaves and stalks around us, I know in my soul there's a lot more to it.

Part of it is related to the non-homesteaders themselves — people who are surprised to hear that it's actually possible for ordinary people to make cheese and bread and sausage — people like the salesman in the COUNTRYSIDE office the other day who examined the wood-burning stove and exclaimed, "You mean there's an actual fire in there? Isn't that dangerous?"

Consider, as I did when pausing to sit on a rock beneath the rustling dry leaves of an oak tree at the edge of a harvested corn field, where we have come from and what it means.

My grandfather, Napoléon Bélanger, grew up in eastern Canada, on a farm not much different from those of his French ancestors. When he moved west to settle on the thin, rocky soil of northern Wisconsin, nothing changed very much. He still cared for his horses, milked his few cows by hand, planted his rye and barley. His life would have been little different had he lived in the time of George Washington, or even Julius Caesar for that matter.

His children learned by watching and doing. They had a culture, which is the integrated pattern of human behavior that includes speech, artifacts, action, and thought.

But things were changing. Rapidly. The children left the thin soil as farming became more "efficient." They fanned out through Green Bay to the new industrial jobs in the Fox River Valley, and as far south as Milwaukee. And they, and their children, progressed.

Within the twinkling of an eye a world and a culture that had changed but little for centuries was transformed into something entirely alien. There were motorcars and tractors and airplanes, radio and television, and men walking on the moon. Nothing was impossible anymore. Even the atom was harnessed to do man's bidding, and one farmer could feed 57 other people. It seemed as if the world were on the brink of utopia.

But there is no such thing as a free lunch. What have we given up to accomplish these wonders?

Yes, there is pollution, depletion of natural resources, and a great deal more. But it seems to me, as I light my pipe by hunching down out of the wind, that the most valuable thing we have given up is our heritage. An entire culture, handed down from generation to generation for ages.

Perhaps a culture can be replaced, but ours hasn't been, yet. The best most people can do is to dismiss it all by speaking of culture shock and future shock, and by claiming that homesteaders wallow in nostalgia.

Nostalgia? We have lost our birthright, as surely as the Eskimos and aborigines have lost theirs to "the white man's ways," and you dare to call it nostalgia?

Nothing substantial can be built without a solid foundation. The foundation of our society, our heritage, has been shattered by rapid industrialization and urbanization. We have flirted with new and dangerous technologies like schoolgirls with sailors, while the hometown boys, with whom the only stable future lies, are disdained.

The skills and knowledge and ideals of Grandpa Napoléon are important to me because they are what make me human. The culture they comprise was his legacy, and without it, I have nothing to build on.

A flock of crows wheels over the oak tree, starts to land in the cornfield, and spots me and the dogs. They bank sharply and cawing raucously, fly off into the haze in the west. It feels like it might be starting to snow. I tap the ashes from my pipe and rise from the rock, then set a course for the house.

As I trudge through the twisted cornstalks I think of Grandpa Napoléon again. What would we talk about if he were here now? What would he think of all of this?

Would he understand that I homestead, not because of any blind adherence to tradition or because I enjoy being old-fashioned, but because I don't really think of my grandfather all that often?

You see, I also think of those who will walk these fields long after I am gone... my grandchildren... beyond the sidewalks.

2014: Again, note this reference to future generations.

84. December 1979

Timber stand improvement on the homestead

When I burn my "beyond the sidewalks" brand on the end of this column, I'll have completed 10 years with COUNTRYSIDE.

It's been an interesting decade. A great deal has happened in the world, and this seemed like a good month to review how those changes have affected homesteading. But when I sat down at the typewriter I found there was too much to say and one page was not enough space. The job looked impossible, and eventually I set the project aside.

I left the house in a light drizzle and a heavy sweatshirt to do some "timber stand improvement." That's in quotes because it's a family joke. We have about an acre of woods, and the rest of our "timber" is in mostly brushy fencerows. Calling it timber is like referring to the garden behind the garage on a city lot as the back forty, and we laugh about it.

It's a pastime. After the routine chores, timber stand improvement probably ranks about 97th on my list of priorities. That's probably one reason it's such a pleasure when I cheat a little and make it number one.

Yet, it has value even beyond improving my trees. Today, as I pruned branches and selectively thinned out weed trees, I had time to think about this anniversary column. I had wanted to make it a special one, ringing with crystal-clear logic and thundering with mighty thoughts, but instead it seemed to be suffering from damping-off disease.

But when I work with my hands, what I'm doing at the moment often lolls around my idle brain and gets entangled with other things I've been working on, until the simple task takes on added significance and even a tough problem looks simple.

Stretching to lop off the deformed branch of a young hickory, I recall that 10 years ago my woods was little more than an over-grown fencerow. With the passage of time and just the whisper of encouragement from my bow saw and me, it now heats our home, year after year. Ten years from now it will provide even more fuel, as well as nuts and berries, wildlife cover, and other benefits besides.

Ten years ago, the ideas I explored in this magazine were mere seeds. Some were just being planted, some had already started to germinate, and a few were already small saplings. What they all led up to was a dramatic change from what had become known as The American Way of Life, to a simpler, more sensible way of living. I, and the readers who wrote to me, explored and discussed solar energy and wind power and organic farming; we talked about radiation and chemical and other forms of pollution; we reflected on the satisfaction of living simply and close to the Earth.

It was all silly at that time, of course, because very few people saw anything wrong with The American Way of Life or any reason to prepare for anything else. Most farmers were grubbing out fencerows, instead of planting more trees in them. Just as I didn't see the seedlings I was planting, but rather the trees they would become, I didn't see unorthodox ideas, but the new way of life they would become a part of.

Studying a clump of good-sized maple trees growing out of an old stump, I realize that part of my frustration when looking back and trying to compress it all into a single page stems from the fact that I thought a lot more would happen, and faster. A few years ago these trees were mere shoots, and look at them now! If I'm amazed at how fast the trees have grown, then why aren't I equally amazed by the fantastic changes that took place in the world?

Maybe it's because trees are solid, permanent, godlike things, which is what makes it almost as hard for me to cut down a prime tree as it is to butcher an animal. It's easy to imagine a tree as having stood tall and sturdy forever. These trees have grown, however, even though I could detect no day-to-day or even year-to-year changes in them. Perhaps other growth has been similar...

Then too, it strikes me as curious that I should look back on what I've written and done and be disappointed that it hasn't been more productive. Would anything I could say really make any difference anyway? It's true that perhaps I've helped the trees along just a little bit with my weeding and pruning, but they would have grown without me. The ideas whose time has come don't need anybody to sit around and talk about them to make them grow either. Greater forces are at work.

I cut off a broken cherry branch lying across a tiny oak seedling, and drag it out of the way.

Then it dawns on me that if almost anyone else had bought this farm, the trees wouldn't be here at all. They were nothing but rows of brush, wasting space, dividing the fields into too-small units, posing nothing but a nuisance to modern agribusiness. They would have been bulldozed.

So even my small efforts have done some good. I didn't make the trees grow any faster, but at least I gave them a chance to grow, and I helped them grow better by thinning and pruning them.

Maybe my writing falls into the same classification. I've been frustrated whenever it seemed like other writers were accomplishing so much more than I was; I haven't done very well at getting my ideas across to great numbers of people, but maybe that isn't important. I can see now that we all change the world, little by little, often without realizing it, just by performing our everyday duties. We don't have to be activists to be part of a revolution.

The drizzle has turned into a light, cold rain, and the sun is getting low. I'm wet in spite of the exercise. It's time to quit anyway, so I sling my saw over my shoulder and head back to the house.

And walking in the rain, I ask myself what important lesson I've learned in the past 10 years that would fit on one page. The answer is suddenly clear. I should have seen it all along.

I learned that the most insignificant deeds and events are often the most important because there are so many of them that their effect is far greater than that of the occasional earth-shaking deed or event.

Homesteaders may become actively involved in changing the world for the better through lobbying, or demonstrations, or writing. But perhaps we are all doing more just by maintaining and improving our tiny portions of Spaceship Earth, by reducing the world's dependence on finite resources, by bringing a more human dimension to life, even if it only seems to affect those closest to us. Our miniscule efforts — the few eggs we produce — are lost among the massive ones — the millions of dozens of eggs agribusiness produces. But the forest is full of barely noticeable tiny oak seedlings...

Today I learned that when we become discouraged with our progress, it's a good idea to step back and distinguish the trees from the forest. We may be accomplishing more than we suspect, simply by acting out our lives beyond the sidewalks.

Part X: 1980

$1 in 1980 is worth $2.45 in 2011; Inflation: 13.58%; Federal Reserve interest rate, year-end: 21.5%; DJIA, year-end: 963; Gas/gal: $1.19; Average income: $19,500; Start of Iran-Iraq 8-yr. war; US heat wave causes 1,117 US deaths; Mt. St. Helens eruption kills 57; First fax machines (in Japan); First Post-It Notes; Jimmy Carter, president, Ronald Reagan elected president

85. January 1980

New Year's Eve fireside chat

Hello there! Come on in out of the snow and cold, take off that coat and sit by the fire and warm up.

I know, I know. You usually find me doing chores or fieldwork or puttering around with something when you drop by for a visit, and you thought I worked all the time! But tonight's the last night of the 1970's, and I was just sitting here by the fire thinking about what a year it's been.

Come on, sit down. That old rocker is more comfortable than it looks. Pull it up closer here. We don't often use the fireplace screen on the Timberline stove, but it's a nice feature on nights like this.

You're right: it's been not only an interesting year, but an interesting decade. But don't you think we're in for even more interesting times?

I remember when COUNTRYSIDE used to print "home-made" ads for things nobody else ever bothered to promote... things like earthworms and snowflakes and sunshine. One of my favorites contained the legend, "'May you live in interesting times' is said to be an ancient Chinese curse." That's something to think about, isn't it?

Why do I think times are going to get even more interesting? Just look at the trends that have started since you and I sat around the fire talking on New Year's Eve 10 years ago. Don't forget that we saw a lot of things other people couldn't see, then. They called us crazy doomsayers, but look what's happened. I'd say we were right on target, wouldn't you?

Well sure, we missed out on a few predictions. We expected a major depression which hasn't occurred — yet. But it was only avoided by flimsy props that are going to make it all the worse when it does come. (Have you noticed that getting ready for it is one of the main goals of most homesteaders?)

We haven't had the major nuclear disaster or food shortages we thought we'd see during the '70's, although you could say we got a taste of both of them.

On the other hand, the energy crisis was right on schedule, and there is certainly a lot more awareness of agricultural chemicals' dangers, soil erosion problems, the plight of the small family farm and its importance, and a great many other things we were discussing when the 1970s were young. Maybe the most exciting thing is that there are more people acting like responsible passengers on Spaceship Earth, and more getting closer to life beyond the sidewalks, and more joining in these monthly chats in COUNTRYSIDE.

Of course, we expected to have many more people in all those categories, and so far as I'm concerned, at least, I'd hoped there'd be more with a deeper understanding of what it's all about. I really thought that if we had enough crises, or one big enough crisis, people would come to their senses and we could get back to the business of living again. That hasn't happened.

Yet more people are starting to think about homesteading, just because of inflation. And when the depression comes, there will be many more. But the big question is, are they going to homestead grudgingly, taking it as a burden and a curse, or are they going to go after it as a joyful way of life the way we've been doing? If they consider it a temporary misfortune, we aren't going to make much progress.

We seem to have managed the turn-around in attitudes toward automobiles and heating and cooling without a whole lot of trauma, and millions of people are finding that gardening is fun as well as a money-saver. We have a long way to go, of course, but at least we seem to be moving in the right direction. Maybe there's hope.

You're right: not everyone wants to be, can be, or should be a homesteader. But do you remember all the trouble we had finding a name for what we were doing 10 years ago? Very few people knew the modern definition of a homesteader, that's for sure! I think during the '80s we're going to hear some new terms. There's homesteading for the countryside, and for urban areas, and while the lifestyles may differ the basic ideas behind it all are pretty similar.

Ah yes, you're right again. (That's one reason conversations with old friends are so comfortable; we can communicate volumes with a key word, or a gesture, because we know each other.) You're right when you say that most people aren't aware of the basic ideas behind homesteading and aren't likely to find out very soon because they aren't even looking for them.

And yet, you and I, who have plowed and planted and mown hay together in this column during the past years, who have milked goats and cows and sheared sheep, who have worked in the garden and woods and have just sat around like we are now enjoying the fire or sunset, we understand each other. We've taken into account the daily headlines and have gone into everything from Howard Ruff on the financial side to Thoreau and Teilhard de Chardin on the philosophical. Altogether, it's simply too much to be able to communicate to someone who hasn't at least taken the first steps himself, or worse yet, who doesn't care. It all has to be built up block by block.

The last few years have pretty well proven that we're on the right track. And the track is getting straighter and more level; we are picking up speed.

Don't you wonder what we'll be talking about here 10 years from tonight? What will the world be like?

One thing is certain.

No matter how we try to change the world through politics or economics or science — as long as we don't blow up the whole planet in one way or another — the sun will rise in the east; chicks will hatch and lambs and piglets and calves and kids will be born; seeds will grow; and nature will follow its course pretty much as it always has. Those are the important things most people take for granted! And the things *they* think are important, like politics and economics, won't change the really important things at all *unless...*

Unless we allow those activities to so interfere with nature that they actually destroy it.

As we look back 10 years from now we'll be able to reflect on even more progress than we've made so far, both in the world at large and beyond the sidewalks.

2014: If only it were so! Now, not ten but *thirty-four* years later, plenty has changed, all right, but for the better?

86. February 1980

Getting the mail

Every day on the homestead is new, different, and exciting. But at the same time, each day is held together by predictable events and routines that lend a certain comfortable stability to life — events such as sunrise, chores, mealtimes, and getting the mail.

If your house is anything like ours, getting the mail is one of the highlights of the day, week in and week out, year after year. And like many other homestead tasks, it's always the same, but always different.

I've often been amused to be driving down a country road and pass one person after another wending their way to the mailbox, like little dancers who come out of a cuckoo clock to parade on the hour. Sure enough, before long I catch up to the mail carrier. Most people don't even let the mail cool off before snatching it up: they await mail call as eagerly as any new army recruit who's away from home for the first time.

A mailbox is a very special part of country living. For some of us, it's our main link to the outside world.

Will there be a letter from Mom or Dad, or a son or daughter? An unexpected note from an old friend? Or just bills? What's the news in the paper from the city, and what else will be waiting for us: maybe today is the day COUNTRYSIDE arrives!

Some days, the mail itself may be disappointing, but even then "going for the mail" can be interesting. If I've been on a tractor all morning, it's good to listen to the quiet as I walk out to the road to pick up the mail. If I've been cleaning the barn, the fresh air and sunshine are welcome. Even drizzling rain or blowing snow can't dampen the enthusiasm for going for the mail.

An apartment dweller might pick up the mail in the lobby, and not even have to go outside. For me, getting the mail is a clean break from whatever I'm engaged in, and a miniature adventure.

I don't own a watch, but I always know when it's time for the mail... just as I can tell when it's lunchtime.

We can follow one of two paths to our mailbox. One is the driveway, which runs between the garden and the pasture, past the barn, and out to the road. The other is a shortcut through the garden and the orchard. I like to vary the route, but it isn't necessary to avoid boredom; every day is different.

Today, I stopped work on the Allis-Chalmers WD carburetor, wiped my hands on a rag, and took the garden path to the mailbox. The garden was snow-covered, but in my mind's eye I could see both last year's effort and next year's dream. I can even plan the new garden as I pass through.

Then, it's good to check the raspberries and the young fruit trees to make certain the rabbits haven't broken through my protective screening.

Later on in the year, of course, the garden is growing, and going for the mail becomes even more of an inspection tour. When the first berries ripen, it can take quite awhile to "get the mail." And then this path deviates a little to take in the mulberries and wild plums growing along the road, too. Even stopping to pull a weed or two while passing through is not unheard of.

Eventually, I end up at the road.

Walking across the road to the mailbox in itself brings a sense of "meeting civilization." I can look right and left and know that cars, bearing people with destinations and goals far different from my own speed past without even thinking of this little spot on the planet. They don't even notice my destination: my mailbox.

It's not one of those fancy or clever ones you sometimes see along the road. Some of those almost seem to mock the importance of mail to rural residents, with their birdhouses on 10-foot poles for airmail and their old pot-belly stoves labeled "bills." Yet, even those make a statement about the importance of mail in the country.

Our poor mailbox has seen better days. It reminds me of a tired nag tied to the hitching post in front of the general store. A workhorse. Necessary, on one level; appreciated; but taken for granted.

The post that supports it is sagging, the victim of heaving frosts and the town snowplow. It has been toppled by vandals and the fellow who mows the weeds along the road. The name and box number that my daughter painted on it years ago have faded — almost in direct proportion to the way she has bloomed since that long ago spring day I remember so well. Now it looks lonely, deserted, uncared for.

But, its appearance means little as I flip down the lid and eagerly reach inside. There is an aura of anticipation... and as I feel the warmth of the papers, heated by the mailman's car, the thought of finding a fresh egg in a nest makes me smile.

I take the long road back. Working the rubber band off the packet, I glance at the newspaper headlines and wonder what homestead life would be like if I didn't bother to read newspapers. Maybe I could get away with it if I weren't a magazine editor, I think. The idea is tempting...

But there are also letters. Letters from people who feel as I do about life. I eagerly seek these out, anxious to make contact with a fellow human who shares my views of our planet and who will help strengthen my commitment to make nature's experiment with *homo sapiens* work. Those letters will have information and ideas I'll never find in any newspaper... and it seems to me that homesteading would be a lot more lonely and less meaningful without them, which, of course, is why I try to share as many as possible with fellow homesteaders through COUNTRYSIDE.

As I pass the barn and the adjacent pasture, the sheep gather and watch me in expectation. Whenever I pass this way they either get fed, or I'm getting the mail, and they're too stupid to tell the difference.

At the house, I can sit back and go through the entire package without fear of losing anything in the wind. The aroma of homemade soup is in the air as I sort it out. How appropriate that food for the mind and food for the body are served up at the same time. After getting the mail, and lunch, I'll greet the afternoon with renewed vigor.

Even on the days when there's nothing but the newspapers and bills and advertising, going for the mail is a pleasurable experience, beyond the sidewalks.

In 1980 I couldn't have dreamed how quaint the ritual of getting the mail would sound in 2014: e-mail and Facebook and cell phones and Twitter — and talk about closing small-town post offices and eliminating Saturday mail? Just another example of how life has changed, and how quickly. And how few even notice. Or care.

87. March 1980

How a journalist measures a field

I t's not unusual for me to reflect on the now-trite saying "Small is Beautiful" while I go about my chores. What made it a little out-of-the-ordinary this afternoon was, I was thinking about the news.

Heaven knows there is little enough good news going around these days, but that's not its greatest shortcoming. The real crime is, it's boring. Maybe that's because it's so unimportant. Or maybe it's just that we've fallen for the bigger-is-better theory, even in the news.

I was measuring a field. I knew it covered 20 acres, but that's too large both for my machinery and my attention span, and I wanted to divide it into three smaller parcels. Moreover, it's rather sloping and will benefit from strip cropping. So I was pacing it off and writing the counts into the small notebook stuck in my denim jacket pocket so I could compute the area and know how much of what seed to order.

It was a nice day. We haven't had much snow here this year, and what little there was was getting mushy under the bright afternoon sun in the clear blue sky. It was a good day to be outside, and the thought of approaching spring planting made it even better. But like a tongue probing a sore tooth, my mind kept going back to the news.

Iran. Afghanistan. Energy. Gold. Inflation. None of it very encouraging, none of it very interesting, and none of it very important.

I always have guilt feelings when I think like that, because I can just imagine the journalism professors and news editors I've worked under rising up in furious rage at my unsophistication. All of that news *does* affect me personally, they shout in unison, and then they vehemently list the ways.

I bend down to pick up an ear of corn the picker missed and stuff it in my pocket with the notebook.

Actually, I was never eager to work for a wire service or a metropolitan daily. In fact, the only reason I got into journalism was that back in the 1950s everybody told me it was impossible for a young man to break into farming (and making a living as a writer was impossible). Journalism was my second choice, but I still wanted to be close to the land and the people who appreciated it, so I set my sights on editing a small weekly newspaper. Nobody told me that making a living on a small weekly newspaper was as tough as farming. But I learned a lot.

Among other things, I learned that a dog fight on Main Street is more newsworthy than a war in China. I learned that everybody likes to see their name in the paper, even if they don't admit it. I learned that small can be beautiful, even when you're selling news.

But what happened? We not only have megafarms, global corporations, and proliferating government: we also have a situation where the only news that's deemed important is in Washington or some foreign capital. The only news worth reporting is *big* news.

"What do you think of that?" I asked a field mouse who had ventured out to enjoy the sun. "Is the price of gold in London today as important as the sun in the sky or the coming of spring? The grain embargo will affect the value of what I plant this year, but will the seeds grow more poorly because of it, will the bread made from my wheat be any less tasty?"

The mouse scurries into a hiding place among the stalks, and I continue my pacing to the end of the field. There I write the number on the rough map in my little book and sit down to enjoy the view.

I can see the entire field from here, and part of the winter rye beyond. All of the top news stories of the day seem so far away and so meaningless... If any of the newsmakers, like the president, were sitting here with me, would we talk about Russia, and interest rates, or would we remark on the number of deer tracks skirting the edge of the field and the spring-like day?

"Hey Jimmy, look at that red-tailed hawk! Isn't it beautiful the way it soars, without even flapping its wings?"

Maybe presidential candidates — and newsmen — try too hard. They flap their wings, when they ought to soar.

I get up and resume counting. Fourteen, 15, 16.

The job finished, the notepad tucked into my pocket, I head for home. But I make it a point to stop by the barn, since I like to check on the sheep as often as possible at this time of the year.

The fat pregnant ewes lie in the yard chewing their cuds, watching me. Some stand and come towards me.

But the one I call Cardigan (her twin sister is Argyle) seems distressed. She's lying in the cranny between the barn and the silo, and looks uncomfortable. As I approach her, she doesn't move, but looks at me with anxious eyes.

And there, on the other side of her, lies a still wet newborn lamb. The first of the year.

I get the two of them into a pen in the barn, disinfect the lamb's navel, and get a bucket of water. The new mother drinks appreciatively, then nuzzles her lamb, and it begins to nurse. Taking the ear of corn from my pocket, I thumb off a few kernels and offer them on the palm of my hand. The ewe sniffs them and nibbles.

In the house, I hang up my jacket and retrieve the notebook, anticipating the brightness and warmth of the kitchen and the sizzle of supper. I'm eager to tell the family about the new arrival… and the added work and vigilance that will be a part of our life as the rest of the flock comes in. Striding from the dark hall into the kitchen, my first words are, "Guess what's new!"

It may not be big news, but it's good news. And there's a lot of that beyond the sidewalks.

2014: And what is "news" now, in the Internet Age? Sex. Violence. Drugs. Young billionaires. Often all four wrapped up together. It's hard to tell if "journalist" is a dirty word or an anachronism, but I disavowed that profession long ago.

88. April 1980

A farmer is a farmer is a farmer

It had been an excellent homestead meal: flavorful chicken, roasted to a golden brown; potatoes and rich gravy; peas and carrots; biscuits and honey; and garden huckleberry pie for dessert. As I crawled into my jumpsuit, the cuffs stiff and aromatic with hog manure, I thought of how nice it would be to settle down by the fire with a good book. I wondered, briefly, what all the other people who had worked in town all day were doing just then.

No wonder so many of them think we homesteaders are a strange breed.

I pulled on my black rubber boots — an absolute necessity in the early spring when the manure is piling up and thawing out. But it's still cold enough to require the orange stocking cap and gloves, too, and even though there's a touch of spring in the air, chores are done in the wintry dark, so the flashlight is thrust into my thigh pocket as a standard piece of equipment.

Picking up the milk pails and heading for the back door, I can see my reflection in the window, noting with satisfaction that few people would mistake that apparition for a downtown businessman. What most people would call the real world was fading behind me, and I was eager to leave it. As I clomped down the porch steps I realized why, when wisps of the business day swirled around me like the fog I knew lay ahead. Events came in snatches, touching my mind then dancing away as if trying to tease me into grabbing for them.

They didn't have a chance.

At the bottom of the stairs, Daphne joins me, her tail wagging, and together we step off into the dark and fog. The gravel in the drive crunches under my boots, and I'm in a different world: the world of homesteading.

Over the years I've been working with COUNTRYSIDE, I've often been asked just what a homesteader really is. I've also heard many people say they aren't really homesteaders, because they only have rabbits and chickens and goats, and only two or three acres, and they work in town. And then there have been all the discussions about small farmers, part-time farmers, and — a term I loathe — "hobby farmers."

Sometimes the terms we use are important. When we write, or speak to one another, it's necessary to use words we both define in the same way. And yet, in some quarters today, none of these terms matter anyway, because they all refer to people who aren't "real" farmers. We don't produce significant amounts of food: the 80 smallest farmers out of 100 account for only 20 percent of the food produced in the United States, so the contributions of the *very* smallest ones are probably insignificant. Worse yet, in the eyes of agribusiness and most of the rest of the world, we don't make very much money.

But I refuse to consider my farming a hobby, as if it were related to stamp collecting.

For one thing, I firmly believe that we small farmers provide a stable base for agriculture. I also believe that the ever-growing big farms have passed the point of optimum efficiency, and that as the costs of capital and energy increase, the most efficient farms will be the small ones. Who will have the skills and equipment to produce food, competitively, when fuel hits $2 a gallon and the money supply is cut off?

But there's more. I don't work in town, publishing magazines, because I have to. In fact I was "retired" when I took over COUNTRYSIDE 10 years ago! I just saw it as something that needed doing, and provided a great deal of satisfaction.

Farming isn't my hobby... but maybe magazine publishing is.

There probably aren't very many homesteaders who are fortunate enough to have a job like mine, where virtually every hour of every day is devoted to one aspect of homesteading or another, in town or on the farm. And there certainly *are* people whose homesteading is only a hobby.

Maybe that's why it's so hard to put any of us into neat categories, or even to adequately define what we're doing, or to explain why we're doing it.

A few nights ago on the trip to the barn, the stars overhead seemed as sharp and cold as the gravel underfoot. I had stopped to lean back and gaze up at those faraway suns. Thinking of their vast size and awesome distance made me feel insignificant in the universe, and yet...

Somehow, at the same time, they seemed to speak to me of my ties with divinity. They said "Others can worry about how much money a farmer has to make to be called a farmer, or whether small farming is merely a substitute for stamp collecting, but we know better. Tending the soil with loving care, thrilling to the first sprouting seeds in spring, caring for animals — and even listening to the stars speak — these are not hobbies. For the spiritual minded, they are not even occupations."

What are they? I waited breathlessly for the answer, but the stars only winked, and said no more.

Now the stars were hidden in the fog.

There was work to do in the barn. As I turned on the lights, the sleeping pigs struggled to their feet and the steam from their warm bodies rose in the dim light like the fog outside. I set about my tasks and quit thinking about applying a title to what I was doing.

It didn't really matter. Those of us who do these things know why. Even if no one else does, *we* know who and what we are, beyond the sidewalks.

"When fuel hits $2 a gallon"? Good grief! I don't know what to say about that in 2014. (It was $3.699 this morning.)

89. May 1980

What's in a name? Much more than a number

A lamb was born in our barn last night. As I wiped the mucus from her mouth and disinfected her navel with iodine, it was plain to see that her name was Squeaky.

Diane frowned, and said that was a very unusual name for a lamb, but I was powerless. I could tell by looking at her that her name was Squeaky, and that was that.

But this little episode started me thinking about the quaint custom of giving things names.

People who are new to farming, and homesteading, seem to name everything on the place. Having a goat or a pig without a name seems as unnatural as having a nameless family dog.

Some friends of ours used to have an ancient pickup truck named Sherman, after the tank. Now, every pickup has a personality of its own, but with a name, Sherman's was amplified, somehow. Even casual acquaintances would glance surreptitiously at Sherman as if expecting him to break out into a grille-wide grin and say something clever, like a car in a Disney movie.

We happen to have a tractor named Alice. That's not very original or clever for an Allis Chalmers WD, but names don't necessarily have to be original. I've driven other WD's, but Alice has her own idiosyncrasies — the ignition switch is pushed in to start, and pulled out to stop, which is just the opposite of what you'd expect. There is a certain way to choke the engine to get her started, and, of course, she has her personal assortment of dents and shiny new parts that stand out like warts among the generally comfortable rust and faded paint of the rest of her. Over the years, we've worked hundreds of acres together, a few at a time, and I could pick Alice out of a whole parking lot of WD's from a half-mile away.

And what about fields? Does anyone name fields anymore?

When we started farming, it often happened that I wanted one of the boys to bring the hay wagon to a field where I was working, or I wanted them to plow or mow or perform some other task on a specific field, and we found it difficult to communicate. We'd say things like "the field out in the back forty alongside the ditch where the willow trees are growing."

"You mean the one where we planted wheat?"

"No! Don't plow that one! There's clover in that stubble. The flat one, on this side of the willows."

So it became Willow Flats Field, which made it easier all around.

Of course, when our soil consultant did soil testing and made recommendations, the fields on his penciled map were all numbered. He could talk about number seven, but I had to translate that before it meant anything to me. Number seven? Oh, that's Wounded Pheasant Field. That's the one where I so carefully tried to avoid a family of pheasants while I was mowing hay, but in spite of my best efforts, one young bird lost a leg in the mower. Any field on the place could be number seven, but there's only one Wounded Pheasant — and the name calls up all of the soil fertility and cropping history and other information that the number would.

I don't know what it is about a name that's important. Surely, we all like to hear our own name. A letter with your name on it is almost certain to be opened before one addressed to "Rural Box Holder." And yet, when some magazine sends me a letter with my name ink-jet printed in letters half an inch high, and my name and "Waterloo, Wisconsin" sprinkled liberally throughout the copy thanks to clever writing and computer technology, the personal feeling doesn't last long. A name is something special, and a computer just can't convey all the subtle implications. The name is nothing but a substitute for a number rather than holding any actual meaning.

And yet, while my name means something to me, does a goat or a dog really care what it's called? A tractor or a field certainly doesn't know or care! Are names important for the things being named, or for the one doing the naming?

For homesteaders, the importance is obviously the act of naming something. Some farmers can use ear tags or tattoos or other means of identification, and have all the information about an animal that they need. But even those farmers almost invariably have their own special animals, with names as well as numbers, simply because in some way those animals have affected the farmer's life or outlook.

A few months ago, Ron Parker observed in COUNTRYSIDE that "anyone who has too many sheep to name has too many sheep." I like the thinking behind that. That's why we have a cow named Sara, a Bantam rooster named Buster, and a brand-new lamb named Squeaky.

Is this foolishness? Is it an idle pastime only for neophytes and part-timers who don't take their farming seriously?

I don't think so. You have to know something intimately before you can give it a good name. And when you *do* know something intimately, it's almost impossible not to name it. And once named, you get to know it even better, to respect it more. It's been that way since the Biblical admonition to name the creatures of the Earth. The American Indians had names for nearly everything, and so do those who today live beyond the sidewalks.

90. July 1980

If the sky falls, join Chicken Little beyond the sidewalks

At the beginning of the 1970's, some people believed that the world was on the brink of momentous change. Far from establishing the American Dream in underdeveloped parts of the world, they said, that dream would fade even in the overdeveloped areas. There wouldn't be enough energy to sustain the kind of technology that was required for what had become known as "quality of life." There wouldn't be enough food. In our mad scramble after the dream, we had virtually sucked the Earth dry of natural resources that could be economically utilized. Energy, minerals, wood, soil and water and the very air itself had been destroyed by our greed and our blindness.

Other people, of course, said this was all foolishness. They said we'd all starve if we farmed organically, and they made jokes about running American agriculture with 30 million mules. They said nuclear power or space technology or some other scientific miracle would save us. Some of them got angry hearing about "laymen" poking their noses into economics and chemistry and nutrition and nuclear physics and other things laymen aren't supposed to know or even think about.

Still others tried to ignore the whole scene, with muttered references to Chicken Little, and doomsayers.

Isn't it funny how there seem to be more and more Chicken Littles showing up every day? Everybody likes to go with the winner, but sometimes it takes a while to be able to see who's ahead.

It's been said that humanity is like a pyramid that's cut into three equally thick layers. The top layer consists of people who make things happen, the middle layer is made up of people who wonder happened, and the bottom layer — the largest — is comprised of those who don't even know anything happened.

It's been interesting to watch how our society has changed some of its ideas in the past 10 years. Small cars, which used to be laughed at, are now status symbols, while big cars, which used to be status symbols, are now scorned. In the future, angry mobs might well attack luxury vehicles and their occupants... and indeed, at least one case of this has already surfaced in Illinois.

Ten years ago, few people were unorthodox enough to heat with wood, or garden organically, or conserve electricity. Today, all that has changed. At the same time, many people are still shocked, and perhaps angered, at what has happened to them. Since they just woke up from the dream, it all seems so sudden.

And then, there are still those who have no idea what has happened or is happening. They still think the Dream is possible, and we're merely involved in a temporary inconvenient phase brought on by the Arabs, or the administration, or business, or high interest rates, or any number of other scapegoats.

We know — you and I — that the American Dream was never more than an illusion, and a not-very-worthwhile one at that, based as it was on materialism even at the cost of higher human aspirations. It was based on undervaluing depletable resources, which amounts to living off capital, and which cannot be sustained. Those who couldn't understand or accept that said we couldn't afford to farm organically, avoid nuclear power, and not pollute our air and water. But their accounting methods were wrong, and we couldn't afford *not* to respect our planet and its finite resources.

None of this is new to serious homesteaders, of course, but it's worth considering again now that it's apparent that the sky really *is* falling, or at least now that so many more people are apprehensive about the possibility. That means that the entire pyramid of which we spoke has shifted: the people at the top are making *new* things happen, and those at the bottom are as oblivious to those new developments as they were to the old ones a decade ago. One indication of this is that we know that today there are even homesteaders spread throughout all three layers of that pyramid.

And what *is* that next step?

That, too, is nothing new. For even as we spoke of the death of the American Dream years ago, we also knew we were witnessing the birth of a *new* age. We knew we wouldn't come upon it suddenly, as if walking through a door, but that it would creep up on us as stealthily as old age. We were not, even then, harbingers of doom and gloom, but rather proponents of new challenges and new opportunities for the betterment of humanity and the Earth.

Now that the trials and tribulations have begun in earnest — for we haven't seen anything, yet — it's a good time to step back and ponder what might happen next. The same principles and ideals we've embraced in the past have served us well in this first stage: now is the time to reaffirm them. We'll need all the inner resources we can muster for the days ahead. Chicken Little may have been vindicated, but we aren't through yet. When the sky falls, it falls on all of us.

As usual, one of the best spots to be, both to be able to see the truth and to live with it, is your own place, wherever it may be, beyond the sidewalks.

2014: I'm not sure, now, what instigated this one, but whatever it was, it obviously was no big deal: according to conventional thinking, I was still a Chicken Little Doomsayer. However, it's interesting to observe the changes that have taken place in 34 years. Some of the old minor concerns have become major problems, recognized by nearly everyone; at the same time, the masses have become so accustomed to some of them they simply ignore them.

91. August 1980

Nothing is ever easy
Example: milking a goat

Remember the first time you saw somebody milk by hand? The milk came out in strong, swishing streams to foam in the bucket with a regular pulse while the cow or goat stood quietly, seemingly oblivious to the procedure. The milker worked effortlessly, tirelessly, and the bucket filled quickly.

"Nothing to it," you probably said, especially if you were young. Anybody could perform such a simple operation.

And then the milker rose with a pail of foaming milk, poured it into the strainer and, with a knowing smile, handed you the pail. "Here, you do the next one."

What happened next depends on what kind of person you are.

Maybe you had second thoughts about the whole thing and hurriedly declined the offer. Maybe you timidly took the pail, gingerly touched the teat with one outstretched hand, and drew it back quickly when the animal kicked, thus ending your first milking session. Or maybe you sat down, full of confidence, and began to attempt to milk. You squeezed. You pulled. You got nothing.

If you had a patient animal and a patient mentor, you probably went on to learn how to trap the milk in the teat by blocking it off in the crook of your thumb and forefinger, then forcing the milk out by progressively applying pressure from the top down. Maybe you learned some other method, but, either way, it took some time, and concentration, before you got the first squirt.

Which either went up your sleeve or in your lap — anywhere but in the bucket.

And after a long time of squeezing and pulling and concentrating, you almost had the bottom of the bucket covered.

Easy, eh?

Almost everything looks easy, from a distance. What child, depending on age, location and sex, hasn't dreamed of being a cowboy, movie star, test pilot, nurse, star athlete, or one of dozens of other high-visibility occupations? What more mature person hasn't read or heard about somebody who has made it and thought, "how easy it would be to be rich, famous, wise, powerful" or whatever the mood of the moment might be.

The older we get — the more things we try, the more things we fail at, and the more things we really do get good at through long practice and hard work — the more we can smile at the idea that anything is "easy."

I think this is one of the most valuable attributes of an experienced homesteader.

Maybe it's because homesteaders, by definition, *try* so many more things than "normal" people. How do you really know what's involved in something as simple as milking a goat or making crisp dill pickles until you try it? How can you appreciate the butcher's skill, the gardener's art, the science of buttermaking, until you roll up your sleeves, plunge in, and do it yourself?

Once you start on that path, several things happen.

One is that you begin to think and react differently than the person who watches a football play on tv and grumbles, "For Pete's sake, I coulda done better than that!" or "of course, I *could* be a (fill in the blank) if I really wanted to be one" or "F'r crying out loud, don't those politicians have any sense at all?" You begin to respect other people's skills, training, outlooks, and problems, just a little more than you would if you still thought everything was easy.

But you also have found that with practice and perseverance nothing is impossible. By not giving up, you became a proficient milker, a prize-winning pickle-maker, a gardener who other people now come to for advice.

While some people sit on the sidelines, thinking everything is easy, you have grown in self-respect; you have earned the right to be proud of your accomplishments; and you have learned to be very humble about all the things you still don't know.

Maybe this is why, while some people have simple explanations for and solutions to the energy situation, the economic situation, the problems of ecology and other challenges of our generation, we homesteaders tend to sit back and mull it over just a bit more. Maybe it's not all as simple as it seems...

But it's probably not as impossible as it seems, either, if we're willing to dive in, willing to make a few mistakes, willing to work, and learn.

After years of reading letters from readers and fielding questions from audiences, it's easy for me to spot the person who thinks everything is easy... that everything has a simple solution... that great things can be accomplished without effort.

Tonight, just before I sat down to fill this allotted space in COUNTRYSIDE, I milked my goats.

I've been milking goats for many years. I've written about how to milk goats; I've answered countless questions about milking goats; I've had numberless people try their hand at milking for the first time using my goats or cows as guinea pigs.

But one of my animals has been becoming increasingly skittish of late, and tonight she was all but hopeless. It was the first time in a long time I've had a goat step in the milk pail, and I had all I could do to milk her out. She used to be gentle as a kitten; there were no flies; there are no discernible irritations in or on the teat or udder... I suspect it's psychological, and I'm going to have to put her through goat therapy.

I'm going to have to learn to milk all over again, on a different level.

***

Nothing is easy, and nothing is ever finished. How hard that must be to grasp for some people who live "the good life" according to American standards! But how natural it comes to those of us who are privileged enough — and savvy enough — to live beyond the sidewalks.

A glimpse of the Pearly Gates

I was just finishing up disking a corner of a field that had been too wet to plant to oats last spring. One more of these orphan fields to go, and I'd be ready to sow buckwheat. There was plenty of time to spare before the mid-July deadline.

I had to move the disk a short way down the road, then back along a dirt farm road, to get to the last field. But, sometime along the way, something seemed to grip at my chest.

It wasn't a pain, really. It felt like someone had cupped my heart in two soft but firm hands... and was gently but relentlessly squeezing.

I pulled the tractor in front of the beehives on the south slope facing the marsh field I was going to disc, and tried to breathe deeply.

It didn't help.

I got off the tractor and walked around, trying to relax. The pain-that-wasn't-a-pain persisted.

But it seemed to subside a little — nothing serious, I decided — and, eventually, I got back on the tractor, nudged it into gear, and rolled down to the fluffy black soil of the marsh field. I lowered the hydraulic ram on the disk, slipped the tractor into a lower gear, opened the throttle, moved out... and knew right away it wasn't going to work.

I couldn't bluff it. I couldn't ignore it. The pain was too great.

I drove as far as the end of the field, unhitched the disc, threw the tractor into a higher gear and drove back to the house as quickly and as carefully as I could.

What do you think about when you think you're having a heart attack?

My own father took the car to be washed before he told my mother about the numbness in his left side that resulted in open heart surgery, presumably because he didn't want her driving to the funeral in a dirty car.

But I found myself wondering whether Steve, our second-eldest son who's working the farm with me, would know enough to avoid getting stuck in the lower end of the marsh field when he finished the disking I had barely begun. And, although I am no lover of insurance (that's putting it mildly), I felt a certain comfort in knowing Diane would be able to pay off the farm and have a place to live, at least.

But the real impact didn't come until later.

Oh, the pain subsided quickly enough, although there was a lingering, troubling pressure on my chest. Even my RN wife knew better than to try to get me to a doctor under conditions like that... although I was scared enough that I spent the rest of the afternoon reading and sleeping, rather than working.

I do not like doctors. I don't like the smell of their offices, the crispness of their nurses and other attendants, waiting in their outer chambers reading *National Geographic*, their prices, or admitting that something might be wrong with me. In other words, I'm a pretty normal guy.

But when the pain was still there at bedtime, I thought maybe it wouldn't be a bad idea to have a checkup — just to see. And, when I went into uncontrollable convulsions shortly thereafter, it was decided.

I had an EKG the next morning. It checked out all right, but since I had eaten breakfast, I couldn't have a blood test and I couldn't get in for a stress test until two days later.

So, for the better part of three days, I spent most of my time putting my affairs in order.

Being a homesteader, I'm not exactly a stranger to death. Usually I'm thinking, "Well, Chicken (or Goat, or Rabbit, or Lamb, or Pig, or Cow), you're going to die, and the world will be a little different without you, and I'm sorry to see you go. But it's really quite necessary in the scheme of things, and you've fulfilled your purpose."

It was odd to see my own neck on the chopping block... but also, oddly, it seemed entirely natural.

One of my favorite aphorisms says that if you want to see how important you are in the world, plunge your arm into a bucket of water, withdraw it, and observe the hole that's left behind.

By some strange coincidence, only the day before, Diane had chauffeured a non-driving neighbor to make the final arrangements for her father, who had died of a heart attack. When she told me about her day, I felt a personal aversion to the pomp and expense of funeral splendor... but now that became more acute.

I don't want to be buried in a fancy casket, which will only delay the microbiology I've held in such awe and reverence... and the natural cycle behind it. Long ago, when we started organic farming, we had a family joke: whenever someone was cut and bleeding, we could banish the pain by saying, "Quick, don't waste that blood! Go out and bleed on the compost heap!" Then we'd all laugh.

Maybe this was an extension of the same thought. Just toss me on the mulch pile. Don't even bother to dance on my grave. After the life in the soil has done its work on my carcass, scatter the compost and plant beans.

And remember me joyfully as you pick them.

This would be a lot more dramatic if editor Dave Skoloda could say I finished it up by dictating the last lines on my deathbed.

However, the EKG said there ain't a thing wrong with me, the stress test said I'm in "a state of high condition — for a man of your age," and the blood test said I don't have as much as the sniffles. The pain, whatever it was, was apparently nothing serious.

In retrospect, I enjoyed the whole experience.

First, it's a good feeling to know I'm in such disgustingly good shape.

But even more importantly, it's *very* good to have a glimpse of the Pearly Gates... and know that you've done all right in the things that really count. Not perfect, mind you, but all right.

I'm going to live beyond the sidewalks until I die.

What's interesting about this now is that when I really did have a heart problem, some 25 years later, it was nothing at all like this.

93. October 1980

Changes and contrasts make October a good month for pause and reflection

October is a month of contrasts that holds special meanings for homesteaders. October is a very good month.

The sun rises much later, and much farther to the south, than it did only a few weeks ago, so we know summer is past. And, yet, the morning air is heavy with a Midwest summer mugginess that could almost lull me into thinking that summer will never end.

Even if the day is warm, night can bring frost, and when there's a thin sheet of ice on the stock tank you stop thinking about summer and begin to wonder if the woodpile is big enough.

In October, the garden harvest is in the root cellar and freezer, and the frost blackens only a few leftover stalks and some late cabbages. The thin, watery sunlight isn't needed to cure hay anymore: the hay is safely in the barn. There is grain in the bins, and the new seedings of winter wheat and rye are growing well: they seem to enjoy being crowned by morning frost, and they grow lush and green in October.

There are other contrasts. The pheasant population has reached its peak, and their brilliant plumage brightens the landscape. But the red-coated hunters and their dogs, tiny and slow-moving in the distance — and the occasional boom of a shotgun — indicate that that peak has already passed.

Likewise, the Canada geese pass overhead by the thousands, filling the air with their haunting cry, but before long the sky will be empty and still again.

In October, I drape a sack over my shoulder and wander along the fencerows, gathering hickory nuts. The last time I was here — picking berries — this place was still green with the life of summer. Now everything is red and gold and brown. Some would say lifeless, but I know better.

Maybe that's one of the many ways homesteaders are different from "normal" people. We can see things that more casual observers, that people who are in a hurry, don't notice. Yes, in October, everything has changed... but nothing has changed.

As the sun sets earlier and earlier each day, the evening air takes on a chill that our summer-warmed bodies aren't adapted to. No matter that a couple of months from now, when the blizzards howl, this evening's "chill" would seem downright pleasant! For now, it is chilly, and I kindle a fire in the stove. The fire is laid carefully, as if it were a ritual. In October, I guess it is. As the tiny flames flicker and grow, I add larger sticks of wood and wait patiently for them to ignite.

The hoping and dreaming and planning of spring are all long past, and nearly forgotten. The hard work of summer is now a pleasant memory. The labors of the harvest are over, and the specter of winter is beginning to take shape.

But, meanwhile, it's October.

With the flames dancing, I carefully lay some larger pieces of wood on the fire. The room is already beginning to warm, and it feels good.

You know, I think many parts of homesteading are a reflection of life itself. Life, however, is so vast and so complex that it's often hard to understand and appreciate its whole: some people tend to become experts in one tiny facet of it, while others wander through it aimlessly.

Homestead activities seem to dissect life. They give us snatches of insight in more manageable, bite-size pieces. They make it easier to apply our thoughts and ideals to the much larger tapestry.

I like that. And maybe that's what I like about October. With all its contrast and abrupt changes, October is the ideal season for pause and reflection. A time of transition, it's both an ending, and a beginning. It's a good time to be a homesteader.

With the fire settling down to do its stuff, I adjust the damper, and sit back and pick up my book. The aroma of the hickory wood is as pleasant as its warmth.

But the thoughts and ideas that go with it are the best part of all, beyond the sidewalks.

94. November 1980

A tale of two boys

I f you find this story hard to swallow — because you don't believe in time warps, or mirror-image worlds, or intelligent life on other planets — I wouldn't blame you one bit. But so help me, it's true. Every word.

It's a story of two young men who seem to have a lot in common. They're both 17 years old, and seniors in high school. They both have cars, and girl friends, and after-school jobs. Both of them enjoy the woods and fields and country living, and both have daily responsibilities for animals. Both of them are considering farming among their career options.

However, one of them lives in a world where farming is becoming more mechanized, chemicalized, and capital-intensive, and he doubts whether he will even be able to make a start... or whether he'd really want to. Not long ago, in his land, farms were quite small, diversified, and used horse power. The new style of agriculture somehow doesn't fit his idea of farming.

The other fellow already lives on a farm, and has been operating tractors and other equipment for a good portion of his life. He has taken more than one engine completely apart and put it together again, in operating order.

Actually, his whole world is much more technological than the other's. He has always known television: the other young man has seldom experienced it. He has traveled, even by air; the other has seldom ventured beyond his small community, has never been close to an airplane, and hasn't even seen very many from a distance.

While one of these youths has had experience with computers, and has seen satellites glowing overhead, and knows something about stereophonic speakers (and rock music), to the other these are things science fiction is made of.

There are other differences. While the one lives in a world where political and religious leadership is stable almost to the point of the pope and president appearing to be immortal, the other has lived through assassinations and resignations and fast-paced changes that make it seem like nothing is solid or reliable.

Both have lived through periods of war... but they were different kinds of wars, with very different effects on the youngsters who heard about them.

And while one of these young men lives in a world where a golden age of never-ending prosperity seems to lie just around the corner, the other lives in a world where there is widespread concern about shortages of natural resources and a declining — not increasing — standard of living.

Similar as they might seem on the surface, as much as they might have in common if they were to meet each other today, it's a certainty that their attitudes and outlooks on many important subjects would be — as they *are* — worlds apart.

Sitting at our well-worn, hand-made library table, working on a particularly perplexing problem, I finally gave up, tossed down the pencil, and sat back to gaze out the window.

Ordinarily, I can compose myself by admiring the sheep and goats on the hillside pasture, by looking for the red-tailed hawks and sandhill cranes that frequent the fields beyond, and by marveling at the shadows of clouds that race over the gentle hills in the distance. But, today, I didn't get that far.

My eyes were drawn to the half-dozen pictures of my son, Steve, that were strewn on the table in front of me. He had recently gotten his high school graduation pictures, and they were lined up for the whole family to admire and comment on while he pondered which one to choose.

I couldn't help but look beyond that familiar face, and wonder. What does he really know, what does he really think, what does he really hope for? Sure, we work together, and we talk, but we've both been shaped by very different forces, and I wonder just how well we really understand each other...

It took awhile to dig out a picture of another 17-year-old, one I used to know very well.

Me.

Looking at the two pictures side by side made me realize once again just how rapidly and extensively our world has changed, and, by inference, why I considered homesteading an ideal way to put things into their proper perspective.

Why homesteading might well be the only sane way to live.

What's going to happen to Steve, and all the other people his age, in the years ahead, I wondered? They can't see the future any more clearly than we could when we were 17, but the trends are clear. And not particularly encouraging, for any but homesteaders.

I gathered up my papers, drew open the drawer of the table and tucked them inside, marveling as I always do at the craftsmanship of the simple little piece of furniture. It struck me as being wryly appropriate that it was made by Walter Landskron, when he was about 17, in a high school shop class.

Walter, you see, is my father-in-law, and Steve's grandfather. Maybe I could make this a story of *three* teen-age boys...

But that makes it all the more intriguing to add yet a fourth: one yet to be born. What will *his* world be like, and how will what we do today and tomorrow affect it?

Just as I admitted I didn't know the answer, three cranes, birds that have been unchanged for millennia, came flapping into view. Their eerie cry sounded deafening, and somehow both haunting and reassuring, as if to say "Some things never change — at least beyond the sidewalks."

95. December 1980

Outrunning the blahs on horseback

L ate autumn, early dusk.
Supper was scavenged from my favorite garden, the frost-proof garden, where carrots and turnips and Jerusalem artichokes not only stand out like sparkling gems amidst the frost-blackened tomato vines and the frost-wilted leaves of leftover Chinese cabbage, but they're actually sweeter and crisper than ever. The chores are finished, and the sheep are moving out to the pasture where the rape is still green and tasty, and I'm guiding Colonel, the black gelding, down the drive toward the road. The clip-clop of his hooves is a pleasant sound in the quiet evening, and his warmth against my legs is comforting in the still, chill air. The temperature will surely dip into the teens tonight.

We reach the road and head west, up the hill toward the setting sun. Colonel is glad to be out of the paddock, and I'm glad to be out of the magazine office: you can feel the vibrations of the joint gladness, the freedom. The hill is rather steep, and the horse's head bobs up and down with the effort of the climb. There is a faint afterglow of sunset oozing over the crest, but most of the visible horizon is a mass of leaden clouds that clash with the clear sky overhead.

You might be one who thinks an evening horseback ride represents the ultimate in good living. I might agree, and yet, the thoughts going through my head almost made me forget where I was.

It shouldn't be any kind of a surprise to anyone (and certainly to any homesteader) to hear that even homesteaders have problems and off days. To say that farming isn't all a bed of roses, or that publishing a magazine is not a snap, is even less astounding.

On the farm, our fuel costs are up; machinery repairs are more expensive; utilities and fencing and feed costs are higher than they were last month and last year... but where is the money coming from if the returns aren't keeping pace?

On the magazine, postage costs have doubled; paper and printing costs are in a steady upward spiral; rent and taxes and everything else... same thing. What are the options for keeping the whole thing going? How much further can hard work and more work and belt-tightening take it?

Whether the mental gloom was part of the chill and the gathering dusk, and riding toward a black sky in a darkening tunnel created by the berms on either side of the road and the stark trees rising from them, or whether it was a real case of the blahs, I'll never know. Because suddenly, we reached the top of the hill, and the brilliance of the setting sun blinded me like the rising sun does when the window shade is raised too quickly in the morning. It jarred me back to reality. How could I *not* remember where I was with that mass of molten sunglow spread out before me, highlighting the acres of brown marsh grasses stretching away beyond the foot of the western side of the hill?

Maybe things aren't really as gloomy as they seem, I told Colonel, urging him up the embankment to the north, where a seemingly vast stretch of alfalfa crowned the very crest of the glacial esker. He seemed to sense it, too, and with just the slightest nudge, he began to gallop.

With his sleek black neck stretched forward in eager pleasure, his mane flying, he ran like the wind. I'm not a good rider by any means, but when Colonel reaches a certain speed it's easy to fit in with his rhythm, to feel a part of his power, to sense his majesty and the sheer pleasure of making full use of his gifts. And in some strange way I get to share that power, and majesty, and pleasure.

We make a huge U-turn in the field and end up back on the road. His breath is steaming, and I'm winded, and now it really *is* getting dark, but it's no longer chilly... and it's no longer gloomy.

Tomorrow's another day, all around. I guess I'll make it all right, thanks to a stimulant not found in any pill or bottle. You can't bottle the kinds of stimulants we find beyond the sidewalks.

Part XI: 1981

Inflation: 10.35%; Year-end Federal Reserve interest rate: 15.75%; Average annual income: $21,050; Gas/gal: 1.25; Reagan becomes president; First American test-tube baby is born; Air traffic controllers strike; Reagan fires them; Frequent Flyer Miles introduced; AIDs virus identified; Microsoft releases MS DOS

96. January 1981

Trying to define homesteading

In all the years I've been writing about homesteading, one of the toughest (and most constant) challenges I've faced has been trying to *define* homesteading.

Oh, it's easy enough to list some of the things some homesteaders *do*. You can talk about what homesteaders are *not*. But if anyone can tell me what a homesteader *is*, I'd certainly be grateful.

I was on a radio program the other day, and the inevitable question came up, and I gave my usual unsatisfactory answer. Homesteading has nothing to do with free land; very few homesteaders live entirely off their land; most homesteaders have jobs and drive cars and eat store-bought bakery at least *once* in awhile, just like everybody else;

homesteaders have an Earth ethic, and try to provide as many of their own needs as possible including food, shelter, clothing, entertainment and recreation, and so on.

As usual, it bothered me, afterwards.

In today's *Chicago Tribune* I was reading Jack Mabley's column. He was writing about the energy crisis, saying that there shouldn't *be* an energy crisis. Why not? Because there are trillions of cubic feet of natural gas just waiting to be plucked, like hidden Easter eggs... three miles below the surface of the Earth.

I used to get angry, reading about why we need more oil or gas or coal or nuclear power simply because we'd lower our "standard of living" without abundant energy. But defining "standard of living" is as difficult as defining "homesteader." I find it simply impossible to understand how Plato and Socrates, Leonardo da Vinci and Michelangelo, Confucius and Thoreau and even Ben Franklin and Tom Jefferson were able to maintain a decent standard of living without Standard Oil. How on Earth could they live meaningful lives without ever having seen Charlie's Angels, eating Wonder Bread, using toothpaste and mouthwash with sex appeal?

Does it matter so much that there were "poor" people then? Disease? Ignorance? We still have all of those... but we needn't have them. And none of it has much of anything to do with energy.

Mabley, and millions of others, think we need more energy to live meaningful, fulfilling lives. Homesteaders think it doesn't matter much one way or the other, but that over-reliance on energy makes life *less* meaningful... and raping the Earth to get that energy is a crime without equal.

Is anybody an honest-to-goodness homesteader just because they're afraid the world is going to run out of energy next year, or 10 years from now? Is anybody really homesteading because they're alarmed at the loss of topsoil from the land that feeds us, alarmed at the loss of the land itself due to urbanization and industrialization? How many people are homesteaders because they're afraid of the chemicals agribusiness — farmers and processors — put into their food, because of the nutrients that are missing due to infertile and unbalanced soil and the wonders of modern food technology? How many real homesteaders are doing what they do only because they're afraid someone will start a nuclear war, or the world economy will collapse, or because they expect widespread strikes and riots?

Oh yes, you hear of all of these and more in homestead circles. In many cases, people are doing what homesteaders do — they're acting like homesteaders — because of one or more of these concerns, but it's merely a way of acting. Not a way of thinking, not a way of life.

There are outward signs, and there are inner graces...

Yes, homesteading has an economic basis, but what homesteader has the skill or patience to try to explain the details to someone still rooted in the economics of the past? Is it even worth pausing in your homestead tasks to answer someone who scoffs at your goat milking and rabbit butchering and vegetable canning when you could buy food so cheaply at the supermarket? Sure, it's fun to raise goats and rabbits and chickens, but how can you explain to non-homesteaders that all of that is just a means to an end?

And if you want to talk about nuclear power, soil loss (through erosion, loss of balanced fertility and humus, and urban expansion), undue government interference with private affairs and big business and big government in general, natural foods, education and morality and economics and a thousand other concerns...

But excuse me. I really do have to feed and water my animals, check the hams in the smokehouse, bring in the day's supply of firewood and stir the lamb stew simmering on the back of the stove.

The insulated panels are already locked in the windows for the night, and I'm writing this on an electric typewriter; it's going to be printed on a million-dollar press and delivered to your mailbox by one of the biggest governmental organizations the world has ever seen, and if you want to discuss how my homestead philosophy jibes with all of that, well, it'll just have to wait for another time. It's absolutely amazing, the conversations you can have with yourself when you read a little, think a little... and truly live beyond the sidewalks.

I was often chided for trying to define homesteading. Readers said, "Why not just *do* it?" Sounds good, so far as homesteading is concerned. But it's tough to run a business — to write, edit, sell subscriptions and advertising — when you're not even sure what it's all about.

97. March 1981

Doin' nuthin'... but not wasting time

The mid-winter thaw verged on becoming a heat wave which was made even more tropical by coinciding with a full moon. Great night for a walk.

It was almost midnight: not the time of day most people are inclined to take a stroll. But the dogs didn't think it was the least bit unusual. They romped through the remaining patches of crusty snow, in the glare of the rising moon, as if this were just an ordinary Sunday afternoon outing.

Leaving the house, we crossed the pasture, passed through the fencerow where we keep the beehives, skirted the field where the corn stubble cast Halloween-like shadows... and found ourselves under the huge, dead elm tree in the hill field that nestles against the marsh.

I sat under the tree, not to rest, but to enjoy the night. The dogs nuzzled me, expectantly, as if to say "Hey, what are we doing sitting here when there's a whole world to explore?"

When it became apparent that I was engaged in a pleasure they couldn't understand, they loped off to investigate more exciting possibilities.

Watching them fan out, noses to the ground, picking up the scent of a deer or a rabbit or maybe the possum I startled in the granary last night, I wondered whether my presumably better brain and decidedly more expensive and painful education was a blessing, or a curse.

M ost intelligent, educated readers would expect some more-or-less Earth-shaking discovery or pronouncement at this point. Sure, it always takes civilized thoughts awhile to settle down in a situation like this. So I ought to breathe in the fresh air, get inflation and nine-digit zip codes out of my brain, and zero in on some deep and immutable truth, right?

Shucks.

If life is being born, living, and dying, dogs have it all over us so-called more intelligent beings.

If life is something more...

I'm still not so sure we know something dogs don't know.

The moon was so bright that none but the brightest stars were visible, but the night was punctuated by the pinpoints of headlights that to my perspective were creeping along the land where I knew Highway 89 wound around the hill beyond the marsh.

Where were those people going, where were they coming from, why...? What were they thinking?

And here I am, sitting at the edge of a marsh in Waterloo, Wisconsin! What about the headlights, the people, in Chicago, New York, San Francisco... London and Tokyo and Paris and Moscow and Teheran...

I recalled walking back to this very field with visitors, under the bright warmth of a summer sun. Some, who knew something of farming, looked at the crop and said, "This land sure can't be worth much." Others, to whom I pointed out the red-tailed hawk who habitually rests in the old elm until you get too close, said "Uh-huh, can we go back now?" Still others only complained about the mosquitoes.

A t least there weren't any mosquitoes. At least it wasn't dark. It wasn't cold, to my northern blood. The only thing that made me even a trifle uncomfortable was that I was sitting under a huge dead tree in the middle of the night in the middle of winter, lazily thinking about the rest of the world — but not getting involved. Letting my imagination soar past the faint sky-glows of nearby towns, I wondered how many people in the world were being raped or robbed, being born or dying, at that very moment, and the guilt I felt at enjoying the peaceful night was no less than I'd feel if I were eating a prime steak in the midst of a crowd of hollow-eyed starving people...

But that's a myopic attitude, and a stupid thing to worry about, I told myself, realizing that sitting there wasn't enjoyable any more. I whistled to the dogs as I got up.

Moments like this are not a luxury. Most people probably wouldn't even appreciate them. More importantly, just sitting, "doing nothing," is not a waste of time, nor is it merely a benefit of being apart from the rat-race.

I think it's a necessity for human development.

With the dogs bounding back to my side, I put all thoughts of changing anything, of planning, of doing, even of coping, out of my head. We strolled back to the woodlot, circled through the sweet clover and ended up at the barn before I went back to the house and a hot cup of tea, and bed.

It was a good night, beyond the sidewalks.

98. April 1981

An early attack of spring fever

It was one of those wondrous spring mornings when you know, beyond any doubt, that homesteading is the only way to live.

Walking to the barn became a game of stepping-stones among tiny, gurgling, sparkling streams of snow-melt. An early flock of wild geese was taking advantage of the steady south wind to wing its way north. A new lamb was barely dried off but already following its mother. It looked like a tiny sawhorse trying to walk, and I watched it with that combination of amusement, pride, satisfaction and humility that has no name and which I've been able to find only in homesteading.

I took care of the lamb, then fed and watered the sheep and pigs. While milking the goats, I noticed that none of the ducks or bantams were missing yet. Any day now, one by one, they'd retire to their hidden nests, reappearing a few weeks later with their new families in tow.

It was a perfect day for an early attack of spring fever, and walking back to the house with the milk pail, a passage from an old book came to mind:

"I had a job, once. Worked as a magazine writer, flying around the country getting information, then sitting in my little cubicle in the home office writing it up and waiting for the whistle to blow so I could go home and putter in my garden. And one fine spring day as I came to the end of a row, I leaned on my hoe and felt a south breeze laden with the fragrance of plum blossoms caressing my face and thought, 'Wouldn't it be great if life could always be like this?"

Today, those words were like salt poured on a raw wound.

The guy who wrote that so long ago, in *Country Living*, was me.

And today, due to a wide variety of complex developments, I was again assuming the role of COUNTRYSIDE'S sole editor. The combination made me feel like I was regressing at least 15 years. That was depressing.

❝Since I believe we are masters of our own destiny, I quit the job.

Soon the garden filled the freezer, and a few drawers in the locker plant; we added chickens, dairy goats, a pig and some sheep, and I operated a one-man print shop to bring in enough cash to pay the taxes and other unavoidable financial obligations."

The Countryside Print Shop will be 20 years old this summer. COUNTRYSIDE magazine — the name came from the print shop, and I haven't gotten any better at naming magazines since then, in spite of all my practice — was supposed to be nothing but a small newsletter. Something to help keep the press busy, and to satisfy — something — something very personal — but what was it?

At one point I was writing, typesetting, printing and mailing four publications, with one part-time helper, and I still had plenty of time for homesteading. I never had the feeling of "going to work."

Now we have seven publications, but we also have a dozen full-time employees, and I face the dull dread of "having to go to work."

It could be worse: *Mother Earth* has 150 people working on it. Or maybe it could be better: most of the other magazines that started when we did are out of business. What we have is neither a success, nor a failure, and I feel that, in spite of the years and the work, we haven't accomplished much.

Diane and I drive past the still-slumbering garden at a crawl, remorsefully, guiltily, even though it's too early to think seriously about gardening. We creep past the hog pasture and note the fencing repairs that will have to be made before the hogs can leave their winter quarters. We slowly pass the hayfield, the wet soil glistening in the winter-ravaged stubble of last years' crop. I can envision the hot but happy work that will be waiting for me there almost before I know it, certainly before I'm ready for it, and I wonder how on Earth I'll get it all done.

Once past the boundary of our land, we speed up and head for town.

Events of the past years spin through my brain like the fence posts flashing past the window. My original ideas and goals; all the multitude of forces that shape a magazine and a business; the competition for readers, the financial problems, the people who worked with me to try to improve COUNTRYSIDE and to bring its help and its message to a larger audience... Today is an opportunity for a fresh start, but what have I learned, and where are we going next?

If I were merely going to work, I wouldn't do it. I'd simply hang it up as I did before I wrote *Country Living.*

But COUNTRYSIDE isn't just a magazine, it's not just a business. It's actually part of my homestead, and my concept of homesteading. It's my own, personal opportunity to share, to help others, to be a part of something that's much larger and more important than merely tending my own flocks and fields. I can bring something to it that no one else can... and it can provide me with something I can't achieve in any other way.

Diane is going downtown to the Countryside General Store, but the publications office is a few blocks off the highway, so she drops me off at the corner and I walk the rest of the way. As I walk, the old enthusiasm returns and I find a new determination. Even though everything has changed since I put together that first issue of COUNTRYSIDE, there is still a need for a countryside magazine, and I can still do it with the ideas and the ideals I had then.

"Our purpose, then, is to help guide those who have no starting point at all, to encourage those who aren't too sure about what homesteading offers but who might want to join us, and to entertain and inform anyone else who's interested."

And what's so bad about that, as purposes go? So what if we can't attract big advertising money, and thousands of readers, and high-priced writers? So what if we can't afford an editor, and I have to do it myself? Being a serious homesteader certainly entails much more than milking goats and hoeing the garden, and if I can make my contribution by editing a magazine and running a business, and doing it my way, according to homestead principles, why should I consider myself any less of a homesteader?

Then a strange thing happened.

I was still a couple of hundred yards from the office... and I suddenly came to the end of the sidewalk. I had never paid any attention to that before, but today, it appeared as an omen. I found myself smiling as I followed the narrow muddy path the rest of the way.

A homesteader can even edit a magazine, beyond the sidewalks.

I used to consider myself a has-been who never was, but now, re-reading these columns, I think maybe I achieved exactly what I set out to accomplish. It didn't meet the more customary idea of success, which sometimes gave me pause, but in retrospect, it was a worthy attainment.

20 years of homestead business

L ittle did I realize that by deciding to write on this month's theme — homestead business — I'd run into one of the toughest writing assignments I've ever faced.

After all, it was 20 years ago this month that I started my own homestead business: I've never even mentioned that in COUNTRYSIDE so there's a lot stored up and I expected the words to just flow onto the paper.

They did. But it didn't feel right. It wasn't COUNTRYSIDE. So I started over again. And again, and again.

It was ridiculous. I was getting frustrated.

L oretta, one of our editors; Delores, our part-time bookkeeper; and I were discussing a minor problem that had cropped up here in the shop. We were weighing the effects of the possible solutions and Loretta said, "Well, do you want to be a nice guy or a businessman?'

WHAT!?! Say that again, please!

To her mind, she said, you couldn't be a nice guy and a businessman too.

I knew at once what had caused my writer's block.

Twenty-five years ago, I would have agreed that business was not a nice occupation. That's why I wanted to become a homesteader.

But my desire to be a homesteader led to my becoming a businessman, and the two became so entwined it was hard to tell where one left off and the other started. I learned something about business, and I came to enjoy it, without even realizing it. But that just didn't fit in with the homestead focus of COUNTRYSIDE, so I kept it to myself.

There's something else. COUNTRYSIDE has never printed home business articles, because I've seen too many "How I Wash Windows Three Days a Week and Live Like a Millionaire" stories in other homestead publications. I consider that idea as misleading as any other that portrays homesteading as being all blue skies and rosebuds. But who wants to read about how *tough* it is?

Many polls have shown that most Americans know very little about business. They don't understand margin, markup, profit, return on investment, advertising, inventory control, government regulations... and they don't especially care.

At the same time, breathes there a homesteader who has never dreamed of being self-employed? Is there anyone who hasn't yearned, at least once, to escape the 9-5 grind, brown bag lunches or greasy food in noisy cafeterias, impossible demands or lack of challenges, all personified by a boss who knows less than you do? Isn't that one of the reasons people aspire to homesteading in the first place?

What homesteader can be truly happy leaving the homestead to work elsewhere when the sun is shining and the garden beckons and the goat kids are frolicking in the spring grass?

What homestead couldn't use a little extra money to fix up the house or barn, to buy fencing or tools, or start an orchard?

"Pure" homesteading, where you provide all your own food, clothing and shelter, pay no rent or interest or taxes, have no dental or medical or insurance expenses, purchase no nails or window glass or books, is impossible. (If you sell or barter homestead products you're in business.)

We clearly have a problem. We cannot homestead without the business activity we profess to disdain.

Wouldn't we be better off, and happier, if we could reconcile our homestead principles with our dependence on commercial activities?

Not all homesteaders are antagonistic toward business, of course, but even then few of them understand the relationships between the two unless they've actually been involved.

The two *are* related. The new society we've been evolving toward needs both, and it needs to understand both... *and it needs to understand how our changing world is changing both homesteading and business.*

What is a homesteader? A person who bakes bread, or grinds grain, or gardens or preserves food or raises livestock or lives in the countryside... or a person who thinks about Spaceship Earth in a certain way?

When does a person become a businessman? By selling a few dozen surplus eggs, by selling a certain dollar volume of goods or services, by reaching some other magic quantitative mark? And how do a person's attitudes change at any point on this sliding scale?

When we've discussed the "homesteading' question in the past, most readers agreed that it's a matter of attitude more than anything else. That brings up two interesting points about business, and how our world is changing... and coming closer to the ideal professed by serious homesteaders.

If you ask a hundred people what the primary mission of any business is, at least ninety-nine will answer "profits" or something akin to it.

Not so, says Professor Garfield Stock, a specialist in management and human relations for the Department of Business and Management, University of Wisconsin-Extension, and a consultant to many large and small businesses.

Dr. Stock believes that the primary mission of any business is to *help make people successful.*

Think about that. The mission of every business is to make people successful — and with a homesteader's definition of success, yet!

If you sell sweet corn at the side of the road, your mission is not making money, and it's not building the fence you're going to buy with the money. A father who brings home corn for supper when his wife was wondering what to serve; the wife who pleases her family by serving delicious fresh corn; the child who is happier and healthier for having eaten the buttery delight; all of these people have become more successful (in very minor ways, of course, but so what) because you sold that corn.

Money in your pocket is a by-product.

Obviously, the business that doesn't contribute to peoples' success doesn't make a profit. And those that do make a profit almost as a by-product.

Profits, of course, are absolutely necessary. You wouldn't plant 10 kernels of corn if you didn't expect to get more than 10 back at harvest time. If you depended on that corn to live, it would not only be foolish: you'd starve.

I attended a seminar conducted by Dr. Stock, and as I listened to him piece this concept together and give examples of companies that followed it as a management technique (especially in Japan and other areas that are outstripping the U.S. in industrial productivity) I don't know if I was more delighted as a homesteader, or as a businessman who'd been struggling to make use of Schumacher's "small is beautiful" concepts.

(Here are a few more of Dr. Stock's comments, from my notes: "Money doesn't motivate people: work motivates people — and money results... work should be as enjoyable as play or rest... but a country club atmosphere, being 'nice' to people," will backfire because people will take advantage of a management system without a structure and without goals... good management gives equal emphasis to tasks and to people, unlike the task-oriented slave-master relationship which results in very low productivity...")

It seems to me that this is extending what homesteaders already know and believe, to another aspect of life.

We mentioned small is beautiful: could it be that "small" businesses are somehow better than big ones?

If you plant a seed, it depends on soil fertility, rain, and sunshine, to grow strong and healthy and produce a crop. These same forces apply whether the seed is planted in a window box or in a thousand-acre field. The growth of each is governed by the same basic principles.

No one has yet come up with an acceptable definition of a small farm. There are "farms" of one acre growing extremely high-value crops and grossing more than $1 million a year; there are farms with thousands of acres, perhaps grazing a few sheep, grossing much less.

Some enterprises simply demand greater size, but some people have become so enamored of smallness that any day now somebody's going to say that a four-man football team is better than one with 11 players because it's smaller.

There are no blacks or whites in anything, but we can't distinguish the shades of grey until we develop the ability and take the time to focus on them. Since commercial activity does play such an important role in our lives, it behooves us to develop the ability and take the time.

But there's something that may be even more important for people who are serious about homesteading at this point in the emergence of the new age we've been talking about for so long:

If homesteading is *not* simply gardens and goats, wood heat and windmills, conservation and country living — if homesteading is a philosophy and a way of life that ties in with our religion and politics and what we teach our children about life — how can it avoid interacting with something as all-pervasive as commercial activity?

***

I aspired to homesteading *because of* my anti-business bias, but I wasn't able to become a homesteader without becoming a businessman too. As I learned more about business my attitudes changed. The homestead and business merged, as it were, into something bigger than either one alone, more important than either one, and I got a better view of Spaceship Earth and what I had formerly thought only homesteading was all about.

***

Twenty years ago this month our business consisted of nothing more than a rented typewriter, a T-square and glue pot and the kitchen table for laying out magazines, a strong desire to communicate ideas and information not available elsewhere, and a dream of our own homestead somewhere down the road.

***

Homestead businesses, like homesteads, are often kept going with baling wire and make-do and do-without. We cut type from other printed materials and rearranged it into our magazine headlines.

One memorable headline came from a box of corn flakes.

***

When we bought our first small offset press (with a credit union furniture loan) it was kept in the bedroom of our rented farmhouse.

One day, Diane wouldn't let a repairman repair in, because the bed wasn't made.

***

The truck that delivered our printing paper couldn't travel on our country road during the spring thaw. The trucker called from town, and I had to drive out to the paved highway and transfer the cartons to our Nash Rambler.

I was making a business phone call and identified myself as the Countryside Print Shop, when a rooster loudly crowed, only a few feet away. The receptionist paused, then asked, "Did you say print *shop or* pet *shop?"*

***

A deliveryman refused to stop at our place because he was afraid of the geese.

***

On one of those rare occasions when we visited friends (you don't make many friends when you work at home and put in the kinds of hours self-employed people must to make a living) one of our young children wandered about, exploring the strange house with its carpeting, tv, new furniture, and other things we didn't have.

Finally he came back to my chair and tugged at my sleeve. I bent down and he whispered in my ear, "Dad, where's their printing press? It isn't in the bedroom!"

***

That son became a printer at Countryside Publications. He now runs a press elsewhere, but our daughter still works with us, designing and laying out magazines. Somehow I can't help but consider all of that a part of our homestead experience.

If you could have seen more of it, Loretta, maybe I could change your mind about business. It's been a good 20 years. And it could only have happened beyond the sidewalks.

2014: That son studied business administration in college, took over the magazine when I retired, and made it far more "successful" than I ever did. Or cared to. We both reached our goals, different as they were.

100. July 1981

The question of "quality"

COUNTRYSIDE has a quality not achieved by other magazines. Like quality of life, not everyone will agree that such a magazine, or its pictures or writing, are of *superior* quality, but their peculiar and essential character gives them a *special* quality.

Let me try to explain this another way: What do you consider quality bread? If you're a homesteader, you'll probably answer homegrown organic wheat or rye, freshly ground, mixed with other wholesome, homestead-produced or at least organic ingredients, and carefully baked, with love.

And yet, you know as well as I do that some people actually prefer mushy, white, tasteless, nutritionally empty mucilage that only passes as bread. Two ways of looking at things; two kinds of quality.

If you're old enough, you can probably remember (and if you're not you can probably imagine) how only one person in the neighborhood was recognized as the top fiddle or banjo player. Whoever it was didn't go to music school or spend hours practicing every day: he was just an ordinary farmer who was pretty good at music, and the main star at every hoedown, hootenanny and Fourth of July celebration.

Today, most homes have four to five radios; cars have speakers that take up the entire back seat; there are tapes and records and tv; and anybody can hear the top musicians in the world (as well as all the popular ones who ain't so hot) without even making it a special occasion.

And when they hear Grandpa sawing on his fiddle, they cringe, because it doesn't sound like the Boston Pops or Kiss. But really, which one has the better quality?

If your attempt at cheese-making didn't turn out looking or tasting like the imported stuff (or even like Kraft's), so what? You did it yourself, it's *you*, and it has a peculiar and essential character — it has a quality of its own.

Does someone use your bread as a doorstop? Is everybody laughing because you harvested only one little zucchini squash? Don't fret about it.

The next time someone says, "This ham you cured is sure salty," just smile and say, "Yes, it does have a quality of its own, doesn't it?" Next time will be better, and you'll appreciate it even more because you'll have achieved an even higher quality.

If our ideas of what constitutes a quality life and quality bread differ from so many others, then it follows that our ideas of the quality of many other things must differ, too, when we pursue a lifestyle beyond the sidewalks.

101. August 1981

Eating the homestead way... almost

As with most homestead families, ours hasn't always enjoyed 100 percent dedication to homestead principles. In recent years especially, with our children going through high school, I periodically despaired over the grocery bill (when we supposedly raise our own food) and the packaging that goes to the dumps. In fact, there's a tradition at our house that Dad refuses to take tin cans and glass bottles and cardboard packages to the dumps, on principle.

I got a chance to put that principle into action.

A few days after graduating from high school, Steve left for Marine Corps boot camp, and, on the same day, Diane and John left to visit son Dave, who lives in Salt Lake City. I was alone, and free to eat the homestead way.

I love to cook almost as much as I enjoy producing food — maybe more. But I've seldom cooked for just one person. Proud as I am of my huge cast iron frying pan and Dutch oven and 20-quart stock pot, they obviously weren't going to get much use in my new bachelor life.

Instead, I dug out the efficiency oven. (Page 9 in your Countryside General Store catalog.)

It was Diane's idea to put it in the catalog: I couldn't see much value in the thing. It's only about nine inches in diameter and four inches high, which means it's not going to accommodate a ham or a goose or anything else I'm likely to roast, I thought. But, then, I hadn't thought of eating at a table for one. It certainly wouldn't do to turn on the conventional oven for one lamb chop!

Then, what to eat?

At first, there was rhubarb for breakfast, and then the strawberries ripened, and later the mulberries and wild raspberries. We have homemade bacon and sausage, and homegrown corn and buckwheat for my two favorite kinds of pancakes, as well as wheat and rye for bread. Although we didn't make any maple syrup this year, we have plenty of honey, and jam. And, of course, there are always eggs and milk.

Not having to hurry back to the house from chores in the morning, I frequently strolled back past the mulberries and wild raspberries — and ate so many that when I began to make breakfast I discovered I wasn't hungry! There wasn't even a dish to wash!

Lunch, during the garden season, means salad. There were several varieties of lettuce, radishes and green onions, peas, and Chinese cabbage, kohlrabi, eggplant, zucchini, cabbage red and green, cauliflower, broccoli, and even more.

There's an old adage that you should never go shopping when you're hungry. That probably hold true when you shop in the garden, too. But who can resist such temptation? Every day is different, with different offerings available, and I mentally blended flavors, textures and colors as I harvested. I often got carried away, but the pigs didn't mind.

Sometimes, for a heartier meal, the salad bowl was fortified with bits of ham and cheese, or a sliced boiled egg or even a raw egg (which people who tell us raw milk is dangerous say is a bad thing to do — but I do it anyway).

Some days, the bowl is very simple, by choice. On others, it's quite elaborate, with a dozen or more ingredients. It's always topped with my private label dressing (made with a secret blend of herbs and spices — "secret" mostly because I seldom use recipes and I never measure anything when I cook) — and it's always delicious.

And all I have to wash is a bowl and a fork.

Then, after chores, I put the meat of the day in the efficiency oven pan. We butchered a hog and a sheep just recently, and made up some packages for one.

The oven works on the stove top, with very low heat.

When the meat is coming along, the potatoes go in the same pan. And, when the potatoes are almost done, there's still room on top for the vegetable.

Accompanied by a small salad, I sit down to a meal as fine as any I've ever enjoyed in a good restaurant... even though I eat it from the oven pan. (That way there's only the pan, the salad bowl, a knife and fork, and the cup which held my herb tea to wash.)

This meal plan went on for several weeks. Not only did I not get close to the grocery store: I didn't even dip into the store-bought stuff the family left, and I sure didn't run out of dishwashing soap!

Then one day I got a craving for Mexican food. We have plenty of homegrown jalapeno peppers and beans and corn and ground chevon, but when I thought of the process of making masa — boiling the corn in lime and grinding it — and then going through the rest to make a tamale, I just didn't feel up to it, for just one person.

But there was a can of tamales in the cupboard, and some rice. I boiled the rice, weakened, and opened the can.

The tamales went in the efficiency oven. The beans (which I'd soaked the night before) were cooked in another pan, and placed alongside the tamales. The rice followed, and I threw a few peppers on for good measure and color.

While washing all those pans and cleaning up the kitchen, I looked at that tamale can with guilt and shame, like a junk food junkie. I would have felt silly going to the dump with one can, but I had to hide the evidence.

So I buried it in the backyard, beyond the sidewalks.

102. September 1981

If so many are serving, where's the service?

Some people have a tough time seeing what's so simple about the simple living we homesteaders are so pleased with. But maybe that's only fair, because we homesteaders find it difficult to see what's so great about some of the things that apparently thrill non-homesteaders. For example, the "service economy" we've been hearing so much about.

"Service" is the fastest-growing segment of the U.S. labor force today, and, according to a recent newspaper article, 59.6 million of us are now engaged in "service."

So how come I have to pump my own gas? How come some supermarkets don't even mark prices on their products? (The prices are on the shelves, and they provide a grease pencil if you want to mark them on the package yourself.) How come there is still talk of eliminating mail service on Saturdays, and dropping some small-town post offices altogether?

As a youngster, I walked the few blocks to Ginke's Meat Market. I can still remember the sawdust on the floor, the blood-stained apron and white hat the rotund and jovial Mr. Ginke wore, and handing my mother's shopping list over the counter. There were strings of homemade weiners and sticks of salami and rings of bologna hanging in the window, and hamburger was ground right before your eyes. The butcher filled the order — and he knew just how my mother wanted the pork chops cut and what size ring of bologna we needed.

Today, the meat is prepackaged in quantities too large for some people and too small for others, and, if you want thick pork chops, forget it: there isn't a butcher in sight. And we call it a service economy.

When I was a kid, we traded at the Stier Tea Company. My father-in-law used to take care of Mr. Stier's horses, which pulled his delivery wagon, but by the late '30s the horses had been replaced by a truck. We never got deliveries anyway. I went to the store with a market basket (there was no "paper or plastic?" in those days) and a shopping list, and waited while Mr. or Mrs. Stier pulled the items on the list from the shelves behind the counter.

I especially enjoyed watching them grind coffee in the huge, red, hand-cranked machine, and I always wondered how something that smelled so good could taste so horrible. It was also neat when Mom needed something off the top shelf. There was a little ladder behind the counter for middle shelves, but for the really high ones, Mr. Stier would get a long stick with grabbers at the end and pick up a box of oatmeal or whatever and carefully maneuver it down to eye level. Sometimes he'd knock a couple of other boxes to the floor in the process. That was fun.

On the way home, there was usually a policeman standing on the corner by the Island Drug Store (with its cigar case near the door and the soda fountain in the cool, dim, somewhat mysterious interior). I can still see him: very tall, with very shiny leather boots and belt with a strap that went across his chest, visored cap and — most of all — a real gun. He was friendly, but stern and more than a trifle intimidating, and I'm certain that thousands of children developed certain attitudes from police officers like him.

And he'd often help kids cross the street safely. Service.

I remember being sick, even with something as simple as a sore throat, and Dr. Anderson striding into my bedroom, talking cheerily while taking a thermometer from his black bag.

He was summoned, of course, by telling the telephone operator we needed a doctor. Imagine trying *that* in a "service" economy.

The trade publication *Industry Week* recently reported that the growth in the number of people providing services is phenomenal — up 40 percent in the last decade, compared with 10 percent in mining, manufacturing, construction, transportation and public utilities.

But we now pump our own gas, get our own groceries, pick up our lunch order at a counter or from a machine, and see a doctor in a hospital if we can find a way to get there and can afford to wait.

Maybe you can explain it, but it sure stumps me.

Meanwhile, the number of farmers continues to decline. One farmer now feeds nearly 60 other people.

This is usually compared with a generation or two ago, when one farm family is said to have provided food for itself, with just a little left over. But that comparison holds less water than a leaky rain barrel, because today's farmer couldn't operate without machinery that has to be designed and built with materials mined from the earth, without the transportation of the machinery and its fuels as well as farm products, without maintenance and electricity and, oh, I'd say probably 40 or 50 other backup people, from veterinarians and bankers to printers and supermarket clerks.

The old farmers provided their own food with very few of these backup people. Their horses and mules replaced themselves, and the farmers grew their own fuel. And even long after the spinning wheel and loom went out of favor, farm families still provided a great deal more than food. Quilting frames and shoe lasts are still common at many farm auctions in our area. Some people who are still living helped build the roads past their farms, and helped maintain them... not as employees of the county or township, but as citizens who didn't see any need for having others do for them what they could do for themselves.

It seems to me that we're coming to the other end of the spectrum: some people today don't want to do anything for themselves.

The real problem in speaking of these things — and in speaking of homesteading — is deciding at what point you're throwing the baby out with the bath water. If you want to be a homesteader, independent and self-sufficient, how far do you go in developing a lifestyle that will be meaningful, yet not demeaning?

And for those who demand more and more "service," how far will they go before they're working harder to pay for their services than we homesteaders work to provide our own?

Maybe when the world reaches that point, we'll have some answers to the puzzling questions.

My bet is that they'll lie in picking and choosing from the best of both worlds as we homesteaders are doing, beyond the sidewalks.

2014: Like almost everything else, now it's even worse: bag your own groceries, ATMs, etc. However, so far at least, most people seem to be balking at those "self-checkout" stations seen in many stores. But it still bothers me that nobody *makes* anything anymore. It's only a matter of time until we're all taking in each other's laundry. What economic sense does that make? What kind of a life does that make?

103. October 1981

Sweltering in the sun, sloshing through the slime... is it just for fun?

A long time ago, when only Santa and a few other eccentrics had beards, there lived an old man with a long, flowing, white beard. He never gave it much thought, until one day a little girl came up to him and asked, "Do you sleep with your beard inside the covers, or outside?"

It was a ridiculous question, of course, and it caught him by surprise. He thought. "Why, ahem, I sleep with it *inside* the covers, of course."

The tyke went on her way, apparently satisfied. But the old man was troubled.

That night, in bed, he smoothed the white hair down from his chin over his chest, and pulled the blankets over it. And smiled.

Why, *of course* he slept with his beard tucked in.

But it didn't feel right.

Slipping his hand under his chin, he whipped the beard out, splaying it over the top of the blankets.

Ah, that's better, he thought. I guess I sleep with it *outside.*

He was still vaguely uncomfortable. He tried putting it in, and out again. He turned onto his stomach, and his side, and the other side.

When the sun came up he hadn't slept a wink, and after briefly considering strangling the little girl, he got a scissors and cut off the beard.

In July, COUNTRYSIDE's Question of the Month was "Why do you homestead?" (Your replies are in this issue.) While I certainly hope the question didn't drive you to the extreme distraction of the man with the beard, it did have some of that effect on me.

The question seemed innocent enough when we were putting the magazine together, but everything looks different in print.

I get a copy of COUNTRYSIDE in the mail at home, to check the delivery time and condition, and so I can go through it with the rest of the magazines I get and try to see it as somebody who doesn't spend most of his working hours *making* it. When I came to the question, "Why do you homestead?" I rolled it around in my mind a bit — decided I put up with the work and the hassles for many reasons and for no reason at all — and turned the page.

A short time later when I was shelling peas — the kind of job where you can put your brain in neutral and just let it coast — it seemed like asking something like, why do you love someone? Who knows, and what difference does it make as long as you do, and whose business is it anyway?

Later, I was pulling the proliferation of weeds that the untimely summer rains nurtured in my garden. Even the normally barren paths along the raised beds were knee-deep in pigweed and lamb's quarters, and they were so thick you didn't have to think much about what you were doing.

But the rains had brought even more mosquitoes than weeds, so I was fully decked out in a long-sleeved shirt, hat, and gloves. And it was hot, and humid. The sweat flowed freely.

I like being outdoors. I don't mind physical labor, or even a modicum of physical discomfort. But I love the sun and usually wear as little as modesty allows, so the sweat-sodden clothes that encased me weren't exactly to my liking. Neither were the mosquitoes that buzzed around my head, landed on my face (to be swatted with a soggy, muddy glove) and even flew into my eyes and nose, they were so thick.

With a smaller garden — say, one designed to provide a few fresh vegetables during the season — a few handfuls of weeds would have made the plot presentable, at least. And if I didn't touch any of them, so what? What great loss would it be?

So why was I a homesteader, tending row after row of potatoes, a hundred tomato plants, enough onions and beans and carrots to last a year, and more besides?

The bugs and the heat got to be too much, and I left the garden long before the job was finished, and long before the question was answered.

Later, I was doing evening chores in the hazy, sweltering, drizzle that seems to have plagued the best part of a Wisconsin summer. And the electric fencer which — usually — contains our pigs, goats, and sheep, and which winks reassuringly from its dark corner in the barn when it's working, was dark and silent.

Muttering, I set out to track down the problem before the hogs discovered the bonanza and rooted up our strawberry bed again.

The two wires leading from the charger pass through the barn wall. The ground wire is connected to a rod driven deep into the earth between the barn and the silo. The live wire is connected to the fence enclosing the sheep pasture, then jumps to the goats' yard, and then to the hog lot. Starting from the charger, I followed the thin strand, looking for a short.

It was beginning to rain harder, a heavy drizzle, and the droplets hung on the wire like morning dew. It also started to wet my shirt — the third I'd put on that day — from the outside in, to combine with the sweat already drenching it from the inside out.

Here and there a blade of grass touched the fence, and I tore those out of the way. But there was nothing serious enough to totally short out the system. It must be farther down the line, I thought as I plodded on.

I passed through the sheep enclosure, and the goat enclosure, and climbed over the fence to the hogs. Their pasture was barren, except for right under the electric wire which is strung inside a woven wire fence. Actually, that's good, because part of the plan is to have the hogs root out the quack and other weeds, leaving a plot that can be planted to small-scale crops that can grow with little or no weed interference, and hog manure... with the crop residue being cleaned up by the hogs when they're rotated back to that pasture again.

But with the rains, the unprotected ground was a lake of slippery, squishy mud. It stuck to my high rubber boots and built up until I felt I was wearing snowshoes. In some places where the hogs had dug wallows, I sunk in up to my calves... and then I fell.

Being completely soaked anyway, the wet mud oozing along my entire left side didn't make much difference, so far as comfort was concerned. But it did lend a peculiar light to the question, "why am I doing this?"

I had more time to ponder that when I found that at the far end of the pasture — it's always at the far end, you know — the hogs had used their horny snouts to shovel up the earth until it touched the electric wire, nine inches above the original ground level. Slipping and sliding back to the barn to get a shovel gave me time to think about many things.

By the time I got the fence cleared of heavy wet clay, the rain had increased in intensity, but I was so hot it didn't make any difference. In fact, the cold rain and the gathering dusk felt good.

Back at the house, I peeled off the sopping clothes in the mudroom and squished my way to the shower. Then, wearing sandals and shorts, I dipped into the refrigerator for a Leinenkugle and asked Diane, who was molding bread dough into pans, "Are you a homesteader?"

"Sure," she answered with a brightness that contrasted with the gloom outside and my mood, even after the shower.

"Why?"

"Because it's fun."

I flipped the top off the Leinie and sat back, looking at the jars of pickles and green beans Diane had taken out of the pressure canner earlier and had set on the counter to cool. The only sound was the patter of rain, and the hum of the dehydrator, which I knew held several trays of rhubarb leather and some cucumber chips and at least one of basil, and probably more.

"What's fun about it?"

"Oh, playing in the garden, and playing in the kitchen, and playing with the animals."

"What about the mosquitoes."

"Oh," she wrinkled her nose, "I don't like them. When they're out I do something else." She put the bread in the oven and started to carry the jars of canned goods to the pantry, stacking them along rows of beets and plums and kraut.

I set down the beer and started to help her.

In a lightning flash — not a bolt, but the kind that rolls in from over the hills and bathes the entire night landscape in revealing light — I knew why I've been homesteading all these years, and why I love my wife, and why I'm a husband and father, writer and publisher, instead of all the other options I've had. It doesn't matter that I can't put any of it into words. That's just the way it is, and what difference does it make to anyone else, anyway?

We went to bed with the rain still gently pelting the windowpane. I sighed in contentment, and smoothed my beard out over the thin summer blanket. It didn't feel right, so I tucked it in...

104. November 1981

Gretchen and the harvest

Compared with the other seasons of the year, autumn is as plump and ripe and as satisfying as the harvest it represents. The dreams and hopes of spring have either been fulfilled, or aborted. The work of summer is just a memory. The long, cold sleep of winter lies in the future like death itself: a certainty, but not today. Not yet. Fall is a time to enjoy, and to harvest, and to give thanks...

Two years ago last summer we bought 21 purebred Spotted just-weaned piglets. In fact, they had been weaned early, since their owner was leaving the state and wanted them ready for the auction. I paid too much, as I usually do at farm auctions, but I convinced Diane (and myself) that I wasn't just buying feeder pigs: I was buying some purebred, future breeding stock.

Since they were so young and so small, we tried feeding them milk with the Pig Saver, but they chewed the nipples off. We had to switch to bottles with lamb nipples.

The process of bottle-feeding animals works two ways. The animal grows to regard the person holding the bottle as its mother — and the person holding the bottle goes a little goofy, too. Whether the animal is a goat, a calf, a lamb or a pig, a strange symbiosis seems to cloud over normal human intelligence and rationale.

My favorite was a mostly white little rascal named Gretchen. "Favorite," of course has nothing to do with a knowledge of livestock genetics or conformation or economics, but rather with an inexplicable rapport that, perhaps, borders on a kind of love.

The little pigs thrived, and grew, and when they were large enough to send to market, we kept seven gilts as breeding stock. Naturally, Gretchen was one of them.

If you're deeply involved with animals of any kind, you can't help but become enmeshed in all kinds of strange, but wonderful — and sometimes unsettling — thoughts. When you see animals breeding, being born, growing, sick, healthy and playing, fighting, dying, you just have to feel a sense of awe and wonder. Eventually, you see a pattern emerging... a pattern that includes you, and the universe.

I can never butcher an animal without recalling something I read, years ago, about experiments with ESP, where rabbit fryers were butchered... and scientists recorded reactions in the mother, who was a considerable distance away. Supposedly, she knew.

Gretchen grew, and prospered, was bred, and farrowed seven fine youngsters. She — and they — were part of the troupe that escaped and, trotting down the road a half-mile, ignoring lush alfalfa and ripe corn on either side, savaged a neighbor's lawn something awful. We had to sell many pigs to pay for the damage. Her offspring grew, and were sold, and she farrowed again, and she kept on growing too.

Soon she weighed 400 pounds, and was farrowing 11 piglets in a litter. She started getting a little ornery. Now, I like to see a certain defensiveness in a sow when she has little ones, but Gretchen was getting ornery *period.*

Of late, my son John felt it necessary to be armed with a stout stick just to go into the barn to turn on the water to fill the various stock tanks.

And the other night, when son Dave and Diane and I were out in the pasture herding two young sows and their new litters to the shelter of the barn, Gretchen lunged at Diane, sending her scrambling over the fence.

Some people speak of "mean" dogs or goats, of "dumb" animals... or of highly intelligent or loving animals. And yet, can a goat that is chained by the neck, neglected and abused, be expected to act like a goat that is well-fed and housed and properly treated? Will a dog that is chained and beaten, or allowed to roam without any control whatsoever, react to a pat on the head, or a command, in the same manner as a dog that is worked with?

How much attention do we pay to animal psychology?

Many working dog trainers claim that training dogs is simple: it's training dog owners that's difficult. Trainer Bob Carrillo recently told me of a lady in one of his training sessions who was only confusing her dog, and scattering sheep by improper directions. He had her tie the dog outside the corral... and made her work the sheep.

She learned what she had to tell the dog to do.

When we try to think like sheep, or dogs, or goats or pigs... something wonderful happens. Not only does our work become easier, but a part of the cosmos, hidden to most people, opens itself to us. While we milk, haul feed, pitch manure, lug water, and repair fences, we slowly discover the infrastructure of the universe.

Chore-time last night was like it always is before market day. Like all good-byes.

I wish I would have done this or that differently, spent more time, paid more attention. In a futile last-ditch effort to make up for my shortcomings, to placate my conscience, I usually provide a last supper.

I hand-picked a few bags of still moist corn. I cut a load of the tenderest new-growth comfrey, which has revived under the autumn rains. And I hauled all of this into the center of the main hog pasture and dumped it in neat little piles.

The pigs should have been full of their regular barley, and rape and alfalfa from the side pasture, but they seemed delighted with the treat. I hunched down to watch them.

Then, one huge, old sow waddled away from the small groups who were noisily enjoying the feast, and approached me. Gretchen and I looked at each other, in the dim light of the autumn evening.

She weighed 600 pounds by then, but from my squatting position, she looked like a battleship. No intelligent hog farmer trusts a sow like that... but I didn't move.

She came up to me, snuffled at my feet, and rubbed my leg with her huge, horny nose.

It wasn't a scratch-those-mites kind of rub, which would have bowled me over. It was more like a kind of communication.

She was telling me, "There's a harvest moon, and to everything there is a season... and it's been good."

I reached out and scratched her behind one gargantuan ear — and she uttered a satisfied snort and trotted back to the last supper.

It was dark when I left the hog lot. I felt strangely — moved. Sad, yet knowing this was the natural order of things, and I was a part of it, and therefore joyful.

I turned out the barn light, and as I came out the door, I heard a flock of Canada geese winging and honking overhead. It was nearly 10 o'clock, on September 21, and autumn would be arriving in just a few minutes.

Everything was on schedule. The universe was in order.

All of us who deal with animals impart a facet of our own personalities to the animals we deal with. Some people dote on their cats and dogs as others dote on children. Some people abuse animals just as they abuse everything else. Some people... think pigs try to teach them about the meaning of Life...

And yet, what difference does it make if our lives are touched by a great novel, a poem, or a pig? If an experience changes us, enlightens us, can it really matter if it comes from a great composer and a symphony orchestra, or anything else that affects human emotions? Even a pig?

The next morning, we loaded 20 hogs onto Larry Wilke's truck, and, as I closed the gate to the loading chute, they moved up the driveway.

Gretchen was with them, but I didn't think about her.

We're going to butcher a hog for our own use, this Saturday, and while I think I'd have a hard time slaughtering Gretchen, I sort of wish it was me instead of some stranger in a factory-type slaughterhouse. But there's no time to think of that, either. For one thing, there's a sleek black gilt, with a litter of seven that needs to be checked.

As I lean over the fence, one fine-looking little squirt comes over, and when I dangle my hand in front of it, it nudges my finger.

The cycle continues, beyond the sidewalks.

105. December 1981

If you have to ask the price...

I got a little excited about the September Question of the Month... the one asking about the best places in the world to homestead. "The Ideal Homestead" is one of my favorite topics, and it ought to be: I've been searching for it long enough.

As I went about my homestead chores, I found myself wondering what *my* answer would be...

While I was digging the last of the potatoes, trying to aim my fork close enough to the withered vines to turn up the whole hill but without stabbing any of the spuds, I was reminded of some of my first farm experiences, when I was just a boy. We only had a homestead, ourselves, with chickens and rabbits and an apple tree and a fine garden, but my uncle had a farm. That's where I used to watch the dozen cows being milked by hand, the mighty draft horses in their stalls, and the huge sow named Alice. I watched while a cow was butchered, I played in the haymow, and I roamed the fields...

And I wondered, as I put the potatoes in the basket, if for all these years I haven't been seeking some kind of nostalgic small-farm experience that no longer exists... anywhere.

While I harvested the last of the green tomatoes — wrapping some of them in newspaper to ripen slowly in the root cellar, and then pulling entire vines out of the ground, to hang upside down from the rafters in the garage — I found myself thinking of all the places I had searched for the ideal homestead in all those years since I first realized I wanted to be a homesteader, when I didn't even know what a homesteader was.

It started long before graduating from high school. Probably the strongest urging came when I watched those magnificent Soo Line 4-8-2's steaming around the bend from the marsh country to the northwest. I never wanted to follow them south — to Milwaukee, and Chicago — but when they headed out toward the wild country they exemplified far-away places and adventure and "something better."

Small wonder I set out to homestead in western Ontario.

It didn't work, of course, but as I pulled out the last of the tomato stakes I realized that I don't regret it. But where *is* the best place to homestead?

Just before the first frost was predicted, I dug some pepper plants from the garden. One is almost as much an old friend as Daphne, our dog: a jalapeno, I started it in the house from seed, transplanted it to the garden, dug it in the fall and nurtured it through the winter and planted it in the garden the following spring... and that's been going on for five years. With all the blossoms I hand-pollinated on it during that time I'm somewhat surprised it doesn't have a name.

But that made me think of warmer climes where I found myself searching for the ideal homestead. Mexico, of course, and Florida and California, and a couple of years in Hawaii...

There were places on Molokai, on the Big Island, and even on Oahu that should have been perfect for the lifestyle I envisioned. But for me, it just wasn't right. I delighted in the rustle of the palm leaves along the beach on balmy winter evenings, but they made me long for the rustle of corn stalks instead.

Rustling palm leaves do sound a great deal like rustling cornstalks, I thought, as I moved down the row, picking corn, even though the South Seas seemed far, far away, with the chill of the north wind and the screaming wedges of geese using that tail wind to fly south.

There's a good, sensuous feeling about grasping a solid ear of ripe corn, wresting it from the golden brown stalk, and thrusting it into the sack. You hate to see the geese go, because you know what they're going to avoid, but the weight of the golden ears of grain serve as a sort of ballast that helps keep you from following them.

In fact, hearing the geese, and still dwelling on the ideal homestead, I found my thoughts floating in the opposite direction, the direction the geese had come from.

The far north has fascinated me since my youth, feeding dreams of peaceful remoteness, and living in close harmony with nature, and the need to depend on one's own resources. Pausing in the corn field to turn up my collar against the cold wind, I recalled a night spent in a bar in Churchill, Manitoba, talking with some of the people who lived there, nearly on Hudson Bay. I was on a magazine assignment. One of the attractions was the polar bears. It was 30 below, there were six-foot snow drifts... and it was the middle of May.

Certain aspects of the area fascinated me, yet, there was something missing there, too.

I dug the chicory, lopping off the leaves to plant the roots in boxes of soil in the root cellar to provide welcome greens during the first part of the greenless season in Wisconsin. And digging, lopping, and chucking roots in the basket, I thought of other places I've been, looking for the ideal homestead.

Like the time I was driving through Missouri. The narrow road curved, dipped, and crossed a gurgling stream, and the brush along the road gave way to a tiny clearing. A fine Jersey cow looked up from her grazing as I passed, slowing down as I came to the house.

It was a small, simple, white frame house, with a white picket fence and a colorful flower garden in the front yard. A couple of varicolored chickens were scratching in the dust out by the mailbox, and scattered as I approached. A Border Collie was lying on the porch, beneath the swing, just beyond the trellis with the red tea roses growing profusely across it.

A fat, contented-looking Duroc sow lay sleeping in the shade of the small barn while her offspring cavorted a short distance away.

Beyond the house was a large garden, with rich soil showing between rows of lush, green vegetables. And while I can't be certain — it might have been my imagination — I'm quite sure there was a small orchard and some grape vines; a neat little rabbit hutch and a smokehouse and a respectable supply of stacked dry firewood.

Whenever I pass such a place, I'm always tempted to stop, drive in, and see who lives there... listen to them... find out if they appreciate what they have. Because, you see, I've seen places like that in California and in Maine, in Washington and in Florida, in Idaho and Texas and Minnesota. And right here in Jefferson County, Wisconsin.

One of the final chores of the harvest season... after the carrots are mulched and you're eating as much of the late cabbage and turnips as you possibly can... after the fall hog and the fat lambs are butchered... you have to make horseradish.

Fresh pork demands fresh horseradish, I always say.

I was sitting in the kitchen scraping the roots. I don't have a real recipe for horseradish except that it ought to be dug after everything else in the garden is taken care of but before it gets so cold you can't open the windows while you're grating it.

The kitchen window was open, but Diane was on the floor repotting plants and she felt a draft, so I closed it. And as the eye-watering aroma of horseradish wafted about me, clearing my sinuses, something else became clear too.

If I could start all over again, knowing what I know now, where would I homestead?

I've fished in the surf while the swell of the sea washed over volcanic rock, I've felt the spray of remote waterfalls on my face, tested the tingling waters of frigid glacial streams, sloshed through mosquito-infested (but quietly beautiful) northern marshes. I've hiked in mountains, and in deserts, and camped in rain forests and redwood forests. From the Atlantic, to the middle of the Pacific, from Hudson Bay to the Gulf of Mexico, I looked at the land, and the people, and I asked myself, "Is this the perfect place to homestead?"

Sitting in my kitchen, making horseradish, not very far from where I was born and raised, the answer was clear: other places may have many attractions, but for me, this is it. This is the place, right here.

Of course I realize that *you* might not like my homestead, or where it is. But it took me a long, long time to find it. No, correct that: I didn't find it. I built it — I'm still building it — bit by bit, from my own dreams and aspirations. And now that I think about it, I could have built it anywhere.

Because the best place to homestead is wherever your heart and soul are as much a part of the Earth as the stones, and the birds and animals and insects who have lived there for generations, and the shadows that slide across the fields as the sun progresses across the sky.

There IS no perfect place, except in your own mind, and the whole essence of homesteading is transferring that mental image to — wherever you are.

The dissatisfied person can be dissatisfied anywhere, and most of them are. The satisfied person can be satisfied anywhere, because their satisfaction doesn't stem from their surroundings, but from themselves.

So where is the best place to homestead? To me, the answer is like the rich folks say: if you have to ask the price, you can't afford it.

Oh, sure, I do have one important requirement of my perfect homestead: just make it at least a little ways beyond the sidewalks.

In 2014 we're about 200 miles farther north, and very close to where those long-ago Soo Line trains used to run. (Now it's the Canadian National Railway.) I haven't noticed a great deal of difference, although when I do happen to go south again it does seem awfully crowded...

Part XII: 1982

Inflation: 6.16%; Federal Reserve interest rate, year-end: 11.5%;
Average annual income: 21,050; Gas/gal: 91¢;
First class postage stamp: 20¢; Tomatoes, 39¢/lb.;
Loaf of white bread: 50¢; Terrorist attacks in France (Carlos the Jackal);
All-time record lows in Midwest states; First issue of USA Today;
New York: 700,000 protest nuclear weapons;
US: Severe recession begins; First artificial heart implanted;
World's largest oil rig sinks in North Atlantic;
Potassium cyanide in Tylenol capsules kills 7 in Chicago, drastically changing packaging; First CD player sold (Japan)

106. January 1982

It was a good day
It's the little things that count...

What can you say about a Saturday like that, except that it was a good day?

Of course, it was nothing special. I didn't really accomplish very much, didn't go anywhere, do anything out of the ordinary. It was just — good. And there's nothing wrong with that.

We were still picking corn. By all odds, harvesting corn in December ought to be a grueling experience, but the grain was standing well and the weather was pleasant. So pleasant, in fact, that by late morning the ground began to thaw, and by early afternoon, when the going got tough and the tractor almost got stuck, we just quit.

After a short, late lunch, I decided to tackle a job I'd been putting off for too long: cleaning the garage, so I could get the truck inside should winter come to Wisconsin this year. The biggest obstacle was the Allis

Chalmers tractor which had been parked there since last spring, waiting to be rewired.

I hadn't had time to even look at it, and meanwhile, it had become a monument of sorts, as if it belonged there. A squat orange deity, enshrined in the garage, surrounded by little offerings like some pagan statue hidden in the jungle.

It had been convenient to lean the broken storm door I'm going to repair some day against one tire. There was a makeshift workbench in front of the tractor, hastily erected when someone was working on the machine, and now cluttered with other tools that had never been used on the tractor. The garden tiller and the lawn mower were conveniently stowed out of the way, beneath the tractor. A tent and badminton net and some gunny sacks were stacked on the tractor seat, and assorted pieces of lumber were leaned up against it.

It took awhile to move everything out of the way before we could even move the tractor. When we got that far, we dragged it over to a neighbor who enjoys mechanical work, and put it in *his* garage.

I didn't actually clean the garage: I more or less rearranged it. But there was room for the truck, at least.

In the rearranging process, I ran across a replacement headlight I'd bought a couple of months earlier, but hadn't installed. So I took out the burned-out one and put in the new one.

On mellow, laid-back days like this, I enjoy dawdling over chores. I like to dream that if hogs were $60/cwt or lambs $90, or if I could find a way to sell goat milk or rabbits at a profit, this is how my days would be spent: surrounded by my animals, like the shepherds of old, with no other responsibilities. I'd like to try it for awhile, at least.

We had a nice supper — nothing special, but nice — and we listened to *A Prairie Home Companion* on the radio, followed by the old-time radio shows that have become as much a part of our Saturday nights now as they were 40 years ago: *Henry Aldrich, The Great Gildersleeve, Duffy's Tavern...* Nothing astounding. But fun. Good.

The next afternoon I transplanted some head lettuce and peppers in the atrium-greenhouse, walked down the road with my bow saw to clean up some overhanging branches that offended the school bus driver, and split some wood for the stove. And then, I got out the mandolin and accompanied the music on one of those wall-paper music radio stations. The kind of music they play in elevators, which even someone like me can follow without too much difficulty. It's more fun playing with a group than all alone.

Diane made a from-scratch pizza, and after eating, we put the screen door on our woodstove, and sat listening to folk music on the radio.

And that was it.

I told you it was nothing special.

And yet, back at work — having to write this column — the beauty of it all began to dawn on me.

It wasn't strenuous, like some of my best weekends are: I didn't spend hours in the hot sun, baling hay; monotonous hours on the tractor, plowing; I didn't work up a sweat in below zero chill, cutting and hauling wood.

There was nothing monumental, even on a homestead scale, like butchering a hog or building a solar water heater.

There wasn't even anything particularly rewarding, like finishing planting the garden or a field, or solving some kind of problem such as repairing a machine or discovering why the electric fence doesn't work.

It was simply good. Pleasant. Satisfying. It was nothing to write home about, and yet...

Isn't that what most of this country life business is all about?

If every day were some tremendous adventure — the cow breaking out to go down the highway, the septic tank going kaflooey, being there when a pair of goat kids was being born or witnessing a magnificent sunset — if every day were like that, wouldn't it tend to get boring? Wouldn't we become jaded... and wouldn't it be a terrible thing?

It's the little things that count.

Having a kitten act like it loves you. A goat licking your ears. Raindrops on the windowpane. A crackling fire, a bowl of hot homemade soup, the aroma of fresh-baked bread.

Little things. These are what make a life rewarding. Or unbearable.

Some people would have found my weekend dreadfully dull, but I enjoyed it very much. In a way, it personified the peace and fulfillment I'm looking for, everything I could want in life, beyond the sidewalks.

In no way should a day of leisure like this be confused with chronic laziness, or even with *creative* leisure. But we do need periods of "nothingness" on occasion, just to rejuvenate.

107. February 1982

Our vanishing heritage

America has a living national treasure which is becoming extinct.

I'm not talking about the bald eagle or the snail darter: I'm talking about those human beings who were born in a period of horse transportation and mud roads, and lived to fly in jet planes and to see men walking on the moon. They've lived through some of the most mind-boggling changes and developments the world has seen or probably will see, and perhaps are a testimony to the adaptability of humanity.

However, because of this adaptability, something is being lost. Not just knowledge and skills, not just a way of life, but a heritage.

Like most Americans in the early part of this century, my maternal grandparents were farmers. Of course, with their small acreage, horse power, and handful of diversified livestock, today's USDA wouldn't count them as farmers at all: they'd be homesteaders.

But that's what this story is about.

Aside from living in a new land, their early lives were largely unchanged from the lives of their parents and their parents', fading back into antiquity. They had little or no formal schooling. What they needed to know to survive they learned from their elders, just as naturally and in the same way as we all learn to walk, use a cup and a spoon, talk.

It all changed, virtually overnight.

Grandma Ciske always seemed to be sitting in her big old rocking chair in her large L-shaped kitchen, back in the corner window by her canary cage where she could have watched over both wings of her kitchen had she not been blind. In one part was the oilcloth-covered kitchen table, large enough for all nine of her children to sit down together. In the other part was her wood stove, sink, cupboards and work table, and jutting off at the far end was the most interesting little pantry.

Grandma and grandpa had left the farm some years before, him to work in one of the rapidly growing paper mills that sprawled through the Fox River Valley from Neenah to Green Bay. The period of rapid change had begun. The old ways, handed down from generation to generation for countless ages, had started to crumble.

The children, who had been born into a farming life that had changed little in centuries, grew to adulthood in an entirely different world. All nine of them worked or were married to someone who worked in the paper mills. They had no need for most of the knowledge and skills of their parents, and in just one generation, a heritage was all but lost.

The break was sudden, but not sharp: Grandpa couldn't have forgotten his farming skills, even as he learned the new ones of a paper maker; and he still maintained a wonderful garden. His children retained some of their farm heritage even when living a greatly changed lifestyle; and a very small part trickled down to his grandchildren.

One spring Grandma had a hankering to make some elderberry blossom wine, and I was chosen to pick the blossoms. My mother wasn't at all certain that winemaking was an essential skill for a 10-year-old, but I rode my bike out into the countryside and picked a big sack of blossoms and Grandma and I made wine.

When it was finished, she let me taste just a sip of it, but she gave me a whole bottle with the advice that "It will be just right for your wedding."

Once Grandpa was sick when a load of firewood was delivered, and my mother volunteered me to stack it for him. I had helped him before, but it was a grown-up feeling to be responsible for doing the job alone. I spent a whole day at it, and was proud.

But when he recovered, he tore down the whole pile and restacked it, because the ends of the logs weren't perfectly lined up the way they should have been.

I've never even come close to being a perfectionist, but every once in awhile when I wish I weren't quite as sloppy as I am at stacking wood or at publishing magazines, I wonder what I'd be like if I would've spent more time with my grandfather. Although those were in the days before "mobility," and all nine brothers and sisters lived nearby (most within walking distance: few had cars), and Sundays were generally gala events with aunts and uncles and cousins "visiting," times were changing. Young boys had neither the need nor the opportunity to spend much time with their grandfathers. There was no need to learn to stack wood, when most people used coal.

Of course, I learned a lot from my parents, too, and we did have a Victory Garden and rabbits and chickens which provided some ties to the past. But it wasn't the same. There was school... which concentrated on the ancient past, or on the future. The icebox gave way to the electric refrigerator, the coal furnace to oil, steam engines to diesel... we kids thrilled to the first jet airplane that flew over our little town, felt vaguely frightened by The Bomb... and the ways of the recent past were of little interest or importance.

And when we children had children of our own, the transition, for most, was complete. It was as if a branch had been sawn off down to the trunk and in a few seasons the bark had grown over and completely covered the wood.

While my aunts and uncles all stayed close to home, my cousins started to spread out, and our children... why just mine alone had addresses in Florida, Utah, and California. It becomes more and more difficult — maybe even impossible — to preserve the old traditions, the old knowledge, the old skills, and with them the sense of close belonging, the sense of heritage.

It was a bright, warm, spring day, the Earth fresh and full of promise, when Diane and I announced that after being engaged for two years, we were getting married in May.

We were at Diane's parents' farm when I got the phone call. Grandma Ciske had died.

I didn't think of the elderberry blossom wine at the wedding, and it was a long time before we tasted it.

It was a good wine. With the memories, maybe even an excellent wine. At least for someone who lives beyond the sidewalks.

108. March 1982

I'd rather be a gardener

Gertrude Stein once said, "I've been rich, and I've been poor. And believe me, rich is better."

Although it's not nearly as poetic, I would prefer to say, "I've been a gardener, and I've been in situations and places where having a garden was impossible. And believe me, gardening is better."

What's the attraction?

It's probably different for everyone who ever pulled a weed from a row of carrots, but there are a few highlights in my own gardening experience that stand out.

When we'd been homesteading a couple of years and had some experience — enough to really get into self-sufficiency and organic methods and all of that — we began to *depend* on our garden.

Naturally, that's when we ran into our first crop failure. It was something important — potatoes, as I recall — but I was really depressed about it.

But my sister, who I thought was in tune with these things, was amazed at my depression. "Good grief." she chided, "it's not like you're going to starve to death. You can always go to the grocery store."

Maybe it was the way her eyes told me I was crazy for worrying about a few bushels of potatoes when the grocery store had plenty of potatoes, but whatever it was, I was even more depressed.

Garden productivity has always been important to me, and it still is. But in recent years — I won't say I'm slowing down, but maybe I'm mellowing out? — I've discovered other pleasures in my garden. Example: straight rows.

I used to opine that if the shortest distance between two points was a straight line, then it figured that a *crooked* line of beans meant it was a longer row... which meant there were more beans in it.

Lately, I've come around to agree with those who regard a garden as a thing of beauty, with one of the beauties being its symmetry.

I've never been able to plant an entire garden with straight rows of neatly laid-out plots (although I did have one straight row of carrots, once), and I've certainly never even come close to arranging beds and rows so they were geometrically pleasing and color-coordinated.

But you know, I've come to *appreciate* such gardens. I admire people who can execute them. They're artists, working not with clay or stone or paint and canvas, but with a most difficult medium: a medium that changes day by day, is subject to the vagaries of weather and the ravages of disease and insects and crawly animals, and which is wiped clean as a slate board a few short months later.

And you even get to eat it.

There's yet another, even more wondrous attraction to gardening. Imagine: you take this tiny little brown speck of a seed and poke it into a cupful of potting soil and put it on the windowsill (where the snow is still peaked up against the glass on the outside). Shortly, a green shoot appears. It grows, and when the soil in the garden warms, you transfer the little plant outside. Day by day it spreads... produces blossoms... little green tomatoes... then large, ripe tomatoes. The first one is savored, maybe on BLT sandwiches. Then you get a little more extravagant, and eat one whole. Later, you're eating whole salads of tomato wedges... and pretty soon you're sick and tired of tomatoes.

Then, the nights get frosty. You pluck as many of the ripening fruits as you can and store them, wrapped in newspaper, to prolong the season. You start using green tomatoes, maybe lightly fried.

And then, one morning in fall, the sun rises over a frosted landscape, and the once-little tomato plant sprouting on your windowsill is now a sprawling gnarled octopus with blackened leaves and whitened, mushy fruit.

That's amazing... all of it... and if you're a gardener, you can't help but be moved by the wonder of the cycle.

It's been said that every home needs at least two books: a Bible, telling of God's miracles; and a seed catalog, proving that miracles still happen.

But the main reason I garden is for the bounty.

I love to eat, I love to cook, and I love to garden. And I hate to spend money.

So imagine the pleasure I get when it's time to make supper, and I swoop up my harvest basket and stride into my garden to do my daily grocery shopping.

The leg of lamb is already out of the freezer: now, what will go with it?

The salad garden is closest to the house. What looks good today? The lettuce is past its prime, but the chard is nice. Mmm, a few leaves of mustard greens will add just the right touch to lamb. A garlic clove is a necessity, of course, as well as some lemon balm, which is over in the herb section, along with the parsley.

Radishes and green onions go into the basket.

I select a few prime tomatoes, a firm cucumber, and a grade A head of cauliflower. And in the process, I pull a pigweed from the row of okra and fling it on the compost heap.

Feeling just a little bit naughty, I feel under the mulch for some small, new potatoes. Drawing them out from the moist straw is like plucking a warm egg from a nest. I take only what I need for supper, and leave the rest to grow larger.

If I don't pick that zucchini, tomorrow it'll be bigger than a log. And that eggplant is ready, too: it'll make a good breakfast, breaded and fried.

When I go into the kitchen and plop my basket on the counter and announce with the air of a great hunter, or at least provider, "Here's supper," Diane looks at the booty as if I'd dumped a bear carcass on the table and said, "Make me some steaks and a pair of gloves."

But I don't mind. I love to garden.

It's just one of the forms of dementia that come with living beyond the sidewalks.

109. April 1982

April showers: To the homesteader, they mean more than just May flowers

April showers.

What imagery those words convey! What magic!

Maybe that's why, although I was never much on poetry, I've retained the words of Chaucer from my high school days:

Whan that Aprille with his shoures soote
The droghte of Marche hath perced to the roote,
And bathed every veyne in swich licour,
Of which vertu engendred is the flour;
— *Chaucer, The Canterbury Tales*
And
"April is the cruelest month, breeding
Lilacs out of the dead land, mixing
Memory and desire, stirring
Dull roots with spring rain."
— *T.S. Eliot, The Waste Land*

April is, of course, a wonderful month. Especially for those of us who have spent the past few months trying to live normal lives under tundra conditions we aren't equipped to cope with.

But the April showers... ah, there's something worth living through winter to experience!

They start in late afternoon. The sky is dark grey, almost black, but you can never be quite certain that the mist that begins to form will turn to rain or not.

By dusk, you know: rain. *Warm* rain!

Lying in bed, you can hear the gentle patter. You can picture it spattering against the windowpane even in the dark. You can hear it on the roof, and you can imagine the grime of winter getting washed off the roof and the roof enjoying it, like a hog under a fine mist from the hose on a hot and sunny day.

And the fields, the garden! Why, you can almost *feel* the warm water soaking in, eating away at the last wisps of frost, whispering to the earthworms and saprophytes and springtails, "Wake up! It's April!"

If God hadn't made April showers, poets would have had to invent them.

There have been a few Aprils since I've been farming when there *were* no showers.

The frost hangs in the ground, rotting out from beneath as slowly as from above. You walk out into a fall-plowed field and kick at the dry clumps of clay, search the clear sky at bedtime... and lie there listening to the silence.

Oh, it generally clouds up pretty good, now and then, even during a dry April. That gets your hopes up, but makes it all the worse when the rain doesn't come.

Eventually you concede that time is running out, so you hook up the disk and bounce over cement-like clods, and sow oats into a gravel seedbed and wait for the rain that will make them sprout. And wait, and wait...

It's truly amazing, when you stop to think of it, how we take water for granted. April showers, summer showers, any kind of water.

Like the time last winter our pipes froze up. It wasn't the first time and it won't be the last; those minus 70 degree wind-chill-factor temperatures we had here last winter have a way of thwarting even the best of preparations.

But you can live with it. Sure, water is a necessity: you can live longer without food than you can live without water. Yep, it sure is a convenience. Anyone with any water-rationing experience at all ought to be able to do their morning washing-up and tooth-brushing with a cup or so, but it's nice to have a little more. Toilet flushing, coffee making...

there are ways to deal with all that, and besides, you can always regard being out of water as a test of your powers of self-sufficiency. It's *macho* to see how far you can stretch a gallon jug of water.

But then you find out somebody used the frying pan for a midnight snack, and you take it over to the sink to wash it. You turn on the faucet, and — nothing.

Of course you knew there wasn't any water! But it's irritating. Like falling for a dumb joke when you woke up knowing full well it was April Fool's Day.

So you use a different frying pan, and cook up the bacon and eggs.

My favorite way to cook an egg is to break that egg into the pan, then dump a little water on it, and cover the pan to let the whole thing sort of steam. So I reach for the tea kettle... it's empty, and oh no, I won't get caught at the spigot again!

So we eat the eggs with slightly crusty brown edges. They aren't all that bad.

When I take my plate to the sink, the uppermost thing on my mind is my greasy fingers. I don't know why I ate the bacon with my fingers: no class, I guess. But when I turn on the faucet to rinse them off...

Of course.

And so it goes. I want to water the tomatoes and peppers and other stuff we grow in the house over winter, and mist the houseplants, and there's no water. When I go to the tap to draw some warm water for the dogs, I suddenly remember. The vitamin capsule is in my mouth, and...

Oddly enough, the pipes in the barn didn't freeze at any time during the winter, which may mean our animals enjoy better housing than we do. On the other hand, those pipes have frozen in much milder winters, and we found ourselves hauling bucket after bucket from the house to the barn, for stock that never acted that thirsty on 100-degree summer days.

And there have been times, when both house *and* barn were waterless... we hauled milk cans of water from town.

The point is, you don't really appreciate what you have until you don't have it anymore.

Especially if it's something as common, and as *important,* as water.

We can't really count on it, you know.

Oh, sure, the pipes thaw out eventually, the rains come, eventually. And yet, when you really sit down and think — really think — about our water... where it comes from, what happens to it, what we do with it, how important it is to us...

Maybe I'm weird, but I can't stand in a drizzle without thinking about that water falling on my face. It's solar energy, of course, having been evaporated by the sun's heat and transported thousands of miles by the sun's winds.

But...

Water is indestructible. The water we have now is the same water that Fulton's steamboat navigated, that Columbus sailed, that Cleopatra floated on, that Noah survived.

The water Caesar drank, Hannibal's elephants eliminated, and Archimedes was bathing in when he shouted "Eureka!" is the same water we depend upon for survival today.

Thinking of all the things that might have happened to that water falling on my face as I stand, gratefully, in an April shower, makes me feel very small. Like standing in a grand cathedral, or listening to a masterful symphony.

Thinking of what each of those tiny droplets has seen, where they have been, what stories they could tell...

Was this drop on the tip of my nose, right now, ever lapped up by a dinosaur? How many times was it at the very bottom of the ocean... swept away by some convectional current that brought it to the surface, where it was transformed into vapor and carried away to form a snowflake, which joined the great glaciers, which carved away the mountains that used to rise where I now stand?

And, then, did that droplet melt, and join the flood that swept over the land to help form the fertile prairies to the south of us? What happened to it on the way? What could it tell me?

As I stand with my face uplifted to the clouds, the raindrop drops from my nose to the gravel driveway, and joins a rivulet. Looking down at it, three more drops join the tiny stream.

They'll be back. I know they will.

That's part of the reassurance you have when you live beyond the sidewalks.

This makes me think about all the people in California (and elsewhere) in 2014, who have no water, but intend to get more by drilling deeper wells. Why can't they see that's no real solution? But then, that's how most humans today regard Earth's resources.

110. May 1982
Rare breeds... of all kinds

The special focus of this issue of COUNTRYSIDE is rare breeds of domestic livestock.

I have to admit, I wasn't too excited about the topic when this issue was in the planning stages. As a publisher, I really had no idea what kind of material we'd be able to come up with. As a writer, I've been somewhat chagrined now and then by readers who, it seemed to me, got too enthralled by exotic animals simply because they were unusual. As a practical homesteader, I can't see paying buckets of money for an animal that isn't going to produce any more meat, milk or eggs than a "common" specimen — and probably less.

But I've been having second thoughts.

Sue Pfrang was the editorial coordinator for this special section, partly because she has a knack for ferreting out obscure information — and she loves to make long distance phone calls almost as much as I *hate* to make long distance phone calls. She ran into a lot of dead ends in the beginning, but day by day her persistence began to pay off. We actually ended up with more than we could use.

And, as I watched her delve into the subject and saw the issue evolve and develop, I found myself thinking more and more about rare breeds.

We've always considered our homestead practical, but it's never been super-efficient. We've always had a cow, or pig, or goat, or chicken, or rabbit that didn't really pay its way but was kept anyway, on pet status. What the heck, money ain't everything.

Most years we raise Rhode Island Reds for both meat and eggs. Other years we experiment with other breeds, or we raise Rock Cornish for meat and Leghorns for eggs. And then there was the time we bought a batch of "mixed heavies." This was a grab bag of the hatchery business.

The day-old chicks looked normal enough. But, as they grew, the flock began to take on the appearance of creatures who might be seen milling around the terminal of an intergalactic spaceport.

They were all colors, shapes, and sizes... and they weren't all heavy. There were Wyandottes, Orpingtons, and even a crested Polish. But the real stand-out, the gem, was a magnificent Black Minorca.

There was something about his iridescent feathering, blood-red huge comb and wattle and pure white earlobes that made him a pleasure to behold.

He didn't lay eggs and he died a natural death, but he contributed something to our homestead nevertheless. He contributed something to our life.

Of course, the primary reaction to any mention of rare breeds is most likely an ecological one. The term conjures up visions of exotic creatures on the brink of extinction, but we tend to think of snail darters and whales and American eagles.

I'm ashamed to have to admit that, in spite of my livestock writing career and ecological bent, I really haven't given proper consideration to the ecological aspects of rare breeds of *domestic* animals.

An extinct breed of hog or chicken is as much a loss to the world as an extinct passenger pigeon or dodo — perhaps greater. For instance, we depend far too heavily on Holstein cattle for milk, with just four other breeds producing virtually all of the small amount that doesn't come from Holsteins.

And, yet, as Sue points out in this issue, these major breeds have been developed to suit particular conditions and situations. When conditions change (as they are wont to) where is the gene pool to draw upon? This can be viewed as something akin to the corn blight of a few years ago: if there had been no resistant strains of corn from which to develop new varieties, corn conceivably could have ceased to be a major crop, with far-reaching and disastrous consequences.

It's important that we maintain a diversity of genetic traits. It's important that we preserve "un-economic" breeds of livestock, just as we preserve strains of seed that are not in widespread use today.

And if it's important that we humans be reminded of the grand diversity of nature, then it makes no sense that all cows should be black and white, or all pigs and rabbits and chickens the same. If they were, life would be as drab and monotonous as it would be if we ate nothing but beans: kidney beans only. No navy beans, lima beans, black beans, Jacobs cattle beans, adzuki beans, mung, soy or fava beans, or the multitude of others.

Today was Friday. A couple of us ended up sitting around the office after working hours, discussing, winding down. It was dusk when I started doing chores, and I was still mulling over this issue of the magazine; it wasn't an intense effort. There was no real need to be thinking of magazines, or rare breeds, as I fed and watered the animals, and it was as if I was looking at the topic from a long way off. That's probably why it hit me so hard and so suddenly:

WE are a rare breed! Human beings!

Look at natural history, and it's plain that we "have no right" to be here at all. In planetary terms, we're useless and uneconomic, destroying more than we build up, taking more than we give, plundering and wasting as mindlessly as a herd of goats chomping on the apple trees and rosebushes or denuding a South Sea island. We've elbowed aside the passenger pigeon, the bison, the dodo... and we've been working on the brown pelican and the whales and many others... but under what pretense, and at what expense?

Then how much rarer still are those of us who consider ourselves homesteaders, those of us who cherish diversity, and beauty, and other uneconomic values?

At that point, any reservations I may have had about a special issue on rare breeds of livestock disappeared.

After all, we have to stick together, we rare ones. Dexter cattle, Tamworth hogs, open-pollinated corn, homesteaders... we might just be the glue that holds the world together, and provides its future.

We can't expect much help from the crowd that wants only cheap food and cheap power, from those who can't appreciate the expansive view we have from our special perspective, beyond the sidewalks.

2014: Rare breeds have become surprisingly popular in some places — as food. Just as heirloom vegetables became popular, heritage hogs, poultry and cattle have become sought-after by a certain class of consumers, resulting in a farming niche for small operators. It's ironic: former rare breeds are now less endangered because we're slaughtering them.

As for Man being a rare species... endangered, yes, but not so much rare as *invasive*.

111. June 1982

Has milk lost its magic?

D airy animals have long been a staple topic in COUNTRYSIDE, but it's been a long time since we've devoted our entire feature section to that amazing product, milk. And one of the interesting little facts I learned — although I suppose I already knew it, subconsciously — was that milk isn't held in the same high esteem it was when I was a lad in America's Dairyland.

In fact, milk trails behind soda pop, coffee, and beer, in popularity as a beverage.

In some ways, that doesn't surprise me at all. Yet, it rather saddens me.

When I was a kid our milk appeared on our doorstep every morning as if by magic. It came from a "Golden Guernsey" dairy, and I can still vividly recall reaching out the door on a snowy morning to pluck those square glass bottles off the porch... bottles with a painting of a Guernsey cow's head in gold... and finding the cream poking up the paper cap like a frozen popsicle.

When we started getting homogenized milk, it was some kind of a wonder, and supposedly a great breakthrough in convenience. I mean, you didn't have to shake the bottle every time you poured a glass of milk to distribute the cream!

There was no talk of cholesterol and other such nonsense in those days. Milk was *good* for you... and it tasted good, too!

Later on, when I went away to school, and roamed around a bit, and joined the Marines and roamed some more, I found out that reliance on milk and dairy products as a staple food wasn't a universal trait, that we Wisconsinites were something of a strange breed when it came to malts and cheese and butter. I even met people who had never even tasted good cheese — who wouldn't recognize it if they did — and I began to realize that a taste for good dairy products is a learned trait.

With this kind of background and upbringing, it isn't too surprising that one of the far-out vegetarian claims that rankles me most is that "milk is food fit only for babies." That goes along with the cholesterol stuff as being entirely alien to everything I was brought up to believe.

On Diane's parents' farm, we'd go down to the milk house and dip buckets of cold, fresh milk out of the bulk tank. Not only was it nutritious, I thought — one of the basic food groups we'd learned about in school — but it was delicious! Cream and all...

Why does a homegrown tomato taste so much better than the store-bought variety? Why is a homestead chicken so much more flavorful than the bland watery things available in the supermarkets? Why is milk from your own goat or cow so far superior to the chalky stuff that comes in waxed paper cartons? And homemade buttermilk is even better!

I have no doubts at all that part of the reason is real, actual quality. Tomatoes grown for shipping quality and other similar economic factors and ripened with gas *can't* compare with vine-ripened fruits; cage-free chicken just naturally tastes more like meat than chicken raised on computer formulated rations... and real milk has no relationship with the chalky water produced by the economics-minded dairy industry of today.

Part of the problem we goat raisers have always encountered — if it is a problem — has been that people who taste our goat milk think it's "richer" than cow milk. But, of course, what people are used to is standardized cow milk... water, really... that has no butterfat, and no taste. Good, fresh cow milk (especially from a Jersey, to my taste buds) is quite similar to good goat milk, and neither can be compared to the stuff available to most Americans.

But there's more.

Why does a meal cooked outdoors seem to taste better than the same food prepared on a kitchen range? Why is a fresh trout, fried at streamside, better than the same fish cooked inside?

There is nothing I enjoy more than bringing buckets of warm frothy milk from the barn into the kitchen.

And when I drink a glass of homestead milk, it seems to embody the aroma of fresh straw, the feel of the animals, and the knowledge that, doggone it, I'm the one who produced this beverage.

It's good for me, and it tastes good. That's the way I was brought up.

And when that milk piles up in the refrigerator, and we make loads of cheese and butter and yogurt, the feeling of participation grows even stronger.

It's a feeling that not only am I producing my family's food... I'm in control of my *own* life. And that's a *good* feeling.

Every so often, I still like to dip into the refrigerator just before bedtime, and pour a small glass of milk... off the top. Pure cream. Diane says I don't need it, and I *am* developing a bit of a paunch, but surely it can't be any worse than a soda pop, or coffee, or beer. Even the health nuts who tell me I shouldn't drink so much milk couldn't argue with that.

But the best part is, it *tastes* good.

Maybe it's one of those evil little enjoyments that people can only appreciate when they raise their own dairy animals, beyond the sidewalks.

2014: Much could be added to this update, including comments on an ongoing legal battle concerning the sale of raw milk in Wisconsin, and the current availability of organic milk, which to my taste, is worth the added cost, if you can't produce your own.

112. July 1982

A family's future comes from its past

Dear Steve,

I'm really supposed to be writing a magazine column tonight... preferably something on "homestead families" (the theme of this issue)... but it doesn't seem to be coming together. And of course, thinking about family made me think of you, out there in California. So here I am, writing to you instead of to COUNTRYSIDE'S readers.

We're all busy... your mother, sister, brothers, and me too. It's spring here (something you're missing!) and the lilacs and plums are in bloom, and the weather has been a delight. Temperatures have been in the 70s and 80s — and no flies or mosquitoes! No wonder this is considered such a great time of the year around here.

A good part of the garden is in. Your mother and I planted 700 feet of row in potatoes. She commented that that ought to be enough to keep even *you* in potato salad for a year, if you were here! I declare I never saw anyone who enjoyed potato salad as much as you!

Naturally we have lots and lots of onions. I'm not sure whether we always plant so many onions because we really like them that much, or because it's something of a family tradition, going back to the time I was in college and taking care of Anne-marie, and your mother was working — and she came home from the night shift at the hospital to find Anne-marie in the high chair eating onions and chocolate cake for breakfast. I *know* that's not what I fed her, ordinarily, but over the last 20-some years it's become a family joke.

We had some nice rains, and we're looking forward to a productive gardening season.

Natasha kidded the other day. The kid was dead — it *had* been dead for some time, apparently — and I was concerned about Natasha. Especially at her age.

It was kinda funny, but just a few days before, I had mentioned to Mother that we ought to get a picture of Natasha, and John, just for fun. We don't have a lot of pictures of you people kids, because I was always taking pictures for the magazines. The shoemaker's children going barefoot syndrome, I guess.

Anyway. There was a picture of John and Natasha on the cover of *Dairy Goat Guide* way back in 1971. They both look quite a bit different, now, and I thought it'd be fun to have a "before" and "after" version.

Then she kidded... and the complications... and I figured it was too late.

Funny how that creeps into so much of life, especially where families are concerned. When you're young, it always seems like you have so much time and so much life ahead of you... and then one day you wake up and realize you're not young anymore and your kids are grown and have gone off to live in Florida and Utah... and California... and you didn't do half the things you'd always dreamed of doing.

Where does the time go?

But of course, even us old fogies have to go on living, and it doesn't do any good to dwell on the past. Well, not on the omissions and mistakes, at least: past pleasures? That's something else.

For example, some of the things you seemed to enjoy most — haying, shearing sheep, even barn-cleaning and *certainly* machinery maintenance — have really gone downhill since you left last spring. When I'm doing those chores, I really miss you!

Oddly enough, it's not just because I could use some extra help around the place... It's a whole lot more. Little things. Family things.

Remember that time something went kaflooey with the baler, and we ended up with that bale that was about 10 feet long? You were clowning around, trying to get it on the hayrack, and how we laughed!

Or how about that time we were moving a 200-gallon gas tank, and you dumped it right in the middle of the highway? Come to think of it, you did pretty much the same thing with the cement mixer.

But then, I still have fond memories of how faithfully you took care of and milked your cow... and that time the manure spreader broke down, and you did a fine welding job on it all by yourself, and I suddenly realized that you had become a man... I almost said you "had become a man, and didn't need me any more," but that's not true. You'll always need a father, just like I'll always need a son.

No, you don't need me to show you how to skin rabbits any more, and I don't need you to help milk or clean the barn or bale hay.

We need each other for the memories that make a life full, and rich. We need each other for the support, in the good times and the bad times that have been, and are yet to come. We need each other for the love that just doesn't develop between neighbors, or good friends, the way it does among kinfolk.

I guess maybe that's what families are all about, huh?

Especially where there is so much interaction, so many memories... so many good times, and bad times... on the homestead.

Oh, by the way, Natasha is doing just fine. I guess, in a way, she's part of the family, too — just like the other goats we have fond memories of, and the horses, the cats and dogs, the cows and pigs... It all comes together, in something I can only call Life. The *Good* Life, beyond the sidewalks. — Love, Dad

2014: The family has grown. Steve (and Tammy) now have two sons of their own — both older than he was when I wrote this. Where did that time go?

113. August 1982

Those rewarding dog days

I n August come the dog days.
Some purist will probably insist that the name is connected to the heliacal rising of Sirius, the Dog Star, but we country folk know better, even if we're acquainted with the stars.

Dog Days are those hot, sultry days of August when the family mutt prefers sleeping in the shade to anything else... and the dogs aren't the only ones.

During dog days, *nothing* moves, unless it has to.

This is the time of the year when the days seem to follow one another with almost monotonous regularity. Here in the Midwest we can count on day after day of cloudless skies and hot, humid air. Not only does nothing move — nothing changes. After a few weeks it's like looking at yourself in two mirrors, where your reflection marches away into infinity. Every day is the same, and you begin to wonder if the sameness will ever end.

T his is when city friends and relatives show up at the farm on their vacations. We're always glad to have them, of course. But I'm afraid some of them might get a slightly distorted view of life beyond the sidewalks when they visit during Dog Days.

Because Dog Days, you see, are a prime excuse for the myth that nothing much happens in the countryside, and that country living transforms even former city people into slow-paced, dull-witted bumpkins.

I find it exhausting to be vibrant, and witty, and vivacious, even under the best of circumstances, but with the temperature and the humidity both in the 90s, even attempting it doesn't seem worth the effort.

Then too, with the corn cultivated and the first-crop hay in the mow and the tomatoes not quite ready for the main canning push, it's time to relax a bit. And what better excuse is there for relaxing, than to spend some time with friends you don't see very often?

Of course, there's the danger that they'll think we *always* sit around like this, sucking lemonade and sun tea and swatting flies, but what's the harm in that? Let them have their illusions. Let them take that experience back to the city, and envy us all the more, the next time they get caught in rush hour traffic and it's 100 degrees on the freeway. Maybe, thinking of us then will lighten their burden a little.

Of course, when you have company, you don't just sit around all the time, even in the countryside. You eat a lot. But here again, the homestead visitor in August is a sitting duck for the perpetuation of hayseed myths. Because whatever negative aspects Dog Days have, lack of food (or variety) isn't one of them!

There is, first of all, in this part of the world, corn-on-the-cob. *Fresh* corn, that will make even the most epicurean city-dwelling visitor to the country drool for months afterward at the memory. Truly fresh corn isn't even plucked from the stalk until the water is boiling (although we now steam, rather than boil) or the coals on the grill are ready — an impossibility in the city.

Serving corn on the cob daily, or even twice daily, (which is often necessary during the height of the season), might give the impression that we country dwellers eat a lot of corn. And if the visitor stays more than a few days, you might encounter more awe and sympathy regarding diet than you do regarding such cultural effects as an outhouse, or a lack of cable tv. But that's life, in the countryside.

Corn is by no means the only food product in abundance in August. The goats are still milking well, the hens are still laying up a storm, and the garden is a veritable Eden.

Try to imagine, if you can, the thoughts that must course through a city person's mind as he bellies up to your picnic table groaning with the weight of your garden's bounty. Memories of guiding a shopping cart through jammed supermarket aisles and listlessly picking over wilted (but still expensive) vegetables, are ruthlessly overshadowed by the vision on your homestead table.

There are tomatoes, naturally. Big, sun-ripened, juicy, fresh, naturally-grown *delicious* tomatoes! There must be a zillion ways to present tomatoes at a table, but to most people who shop in supermarkets, any homestead tomato just has to be a treat for the eye as well as the palate (especially when it's an heirloom variety).

Some days, maybe, the tomatoes will be part of a salad (although in August, we often have salad *and* non-salad tomatoes). But what a salad!

While the city dwellers may be content, from custom, with a small plate of nondescript iceberg lettuce (California's way of exporting water), we serve up heaping bowls of chard, cress, kale, broccoli and cauliflower buds, tiny Brussels sprouts, radishes, peppers, scallions and leeks, cucumbers, peas, beans and half-a dozen varieties of lettuce and bok choi and...

What's growing in *your* garden?

Oh, yes. In August, the first new potatoes are ready. Little round ones with papery skins as delicate as a baby's breath. We simply wash them, steam them, douse them liberally with butter and salt, and garnish them with plenty of fresh parsley.

No wonder fancy big-city restaurants always seem kind of second-rate to me. I live on a four-star homestead!

With all of that, a meat course almost seems superfluous... but in August, meat is another item in abundance on homesteads. The spring lambs are fattened and prime, the fluffy chicks of spring have become feisty fat roosters, and the rabbits are reproducing like flies.

For dessert, while I have nothing at all against a peach pie, or even an early apple and a hunk of homemade cheese (which can be particularly satisfying after a heavy meal), I feel dog days require ice cream.

Homemade, naturally.

And you know, when those city friends sit out there in the yard and watch the kids playfully fight over who gets to turn the crank on the ice cream freezer (after exclaiming over the homegrown milk, and the simplicity of making something most people assume has to be made in huge factories), I get a good feeling — a *better* feeling — about what I'm doing. About how I'm spending my life.

So I'm not a city sophisticate. I was on a subway, once, and it scared the daylights out of me. There are lots of things that are routine to these friends of mine that I couldn't cope with. I *wouldn't* cope with.

And yet, there are so many things I take for granted that simply amaze city people that I can't help but feel a tad good about myself. Maybe it *is* a bit of one one-upmanship, but I can think, "All right, so you know how to deal with traffic lights and parking ramps and cab drivers and tipping — and I don't — but I can grow corn and tomatoes, and milk goats and make ice cream. Maybe I'm a Midwestern hick, but I'm not entirely useless, or ignorant."

My friends, of course, never entertained the notion. It's all in my own head, from watching tv ads and reading about the really smart people on the East Coast and the really savvy people on the West Coast. Those of us here in the middle, in flyover country... especially in the countryside...

can easily get the idea that we're second-class citizens. Not too bright, not very ambitious, and not really getting our share of the pie.

But...

When the child turning the crank on the ice cream freezer calls out, "I can't turn it any more! It's too *hard!*" the shoe is on the other foot.

Even if it was iffy during the afternoon lounging in the shade during the sweet corn course, the salad and vegetable courses, the homegrown meat course, now, I'm really and undeniably a hero.

The child willingly offers up the crank to my experienced touch. I test it and...yup, it's just right.

When the cover comes off, tiny unwrinkled fingers dip into the ice cream and reach small puckered mouths while I make mocking threats amidst frolicking laughter and glee.

The sun is down. The oppressive heat of the day has dissipated, somewhat, but you know there'll be tomorrow... and sleeping tonight won't be all that comfortable, either. The children, tired and sunburned, have been trundled off to bed. The fireflies are flickering their love messages, and the stars... Sirius included... are blazing overhead. The old swing is squeaking.

And your friend, who has chosen a different path to follow, says, "Y'know, you really know how to live."

Maybe you never thought about it much, or in just that way. But it makes you think.

There are lots of ways to spend a life. But you only get one chance. It's easy to lose sight of why we chose a way that seems harsh, and at times unrewarding, but moments like this make it perfectly clear.

We have the best of all possible worlds, when we live beyond the sidewalks.

114. September, 1982

#$@!~ machines! Who needs 'em, anyway?

Machines and I do not get along. We don't get along at all.

I know absolutely nothing about cars, trucks, motorcycles, washing machines, or toasters. I know *almost* nothing about tractors, hay balers, and mowers, and very little more about combines. (The reason I know a little about combines is that my antique one is broken down more than it's running. Therefore I spend more time fixing it than I spend combining with it, and I've learned a little.)

But this isn't about any of those machines. This is about tillers. Plain old garden tillers, that anybody with any kind of a respectable garden has, and seems to be able to use anytime they want to, as easily as turning on a faucet.

Well, not me. Garden tillers are machines, right? Machines and I don't get along, and it seems to be getting worse.

I've just completed my second year of gardening without using a tiller. It wasn't intentional, but maybe next year it will be.

Down through the years, a variety of tillers have been used to care for our gardens. They never caused many problems that I can recall, but lately...

Three years ago the rear-tine model (you know the big red one I'm talking about) stopped. My son Steve, who has taken apart (*and* put together again) more cars than I've owned in my entire life, volunteered to fix it.

Of course, he didn't get to it until late winter... and then he found out it had a broken piston and some other stuff I know nothing about but for which he didn't have the necessary tools to do whatever it was that had to be done. So we took the engine to a repair shop... which couldn't get one of the parts we needed. The repair shop called me this past March — one year after I'd taken the tiller in — and said it was ready. By that time I couldn't find the hardware required for mounting the engine on the tiller.

Well, I improvised, and I got the thing going, eventually.

But not for long. It stopped, cold, and it just wouldn't start.

Not wanting to risk waiting another year, I didn't go back to the small engine repair place, but hauled the whole rig just down the road to Larry Smith, who is one of those guys who actually *enjoys* working on infernal combustion engines. (Steve had long since moved to California.)

Whatever was wrong wasn't very serious, Larry said. And he wanted to use it to till *his* garden, which was fine with me because if anything else went wrong he'd be able to get the bugs out of it.

One evening he came over to my place, with a very long face.

"Bad news," he said.

The contraption had thrown a rod, and there was a hole the size of a silver dollar in the engine housing. Apparently the guy who had put the new piston in hadn't done it right.

Machines: who needs 'em, anyway?

We must have close to an acre of garden, in four different plots. One of them I could work with the tractor and plow, so I did. That's where I planted sweet corn, beans, and pumpkins, and all it took to keep most of the weeds down was a couple of trips through with my Ro-Ho — which does not have a motor and therefore is compatible with me — and an occasional walk with the hoe, which is necessary even with a tiller.

Another section of the garden is raised beds, which I wouldn't till even if I had a tiller. The soil in the beds is loose and uncompacted, and digging in them with a garden fork is almost as easy as playing in a sandbox.

Still another section is under permanent mulch, a section that gets enlarged every year I garden without a tiller. For bedding plants, I simply sweep aside the mulch at the spot I want to plant in, and dig the hole I'd have to dig anyway even if the whole garden had been tilled. For onions, beets, carrots and the like, I rake off the mulch where the row is to be, and spade it by hand. The soil under that mulch is mellow and friable, and easy to work. I certainly wouldn't want to spade a whole acre by hand, but you don't plant seeds in the whole acre anyway. Why dig up ground that you're just going to walk on, or that the squash and cucumber vines are going to spread over?

Also, most of our plantings are in narrow rows. Instead of spading a spade-width row down the garden and planting one row of onions, I spade *two* spade-widths, and plant *four* rows of onions. Or carrots or beets or whatever. Since I don't have the tiller to cultivate between the rows with anyway, it's much easier to hoe or pull weeds from a small space than from a wide path. But the best no-till trick of all was reserved for the muskmelon and watermelon this year. Both of these are pretty hard to grow to maturity in our soil and climate, but we had the best crop ever.

I laid down sheets of clear plastic, dug trenches around the perimeters, and piled that soil on the edges. Then I cut X's in the plastic, and planted the seeds through the openings. I also planted some seeds without the plastic, just to see what would happen.

The difference was amazing. The clear plastic allows the ground to warm up, and of course, melons love hot weather. You'd think black plastic would get hotter, but apparently it doesn't work the same way.

In any event, the plastic-mulched melons came on strong and early, the weeds that sprouted beneath the plastic soon wilted and died, and the vines set an abundance of fruit — early enough to ripen. The vines growing in the open ground won't produce anything before being caught by frost.

Larry's putting a short block on the tiller, but I don't have much use for a garden tiller during the winter. By next spring... who knows?

Maybe I've discovered another silver lining behind another of those clouds that so often seem to gather out here, beyond the sidewalks.

By 2014 we are using the broadfork, which is basically a very large garden fork; it simply loosens the soil without turning it over. Raised beds and mulch are still important, and we're making increased use of containers. I haven't owned a tiller for years.

115. October 1982

Hurrah for the first frost: *No more mosquitoes!*

At this time of the year in Wisconsin, dawn breaks noticeably later every day, lengthening the night.

And dusk swoops down more swiftly, catching us unaware as we dawdle at evening chores that used to be done at the same time — but in broad daylight.

In between dawn and dusk, the air wears a dark veil of weary experience and sad expectation.

It's fall in the northern Midwest.

The season when the birds (perhaps with better sense than most of us can muster) gather up, and fly south. The time when those of us who are left behind to face another northern winter line our burrows in preparation.

And yet...

Even though I know full well that winter is coming, even though I know full well what to expect (having chipped ice from many a stock tank supposedly protected by stock tank heaters, having dug out from many a snowdrift as high as the cab of my pickup, having made many a visit to the woodpile with blizzard-driven icy snow stinging my face as I struggled through the drifts...) even though I know what winter is like here... I welcome the frosty mornings of October.

The reason:

MOSQUITOES.

I am not a vindictive person. I have a great deal of respect for all life forms. A mouse or a rat or a hornet, here and there, now and then, doesn't upset me much. They have a right to live too.

A weed in my garden doesn't send me into apoplexy. I don't even mind a cabbage moth or an armyworm once in awhile. I've had raccoons and deer steal my sweet corn, and my garden has been invaded by badgers, skunks, gophers, rabbits, chipmunks, and assorted other creatures whose survival didn't depend on my homesteading skills and efforts (even though those skills and efforts certainly made life easier for them!)

None of it has bothered me, much.

But then, even the mosquitoes didn't bother me much, at first.

Oh, there was the occasional buzzing, and a slap or two, and once in awhile a slight burning that stung and itched for awhile after I'd left the garden. But then...

I'd be out trimming the weeds from under the electric fence enclosing the hog pasture, weeds that reach up and zap the energy from the wire in a self-destructive kamikaze effort (and when the fence finally loses its jolt, the pigs somehow know it, and immediately break through the wire and head for the garden) and clouds of mosquitoes would rise up, swirling about my face like lather. They made the job uncomfortable, at first, and then one day they were so thick it became impossible.

*   *   *

Like almost everyone else, I'd read that this was the worst infestation of mosquitoes in the quarter-century I'd been homesteading. But they didn't seem that bad on *my* homestead... or it could have been the recollection of the mosquitoes that plagued my first attempt at homesteading, back when we thought you had to move to Canada to be a real homesteader. I honestly thought I'd picked up an immunity, up there: the little stingers really hadn't bothered me much in the 25 years since then.

And even when I did get the occasional mosquito bite, I figured I could accept it, just as I accept the occasional bat in my house, mouse in my root cellar, and gopher in my garden.

But then the mosquitoes got so bothersome I took the extreme measure (for me, at least) of using a repellant. I tried *two* repellants.

It almost seemed as if they were *attractants*, because when I was picking beans, the insects would swarm about me just like the bees do when I inspect a hive on a fine autumn day when the bees don't have much else to do but protect their honey from me. Their very *presence* was maddening.

It was hot — but I wore a long-sleeved sweatshirt, to keep *some* of the mosquitoes off my arms and to keep the sweat from attracting more of the swarm to a meal. I wore a bandana knotted around my neck to keep the pesky critters from crawling down my back.

They landed in my beard, and crawled skinward, and buzzed hideously, making a dandy substitute for Chinese water torture.

They squirmed and buzzed their way into my ears, they flew up my nose, they landed on my eyeballs and started drilling...

We had a lot of garden produce this year that was not lost to coons or rabbits, bugs or worms. It was abandoned. To mosquitoes.

As I did chores, the sweat pouring off of me into my heavy protective clothing, the feathery little buzzards would cover my hands, and my nose (which was about the only unprotected target I offered). They'd actually bore through two layers of heavy clothing, and fly up my pants legs.

And my dog, Bear, would have mosquitoes covering his face, thoraxes to antennae (or however mosquitoes line up) so that I'd feel so sorry for him I'd let him in the house for protection.

Of course, he always brought a few hundred of the little monsters in with him, which kept me busy with the fly swatter until bedtime... and beyond.

And then...
FIRST FROST!
The tomatoes were whitened and done for. The peppers were blackened. But oh joyful bliss... *no more mosquitoes!*

I've always known I could live in harmony with just about anything: bugs, gophers, skunks... even politicians. I just go about my business, and let them go about theirs. There are some things you just can't fight.

But nature balances everything out.

That's one of the things you learn, when you live beyond the sidewalks.

116. November 1982

The indefinable art — and enjoyment — of homesteading

I've been a "homesteader" for a good many years, now. For a long time, I've worked on a magazine that deals with "homesteading." I've written a bunch of books, with titles like *Raising the Homestead Hog.* And over the years, I've learned not to get disturbed by letters that begin with, "We're not really 'homesteaders' because we only have one acre, three goats, a pig and some chickens..." But finally, I give in. I'll admit that, despite all the definitions I've heard or concocted over the years...in spite of the ads I've written trying to convince "homesteaders" to read our homestead magazine and to convince advertisers that "homesteaders" weren't long-haired hippies running naked through the woods living on roots and berries, I really don't know what a homesteader is.

Momentous announcements like this don't just come out of the blue, of course. They incubate, under various forms of broody hens. Then, on the equivalent of the 21st day, something happens...

Part of "what happened" came yesterday afternoon, when Diane and I got home from the office. It was going to rain, and I didn't feel like going down to feed the livestock in the rain after supper, as I usually do, and the last wheelbarrow load of potatoes that was curing in the open air shouldn't get wet, of course.

When two people live and work together as long as Diane and I have, it doesn't take much time or many words to make decisions and get things done. By the time I reached the barn, I could see her sorting potatoes into bags.

I fed and watered the pigs, the sheep and goats. We don't have a cow, or horses, or even rabbits, at present. Those seemed to fit into the homestead scheme better when our children were still at home. And oh yes, we aren't milking any of the goats — after how many years? There are lots of reasons. "Excuses," I would have called them, a short time ago.

I didn't feel much like a homesteader, as I trudged back up the driveway, with neither milk pail nor egg basket.

Diane was still picking up potatoes. And there were a few baskets of onions there, too.

The clouds were blacker, the wind was picking up — and was that a raindrop I just felt on my arm?

I left Diane to her labors, and went to the garden to pick supper.

Ours is a homestead garden. Definitely homestead. Sometimes I marvel at how, driving up the driveway, the whole thing looks like nothing but a patch of weeds and yet I *know* how many tomatoes, cabbages, potatoes, onions, peas, okra, beets beans and a seed catalog of other good stuff is prospering behind that façade.

And tonight, I can't help but think of the most picturesque garden in the township, this year.

It had been weed-free all summer, in rich black loam, and could have posed for the cover of any gardening magazine without any retouching. A serious gardener like me couldn't help but notice and admire it. But the other day as I passed it, the whole thing had been tilled under. It was as black and as smooth as a cleaned slate on a classroom wall.

Mine still looked like the dickens — but I'd have no trouble at all finding a meal in it. In fact, since frost still hadn't hit us, even in October, I'd find *more* than a meal.

I plucked a bunch of tiny, late-crop onions from the ground. They came out like white teeth, and left depressions in the earth that looked interestingly like — tooth-holes, or whatever they're called. I took kohlrabi from the row, and eyed up all those that were left, planning future autumn meals. They'll take the frost, when it comes. So will the turnips, and cabbages, which don't quite fit into tonight's menu.

But there are still frost-prone tomatoes... and second crop green beans, and even a green pepper that somehow missed the "final call" when we were sure frost was going to ravage the garden in September.

Celery... Swiss chard... beets... parsley... carrots...

As I took a load to the kitchen I wondered about those people with the picture-perfect garden. I wondered what *they* were eating tonight...

And I wondered, again, about the definition of a "homesteader."

I had made the final trip into the kitchen and had begun scrubbing the vegetables, when I saw Diane jog toward the root cellar with the last of the potatoes.

The rain spattering against the window made a comforting sound as I cut the tops from the carrots, and I smiled, inside. Maybe I can't define being a homesteader. Maybe I can't explain it to anyone else. I sure can't sell the concept. But I can recognize it when I feel it... and it feels good, and proper.

I asked Diane if she wanted my seven-course Monday night homestead special — or everything tossed in one pot.

One pot, she said. She didn't want to clean up my mess.

But with the gathering dusk, and the rain, and my homestead feelings, I just couldn't do it. (Besides, I clean up my own messes, when I have time.) I boiled the tiny onions, gently, and added a white sauce. I candied the carrots. I shredded the kohlrabi, and fried it lightly. The tomatoes were quartered, and garnished with chopped peppers and onions and celery and parsley. Some leftover chicken was warmed in a frying pan.

And when everything was done, I arranged it all in a pleasing manner on a large platter and added parsley to make it look something like the covers of one of those fancy cooking magazines.

One of our sons showed up, unexpectedly, for supper, but there was plenty to go around. And since there was no way we could have used the broccoli and cauliflower I'd brought in, we blanched it and put it in the freezer. There'll be more — fresh — tomorrow.

As we dug into a homestead-produced meal (whatever a "homestead" is) and we all raved about how *good* it was, I had to perform a time-honored Belanger homestead ritual. I said, "Do you know how much all of this *cost?*"

Nobody answered. They never do anymore.

But it never fails to amaze *me*. To please me, and excite me. And I'm not sure you can convey that to someone who hasn't experienced it. Maybe that's why you can't explain what homesteading is, or why life is so enjoyable, beyond the sidewalks.

Part XIII: 1983

Inflation: 3.2%; Fed interest rate: 11%; Average annual income: $21,070; US unemployed: 12 million; Deaths in Ethiopian drought: 4 million; First mobile phones introduced (Motorola); ARPANET officially uses the Internet Protocol, creating the Internet; COUNTRYSIDE hits a new low, back to a one-man operation

A New Year's message
A time for new lessons — by looking backwards

As the months roll by, changing from one to the next most often means nothing more than tearing a page off the calendar and waiting for the onslaught of bills to arrive.
But not January.

One of our favorite "spiritual predecessors"—the editor of the *Wisconsin Farmer*—said it well (if wordily) in the January 1857 issue of that paper:

"Once, at least, in each twelve months, every thinking, reasoning, systematic mind, that controls and engineers a human body and deals with the issues and destinies of an immortal soul, should calmly examine itself, and take new soundings upon the sea of time—should look back over the wake of the past year's voyage, noting its haps and mishaps, its calms and its storms, its forward and backward movements, its deviations to the right and left, its wisdom, its follies, its joys and sorrows, and all the causes from whence they sprung; for, what is the worth of experience if it profiteth us nothing?"

He went on to point out that every incident of life, good and bad, has its cause and origin as well as effect. If we want to change the effects, we have to change the causes. And there's no better time to study the two, than January.

Or, as our friend of 126 years ago put it, "What time of the year is so appropriate as the opening of a new year, for the thorough review of the subject, and the commencement of a new lesson?"

Ah. The beginning of a new lesson, by looking back! A novel idea, no doubt, to those who think progress involves the latest news, the newest gimmicks, and the blazing of sundry other untrod paths. But listen, please, to these paragraphs from the past:

"How many of the numerous readers of the *Farmer* can, on review, fully approbate their past year's operations? How many have tilled their farms so wisely and well, in all details and particulars, as to be willing to copy without change the coming year? How many have harvested their crops as judiciously as they might have done, and realized as large results as they expected?

"How many have rigged up as well, at house and barn, for our cold northern winters, as they ought? How many have diminished their debts, and how many have increased them needlessly, by buying what they did not need, or could have settled up their affairs, as we suggested in the December number, and how many can now tell just where they stand? How many, in a word, kind reader, and are you one of the number, that can put your hand upon your heart, before you close your eyes in sleep on the first night of the new year, and say, 'I know of no duty I have left undone, or of anything that would give unnecessary trouble or perplexity, to those I should leave behind, if I should not wake again?'"

As we begin our journey through 1983, let us make every effort to improve our homesteads, and our homestead lives. By renewed industry and ambition, yes; by improved techniques and efficiency, certainly; by searching out new ideas and methods and equipment, sure.

But let's not forget that the greatest progress, the most efficient gains, probably won't be made by using anything new and startling: the surest progress will be won by making improvements—even though slight—on what we did last year. And no book or magazine or machine or vast sum of money can take the place of *your* insight and determination. Have a happy new year.

118. February 1983

Diversify! Diversify!

Isn't it interesting how everybody has different tastes?

Some farmers like to milk cows, but they hate pigs. Others like pigs but not cows. And still others wouldn't think of raising anything but sheep.

And of those who love cows, some prefer Holsteins, while others wouldn't have anything but Guernseys or Brown Swiss or Jerseys in their barns.

We all have our own likes and dislikes, our own ways of looking at things and of doing things, and that's wonderful. How dull it would be if we were all alike!

Can you imagine how drab the world would be if all cows were black and white? How drab life would be if nobody loved goats the way some of us love goats... and by implication, how drab it would be if everybody loved goats!

Diversity is part of the scheme of nature. There are thousands of plants and insects that mankind hasn't even gotten around to classifying yet. There are different climates, and different weather patterns—and different plants and animals for each of them—and different kinds of people to enjoy living in them.

And my goodness, are there ever a lot of different kids of people!

Homesteaders appreciate all this diversity more than any other group I can think of. Maybe that's because we're a little "more different" than most, ourselves.

It's always something of a shock to meet a city person who is astonished to learn that people like us even exist.

"You raise goats? What do you do with them? You milk them? What do you do with the milk? You *drink* it? Oh my gosh." They're incredulous.

If those people could actually see the mud and smell the manure and feel the aching muscles and sweat and sunburn that we seem to sadistically seek out, they'd think they were caught in a time warp, or they'd think we were crazy... and you'd never convince them that more than one family lived like that in this enlightened age!

A normal person will look at a run-down unpainted leaky-roofed abandoned farmhouse and either tell the real estate agent to keep right on going or inquire about the availability of the nearest bulldozer.

The homesteader will look at that same house and cry out in delight, "It's perfect! With a little fixing up it'll be just what we wanted."

The homesteader will stand overlooking a row of tract houses that most people would be delighted to live in, but the sameness and closeness will cause a constriction in the chest and pounding in the head and an irrational desire to get away... anywhere... fast.

Homesteaders crave diversity.

Most of us are aware of the ecological folly of monoculture. But the most dramatic effect of driving past mile after mile of corn or wheat is that it's boring.

I seriously considered farming as a career in the early 1950s, but the traditional diversified farms were on the way out. Farmers were being told they had to specialize to succeed, and they had to get bigger. They had to copy industry, and become assembly lines.

I couldn't imagine anything more boring.

I wanted a farm with chickens and pigs, cows and sheep, ducks and geese and goats, with pastures (none of that slatted floor confinement stuff) and a garden and orchard and woodlot.

Nostalgia, for the farms of my youth or the good old days? Heck no. Diversity!

A "modern" farm for a hogman like me (I did become a farmer, eventually) would mean I'd grow nothing but corn, the pigs would be cooped up all the time... and I'd feel cooped up too.

No thanks. If that's what it takes to be a farmer, then I guess I don't really want to be a farmer after all. Don't even call me a small farmer because that implies that I'm just not smart enough or ambitious enough to be a big farmer. The truth is, I'm something entirely different.

I'm a homesteader. Someone who truly believes that variety is the spice of life... and that life ought to be spicy.

Of course, there are plenty of people who think that the cities are where all the action is: the hustle and bustle, the diversity of people, the plays and restaurants and the athletic events and sirens and traffic... those people think country life must be dull, indeed.

They're welcome to their opinions, and I wouldn't even dream of trying to change their minds. After all if everybody was a homesteader, there'd be just that much less diversity for us to take pleasure in. Even in the most wondrously diverse places of all, beyond the sidewalks.

***

And speaking of diversity, you'll probably notice that this issue of COUNTRYSIDE is a little different from most other magazines you see. You might be interested in some of the reasons.

- This is what I think COUNTRYSIDE ought to look like, and since I put the whole issue together myself (and there wasn't anybody here to argue with me) I just did it.
- There are plenty of magazines with articles and pretty pictures, but there aren't any where us average people (who are the real experts—maybe the only experts—at homesteading) can share our expertise *and* have our diverse opinions heard.
- This is what COUNTRYSIDE started out to be, and was, until a bunch of other back-to-the-land magazines came along and I started working with some real magazine people who thought we ought to compete, instead of just being ourselves.
- This attempt to compete didn't work.
- It doesn't make sense—it probably isn't possible—for a magazine with an editorial staff of one to answer the amount of mail COUNTRYSIDE gets—and then throw out that research and scurry about to find "articles" to put in the magazine.
- There are only so many ways to say the same things, the basic homestead stuff we've been saying month after month, for years. Long-time readers are getting tired of it, and so are we.
- Letters from real homesteaders are more interesting than "articles" from "authors."
- "Non-articles" don't lend themselves to conventional magazine graphics.
- Conventional magazine graphics waste an awful lot of space: they're for readers who don't really care all that much about the information involved, and for winning magazine awards, and for advertisers—none of which applies to homesteaders or to COUNTRYSIDE. People who just want a pretty magazine have many to choose from: people who want a down-to-earth personal communication experience deserve COUNTRYSIDE.

But by far the most important reason of all for me, a career homesteader who just can't kick the writing habit and who loves to discuss things with kindred souls who don't find me strange at all (and naturally I think they're wonderful) is that this is *my* kind of magazine! Or newsletter, maybe. There's a give-and-take, a personal closeness, that simply isn't possible when a publication tries to sound high and mighty and looks like its put together by the Eastern intelligentia to change the world and sell advertising (not necessarily in that order). COUNTRYSIDE was looking too much like a successful magazine, and frightening off too many people who thought we didn't need their ideas and contributions.

I started COUNTRYSIDE because other magazines wouldn't print my articles or even my letters to the editor (they still don't) because they didn't have "mass appeal." So why on Earth should COUNTRYSIDE be like them?

I had a very good time coordinating this issue for you, and I sincerely hope you enjoy it enough to be a participant, next time.

Even if it does look different.

2014: The magazine redesign referred to here took us from a rather modern, "professional" look to a much simpler and old-fashioned appearance — something like this book, now that I think about it. No pictures, nothing fancy, just good information.
Some readers hated it.

119. March 1983

Thoughts on football, trees and cannibalism

What were you doing on January 30, Super Bowl Sunday? That might sound like an odd question to be asking in a homesteading magazine—but it's going to get odder.

It's January 30. It's overcast and chilly, but still as unseasonably mild as the rest of the month has been. All the "must" work is done (and there's mercifully little of it, this time of year) and it seems like a good day to spend a few hours on my "timber stand improvement" (TSI).

I pull on my jacket and as I duck my head into the living room to tell Diane where I'm headed, I notice the tv is on. Tuned to the football game, naturally.

John had turned it on. I'm not absolutely certain, but I think he might be the only serious athlete in the entire history of the Belanger clan.

But he isn't even watching. He's sitting in front of the fire, working on a speech. The speech is supposed to be about something unusual. He's going to talk about cannibalism.

On the tv set, No. 85, in a green and gold uniform, is just plunging over the goal line. Something primal stirs inside me.

"Hey," I say. "That's Max McGee!"

Odd. I was never a sports fan. Even in grade school, when the other guys were playing ball, I was sitting with my pigeons or rabbits. But

344

when a mania sweeps through a region it's hard to escape. Ask me to name a baseball player and the only name I could come up with, besides Babe Ruth, would be Eddie Matthews, whose name was a household word in Wisconsin when the Milwaukee Braves were hot. That had to be why I remember that No. 85 was Max McGee...but I didn't even know the Packers were playing in the Super Bowl.

Turns out, they weren't. The play on the tv screen was a film clip of Super Bowl I... 17 years ago.

And to think I can't even remember where I left my glasses, five minutes ago.

I leave the house, and head for my trees.

M y "timber stand improvement" is a family joke of long standing. We have a small woodlot—actually two of them, but one is nothing but weed trees—and a great deal of overgrown fenceline. That's one of the things that attracted me to this place.

When the realtor guided us over the property, he waved his arm towards the rows of scraggly trees and said, "You'll want to bulldoze all this trash out, of course," and when I looked at Diane she was giving me a sidelong glance and smiling. She knew about Jerry's Jungle—the "forest" I had planted from seed on our one-acre homestead, long ago.

Anyway, I've been pecking away at my fencerow forest ever since, and in some areas I've made a lot of headway. Although it still bothers me to cut down a tree—any tree — over the years I've learned to look at weed trees and crowded trees the same way I look at weeds and closely spaced plants in the garden.

And what's even more helpful, I'm beginning to see some of the results of my efforts, as some of the trees I selected years ago are growing tall and straight since I gave them room to grow by eliminating their competition.

Today, I'm working along the road, in a section that was nothing but tall brush when we moved here. Mostly box elder, or "Morden Maple" as at least one nursery dubs it, a name I once used, jokingly, when a neighbor asked me what a certain tree I was pruning was. He was impressed, and I was embarrassed because he certainly should have known better, but the experience showed me the importance of a name.

Actually, box elders aren't all that bad. We have so many of them in our fencerows that they're one of our main sources of firewood. They certainly don't take the place of a good hunk of oak on a cold winter night, but they grow a lot faster. And they burn, and they throw off heat.

I've tapped box elders, or Morden Maples... which really are a member of the maple family... to make syrup. Box elder syrup, I guess it was. It's maple syrup: it just takes more sap to make a gallon of syrup.

When I grub out box elder in the spring, after the leaves have come out, I put the branches in the goat pen. They ravish both leaves and bark.

But today, there isn't even a sign of a bud, and most Americans are in front of their tv sets, watching a football game in sunny California.

With the passing of the years, the box elder shrubs in this section of the fencerow have grown into small trees.

But along with them, in the absence of foliage, I can see some mighty promising young hickories, some cherries and an occasional oak. The slower-growing but more valuable trees will be choked out by the box elders, so my job today is to give the good guys some breathing space.

In some places, the chain saw is the tool that does the best job. Sometimes there's nothing but a clump of small saplings where the bow saw is both easier and more efficient, and safer, too. In other places, the axe works best.

Here I saw off the weaker of a double-trunk hickory; there, I lop off a poor joint in a cherry. In one long section, there's nothing but box elder, so I look them over, choose those that are well-grown and straight and properly spaced, and give them the air and light and moisture and nutrients they need to become good trees by sacrificing the lesser ones around them.

Cannibalism! That seems like an odd thing to give a speech about. At least it's not a mundane, boring kind of topic...

I work methodically. This isn't like felling timber, like the huge oaks out back. It's more like weeding the garden, only without the mosquitoes. And it's not even like work. It's something I want to do, and it doesn't really have to be done today. Trees have a slower pace, and they give you a slowed-down outlook on life.

I stop, often, not so much to rest as to size up the next move. Every time I squat on my haunches, Bear comes up, wagging his tail, and puts his head in my lap.

It still amazes me to think I'd remember number 85. But then, how many people are watching that game right now? I forget, but advertisers are paying something like half a million dollars to talk to them...*for 30 seconds.* If I had half a million dollars to spend on advertising, how many new COUNTRYSIDE subscribers would I buy? Half a million dollars would print COUNTRYSIDE for... what, about five years? But then there's postage and...

It's a ridiculous thought anyway and... look at that grape vine strangling that cherry tree over there. Wild grapes are a real problem, here. Much worse than box elders. Out in the back woodlot, I've hacked though some as thick as my wrist, that snaked 50 to 60 feet up into the trees like gigantic pythons, killing huge branches and wilting entire trees.

Is that cannibalism? Parasitism is probably something else... but grapes aren't even parasitic.

This kind of work-that-isn't-work gives you a lot of time to think. Maybe too much, because you know you'll never get the time to think all of it, or maybe even any of it, all the way through.

Sometimes I wonder what it would be like to live this homestead life without having any contact with the outside world. What did the farmer who first carved a field out of forest where I'm working now think about?

Not the Super Bowl, certainly. Probably not cannibalism, and certainly not COUNTRYSIDE and television commercials that cost half a million dollars for half a minute.

And that's not even considering the truckers' strike, the possibility of a new volcano in California, Lebanon, OPEC and the fact that the gas tank of my truck has sprung a slow leak.

There are people who read COUNTRYSIDE who have… successfully, so far as I know…done away with all these outside influences. They live on their own little Walden Ponds, and I don't know whether to envy them, or to feel sorry for them. They're a galaxy away from most of the people watching the football game… and most of those people, I feel sorry for.

I've said that much, in polite company, and was lambasted for my holier-than-thou attitude.

I like trees. They ask you questions… make you think… but they don't put you down. As I look back on my afternoon's work. It doesn't look like much. I didn't really do much damage, after all.

After supper, as I head to my downstairs dungeon to write *Beyond,* I'm so full of fresh air and ideas I have no idea where to start. As often happens, I ask anyone within hearing distance what I ought to write about this month.

John says, cannibalism.

I roll a sheet of paper into the typewriter.

Cannibalism. I've had crazier assignments in the past 25 years.

I think about chickens pecking each other to death, and the pine tar we used to spread on their tail feathers to thwart that peculiarity (red pine tar works the best)… and the lighting hints we've written about in COUNTRYSIDE (red lights are supposed to help) and debeaking, and even special glasses you put on chickens to keep them from pecking each other to death.

I think about mother rabbits eating their young… and the controversies that have raged in these pages over the years about such things as hanging a hunk of raw bacon or salt pork in the rabbit hutch to avoid disaster…

I think of the sows we've had, who, for some inexplicable reason, took to eating their offspring. The time I didn't check a Ketch-all mouse trap in some remote corner for a few days, and found a bunch of eaten mouse carcasses… and one very fat live mouse…

Yeah, I think I could probably write something about cannibalism, grotesque topic that it is. But something tells me that I already have.

Out of curiosity, I looked up "cannibalism" in the dictionary.
    1. To dismantle (a machine) for parts to be used as replacements in other machines.
    2. To deprive of parts or men in order to repair or strengthen another unit.

Maybe I'm stretching things to make use of John's suggestion, or maybe I just spent too much time in the fencerow. But it occurs to me that we're all cannibalizing — ourselves. We all deprive ourselves — of something — in order to have something else we value more.

I hope I remember that, the next time I start feeling sorry for myself, with all the choices that we have to make, beyond the sidewalks.

Update: In 2014, a 30-second Super Bowl ad cost $4 million.

120. April 1983

The signs of spring are written in color
Everyone can see them, but only a few get the message

News from the COUNTRYSIDE homestead: Even though this is being written in February, it's easy to imagine April, today. I did some planting. Yes, in the snow.

When we plant winter wheat, in September, we can't plant the clover I like to grow along with it, because it won't overwinter up here. That means that in early spring, when we have warm days but freezing nights, I get to trudge across the fields sowing clover, by hand. The alternate thawing and freezing works the tiny seeds into the soil, and they sprout. Without plowing, disking and drilling or otherwise working them into the ground. I love it!

I have a pretty decent grain drill, since small grains and forage are so important to my farm plan. Sometimes I miss the old wooden, steel-wheeled Van Brunt I used for so many planting seasons. But the old cast iron gears and cogs finally got too worn to mesh. When I planted a July field of buckwheat—finishing up a heavy downpour—and got back to the shed to find out I hadn't dropped but an occasional seed—and the wet conditions persisted so that I never did get back into that field that year—I decided I needed something a little more reliable. Besides, when you divide the number of acres I planted with that thing into the $75 I paid for it, it was a good investment and deserved to be retired.

The new one cost three times as much, has rubber tires, does a much better job, but isn't nearly as much fun, for some reason.

Maybe it's because it doesn't have that neat little running board on the back that the kids used to stand on, when they were small, to help me plant oats. That was before they were big enough to drive a tractor, or to go off to seek their fortunes in strange places like Florida and Utah and California. But planting with the Van Brunt reminded me of them, and of many other things…

Or maybe it's because I just knew that machine! Every mechanical device has its own foibles and characteristics, its own personality, and while I publicly claim to despise machinery, I don't always. Not machines that I've taken apart and put together and jerry-rigged and cussed and spent many happy hours with.

Like anything else, a machine has to earn that esteem…but it also has to earn its keep. Hard fact of life.

The new drill, a metallic IH, works so well (so far) that I haven't really gotten into its guts. That, no doubt, will come.

But today, in a field almost covered with snow (and the uncovered parts so squishy and muddy I'm glad there aren't more of them) I'm working with the good ol' Cyclone Seeder, the $36.95 jobbie from the Countryside General Store.

I had one, once, I bought at an auction, probably for less than a buck. I hung it in the shed, and the mice chewed the bejeebers out of it. But the new model, made by the same company, is actually improved, and now I know enough to take better care of it by emptying *all* of the seed out of it and keeping it in a mouse-proof container.

It must seem like a lot of work, walking up and down a field with a sack of seed slung around your neck, turning a little red crank. I can tell, when the neighbors pass by and are too open-mouthed and wide-eyed to toot their horns at me (and of course, I'm in no position to give them a friendly wave. It's worse then having to walk and blow bubble gum bubbles at the same time.)

But it's not work, really.

For one thing, there's the satisfaction of being outside again, and not only outside, but on the land. Those neat little rows of wheat plants are just straining to reach out to the sun. It's like walking in a garden…even though the land is almost totally covered with snow. It gives you a jump on the season, which is something you need when you live in Wisconsin, and when you live for growing things.

There's a definite satisfaction in plodding along, inspecting the results of last September's planting amid the patches where the snow has been eroded through by our unseasonable winter. (Usually, we do this planting in March. We never really had winter here, this year, by my standards.)

There's also a certain satisfaction of doing something, on a more or less grand scale, without the rumble of a tractor and the clang of machinery. Just the plotch, plotch, plotch of my boots and the whirr of the Cyclone and the hsss of those tiny little seeds spitting out to meet their destiny.

I was grateful for the snow cover. It made walking easier, for one thing. But it also let me see where the seed was falling, and how thickly.

When I plant with the Cyclone, I like to sow a little on the heavy side. Broadcasting takes more seed than drilling, which is one reason Jethro Tull (no, not the singer) invented the grain drill. But forage and ground cover seed prices have gone through the roof this year, thanks to PIK, and even though it never makes sense to waste seed, there's more economic incentive to skimp a bit this year.

But I'm sowing homegrown sweet clover... a crop some modern farmers don't have much use for, but one which most old-timers still say is the best soil improvement legume around. And it makes good honey to boot.

I like to put it on heavy, and the snow cover lets me know when I'm not turning the crank fast enough (to avoid bare patches) or when the opening isn't open enough (or gets clogged with a dead grasshopper).

But best of all... I'm marching. Slosh, slosh, slosh.

Turning the crank. Sssssss.

And then I hear it. Faint, at first. Faint, but unmistakable.

I thumb down the spring latch to stop the flow of seed, stop my northerly march, and turn toward the sound.

The vane of the windmill back at the house presents no silhouette at all: the wind is from due south. It carries the sound, making my ears more aware than my eyes. Finally, I see them.

The first Canada geese of spring! Heading north, heralding the birth of a new season, their plaintive honking stirring the same emotions and memories in my old bones as a Soo Line steam engine would if it rolled down the tracks behind our farm!

SPRING! FREEDOM! Natural cycles... the reaffirmation of life... and a lot more besides.

By the time I finished, thousands of geese had passed over. About 200 of them, by my estimate, landed in the corn field behind the barn, apparently not knowing that our sheep were so fat and contended because they'd been over every square inch of that field in the past couple of months. But it was a beautiful thing. A wonderful thing. The kind of thing that makes you forget about tractors and grain drills and PIK and the price of wheat and all of that.

Because it was an experience that only certain persons are privileged to witness. Farmers in big tractors don't hear it: the machinery is too loud. City people can't appreciate it: they're too far from the awakening wheat (and I don't even know if geese fly over cities). People who simply dwell in the countryside can't really feel the thrill, because they're not attuned to birth and death and the subtle changing of the season.

It was one of those things reserved (and how could I possibly help but feel a bit smug about this?) for true homesteaders, those people who are at the right place, at the right time, because they live beyond the sidewalks.

Homesteads can be fun *and* efficient
Look at time-savers as homestead vacation-makers

A former reader wrote to tell me he doesn't subscribe to homestead magazines anymore because all of them seem to be telling people how to become more efficient, and he's never felt any compulsion to be efficient.

That's an interesting attitude. I assume he has a decent job and can afford to waste time and money on inefficient homesteading On the other hand, since there are people like me, who try so hard to be efficient but seldom succeed, is it possible that there are people who can be efficient without trying? Life does play dirty tricks like that, sometimes.

"Efficiency" is one of those strange words (like "profit") that, to many people, seems out of place on the homestead. And yet, can an inefficient place really be a homestead? I wonder.

My dream homestead—quite unlike my real one—is a model of efficiency. There is a place for everything, and everything is in its place. There is always the right tool for the job. A stitch in time saves nine, so a few hours a week are devoted to those little maintenance jobs that anticipate and head off trouble. Neatness counts, and you can't maintain a positive mental outlook when you live in depressing atmosphere, so everything is kept neat and in good repair and freshly painted.

Records are kept, carefully, and they're used. Culling is ruthless, but the milk pail is always filled, there are fresh eggs every day of the year, and the steer, the lambs, the pig and the young rabbits are fat and sleek. And chores are done efficiently, of course.

Everything is accomplished on schedule and under budget. There are never weeds in the garden, the bees never swarm, the fruit trees are pruned on time and the woodshed is always filled a year in advance.

It's the kind of place where the screwdrivers are always lined up according to size on that little rack at the back of the workbench; where you can always find just the size bolt you need, when you need it (and not a week later, when you can't find the size nail you need); and the checkbook probably balances, too.

The reality is something else. I'd love to be efficient, I try to be efficient, but I usually seem to be incapable of it.

It's always the little things that trip me up.

For example, some months ago the pigs rooted the protective cover off the float valve in their water tank, and destroyed the float valve. I bought a new float valve a few days later, but when I got it home it was the wrong one.

That means that instead of filling the tank every other day or so, I have to run a little water into it at least once a day because if I filled it up the water would all run out, without the float valve to regulate the depth.

To make matters worse, my usual winter practice, when I can't run a hose to the sheep water tank, has been to dip buckets of water out of the hog tank which is located under the frost-proof faucet in the barn, and carry it to the sheep. But since the water level in the hog tank is too low to dip buckets into, I have to fill them at the spigot.

It takes longer...and of course, I never did get around to building a proper gate in the barn, so I have to lift all those pails of water over the stock panel that keeps the pigs penned in the barn during the winter. With the float valve working properly, I was able to just lean over the stock panel to scoop up water but since the faucet is located at the other end of the tank, I've been climbing over the fence, filling the bucket, then climbing back out again.

It only takes a few minutes, of course, so it's no big deal. Or is it?

Let's see...one minute a day would be 365 minutes a year, divided by the 60 minutes in an hour... gosh, that's more than six hours a year. If I had an extra six hours I could probably clean up the workshop well enough to find all the screwdrivers and put them into the rack, so the next time I need the large Phillips I don't have to spend 10 minutes rummaging around looking for it...

No, I don't have any *compulsion* to be efficient: that's too strong a word. But I sure wish I were a lot more efficient than I am, not only in the big, glaringly dumb things but in the dozens of little things that are hardly noticed.

That's because time is one of the most precious commodities on the homestead. And we all waste precious minutes every day. And if one minute a day adds up to six hours a year, then a mere seven minutes a day means more than 40 hours a year, and what homesteader wouldn't be absolutely thrilled with an entire 40-hour week that could be used in any way whatsoever? And how many of us waste *more* than an average of seven minutes a day?

It's possible to rationalize anything. Some people might tell me the exercise I get from clambering over fences with heavy pails of water is good for me. "They're black buckets: pretend you're bowling," They might say. "It's cheaper than bowling, so that's a form of homesteading efficiency."

Or they might point out that I get to observe the sows a little longer, or even that my pet pig gets a few extra rubs behind the ears while I'm waiting for the pails to fill.

They might say, "That was no waste of time when you were looking for the Philips screwdriver the other day. After all, you found the crescent wrench you were looking for last week."

Maybe so, maybe so. But I'd like to be a lot more efficient anyway. Those extra hours gained appeal to me: I'd like to do a little fishing this summer.

All of this is a far cry from the "efficiency" of a modern farm, where one man does the work of 20 or 40 or 60 by using mammoth equipment and lots of electricity and diesel fuel and county-wide fields. No, efficiency on a homestead scale involves little things that add up.

How many time-savers — let's call them "vacation-makers" —can you come up with? Here are a few that come to mind readily:

1. A little extra plumbing—even a float valve—can save a lot of time and effort otherwise required to haul water.
2. It takes less time to build a proper goat fence than it does to continually chase the goats out of the orchard.
3. An extra set of rabbit watering utensils is a good investment in the winter. Bring the frozen ones into a warm place to thaw out, and provide warm water in the other set. Beats trying to chip ice out of it or thawing a single set.
4. Don't keep or plant more of anything than you need or can use. A few extra goats or rabbits might be fun, but they cost money, and take time. If you don't need a zillion tons of zucchini, why plant it and take care of it?
5. Mulching is a great time-saver in the garden.
6. I find it faster to bring eight- or ten-foot small diameter logs from the woods, and doing the bucking right at the woodshed.
7. Preventive maintenance pays.
8. Planning ahead pays. Running to town for a part, or a tool, or an ingredient for a special recipe, is a total waste.
9. Budgeting—time and money—can often mean doing more with less.
10. Locating hay and grain and animal pens in such a way as to save steps will also save time.

How many vacation-makers can you think of? What special little tricks have you found that save you time? We'd like to hear about them.

Because even though most of us probably have no compulsion to be efficient, we have no desire to waste time, either. There are too many other things to do, beyond the sidewalks.

122. June 1983

Luxuries can become necessities, for some
Maybe it all depends on how you were brought up

One of the problems with modern America (someone said) is that luxuries have become necessities, and the necessities have become too expensive. And one of the things that distinguishes the homesteader (I think) is that we're more selective when it comes to luxuries.

Take telephones, for example.

Actually, the phone company *did* take ours, and it gave me a few things to think about in addition to trying to figure out how to sell a few more subscriptions or ads so we could pay the bill.

You see, I don't like telephones very much. Oh, I'll admit they have their place — I couldn't have spent 14 years writing advertising and PR for small independent phone companies if I couldn't see any value in them—but I, personally, just do not care for them anymore.

One of the reasons is that what should be a useful tool, used with discretion, has become a pervasive interference because of its commonness. The idea seems to be "it's there so we might as well use it" whether the task at hand calls for that particular tool or not.

I was brought up in a time and place when a long distance phone call was something that happened when somebody died or when something of equal importance took place. Picking up the phone on a whim just to chat with somebody halfway across the continent makes me uncomfortable, even though I realize that the cost of a call today is a fraction of what it was when my telephone habits were being formed.

Some people aren't like that. They'll call anybody, anywhere, anytime, for any reason... or no reason at all. Sometimes they even call me, but, aside from calls from family members, I almost never got a phone call I appreciated.

A phone call is intrusive, and jarring, and disruptive. If my phone were to ring right now, I'd stop in mid-sentence to answer it and switch my brain into another gear, then come back to the typewriter to grope for whatever it was I had meant to say next.

If the call was important, it might be worth it. But very few of the business calls I get are important. Even if I'm answering a stack of mail and someone calls with the same kind of communication that's in those letters, why should the caller get immediate preference while the others wait?

That's what happens, of course. It's the nature of the beast. Maybe that's why so many of the callers are salesmen: They know that a phone call can't be ignored, that it takes them right to the top of the pile of things to do, immediately.

Most of the calls I get are pretty useless. For instance, when someone calls to tell you that they just mailed you a letter, what are you supposed to say?

Even some business calls that may be legitimate are tough for me to handle. After all, when some people write to say they can't afford a magazine subscription, it's hard to imagine why other people would telephone across the country just to ask the price, or to say that their magazine is three days late.

It's even harder to cope with such calls in the middle of the night. I don't know why the caller didn't get his magazine. I couldn't tell them at this time of the night even if I were at the office, because Pat would have to check on it. I certainly don't keep the circulation records in my kitchen.

On the other hand, when somebody calls in a panic because their goat has a lump on her neck and their vet says the animal should be destroyed, it's nice to be able to offer advice and assurances.

But that's the whole point. Sometimes the telephone is a useful tool. It wouldn't make any sense to write a letter to the fire department when your barn is burning. But that doesn't mean we have to use the telephone to check the spelling of a word with the New York Public Library when we have a dictionary right at hand.

This also applies to many other appurtenances that, not long ago, were luxuries, but which are now so common we take them for granted. Automobiles. Electricity. The world is filled with luxuries that were unknown not long ago, but which have become "in." Treating them as necessities is akin to discovering that salt is essential to life, and using that as an excuse to consume large amounts of it. Too much of a good thing can kill.

It sure was nice and quiet here, without the telephones, although life wasn't necessarily simpler. I took a lot of flak from my associates who don't share my attitude and some people who tried to call us apparently assumed we were out of business, because don't all businesses have telephones? The phones were hooked up again.

And yesterday, someone called to ask us what movie was playing at the Mode. When the person who answered said she didn't know, the caller insisted that she go outside and look down the street at the marquee. Things are back to normal.

With one exception: I no longer talk on the telephone. If it were up to me, the phones would be out permanently, but since I'm the odd minority, I just leave the phone calls to the people who enjoy that sort of thing.

Besides, I have all these letters to write.

N *ews from the Countryside homestead—*
   Actually, there's quite a bit more to this story, but it tends to get jumbled, like this...

The truth is, The Countryside Print Shop used to print advertising and PR materials I wrote for about a hundred small independent telephone companies around the country: That was our main homestead business for 14 years. And one of the things I used to love to write about in the early 60s was how people would someday be able to work at home, no matter where home was, through the wonders of telecommunications and computers. The implications for homesteading were obvious.

I'm working at home, again, because I've found that's the only way I can produce a decent homestead magazine—but I do it without a telephone or computer.

However, despite the increased efficiency I've been able to achieve, I'm still way behind on some very important things—such as answering mail. My policy has been to answer every letter that arrives here, but the burden has become too great, and between putting together this issue and spring fieldwork and getting the garden in, I've fallen hopelessly behind.

I apologize to anyone who's been waiting to hear from me, and I resolve to do better in the future.

Now, one other thing that might interest some of my friends (and probably my enemies) is the financial condition an unpaid phone bill might indicate.

What's happening with COUNTRYSIDE? According to the newspaper, AT&T disconnected 47,000 more phones than it hooked up last year—in our four-state area alone. We have lots of company.

Also, as of April 21, business failures reached a 40-year high for the week, with 751 going under, according to Dun & Bradstreet. Many of our advertisers, who tend to be small firms, have been hard hit, and with this issue ad revenue has dipped to a five-year low.

(I can't help but think of all those who wrote in response to the December Beyond and said "We *need* COUNTRYSIDE! Don't worry about the money!" Oh, yeah?)

On the brighter side, last month our renewal rate picked up by a healthy two percent. We've only had two cancellations since our facelift, a handful of complaints, but almost 500 letters of support. And we've pared our costs to the bone, which will not only allow us to thrive, once we weather the current crisis, but which, I suspect, will also make COUNTRYSIDE a much leaner and hungrier and more aware homestead magazine.

2014: Wow, not much I can add to this! Yes, it was a rough period — but it was going to get a lot worse. On a lighter note, if

that was my attitude toward telephones in 1983, before cell phones, imagine what I think *now*. (Obviously, I do not own a cell phone, although I was an early adopter of the Macintosh computer.) I also still dislike lawns, as the next selection indicates.

123. July 1983

Lawns were for sheep—and some still are

A surprising number of people cringe, or even take offense, every time I use my columnist's prerogative to express my personal opinion on lawns, but even if you absolutely adore knocking yourself out taking care of an ornamental lawn (and I do understand: I have a son like that) you'll probably enjoy this bit of knowledge.

It's from Robert West Howard, identified as an "agriculture historian and author" (had I known there was a job like that, I would have applied) who wrote an informative piece for *Gardens for All*. He points out that lawns are a hand-me-down from feudalism.

"The word lawn meant 'an open place in the forest.' Europe's feudal lords changed the meaning when they realized that open fields around their castles offered better opportunity for observing enemy forces before hurtling rocks, arrows and hot lard down on them."

Besides, horses eat grass and since they had to come into the castle grounds whenever danger loomed on the horizon, it made sense to keep them right outside the gate.

By the 16th century, manor lords were copying the green grass layout for their mansions. Sheep and horses kept the grass trimmed.

In 17th century America, this "lawn" had become a status symbol, not only on the southern plantations and the northern colonial mansions of New England merchants, but "in every village and city home more than five feet from a cart path.

"One of the rigid laws of lawn care is that its dignity must not be sullied by food plants. This, like the taboo against eating horse meat, was another hand-me-down from feudalism. Food plants were grown by peasants and farmers, not by ladies and gentlemen. It would be socially demeaning. The British homeowner who enjoyed gardening and its harvest secluded the operation at the rear of his residence. Americans copied this *idée fixe*."

Because of increases in land values, most gardens in American cities had disappeared by 1890, although when the commuter train, horsecar, trolley, bus and automobile enabled many city people to leave their tenements for more open spaces they took the feudal hangover—grass lawns—with them. Realtors and zoning laws assured the perpetuation of the lawns.

"Further investment in a sprinkler, a truck-load of 'turf builder,' and excessive use of the community's water supply might produce an emerald fuzz that, in a year or two, could be mowed every Sunday afternoon, with beer and pretzels as a reward on the redwood lawn table. Further beautification demanded by a landscape specialist put two blue spruce shrubs as a 'foundation planting' beneath the living room window and four red calla plants beside the mailbox."

Mr. Howard reports that estimates made in 1977 indicated that 200,000,000 gallons of gas and 3,000,000 tons of fertilizer were used annually to keep lawns green—and he didn't even mention water or man-hours.

Grass lawns have a total acreage equal to that of an entire Midwestern state: Maintenance costs must exceed $20 billion a year, he estimates.

Well, not at our house. Ever since the pigs got out a few years back and savaged the small spot of lawn we had...and did a job on the neighbor's half a mile down the road...we've been planting corn, beans and pumpkins there. I had to replant the neighbor's lawn, of course, but at least I don't have to mow it.

We do have a small patch of lawn, on the other side of the house, and I'll admit it looks pretty. But I don't mow it, myself, and I don't walk or sit out there. All my leisure time is spent in the lawn/garden.

Then too, I have to admit, I might be even more feudal than some of the people with large lawns, because I do have a huge, beautifully manicured view right outside my living room window... dotted with sheep and lambs that do the manicuring. Feudal, perhaps, but it's the real thing, which is just what I'm striving for, beyond the sidewalks.

I have as little love for mechanical devices as I have for lawns. I have two garden tillers, but they're both spending a third consecutive spring in the garage, even after having still more mechanics poke at them.

I can't bring myself to simply junk them, and I don't have the heart to foist them off on any other unsuspecting soul, although I'm sure the right mechanic could turn a screw here, adjust something there and make them hum like my bouzouki on Saturday night. I really envy people like that. Me? Any talents I might have must lie elsewhere.

That's why it was almost funny the other day when Diane drove in, and said something smelled strange in the car engine. (The funny part was, she wanted *me* to look at it.)

I had a hard time even getting the hood open, and when I did, looking at those hoses and belts and wires told me about as much as I would learn about next year's weather by looking at the entrails of a goat.

Actually, it did smell odd. It reminded me of the time a cat had crawled up on a warm engine during the winter. Someplace close to the fan belt, it took a nap, and never woke up. This smell was pretty similar. But I couldn't see a thing, there wasn't any smoke or anything else coming from any of those strange parts that my '37 Chevy didn't have (and I wasn't too adept at taking that apart, either), so I gave up with a shrug.

Diane drove back to the office, later, and the smell returned. She asked Jim about it. Couldn't figure it out. She and Anne-marie drove home together that night, and neither Anne nor Chris could tell what the smell was, or where it came from. Over the next few days, she asked half a dozen more people about it. Everybody could smell it; nobody could offer a solution.

Tonight when she drove in, son Steve was here, getting ready to give the new pigs their iron shots. The car stunk. Naturally, as the mechanic in the family, he was drawn into the mystery. He raised his nose and sniffed. "Smells like a dead cat," he said. Then he got down and looked under the car... where no one had thought to look, before. With a stick, he scraped a clump of manure off the muffler. "Try that once," he said.

We'd been cleaning the barn the other day, and some of the black gold was inevitably dropped from the spreader onto the drive between the barn and the road. The car somehow picked it up, and...

Mystery solved, anyway. It's not the kind of thing a factory-trained mechanic is used to, but I suppose you have to expect just about anything, when you live beyond the sidewalks.

Steve tried the magazine business — as a projects editor who built such things as solar ovens, hand well pumps and moveable chicken coops for articles on those topics — but he didn't care for it. He became involved with maintaining much more complicated machinery in factory settings. If you have a talent, use it.

124. August 1983

Stretch your mind

"A mind, once stretched, can never return to its former dimensions."

I hadn't realized just how true that was until this summer when I undertook a number of homestead projects that required skills I hadn't used for awhile... and then found myself thinking about this quotation.

Like riding a bicycle, many homestead skills take time (and an occasional spill) to learn. But, like riding a bicycle, once you know how you never forget.

This happened to me back during planting season. I was putting in a few acres of buckwheat with a grain drill when a clump of straw got stuck in the machine. I kept hoping it would dislodge, but of course it didn't, and soon I was bulldozing a sizeable mound of soil in front of the drill. By then I couldn't pull the rope to raise the coulters...so I backed up.

Almost immediately I knew I shouldn't have because, sure as the sun rises, the openings from which the seeds are placed in the ground plug up with soil.

The reason I know that is that the first time it happened to me, years ago, I continued "planting" nearly an entire field, only to find that I hadn't dropped any seeds at all: the holes were plugged. It took a long time to clean them all out, and then of course I had to go over the field again.

My mind had been stretched, and I wasn't likely to make the same mistake again! But of course, I did.

Maybe it's just because I was thinking about it, maybe it's because I was doing things I hadn't done for a long time, but whatever the reason, I noticed the same "stretched mind effect" again and again.

I planted tomatoes in a part of the garden that had a severe quack grass problem last year, and although I "always" mulch tomatoes—my mind was stretched on that point a long time ago—I didn't mulch these.

The reason was that last year I tried to kill out a patch of quack grass with mulch, and the quack loved it. Grew better than ever. This year I raked out as many of the roots as I could, planted the tomatoes, and kept hoeing out new quack shoots for half the summer, then laid down the mulch.

Maybe that means that learning something isn't always the last word... or maybe it indicated that a mind can be stretched in two directions at once.

I feel pretty stupid now just talking about it, but believe me, when you go over every inch of electric fence wire with a fine-tooth comb to eliminate every last strand of grass that's even close, no matter how fine; when you check and re-check the barn fuses; when you practically tear the charger apart looking for the fuse that must be there *someplace* (there were two of them right out in the open on the side of the old charger I had); well, your mind is stretched when somebody shows you how simple it is to poke the fuses out of the plug, on the cord. Who would've thought of looking there?

You never forget little things like that: your mind never returns to its former dimensions.

There were dozens of little things like that, once I made a game of looking for them. Things some people take for granted, but which many other people still don't know about because they've never needed the knowledge. Things like these:

Castrating pigs. Jacking up the sagging beams of the old barn and putting in new posts. Butchering, and making sausage. (You'd be surprised at how many people want to put the blade of the sausage grinder in backwards, because they can't figure out how it can cut if it's facing away from the meat coming through the auger.) Growing melons under plastic. (Heat helps tremendously, but the plants have to be watered regularly, through the slits, even if it's been rainy.) Managing chicks and goslings. Knowing to check the flywheel key in a small engine that won't start. Knowing when to cut hay, and when to bale it... and I mean really knowing, not just looking down the road to see what the neighbors are doing. Knowing where trouble is likely to develop in the combine and, by checking those points regularly, avoiding the most common problems.

Oh, there were dozens of things I didn't know when I started farming, and dozens more related to homesteading, that I found myself taking more or less in stride, this year. Everything went much more smoothly than it did 10, or even five years ago.

And I learned some new things, too: the mind continues to be stretched.

There's another dimension to this. This summer I "reverted" to working at home... a rather long story in itself, with many aspects of it relating to stretched minds. There were fairly long periods when I was a virtual hermit, and that made me think of how homesteaders differ from both city people and most country people.

There were times when I didn't go to town for weeks on end. It would have been very easy, maybe even comfortable, to consider my little plot of land the center of the universe. Poland, Central America, national politics and economics, none of it really mattered at all. I was, I suppose, self-sufficient, at least for the moment.

And yet I wasn't really apart from the real world at all. It wasn't only because I continued to work on a national magazine, read letters from all over the country and all the magazines and newspapers and other material an editor must read to stay in the mainstream.

It was more that my mind had been stretched, and there's no way I could ever become a real "hermit." Even if I permanently reverted to a plodding, provincial, pastoral way of life, it would be impossible to confine my mind to that existence.

More than 10 years ago I wrote of butchering chickens, and standing there in the yard with blood up to my elbows, I looked up to see the contrail of a jet far overhead. I couldn't help but bust out laughing.

I used to spend a lot of time on planes, so I knew what it was like up there. I could imagine the people. The conversations, the view, the food and drink, the memories of the last stop (whether home or destination away from home) and the anticipation of the next landing (whether a reunion with the family or my next magazine assignment).

And I could also imagine what most of the people up there would have thought if they could have seen me, far below, pulling entrails from chickens—and that struck me as funny.

You see, although I know what it's like to hail cabs in New York and attend meetings in San Francisco and Honolulu, most of those people wouldn't know how to begin to butcher a chicken, castrate a pig, or even dig a potato… and I was doing all these things by choice.

Some correspondents have called this a "holier than thou" attitude. They've seen it as a city-vs.-country confrontation, but that's not it at all.

Because when your mind has been stretched as a homesteader's mind has been stretched, you actually enter a new dimension.

If you and I had been born in the wilderness and we couldn't even imagine what it was like to see towering skyscrapers and six-lane traffic jams and bustling airports, we'd probably know a lot more about homesteading, but would we be in a good a position to evaluate the world and our role in it?

If, on the other hand, we knew only the urban jungle, and had no idea how coarse the wool of a newborn lamb feels, or how silken a baby pig is to the touch, or what a freshly-pulled carrot or sun-warmed tomato tastes like or what it feels like to cup a newly hatched chick in your hand or how to adjust the carburetor on a tractor or thread the needles on a baler or what a sunrise is like when there's no traffic or garbage trucks for miles around… then we wouldn't have a very good grip on the real world either, would we?

I'm more convinced than ever that homesteaders, who have one foot planted in each of two worlds, are a very special breed. Their minds have been stretched to dimensions most other people can't even begin to imagine, unless they too live beyond the sidewalks.

125. September 1983

Nothing like a baby to change your life!
Even if it's a newly arrived Holstein

We picked up a Holstein bull calf the other day.

It was no big deal. We got him from a neighbor who lives on the farm where we used to live—practically next door—so it took only a few minutes to drive over and back in the pickup. It was a trade for some hay the neighbor had picked up last spring, so there was no financial haggling. We've had cattle before, so it was no new and exciting experience. And yet…

It's been at least five years since the last cow left our place. It's been a lot longer than that since we had 20 of them. And to tell the truth, I'd forgotten a few things about bovines.

Of course I'm a goat person. Oh, I used to enjoy our Jersey milk (and certainly the cream and butter). But I prefer the taste of goat milk, and cheese, and there are many reasons I'd rather milk several goats than even one cow.

But that's not what this is about.

This is about what *babies* calves are: innocent, inquisitive, dependent, vulnerable, tender... and very obviously new to the world. I'd forgotten about that.

Pigs—our main livestock (except for the geese during the summer) are street-savvy (or straw savvy?) within hours of seeing daylight for the first time. Oh, they wobble a little, but you can tell by their actions and mannerisms that they think they're perfectly capable of taking care of themselves. And they are.

Goat kids? Well, by the time a goat is a day old, it's ready to start first grade. (And some of ours have. It's great to live on a homestead when it comes time for show and tell!)

Chicks, whether hatched under a hen or in an incubator, really don't need anybody to tell them what to do: they have minds of their own.

But there was something about this calf that made me sit up and take notice. He's about the same size as our large, nine-year-old buck goat, he's much, much taller than our most ferocious sow, and yet, he's a baby.

When the week-old calf saw my son John coming out to his house in the pasture with the bucket of milk in his hand, he came running. After draining the bucket dry in a flash, he never left John's side.

When John came over to me at the sheep and goat pasture, the calf followed.

The sheep shied away. The goats pricked up their ears, the hair on their necks bristled, and they watched every move the baby bovine made.

He ran and leaped in juvenile exuberation... then stopped suddenly with all four feet splayed out and sniffed at a cat that was cowering and snarling and bristling at his approach.

He licked at it. It submitted, and when the calf romped off, the cat fell back on its haunches and licked itself where the calf had left off.

The calf has brought a breath of fresh air to our homestead. (And this is not a reference to the signs on the fences around cows in some of those vacation-type farms that ask, "Don't fresh air smell funny?" or "Come smell our dairy air!")

Taking care of a newborn baby is part of it, no doubt. The calf doesn't require 4 A.M. feedings, like some of the lambs and baby pigs who were brought into our kitchen this spring (and every spring, now that I think of it). I don't have to check his heat lamp, because he doesn't need or have one. And yet, his vulnerability overwhelms me. Here is an animal that follows us around like a puppy, who cavorts like a goat, who is as pleased to be petted as is the tamest barn cat... and who in two short years will weigh a ton. It makes you think.

He'll live here 18, maybe 24 months, depending on the feed situation and other considerations. He'll have a good life, for that time. He'll certainly have plenty of good food, fresh water, a dry place to sleep, and lots of companionship. That hard-to-reach-spot between his ears will be scratched regularly.

And two years from now or thereabouts, I'll be eating prime, mature, marbled, grain-fed beef. And since at my age two years seems but like a fleeting week or two, I'll be amazed that such a frolicking calf could have grown so fast.

I know, because it's happened before. With other calves. With my own children. With myself.

There's no way to stop time, and time passes faster with every passing moment. There's nothing like a fast-growing calf to make you realize how fleeting life is, and how important it is to take advantage of every moment of it.

You don't need a calf to experience these thoughts on a homestead. I've had the same experience with a tomato that was started from seed on the window ledge, and killed by frost a few months later, a gnarled, tangled mass of fibrous stem with whitened leaves.

I imagine that people who love to analyze serious literature, but have no experience with calves, would be puzzled by an essay like this. And maybe some people who raise calves for a living or as a routine matter would say, "Yeah, but what's the point?"

But I know there's a certain, small group of people who know what I'm trying to get at. People like me, who live in a blend of mud and stars, beyond the sidewalks.

126. October 1983
Time goes fast for busy homesteaders
Profits are elusive, but each day's an advance

As we grow older, time passes faster. It makes sense that a two-year-old thinks Christmas is a once-in-a-lifetime event, while a 20-year-old can get pretty blasé about it. But if next summer is going to go any faster than this past one I'm not even going to bother putting away my winter underwear.

Time flies when you're having fun, of course. Being busy helps the hours, and days, pass swiftly. But nothing speeds up the clock and the calendar like trying to cram a day's work into four hours, a week's project into a weekend, a summer's goals into a month... a life's dreams into a summer.

The inequity of it all bothers me sometimes.

I've been reading about the people who've lost their good-paying factory jobs, and have given up looking for other work. Our nearest big-city newspaper detailed how several of these folks had to sell their boats, get rid of one of the cars and were feeling pretty down because they wouldn't get a summer vacation this year. Time hangs heavy on them.

It just doesn't seem fair that their misery was stretched out into an interminable summer, while my happiness was cut so short by a fast one. I wish we could have traded hourglasses, my fine sand for their gravel.

I'm not sure where it all started—you never can be sure about things like this—but I suspect it germinated in a bunch of things at once.

Faithful (or at least *patient*) readers will know that last winter I was getting pretty tired of putting out a little magazine that didn't seem to be going anywhere. Bless you all, you got me off *that* kick in a hurry!

You not only renewed my enthusiasm for putting together good homesteading information, but you revived my excitement for my own homestead. So I laid plans for the then-coming summer in terms of garden, chickens, new woodshed (when we never had an old one) and much more.

And then, son no. 2 showed up, looking for a job on the farm. Most of our land has been worked on shares since he left a few years ago, so there was another rapid shifting of gears.

To make a long story short, we tore down the old falling-down granary, and used some of the beams to brace up the falling-down barn. Then we were able to replace the rotting-out portion of the haymow floor. (I don't mean to be callous, but I really have difficulty understanding how anyone can be "unemployed," at least in the countryside.)

We built a new granary.

We also erected—finally—the two thousand-bushel grain bins I bought cheap about five years ago, and which had been laying out there in the yard like sick or dying spaceships all that time.

A lot of weeds that would never have been cut were mowed. And, just for something to keep busy (and to make use of our facilities) we put down 1,000 day-old goslings, even though our past experiences with projects of that nature and scope had inclined me to foreswear getting sucked in again. *(2014 note: I definitely should have listened to that experience. This was a catastrophe, and not only economically.)*

Son John even took care of the lawn, and the place began to look like a real home instead of a way station where a magazine publishing husband-and-wife stopped off to bathe and rest up once in a while.

We never did get the chickens—next year for sure—and the garden became over-run with weeds (the vegetables were far enough along so that they didn't suffer much) and I'm behind on woodcutting...

But we got some sheep sheared, some hogs butchered, some painting done and the fences are in good repair and we've had some nice litters of pigs and the calf is doing fine and the old grain auger was repaired and put into service filling the new grain bins and the combine ran like a champ and...

Well. It's been a busy, full, happy, fulfilling *short* summer.

With the geese the owls and hawks and fox got, the rained-on hay, the drought-plagued wheat crop and recent hog prices, we probably earned less money than the out-of-work people I've been reading about.

But life is grand! Each day is a new challenge, with new rewards. Every moment is an experience to be savored.

I'm now looking forward to next summer. And you know, I'm hoping it doesn't go quite as well... so it passes a little more slowly... so I have time to savor it just a little bit more... beyond the sidewalks.

Country living, by its very nature, is often solitary. Oh, some jobs, on some places, can involve groups of people and the chatter and interaction that brings, but still, most country folks spend long hours alone, with plenty to think about and the time to think about all of it.

Maybe that's one reason country conversation is so different from other kinds of conversation.

For one thing, since many country people are accustomed to silence, they're quite comfortable with it even in a group. We have a reputation for being taciturn, when in reality, we simply don't feel the compulsion most city people seem to have to babble on endlessly just to dispel the silence.

For another, country conversation down at the feed mill, where men lift heavy bags of ground grain into aged pickup trucks, involves shouting to each other above the whine and roar of the grinder and mixer.

You'll hear it on the lawn in front of the country church on a Sunday morning, at crossroads taverns, on the sidewalks and in the stores of small towns, and most of all at farm auctions and sales barns and grain elevators.

It's a pleasant diversion. Sometimes, it can be informative. For some, it's a way to stay in touch with the wider world and with reality, to touch souls, as it were, and to take a little piece of them back to the solitude of the countryside, not to alleviate that solitude, but to enrich it.

You'll encounter country conversation in many diverse places, but the best place to listen to young and old, experienced and in-experienced, to people from all over, is right here, in COUNTRYSIDE.

127. November 1983

Thanksgiving is the homestead holiday
A full root cellar is better than a well-stocked supermarket

I f there were a national holiday for homesteaders, it would have to be Thanksgiving.

Who but a homesteader can appreciate what went on in the minds of the Pilgrims on that first Thanksgiving? Who but a homesteader can really and truly appreciate the meaning of a harvest festival? Who has more to be thankful for than a homesteader after the harvest?

The fields and gardens have been readied for winter. The carrots and Jerusalem artichokes have been mulched, to be dug and enjoyed crisp and fresh even after being buried in snow. Only blackened hulls under the hickory trees in the woodlot testify to the bounty that fell there... bounty shared and stored alike in the squirrels' nests and the homesteader's cellar. The vines and stalks of the garden have been shredded, and are now part of the compost heaps that steam like miniature volcanoes on frosty mornings.

The animals have been culled in preparation for the long dark months of confinement, increased labor and the cost of stored feed. Fat and sleek, the goats rustle in new yellow straw, the rabbits take on a new sheen with their winter coats, and the Christmas goose grows fatter by the hour with the corn provided now that the grass is brown and dry.

The mow is full of fragrant hay, the grain bins are full, the root cellar is bursting at the seams. There are braided strings of onions in a dry place, slatted boxes of potatoes in a more moist location, shelves laden with squash and pumpkins, baskets of apples, stone crocks of pickles and kraut.

There are shelves straining under the weight of fresh new jars of produce, gleaming like strings of jewels. The orange-red of tomatoes, the purple-red of beets and greens of pickles and beans mingle with the sparkling hues of grape and elderberry jelly. There is rhubarb, and jars of golden honey still in the combs.

The freezer is loaded with peas and asparagus and broccoli and raspberries and strawberries and fresh pork and spring lamb and rabbit and chicken and beef.

To the countrysider, this is beauty. Contentment. Security. But it's more than that, and certainly more than just food.

All this bounty is the first fresh breeze of spring on your face as you begin the garden... preserved just as surely as the peas you planted that day. It's the arrival of the fluffy, peeping chicks and the memory of carefully lifting each one from the shipping carton, inspecting it, dipping its beak in the water fountain, then releasing it to flutter away to inspect its new environment. It's working in the garden when the soil is fresh and moist and still cool and weed-free...and it's working in the garden in the blazing heat of a midsummer afternoon when the weeds threaten to overtake everything. The larder holds not only jars of tomatoes, but the pungent smell of the vines as you picked them, the steaming afternoons canning them, the pride and satisfaction of placing the jars on the shelves.

The harvest is more than just payday for the homesteader. Your storehouse holds not only food, but memories, hopes and fulfillment of hopes, sweat, love. We may face the approaching months with some apprehension, but at least now we know where we stand. Now, after the hot and sweaty and dusty days, and before the time to thaw frozen livestock water and milk with numb fingers and fight snow piling up against the barn door, we can assess our mistakes and failures of the past season and plan for a better one next time around.

This is the Thanksgiving of the Pilgrims and the kindergarten pageants: we've made it this far, we'll make it the rest of the way.

This is as true and good as it is simple. Homesteaders have a much keener appreciation of the subtle changes in nature, we always say...and there's nothing subtle about the transition from summer to winter. If you have even a trio of rabbits in your barn and a dozen quarts of tomatoes on your shelf, you're more psyched up for a harvest festival than the person who trundles off to the supermarket for a frozen Thanksgiving dinner and every other dinner every other day of the year.

It's payday in the country: we collect the rewards of our labors. It's the opposite of April 15: we collect the taxes from the environment that depends on us for its survival. It's Independence Day as we survey our storehouses and rejoice in our freedom from grocery bills. It's New Year's Eve; the end of one cycle, the savoring of reflections that go with it, and the beginning of a new cycle and the hopes that go with all beginnings.

Let us give thanks, especially beyond the sidewalks.

128. December, 1983

More chores get done with delayed winter
Looking forward to the certainty of snow and cold

Year-end notes from the COUNTRYSIDE homestead: For this last issue of our 67th year of publishing, I'd planned on making this column a roundup of events and things learned during 1983. But on a day like today it's impossible to think of things like the end of the year—and Christmas, and snow. We were baling hay. In shirtsleeves. True, this is being written in mid-October but even so, it's highly unusual. It was a highly unusual summer, but being the weather we're talking about, that's only normal. It couldn't last.

That's why I got a little nervous when we didn't get the winter wheat and rye planted by September 15, my usual target date, due to tractor problems. And when on the 15th it rained... and the 16th and the 17th... and the neighbors' wheat started to sprout while ours was still in the bag... I nodded wisely to anyone who would listen and said, "Yessir, you gotta have wheat in the ground by September 15th."

But when the skies cleared, and we got about 10 acres planted, there was plenty of moisture for germination (and more rain after planting) and right now our wheat is as tall and green and hardy as the earlier-planted fields.

Then there was the firewood. I always cut wood in late winter, but what with one thing and another, I never got any hauled up to the house, and that diminutive stack of fuel was starting to make me apprehensive. Because I wasn't ready, I half expected winter to strike hard and early.

But then, while we usually start appreciating a fire sometime in September—if only an evening blaze of short lengths of thin saplings salvaged from my fencerow "woodlot improvement" just to take the chill off—this year there was no call for it. As it turned out, I had plenty of time to go out and round up the trees I'd culled last winter, buck them into stove length pieces, haul them to the house and stack them.

And for the last couple of weekends, I did it wearing a tee shirt. With sunny days in the 60s the stacked wood quickly began to lose the moisture it picked up lying in the woods all those months, and it was sure a lot more fun wood-gathering in the autumn leaves than it would have been in the sloppy slush of late winter or the rush of spring or the bugs of summer.

And then—and maybe most amazing of all—we're still eating tomatoes fresh from the garden!

Our first frost date supposedly averages around September 15, and we have had frost. During one night at least, it got down in the 20s. But for some reason, our garden was spared. (It is protected by buildings on the east and west, and trees to the north and it slopes to the south with the land a few hundred yards farther being considerably lower, and yet...)

What a pleasure to pick ripe tomatoes and peppers in Wisconsin in the latter half of October! What a strange sensation, considering how we scurried around the night of the first frost warning, picking as many of the perishables as we could, only to feed them to the pigs while we went back to the fresh stuff!

And then, mowing hay... and trying to get in the mood to write about winter and the year-end holidays. But that gets me back to the year-end notes.

For example, remember a few months back when we were talking about making silage in garbage bags, and I said I was tired of all the talk and was going to *do* it? Well, I did. Today. In a normal year I never would have gotten around to it, but with the season extended at least a month (so far) beyond my expectations, I plumb ran out of excuses.

And then there are the Burpee LongKeeper tomatoes Phebe Whitehead told us about in June 1983. It seemed rather late, but since I couldn't have ordered them before Phebe told us about them, I got some as soon as I could.

And do you know, they shot up and caught up in size with the varieties I'd planted in February, and with much stouter stems? Everything else Phebe said about them held true in my garden, too.

But while I have several baskets of them laid out in the root cellar, we're still eating the regulars—fresh from the garden—including the fantastic "private label" variety whose seeds were sent to me several years ago by a reader who writes every now and then and signs his name "Ham." He called the variety "Kjar," after the friend who gave him the seeds. While romas are our main crop for canning, and we still plant six to seven varieties just to keep on top of things, Kjar has replaced Wisconsin 55 as our favorite regular.

Some things never change. While we always wait for cool, fall weather for butchering (and usually end up doing the job in freezing rain or sleet) we've had some wonderful days for the job — but didn't get to it. Maybe it was just too nice for such a job, and our instincts told us that cutting firewood and gathering hickory nuts and black walnuts had more priority... and maybe our instincts were right. Butchering isn't any fun when your fingers are freezing, but then, butchering is never fun, anyway. Maybe it's better to be uncomfortable when you're doing it.

We still have to combine buckwheat and soybeans, and pick corn; fix the broken pipe in the frost-free faucet in the barn; harvest the late cabbage and turnips and winter radishes and other stuff in the garden and put the garden to bed for the winter and a lot more. No matter how late winter comes, we won't be ready. Not really.

And yet, the longer it lingers, the more uneasy I become. It's inevitable, in Wisconsin, and the reprieve is a shockingly pleasant surprise. Nonetheless, I'm eager for the first snowfall. It's going to assure me that, even if there are minor deviations according to my calendar, there is still a certain order to the universe. I won't have to wonder how much longer I can pick fresh tomatoes and leeks and greens from the garden or when the last possible moment to save the rest of the Long-Keeper tomatoes will present itself. There won't be any excuses for not topping off the woodpile, making last-minute checks on antifreeze, and all the rest.

Winter will set in, eventually, and I for one will be grateful. You *need* a season like winter, when you live beyond the sidewalks.

Part XIV: 1984

Inflation: 4.3%; Federal Reserve interest rate, year-end: 10.75%
Average income: $21.600; Gas/gal: $1.10; Bacon, $1.60/lb.
Year-end Dow: 1211; Bhopal (India) pesticide plant leak kills 3,500
More than 70 US banks fail; AIDS virus identified
AT&T broken up; Apple Macintosh goes on sale (Countryside gets one)
The Countryside General Store closes

129. January 1984

Take a winter walk through the marsh
Destination: Countryside, with stops along the way

Sometimes I walk to the Countryside Print Shop and office.

It's about three miles, by road, but I never take the road. I take a shortcut, through the marsh. The steps saved vary with the time of year but my goal isn't saving steps. My goal is to delight in the sights and sounds of the marsh, to observe the changing seasons more closely, to draw inspiration from the real world before withdrawing into the world of business and commerce.

Would you care to join me?

***

Step out the back door quickly, so we don't let the cats in the house, and—"Bear! Down, boy! How come all you animals have to congregate here on the back porch when your beds and food dishes are in the garage?"

I see the sheep are still gleaning that cornfield on the hill behind the barn. Pretty, aren't they, even at that distance? They're even prettier in the spring when they're in the pasture right behind the house here. The goats are out there this morning, too. They usually prefer the barn, this time of the year...but it IS a beautiful morning for a walk. Let's go.

No Bear, not you. This isn't just a walk around the farm, and you know how you hate laying in the print shop all day waiting to come back home. You stay here. Atta boy.

When you get to the top of the hill here, just west of the house, you can see for miles. We'll be heading due west: you can see the path we'll be taking, down through the woods there, then through the marsh and up the hill on the other side. The shop is just beyond that hill.

Doesn't look very far, does it? It isn't of course, but sometimes it feels a lot farther than it looks! And the first part here, going downhill, makes the whole trip seem very easy.

Isn't it interesting to look at a distant objective and feel it's so close you could reach out and touch it, and, yet, know there are so many obstacles in the way? When the marsh isn't frozen like it is now, you'd never make it through there at all. You'd be in water up to your hips, and that isn't even counting the river that flows through down at the bottom of the valley. When the marsh isn't frozen we have to head south, past the beehives and through the winter wheat in the back 40, to the railroad tracks, and still get wet feet most of the time.

Here's the western boundary of my farm. All this out here in front of us is the Waterloo Wildlife Area. It's a long, narrow marsh, and we're cutting across the narrow part. Good thing: it covers more than 3,000 acres.

Keep your eyes open for deer, and pheasants. You don't often see them, but there are plenty of both. One early morning last spring—that's when I take the railroad tracks—a young deer jumped up on the embankment right in front of me. I stood and watched it and another deer—obviously the mother—much wiser and more cautious—followed up behind.

I stood stock-still.

The youngster took a nip of new grass, ran back to its mother, and cavorted from one side of the tracks to the other. The older doe saw me and stood as still as I was.

I don't know how long we stood there looking at each other, with the younger deer leaping back and forth between us, but it was a very long time.

Suddenly the doe bounded off, her fawn following.

Isn't that a better way to go to work than driving? Especially on those days when you get stuck behind the school bus that stops at every house along the way, and it seems every kid that gets on drops his lunch or books or loses an overshoe while crossing the road, and you know walking would be faster?

Here's where we get to the part I really enjoy. These marsh grasses stretch for miles. If we headed north from here, the terrain is just about impenetrable. You literally have to crawl on your hands and knees in some places. And look out for the springs that never freeze! It's hard to imagine (or easy to forget) that my house is just beyond the hill that's hidden by those trees on the east, and that town is just beyond the hill to the west, and that north and south there's almost nothing but more of this marsh for miles and miles.

Thousands of people live or pass by within a few miles of this place, but they've never been here. Most of them have no idea what it's like. Oh, during hunting season there's a little foot traffic through here, but surprisingly little. This is state-owned land, but most hunters seem to prefer the farmland surrounding it. Easier to walk through, maybe.

Even the snowmobilers don't use the trail through here, very much. I have little use for snowmobiles, but at this time of the year they do have one good point: even one or two, following the marked trail, pack down the snow so I can walk with relative ease. There have been times, and there are always places, where I've waded through snow up to my knees, and that's work! Sometimes the top is crusted, and my shins actually bleed by the time I make it through.

When the river isn't frozen (and there are places that never freeze because of all the springs down here) you see quite a few muskrats. They don't see too many people traipsing through here, and they're fun to watch when they don't know you're watching.

Ducks—wood ducks always have a nest in that tree over there—and sandhill cranes and herons are a lot more wary. Beautiful birds, up close, in the wild, but you don't often get very close.

Well, we made it through the worst part —which is also the best part. Usually when you get close to your destination you feel a sense of relief. But I don't: not here. The shop is only 15 minutes from that big oak tree up ahead (under good conditions) but the hill we're headed for is a dandy, and the snowdrifts make it even more breath-taking, but worst of all, it feels too close to town.

Ah, we made it. Atop the hill here you can see my house back across the valley, and you can see the route we took. Looks different now, doesn't it? Now all we have to do is pass these houses up here on the ridge, drop down the other side through the corn stubble, and we're at the back door of the shop.

And once inside, we'll stomp the snow off our boots and pour a cup of hot coffee and be ready to go to work, full of fresh air and enthusiasm picked up in an early morning walk beyond the sidewalks.

* * *

The boys and I were cutting firewood in the back woodlot the other day, and when the pickup was loaded I elected to walk back to the house.

I passed the bee yard and found my best colony strewn all over the fencerow. It was 20 degrees in the sun, but the wind chill factor was below zero. The bees were swarming around the bottom end of a honey-laden super, which was cemented by propolis to several other supers. I couldn't lift the thing, even after being warmed up by an afternoon of cutting and loading good solid oak.

I did manage to break the supers apart, but the bees didn't like that very much. I got the hive body back on the bottom board, but there were so many bees swarming over the tops of the frames that I figured I'd squash too many if I tried to put it all back together before they settled down a bit.

So I waited...they did settle down...and I did get the stack back together. Everything appears to be all right, but only time will tell.

Some people think that one of the marks of a true homesteader is driving a beat-up pickup truck. If that's true, I'm about as true a homesteader as you'll find anywhere. Mine is a '73 Ford.

If you get out on the driver's side, the door tends to fall off. It doesn't actually fall off, but you can't close it again without a lot of time and effort.

So I try to remember to slide over and use the passenger side door. But that doesn't open from the inside, so you have to roll down the window to reach the outside handle.

The floorboard is rusted through so that driving on wet roads sends up a spray that soaks your feet and legs, and sometimes hits you in the face. It's like riding a bike with no fenders.

That's the truck that hauls your magazine to the post office...and also transports hay, feed, firewood, other commodities, and hauls your editor to the office. Small wonder I prefer walking.

It would be impossible to get along without a truck, just considering the magazine's uses, but looking at the prices—of both new and used ones—this one is going to have to last a few more miles. Maybe many more miles. My status as a homesteader, by the pickup criterion, will be safe a while longer.

Homesteaders often spend a lot of time and trouble to put a good meal on the table. But not always. The night before Steve went back to California, the whole family was here for sort of a pre-Christmas dinner. Diane fixed a ham, and a lot more.

Afterwards I trimmed out the ham bone, tossed it in my treasured cast iron Dutch oven, added some peas and onions and salt and pepper and covered it all with water, and set it on the wood stove.

I stirred it before we banked the fire for the night, and added more water.

In the morning, I added a log to the fire, even though it looked like a sunny day. (On sunny days, we don't add wood to the fire in the morning: we just remove the insulated panels from the windows of the dome and let the sun heat the place up.)

At noon, the soup was bubbling, and thick, and rich, and delicious. And dirt-cheap.

We almost always have a pot of something simmering on the woodburner, often something made out of leftovers. If it's not soup, it's stew, or baked beans. Sometimes it's *pot au feu,* where you just keep adding anything that's left over. It becomes different, and richer, every day. And it's always delicious, and cheap, and easy... and as convenient as those expensive supermarket "convenience" foods.

When you stop to think about it, we have many conveniences, beyond the sidewalks.

130. February 1984

We're all a bit odd in our private ways
There are different ways to get a kick out of life

"You don't have to be crazy to work here — but it helps."
That message appears on little signs in every type of workplace in the nation. There are times when everybody thinks their line of work, whatever it is, requires (or results in) a special kind of insanity. That's why when homesteaders say "We must be nuts to do all this" or when city people tell us we're nuts to live the way we do, we can just nod our agreement — and smile.

We're not nuts. We just have different ways of getting our kicks.

At the same time, being "different" sometimes makes it difficult to carry on an intelligent conversation with a city person. On the few occasions I find myself in a group of men, the talk seems to concern football, or cars, or tv shows... none of which I have the slightest interest in or knowledge of. Being a basically shy person, I never bring up the subjects that I *am* interested in and know something about — goats, pigs, geese and so forth — but every so often some extrovert tries to draw me into the conversation. If he knows me, the question might be something like, "Well, how are the goats milking?'

"Good, good, real good."

It'd be all right if that would be the end of it, but that type of guy has to keep pressing. He has to ask what I do with the milk and does it really taste like cow milk and is it hard to make cheese and sometimes a lot more. But nobody else gets drawn into the conversation (unless they had a cousin who had a pet goat that ate clothes off the wash line) and before long there's a sort of uncomfortable pause... and then someone says: "That Packer game was really something, wasn't it?" And the discussion is off and running again, and I gratefully fade back into the furniture.

I thought the other night was going to be different. A group of us were sitting around before dinner, which had been prepared by one of the men who is into cooking. Ah, now *there's* a current trend I know something about! Wasn't I a professional cook almost 30 years ago? Haven't I been cooking ever since, and even before that time? Back in the days when masculine cooking was confined to the barbecue grill or campfire, or maybe the occasional pot of chili, wasn't I baking pies and bread and whipping up terrific marinated roasts and building up a reputation for hearty homemade soups? I leaned forward eagerly, ready to participate. Someone was saying, "I don't know how I ever got along without the Cuisinart." Huh? Well, they'll get around to talking about ways to fix collards and turnips or using extra milk or eggs, I thought.

But when the discussion drifted to microwave ovens, and Silverstone, and hot air popcorn poppers, I knew I was still an outsider.

When they talked about their favorite brands of imported mustard, I was going to mention how good my homemade variety is, and how easy it is to make. But I didn't. I got the feeling they wouldn't be interested, and I was certain I could drive the conversation to the same dead-end that resulted from talking about goats if I said anything about growing my own mustard seed, or my special recipe for horseradish mustard, (using homegrown, homemade horseradish, of course).

It dawned on me that I really *am* different from those city people — because I *want* to be. I'd rather cut wood than watch a football game; clean the pig pen than go to a movie; work in the garden than take a trip. For me, it's a whole lot more fun — more challenging and more rewarding — to plan a meal around what's available in the garden, and to plan the garden around what I like to cook and eat; or to plan a meal around the meat that's available, even if it *is* heart or tongue; or to find yet another way to prepare pork, even though we've had pork 12 days in a row.

While some people enjoy shopping around for exotic imported cheeses, I get a bang out of making my own (some of which are so exotic only the pigs will eat them). I think it takes much more skill, and therefore brings greater pride, to sharpen and use a good set of cutlery, and cast iron cookware, and a wood stove, than it takes to use a food processor and a microwave.

Many country people (and even some homesteaders) will disagree with me, of course, on any or all of this. The only point I'm trying to make is that we all do, or try to do, what we *enjoy*, and we all enjoy different things to different degrees, and for different reasons. And if we *don't* enjoy what we're doing, perhaps we should ask ourselves why we're doing it: maybe we *are* crazy!

Some people make a fetish of self-sufficiency because The Bomb is going to fall or because the food production system is going to collapse or because the economy is going to be driven into chaos. They may be right, but I don't consider any of these very good reasons for digging in gardens, feeding animals, cleaning pens and doing all the other things homesteaders get involved in, on a daily basis, year-in and year-out.

That's because I've thought about all of those as reasons for homesteading. And at one time or another I wanted to be self-sufficient so I wouldn't have to punch a time clock, or live and work around crowds, or require the kind of cash income comfortable living demands, and others as well.

But after all these years, none of these have been sustainable as sensible reasons for putting up with all of the work and disappointment that homesteading involves. Friends and readers who did have these reasons for homesteading have gone on to other pursuits, because they simply got tired of waiting for the collapse (or whatever) and they never learned to really *enjoy* homestead activities.

I don't deny my city friends and relatives their pleasures, pastimes, and outlooks on life. But neither do I want them to pity me and my family for our "harsh" existence. We happen to take great pleasure and pride in what we do and the way we do it.

For some people, maybe it does seem crazy to enjoy toil and discomfort... (although for the life of me I can't understand why they think sweating on a homestead is nuts but sweating in a gym is *très rigueur*).

Ah, but there I go again, making the same old mistake: how can I presume to know what other people enjoy? All I know for certain is that I wouldn't want to do anything other than produce and prepare and consume the products of my own garden and farmyard in the warmth of my wood-heated home, doing things my way, enjoying life beyond the sidewalks.

131. March 1984

The quiet season's fiddle time is here
Music practice brings a larger lesson with it

I'm trying to learn how to play a fiddle. Homemade music is certainly a homestead activity, and while my practicing hasn't paid off in any recognizable music yet, it provided something perhaps even more valuable.

This is the quiet season on the homestead. One cycle hasn't ended, the next hasn't quite begun, and we're left hanging between the two as uncertain as the cat between the milk and the liver.

Potatoes, carrots and onions are still plentiful in the root cellar, but the turnips and rutabagas and cabbages are almost gone, and what remains is shriveled. The rows of canned fruits and vegetable are taking on a checkerboard appearance as the filled jars are replaced with empty ones that await the next harvest.

But the next harvest — which will come from ground still frozen rock-hard and hidden under a thick blanket of snow — is nothing but an image in the back of my mind. I have to look real hard to see it: the next harvest is still a long way off.

At this time of the year the woodpile looks dangerously low. It is, of course, at its low ebb, and I'm already at work replenishing it for next winter. That pleasant chore is stymied by the deep snow remaining in the woods, but I feel compelled to chip away at the task, not as much to insure a supply of dry wood for next winter as to anticipate the end of the quiet season, when wood-gathering will be relegated to the list of work that's important, but which can be put off.

Half a dozen lambs have already been dropped, and there will be goat kids, and the new chicks and goslings can't be far behind... and then everything will come at once.

During the quiet season — if you listen with your mind — you can hear the tumult coming.

When I was younger I'd get very antsy during the quiet season. I wanted to make certain everything was ready to go, long before *nature* was ready. It's a good idea, but it can be carried to extremes.

I'd check the tractor and the tiller and all the other tools and equipment, and get them ready for the big rush. I'd check the seeds and plans and work schedules. And I'd start tomatoes and peppers and other bedding plants in the south windows of the house *way* too early. I knew it was early, but I just couldn't wait. Besides, it gave me something to do, a means of containing my nervous energy and enthusiasm. And of course when spring really did arrive, nothing went as planned, anyway.

So this year, I decided to learn how to play the fiddle.

If that sounds like a rather casual decision — it was. You see, I learned to play a ukulele when I was too small to handle a guitar, and since then fiddled with not only the guitar but banjo, mandolin, and bouzouki. (My Dad was a music teacher, among other things.) The mandolin is fingered just like the violin, so I figured it would be a snap.

I could laugh at the squeaks and squawks, the first few days. Then I started to get a trifle impatient. Finally I felt foolish and incompetent.

After all, I'd been listening to people play fiddles for *years*! They make it sound so easy, and even though I had no illusions about becoming an instant maestro it surely should have sounded better than the fingernail-on-the-blackboard kinds of noises I was making. While I'm not what you'd call a good mandolin player, some of the tunes I've been picking at for 40 years sound pretty passable if I do say so myself, but I could hardly play do-re-me on the fiddle!

Then I analyzed the situation. The four strings are tuned the same on both instruments, so the fingering is the same. Since the fiddle has no frets to help you know where to *put* your fingers, you're on you're on your own to a greater degree than the mandolin demands. But that wasn't the problem.

Neither was the fact that you're doing the fingering out there in the air someplace rather than in the more comfortable mandolin position.

All these minor things add up, no doubt, but the main problem was that making a string vibrate with a bow is a whole lot different than doing it with a pick. It seemed — to me, at least — that it should make a very small difference, but in terms of making music it made all the difference in the world.

H omesteading is a lot like learning to play the violin.
If we move from the city to the country, we have much to learn. Homesteading projects might appear to be simple, just as fancy fiddling might appear to be easy. In both cases, it's different when you try it yourself.

It can be a shock to discover you're not as smart as you thought you were, to learn that something that appears so simple is really a very complex combination of talent and coordination and work and practice.

It can be just as much of a shock when we think we've more or less mastered something, and then fail again. It can be as major as leaving one homestead for another in a different climate, or as minor as switching from chickens to ducks or from conventional gardening to raised beds. It can even happen just because the weather is different than it was when we were successful. Even health and financial and psychological conditions change. We're never fully trained, fully prepared.

But — if we can pick up on the tune and rosin up the bow and keep trying, we're going to make it. And we'll have a real good time getting there.

I'm learning to play *Fiddler on the Roof,* and it's coming along nicely, now. For some reason it seems appropriate, beyond the sidewalks.

132. April 1984

"Time travel" suggests homesteading's appeal
Is technology a roadblock or a tail wind?

T oday, I took a walk through time. It changed some of my ideas about homesteading.
While rummaging through a seldom-opened bottom drawer, I ran across the journal I was keeping in the early 1950's. It brought back such pleasant memories I read the whole thing and forgot what I was looking for.

The handwritten pages — written with a real fountain pen before I owned a typewriter — took me back to those "Happy Days," and made me realize how much the world has changed, and how homesteading has not only managed to survive the post-industrial age but, possibly, to thrive in it.

I did a lot of writing even back then, and much of it was poetry (if you could call it that). The notebook is filled with stuff like this:

> *Today I cut a tree up,*
> *albeit with a frown;*
> *Before I cut it up,*
> *I had to cut it down.*

And even worse:

> *Mary had a little bite,*
> *it was the itching kind.*
> *She couldn't scratch it very well*
> *her arm didn't reach behind!*

My first published work was a poem, in *Bowhunter* magazine, in 1955 or so. Fortunately, I don't write poetry any more. But the old journal reminded me of the ways I *haven't* changed in 30 years. For instance, there are pages of aphorisms, some of which are gracing the pagetops of this issue of COUNTRYSIDE. *(2014: The magazine's format had, and still has, pithy sayings built in, as pagetop quotes — another of our innovations subsequently picked up by others.)*

But the most telling entries are those which reflected my interest in both the theories and methods of self-sufficiency.

There's a recipe for potato wine. **"Grind 12 large potatoes, 2# raisins, two lemons and two oranges. Combine with 8# white sugar and 4# brown sugar, one cake of compressed yeast and three gallons of lukewarm water. Let work nine days, stirring twice each day."** I wondered where pioneers got lemons and oranges, but noted that I made some and it was "okay."

There are recipes for dandelion wine, dill pickles, spoon bread and dried salted fish. There are directions for pickling eldershoots, asparagus and onions. There are notes on raising goats and rabbits, a list of what should be planted on a self-sufficient farm and more quotations, especially from Thoreau.

Reading those quotations reminded me of how thrilled I was when I discovered *Walden*, even though it was at least 10 years before it became popular (again), and how alone and out of step (marching to the beat of a different drummer?) I felt because I couldn't find anyone to get excited about it *with* me.

This quote from Emerson probably summed up my feelings, and my reason for keeping the journal:

"The civilized man has built himself a coach, but has lost the use of his feet. He has got a fine Geneva watch, but he has lost the skill to tell the hour by the sun. A Greenwich nautical almanac has he and so, being sure

of the information when he wants it, the man in the street does not know a star in the sky. The solstice he does not observe, the equinox he knows as little. His notebooks impair his memory, his libraries overload his wit, and the insurance office increases the number of accidents."

If you were alive 30 years ago, or even if you've just seen "Happy Days" on tv, you know this was pretty off-the-wall. Those were, after all, the golden years. There was prosperity, and technology was booming ("Plastics! Go into plastics!") and there was plenty more of both yet to come. Farms were being mechanized at an astounding rate, "suburbia" was a new concept, gas-guzzling cars were sprouting fins, and while we hadn't even owned a car a few years before, two-car families were heralded as the wave of the future. Gas was 20¢ a gallon, with full service *and* free glassware. Some of the wealthier and more progressive people in our area even had television sets.

My uncle, who milked 12 cows by hand, used kerosene for lighting, horses for field work, pumped water by hand and kept chickens and a pig for home consumption, went out of business. So did thousands of others. Farms were getting bigger, more mechanized, more efficient and comfortable... and fewer in number.

And everybody thought it was wonderful.

What person in his right mind would collect data on the many uses of cornmeal and make notes on self-sufficiency and simple living in such a heady atmosphere of affluence and bright hopes? And a high school kid, yet! But I now know that I was not, and am not, alone.

It's amazing to reflect on how rapidly technological dreams materialized. The icemen and coalmen of my youth had already disappeared, but new technology kept coming at a furious pace. Freezers became common. Gas-powered lawn mowers, and garden tillers (for the few who had gardens). Steam engines had given way to diesels, but more people were using highways, and some were even flying. The interstate system was proposed... Sputnik was launched... computers came on the scene...

And yet, in spite of all the mind-boggling advances, here I am 30 years later, not only still collecting the same kind of self-sufficiency information I was jotting in my private journal as a teenager, but sharing it with thousands of other people who are interested in at least some of the same things! Not only that, but COUNTRYSIDE is only a very tiny part of the homestead phenomenon: not only are there similar specialized publications, but virtually every magazine and newspaper in the country reflects some of the same interests, from gardening and food preservation to wood heat. This would have been unthinkable in 1954. In 1984, it's still amazing.

But, I wonder as I turn the pages of my journal, is the current interest in homestead things in spite of the awesome changes of the past 30 years, or *because* of them? And that's when something that's been bothering me leapt into focus.

People obviously "homestead" for many different reasons. Some have no use for my "philosophy," or anyone else's. To them, homesteading has nothing to do with one's outlook on life. Some have always lived like that; for others, it's just "homestead chic."

For still others, it's a case of trying to get back to the farm life of the 40s, maybe for nostalgia, maybe in an effort to recapture something that seems to be missing in life today in spite of (or because of) all the technological advances.

I can tell from my mail that there are many other reasons why people homestead... why they pursue different avenues of homesteading... why they embrace different aspects of it with greater or less enthusiasm.

Homesteading in 1984 is definitely not a cut-and-dried affair. It's possible that there are no two of us who think alike, when it comes to what homesteading is or should be and how we should go about it.

There are no rules for homesteaders, no clear-cut guidelines or even definitions. Maybe that's its attraction for so many of us. We must formulate our *own* rules... take charge of our own lives... when we live beyond the sidewalks.

133. May 1984

The underground economy and homesteaders

Something in Alvin Toffler's newest book, *Previews and Premises*, made me chuckle... and think about some possible homestead benefits most people probably don't recognize.

Toffler was talking about the underground economy, and all the money that doesn't show up in the gross national product or other statistics, including tax receipts. Until recently, the most visible and most talked about aspect of the underground economy has been drug trafficking and other illegal activities, but that's changing. Barter, and moonlighting (without reporting the income) have been on the increase, and some economists and tax collectors are beginning to take notice.

But Toffler says there is something inherently more important than the underground economy, something that might have an even greater effect on the national economy and on tax collections. He calls it "prosuming." That's when the same people are both producers, and consumers, of a given product or service.

Wow! Finally, I thought, somebody is paying some attention to us homesteaders. So I read on, with a great deal of anticipation.

But do you know what he used as an example of prosuming? Self-service gas stations. Instead of sitting in the car while someone else fills the tank, and possibly checks the oil and tires and *maybe* even washes the windows, you do it all yourself.

Needless to say, I found this to be a rather disappointing finale so, as I put the book down and went out for another armload of firewood, I made up my own.

All of us who heat with wood realize what we *don't* pay for heating with fossil fuels, of course. But thinking of it in terms of prosuming instead of just plain old homesteading provided some interesting twists.

For example, part of the cost of fuel is the visible tax added to the bill. But just think of the other taxes that are a part of the fuel cost. The fellow who drives the delivery truck is paid a salary, and pays income taxes, all of which is included in the price of the fuel. The truck is taxed, as is the fuel that runs it. The company's land and building and other property are all taxed, and of course you could carry this all the way back to the oil well and beyond, because not only do the insurance companies and pension funds and other investors who own the wells pay taxes, but there are taxes on the companies (and people) involved in making the drilling rigs and hard hats and gloves and so on... and there are taxes on the operations and people who supply *them...* and this is even taxing my imagination!

I don't understand such things, but it almost seems like a perpetual motion machine. And it's easy to see what an impact *real* prosuming — such as homesteading — could have on this pyramid of taxes upon taxes.

I paid a couple of bucks in taxes on my chainsaw, but that was years ago. I've cut many a cord since then, so the tax cost per cord must be awfully low by now. There are taxes on gas, and oil, and parts, but they're also very low on the basis of BTU's when compared with buying fossil fuels.

As I added a log to what I hoped would be the last fire of the season I almost felt like a tax shirker. But you know, it wasn't a bad feeling at all! So I sat back to contemplate my other homestead tax savings.

The biggest one, I decided, came from homegrown products that required little or no processing. My fresh vegetables, for example, must be just about as tax-free as anything can get, nowadays. A tomato grown in California accrues taxes as it moves to a salad bowl in Wisconsin... income taxes paid by the grower and his hired help, by the trucker or railroad workers who transport it, by the brokers and sales people and the folks who work down at the local grocery that sells it... There are real estate taxes levied on all the property involved in the growing and storing of that tomato, taxes on the energy used to transport it and cool it... personal property taxes and probably many others I've never even heard of.

I wonder how they can fit all those taxes into one little tomato!

Taxes on the ones I grow, on the other hand, are practically zip. Who would even bother to figure the real estate taxes on the few square feet of ground it takes to grow a couple of dozen tomatoes, or even on the tiller and fuel involved (which I don't use, anyway)?

There's no sales tax on food in Wisconsin, but again, a portion of the cost of a gallon of milk, no matter how tiny that portion may be, has to go to pay the income taxes of the store owner and workers. The business taxes. The taxes involved in the carton manufacturing and selling, and the distribution of the milk, as well as what the farmer pays.

I went down a whole long list: Homemade bread, homemade cheese and sausage, home-butchered meat and homegrown vegetables... With very many people prosuming like this, it has to make a difference!

Of course, there are still cases where homegrown products cost more than store bought, for one reason or another — usually because of our lack of skill or experience or management, or simply because of the economies of scale we homesteaders can't make use of. But that's no big deal, now that I know about prosuming: Now I can enjoy my homegrown stuff even more than ever, because I know it's not only pesticide-free and additive-free: it's also TAX-free!

And I consider that one more tiny, perhaps, victory, one more blow for independence, one more reason for living beyond the sidewalks.

134. June 1984

Achieving goals: the pursuit of perfection
There's a lot to strive for in a homesteader's life

Everybody has a dream of achieving perfection. One of the goals of rabbit breeding is to produce the perfect rabbit; many homesteaders work — every year — toward the ultimate garden; some people seek the perfect small barn, or the ideal homestead.

In most cases, perfection is an illusion, something that exists only in the mind of the dreamer, and achieving it is well nigh impossible. (There is no perfect chicken, which is why the *Standard of Perfection* has to use paintings, not photos.) And yet, how often do we lose patience when the going gets rough? How often do we despair when we begin to suspect that the perfection we seek really is impossible?

Some people say getting there is half the fun, and that once the ultimate goal is reached it doesn't seem all that important any more. Maybe Alexander the Great was one of the first to discover that, when he wept because there were no more worlds for him to conquer.

And yet, it's often hard for those of us who are still struggling to heed this advice, coming (as it usually does) from people who "have it made." We tend to tell ourselves, "It's easy for *them* to say I should spend more time with my kids and enjoy them now because they grow up so fast: They don't have to work 24 hours a day and half the night just to keep the family going" And even if we do spend time with them, and enjoy them, in a few short years it still seems as if it weren't enough. I suspect it's the same no matter what the goal.

All of this has been going through my mind, because I have the opportunity to actually reach one of my minor goals — to attain perfection. It's only a little thing, and some people might think it's silly, but it seems to me that the principle is the same.

I have the chance to complete my collection of USDA Yearbooks of Agriculture.

I'm not even sure when that became a goal. The first copy I saw was in the early 1950's, and I don't remember a thing about it. Like most early beginnings — a desire to have a homestead, the coming of spring, planting an acorn or falling in love — it's hard to pinpoint the exact starting point and harder yet to predict the results. While I've always enjoyed old books on farming because farming in the 1800s and early 1900s was much more to my liking than modern big-buck industrialized agribusiness, the Yearbooks of Agriculture I'd seen were pretty blah.

But when I discovered an interesting one, here and there, now and then, in the used book stores, I'd add it to my library.

This went on until about 10 years ago. The turning point came when John and Jane Shuttleworth, publishers of *The Mother Earth News,* invited Diane and me out to North Carolina for a weekend. One of their planes was going to be in this area on Friday, they were flying back to Iowa to visit relatives on Monday, we hadn't gotten together for awhile and we had a few things to discuss. Their plane would pick us up in Madison on Friday, and bring us back on Monday.

Their operation in Hendersonville was new at that time, and we got the grand tour. It was quite a change from the little house in Madison, Ohio, where we first met, around 1972. There, books and papers had covered tables and chairs and beds and even the kitchen sink. *Mother* had far outpaced COUNTRYSIDE even then, and even though I was suitably impressed (we hadn't even come close to considering a company airplane), one facet of that visit sticks out in my memory.

John and Diane were walking ahead of me, talking, and suddenly discovered I wasn't with them any more. They came back to find me... in the library.

John Shuttleworth had a complete set of Yearbooks of Agriculture!

For some reason, it had never entered my mind that a complete collection, going back to 1862, was even a possibility. I had certainly never seen most of those volumes in the used bookstores I frequented, but a grateful *Mother* reader had donated the entire set.

From that day on, owning a complete collection of USDA Yearbooks became one of my goals. Being complete, it would be perfect, and it would probably be the *only* perfect thing I'd ever attain.

I never really pursued it as a *collection*, the way serious stamp or coin or beer can collectors go after missing specimens: It was much more casual. For one thing, I seldom venture any farther from home than Madison, Wisconsin, and there are only a few shops there that carry used books, and they seldom have more than one or two Yearbooks at a time. But when I did find one I didn't already have, what a thrill! It would be examined from cover to cover, useful information would be duly noted, and it would be placed in its proper spot on my lengthening bookshelf to be admired every time I passed and, likely as not, to be taken down and read again when I needed a specific bit of information or an escape into the past.

Today, I have 81 of them. And also today, I received a catalog from Henry and Janet Hurley, of Westmoreland, New Hampshire. It's titled *Farming and Rural Miscellany*. I devoured it with a lust usually reserved for seed catalogs: I wanted to order *everything*! And then I came to item 976: U.S. DEPARTMENT OF AGRICULTURE. Annual reports, 1862-1981... And item no. 977: "Most years are available for the above two entries. Please inquire for availability and price."

So. All of a sudden, by writing a single check, I could end the quest. My collection could be complete. Perfect.

But when the initial elation died down, I thought about it. Is that what I really wanted? Is the fun and pleasure, the thrill, in actually having the collection, or in seeking out the missing volumes? Maybe part of the value of the collection is in going into my favorite bookstores, and finding... nothing new. Maybe the search adds as much to the intrinsic value of the collection as *finding* an elusive copy.

My collection will probably be completed, someday. The final volume will no doubt provide a lot of satisfaction, and the shelves of books will stand as a sort of trophy: Like a mounted fish or deer head on the wall, they'll always bring back memories of the hunt.

And by then I'll have gone on to new goals. Maybe a complete collection of the Biggle Books would be in order, or every issue of *Breeder's Gazette* or *The Cultivator* or the *Genessee Farmer* or the other wonderful old farm magazines I try to pattern COUNTRYSIDE after.

But then, as now, getting there will be half the fun. And that's probably why homesteading is so much fun. There is always a lot of "getting there," beyond the sidewalks.

2014: Not only have I not completed that USDA Yearbook collection: in our present smaller house I have shelf space for only about 5,000 books, and the Yearbooks (and hundreds of others)

are stored in boxes. I don't even see them. Greed for material goods — even books — truly is a waste of time and energy.

135. July 1984

Finding treasure in your backyard
There's a pot of gold on every homestead

L ife has not been ideal here, lately. Oh, there's nothing major I can point to, just a lot of little things, piling up. *(Note added: The Countryside General Store's downtown building was sold this month. It became a NAPA auto parts store.)*

But I know that's going to change, because I just saw an omen. You don't believe in omens? Hey, look. When you come to the end of your rope you tie a knot and hang on, but when you start to wonder how long you're going to have to dangle there, any sign of hope is mighty welcome!

One field, which is usually pretty wet in the spring, was plowed last fall after the winter wheat was harvested. It would dry out faster, I figured, and of course that would give us a leg up on spring fieldwork. But it was another wet spring. The field didn't dry out. And by the time we could get on it, the weeds were so thick and tall the disk didn't do any good. It had to be plowed again. So much for planning ahead.

The garden had been partially planted when the electric fencer quit working. The pigs got out... and rooted up the garden.

The steers and goats got in the winter wheat at the same time, since both pasture fences work off the same charger.

There weren't many good plowing days this spring, and when there were, the water pump on the tractor went out and a hydraulic hose sprung a leak and a tire blew out on the chisel plow and several things went wrong with the moldboard plow and when I ran over a huge but unseen buried boulder while disking the hitch pin got twisted in a U-shape and had to be removed with a cutting torch.

There's a lot more, but you get the idea. And as I said, tonight I know it's all going to change.

T oday was what has become a more or less normal day, here: pretty miserable. Hoping to get some fieldwork done so I could plant a little corn while there's still time, I dragged the plow over to a neighbor who has a welder. We found it needed a couple of bolts, so I went to town to get them. When I got back the neighbor was gone, but it didn't really matter much: it was starting to rain, anyway.

I put the bolts on and came home to find another project. It wasn't hard. Like most farmers, I don't go to work in the morning; I just get up and I'm surrounded by it. Even in the off-and-on rain, I managed to keep occupied.

After supper I went to the barn to feed and water the animals, and just as I was finishing up, it started raining again. But it was different. It was a light, warm mist, that made me feel refreshed rather than wet. In fact, after a day in the cold rain and mud, it felt pretty good. That feeling was enhanced because, while thick black clouds loomed overhead, the sun was shining brightly but eerily in the western sky. It felt like there was going to be a rainbow.

And there was. By the time I got back to the house it was perfectly formed, full-spectrum, brilliant and beautiful. Diane came out to look at it, and we stood on the porch in scattered big drops of rain sparkling golden in the setting sun as if we were watching fireworks or a parade passing by.

We were marveling at the perfection of the sight, when a *second* ring started to appear. It shimmered into existence right before our eyes like a genie oozing out of a magic lamp, and in a matter of moments it was as full and as colorful as the first one.

I've seen double rainbows before, but not very often. None were as perfect and as complete as this one. It was a wonderful sight, in the fullest sense of wonder. If one rainbow is fantastic, what can two rainbows, one above the other, be?

But then I noticed something even more startling: The end of the rainbow.

You know, of course, that if you find the end of a rainbow and dig there you'll find a pot of gold. The only trouble is, rainbows always end over a hill somewhere and by the time you grab your shovel and run over there, it's gone.

But this was different from any rainbow I'd ever seen in my life. In fact by now Diane's father was leaning out the window to observe the phenomenon, and he said it was different than any *he'd* seen in his 79 springs.

The arch was vivid and brilliant. I remembered Roy G. Biv and checked it out: red, orange, yellow, green, blue, indigo and violet. All there.

The area beneath the lower span was a startling uniform slate gray. Between the two rings was a much darker, more ominous gray, making the bright colors of the rainbow appear all the brighter. And above both the rainbows clumps of black clouds swirled in an otherwise clear blue evening sky. But none of that, awesome and beautiful as it was, was what was so startling.

Because, you see, the southern leg of that rainbow was dipping down and touching *my* homestead!

The arch rose far to the north and east, soared into the heavens, then swooped back to Earth, meeting it just a few hundred yards southeast of where we stood. I could clearly see the trees in my woodlot, wraithlike, *behind* the shimmering colors of the rainbow.

I'd never seen anything like it. I couldn't have been more shocked if a flying saucer had landed in that field.

Did I run out with my shovel to find the pot of gold? Nope. I'd done enough shoveling for one day, and besides, the rainbow ended in a hog pasture which was already pretty well dug up. No gold there as far as I could see.

But I thought about it, of course. With even a *small* pot of gold, I could clear up the business debts, get some decent fencing and equipment that wasn't always breaking down and in need of patching, and...

And what else? And then what?

As suddenly as the rainbow had appeared I realized that gold wouldn't buy a single thing I treasure. What's more, I already have what's important to me: my family, my health, enough to eat, plenty of work to keep me occupied and enough problems to make life interesting and challenging and to keep from getting bored.

That's my pot of gold. It's all I need. Sure I'm having troubles, but there are plenty of people who'd be willing to swap theirs for mine.

My pot of gold was here all the while. It just took a very special rainbow to make me see it, when storm clouds gathered over my life beyond the sidewalks.

Two weeks later — *Do omens really work?*

We ran out of feed for the pigs, so we sold them. But the best of the bunch brought 47¢ a pound, which was a very good price in our market.

I used $175 of the proceeds to buy a new three-bottom plow, which works like a charm.

* * *

We ran out of the June issue of COUNTRYSIDE even as it was being mailed. There were no extra issues for newsstand sales, or even for the contributors to that issue, whom I always like to send a few extra copies to.

But that's because we printed the same amount as the month before... and circulation took an unexpected leap of 1,500.

* * *

Our 14-month-old grandson fell out of a second-story window of the apartment above the Countryside General Store. Onto the pavement. Miraculously, he appears to be none the worse for the experience.

Hang in there, rainbow.

136. August, 1984

Running a magazine while mowing hay
When things are going well there's time to think

It was incredible: I was mowing hay — and nothing went wrong. The day before, I'd spent a couple of hours riveting two new teeth on the cutter bar, replacing broken mower guards and oiling and greasing... and spent exactly 12 minutes in the field before another guard broke.

Today everything worked beautifully. The first few minutes were unnerving, of course, as I strove to beat yesterday's record. The next hour was a trifle tense, as I waited for the inevitable breakdown.

But it never came. The tractor and mower went round and round the field, the sickle bar's teeth chomping on the alfalfa, and the conditioning rolls spit it out in a rooster tail, leaving long, straight windrows of fluffy aromatic hay.

It got boring.

I thought of all the hours farmers sit on their tractors, for days on end, and wondered what they thought about. Does Earl Spencer compose his COUNTRYSIDE column while mowing hay? Probably. Most COUNTRYSIDE letters are probably composed in the writers' heads while doing chores, before being put on paper.

I thought of some of the letters I'd received recently and wondered how many others were composed while milking or weeding the garden but were never written after the chores were finished. Maybe writing them in their heads made their jobs a little less dreary. At least I hoped so.

Boring jobs do have some value. If you face a problem or a challenge, sitting down and thinking about it often doesn't bring a solution. But when you "sleep on it," presto, the answer becomes obvious. Boring work gives you the opportunity to range over a wide spectrum of ideas, without straining.

Of course, the dialogue is silly, when you're talking to yourself. I was alone in a 10-acre field, but at times it felt as if there was a teeming unruly crowd in my head.

That lady who canceled her subscription because she thought the magazine was going to be about fancy country homes... is there any way to avoid that kind of confusion in the future? Probably not. People have too many different perceptions.

Perceptions. That's been a buzz word for me, lately. Maybe I could write something about how people see things differently. Even magazines.

No, it would sound like an ad.

It is interesting, though. How is somebody who sees COUNTRYSIDE *this month for the first time going to react? It sure doesn't look like other magazines, much less read like them! Some people are probably shocked, but can or should I do anything about that?*

Probably not. Look at all the people who are still offering their opinions on the "old" and the "new-old" format, even though the matter was closed a long time ago. Perceptions are hard to change. Maybe impossible. Anyway, it seems kind of silly to have to explain to someone that the magazine they're reading isn't really a magazine, in the usual modern sense. We've told them about the old-time farm magazines that were reader-written, but that doesn't seem to make any difference. If a person's mind is made up, it's made up.

As the tractor droned on and row after row of mown hay stretched out in a pleasing pattern on the field and the blackbirds flitted about devouring insects, I was no longer just a farmer. I was a publisher again. Away from the office and typewriter, it was easy to mull things over, and from a new perspective.

A cock pheasant hopped out of the uncut hay ahead of the mower and loped ahead of the tractor. A few steps to the left and he would have been out of danger, but he ran directly in front of the machine. Pheasants are odd, I thought. Maybe, just like people, with mind-sets and perceptions! At the next corner he even followed the windrow, turned the corner, and *still* ran ahead of the tractor!

Mind-sets and perceptions. Everybody has them. What if mine are wrong? No, nobody's are wrong: just different.

A reader suggested that we conduct a survey. "Find out what your customers want, and give it to them. Not what you want and what you think they want, but what they want." I told him that's the way they select prime-time tv shows, and look what we get. But did he have a point? The last survey we conducted cost several thousand dollars and didn't tell me a thing I didn't already know, but was that because of my mind-set?

Well, a survey would just tell us what most people want, and it's obvious that more people want a *Playboy* than a COUNTRYSIDE. We don't need to know that. I'm marching to the beat of a different drummer.

Speaking of that, maybe we should start trying to sell some advertising. Heaven knows we could use the revenue... and what are we going to put on the covers? It's hard to print editorial material on them when they're printed so far ahead of the inside pages, and now, without The Countryside General Store, we can't even drop in our own ads.

Maybe I could write some ads for COUNTRYSIDE.

That's silly. The whole magazine is an ad for COUNTRYSIDE, and people either like it or they don't. It'd be a waste of space.

Not necessarily. Advertising CAN be informative... and for instance, how many people, even loyal readers, realize that COUNTRYSIDE is a network?

The debate went on. I was both protagonist and antagonist. Ideas flowed like the hay flowed through the mower, and once or twice I had to jostle myself to keep a part of my brain on the haying job.

I hardly noticed when the pheasant finally tired of playing tag with the tractor and flew off to a tranquil field. And by the time the hay was cut I could hardly wait to get off the tractor seat and onto a typing chair.

Farming and thinking — and writing, for me — seem to go together. The fields, with a view of distant misty hills, the aroma of new-mown hay, and the sun and the wind and the birds, are a much better place for thinking than a book-lined office is. That's what a field is to me: a spacious office with soft green carpeting and the best kind of lighting and air-conditioning — and no telephones.

At the typewriter, I could still feel the effect of the sun on my face, still smell the hay, taste the fresh air. I felt renewed, and much more eager than when I sit at a desk all day. I rolled a sheet of paper into the typewriter and wrote, "Join the network."

Everything in life gets boring, sooner or later. But it's usually later, when you live and work beyond the sidewalks.

I obviously had some big-time business concerns on my mind that day. You'll have to read between the lines to realize how close we were to losing everything — but the worst was yet to come.

137. September 1984

A small ingredient makes a difference
Adding it to everything will change your life

D id your breakfast this morning, or yesterday's dinner, have a secret ingredient? Mine did!

It's nothing you sprinkle on the eggs or stir into the biscuits and gravy. In fact, you can (and you probably do) use this secret ingredient in much more than just cooking. And the only reason it's a "secret" is that it's so common we seldom stop to think about it.

It came to me just as we were sitting down to dinner the other night. I'd been working on the "rural slum" discussion (counting the original letter, this is the fourth month we've been talking about that), and felt vaguely uneasy about it, as if something were missing. I'd also been working on the lengthy questionnaire which appears in this issue as the new *Question of the month,* and felt uneasy about that, too. There had been a few other occurrences that made me wonder whether homesteading — or publishing COUNTRYSIDE — was really worth the effort.

Those doubts vanished as soon as I pulled my chair up to the table. A sudden realization swept over me as quickly as my eyes took in the homestead bounty laid before us.

Maybe it was because I'd grabbed a quick bite at a small diner that noon, and the difference between eating out and eating at home was so apparent. Even at most of the better restaurants I've dined in, something was missing...

To be sure, our evening meal had that somewhat vague *quality* we homesteaders enjoy so much. There was pork from our own well-fed, well-cared-for, home-butchered hog. The new potatoes, golf ball size and thin-skinned, were dotted with butter and parsley... and both potatoes and parsley had come out of the garden less than an hour ago. The salad was just as fresh, and so were the green beans. They'd never been in a refrigerator, much less a freezer or can: there wasn't time. They'd been whisked from the garden to the kitchen to the table.

And yet, none of that was the secret ingredient. Not really. What made it special started months ago, and took months, in some cases, to accomplish.

It started with the pig. We fed, and watered, and cared for that pig for six months. That isn't *anybody's* idea of fast food, and certainly not those who prefer to pop a frozen dinner into the microwave.

The salad looked pretty much like any salad you might find at one of the better salad bars in the country... but the deep red ripe tomatoes had a secret ingredient. It started last winter, when we studied the seed catalogs, and finally whittled dozens of possibilities down to three varieties. It continued when we planted the seeds in flats in the house, while February snowstorms still raged outside the south windows where the tiny seeds germinated. It went on in May, when the tomatoes were transplanted in the garden, and throughout the rest of the summer when we weeded, mulched, pruned, staked and watered them... and came to a climax this afternoon, when we selected those that were at the peak of perfection, and picked them off the lush vines.

After all that, the salad is almost anti-climatic. The entire meal is almost anti-climatic! It only takes a few minutes to eat, and slightly longer to prepare the food, but it's all the result of many hours of caring for animals, hauling bales of straw to mulch the potatoes and tomatoes, hoeing the beans, planting the cucumbers and the lettuce and the radishes and all the rest.

When we dine on our homesteads, we're not just enjoying the moment, savory as that might be: We're enjoying memories and experiences, and tasting again satisfactions (and frustrations) that might have been long forgotten. But meals aren't the only things with ingredients. Everything has ingredients. And everything can benefit from the *secret* ingredient.

By now you know what I'm talking about. It's the dedication and commitment and involvement and labor that love induces.

This secret ingredient can be applied to just about any human activity... and you can "taste" it, when it's there. It results in a wholesome form of pride, and it shows. Even others can see it, if they look for it.

You can find it in hand-knit sweaters. In certain automobiles. In crafts of all kinds. Even in certain families.

And yes, you can find it on certain homesteads — and, I hope, you can even recognize it now and then in COUNTRYSIDE.

The secret ingredient doesn't insure perfection, or even uniform results. It doesn't mean that every batch of cheese or sausage or every loaf of bread will turn out just as you'd hoped it would. It doesn't mean that a table or chair made in the workshop with the secret ingredient won't have a flaw; that a carefully tended garden or flock of hens or hutch of rabbits will necessarily be an unqualified success; or even that every issue of a magazine made with the secret ingredient will be the epitome of that craft. Even a child raised with the secret ingredient can't be expected not to exhibit a blemish now and then, but it definitely adds to the quality.

However, there's another angle to this. If a grandmother knits her grandchild a pair of mittens, who gets the most pleasure from the effort? The child might appreciate the thought and the warm hands, but could also easily wish Grandma had gone out and bought mittens that were softer, or prettier, or had better-fitting thumbs. You might think you're wasting your time when you add the secret ingredient to a fine loaf of whole wheat bread when relatives are coming for dinner, and then find that they only eat white bread. Your own family might not appreciate the effort you expend to add the secret ingredient... to anything!

But that doesn't matter. Not really. Because *you* know.

You might drop a stitch in the scarf you're knitting, or I might let a typographical error or two slip through the 50,000 or so words that appear in COUNTRYSIDE each month — or we might even make more serious mistakes that might lead some people to scoff that we're not "professionals," or that our products aren't as "good" as machine-made ones.

But that's not going to stop us. It's not going to keep us from trying again, and trying to improve. If we're able to muster up the secret ingredient in the first place, we *can't* stop! And if we add the secret ingredient to our *lives,* life will always be great, no matter what happens, beyond the sidewalks.

138. October 1984

Make life more fun by being an expert
How the raspberry expert shared bacon-curing skills

There was a time when I had little use — and no fondness at all — for "experts." (That's why I wanted to be either a farmer or a writer — jacks-of-all-trades.)

Recent correspondence indicates that a number of readers feel the same way, but since I've become something of an expert on experts, maybe it's time to share some of what I've learned with you.

An "ex" is a has-been, and a "spurt" is a big drip. Who wants to be a has-been big drip?

In some fields, an expert is anyone more than 100 miles from home, carrying a briefcase.

An expert is a person who learns more and more about less and less.

And of course, PhD stands for "piled higher and deeper."

These might be good for a laugh, but more likely, they serve to hide our distrust of people who talk about things we can't even understand, and maybe they're an ointment for the deep-seated conviction that we'll never be experts, ourselves.

But what is an expert? According to the dictionary, it's simply a person who has acquired a special skill in, or knowledge of, a particular subject. There are experts all around us, even in the countryside — you might be one yourself — and we'd be in a sorry mess without them.

Along with commonly thinking that an expert must be a genius of some kind, or that expertise requires a lot of alphabet soup after your name or a wide recognition, we also mistakenly think that an expert has the final word. However, sometimes we have to determine what an expert is really expert *at.*

For example, about 15 years ago, I contacted an "expert" at the university for some information on curing bacon and ham. There was a moment of rather stunned silence, and then this person, highly educated in meat and animal science, laughingly said, "*People* don't make bacon: *Oscar Mayer* makes bacon!"

I got the recipe and directions from a retired neighbor who didn't finish high school.

But these two men had two different kinds of expertise, on what *seemed* to be the same subject. While one could have provided all the scientific and technical data on modern, large-scale meat curing and processing, he had no experience with old-fashioned on-the-farm meat curing. On the other hand my neighbor, who had grown up on a farm, knew nothing about how Oscar Mayer operated, but he easily recalled how they had processed pork in his younger days.

My neighbor certainly would have laughed if anyone would have called him an "expert" at curing meat, but he had acquired a special skill in, and knowledge of, a particular subject.

Actually, the thing he was really an expert at was growing raspberries. Here again, he had no special training or schooling, but he had nearly 80 years of experience. Perhaps the most important factor was that he was interested in raspberries, he loved to grow and eat raspberries, he studied raspberries both in printed articles and in his garden, and in 80 years he had become an expert.

The countryside is full of experts at various stages of development, and in a grand variety of disciplines. Farmers and homesteaders must be generalists, but those with the most verve, the greatest zest for life, the most curiosity and ambition, almost invariably become specialists at one thing or another.

Perhaps you're acquainted with a goat lady, or a rabbit man, or a poultry person. Every neighborhood has them, even if in some cases the neighborhoods are rather spread out. The term "goat lady" (we seldom hear of a "goat man") is almost an honorary title, bestowed by people who know they can drop in or give her a call and get an answer to almost any question they might have about goats... and generally with lots of side advice tossed in for free. If you have a question on anything pertaining to homesteading and farming — and more — you're sure to be able to find a local expert and mentor if you look hard enough.

I often think of these dedicated, experienced people — particularly when a disgruntled reader tells me we should have more articles by real writers; by *experts.*

Who does a bride call, when she needs advice on baking a cake or roasting a turkey? A freelance writer? Of course not! She calls her *mother!* Mothers are experts at all kinds of things.

And so are we all, whether we realize it or not. Knowledge and skill usually creep up on us, and we often take them for granted. Several goat ladies (and others of their kind) have confided to me that they were rather taken aback when someone asked them for advice... and they were actually surprised at how much they knew! Where had that "expertise" come from all of a sudden?

It didn't come suddenly, of course. It came from someone, or maybe many people, who had helped *them.* It came from reading. Some of it came from just talking with others about their successes and failures... and a lot came from their own experiences, good and bad.

You might not set out to become an expert, in the sense of gaining fame and fortune. But if you are deeply interested in, say, grafting fruit trees, you're certainly not going to set out with the intention of being inept at it! Whether your interest is raising sheep, or spinning and weaving, or identifying wildflowers or birds or rocks or mushrooms, you can become an expert. In fact, if you stick with it, and your interest drives you to study and practice and swap ideas with others, you can't *avoid* attaining some degree of expertise! I suspect that the real value in knowing how to make super pickles, or bread, or anything else, isn't the finished product as much as it is the satisfaction of *knowing how.*

There are opportunities galore for becoming an expert, and if you think about it you'll probably realize you're already well on the way in some field that holds special appeal for you.

My advice is to go for it. You can "learn more and more about less and less" without neglecting all the other things that make life worthwhile. My neighbor was certainly well-rounded: while he devoted a great deal of his time to his raspberries, he also must have been skilled at his regular job... and he knew something of pork processing, and more. But his berries were what made his life special. And if you become an expert builder of birdhouses, knitter of sweaters or grower of daffodils, your life will be all the richer, too.

Being a generalist is a necessity, but being a specialist adds spice to life, when you live beyond the sidewalks.

2014: Funny that I mentioned daffodils. I had no interest in the flowers back then, but since retiring, I have planted more than 35,000 spring bulbs — many of them daffodils. Naturally, a few people consider me an expert, but they're dead wrong. I plant them mostly because they're perennials, and the deer and rabbits don't eat them. I'm more like the guy who has, not 20 years of experience, but one year's experience 20 times.

139. November 1984
A lesson learned from lilies of the field
Grasshoppers survive winter too, don't they?

For awhile, I was afraid we wouldn't have a real, old-fashioned, homestead Thanksgiving at our house this year. The kind where, when Diane sends me down to the root cellar for some potatoes or carrots or onions or cabbage, I end up spending half an hour admiring the jars of tomatoes and beets and pickles and all the other stored bounty of the summer's efforts. The kind where the entire dinner — and an elaborate one it is (you can tell from the two kinds of pie) — was produced on the homestead, by us. And the forces of nature, of course.

This year we discovered how insignificant a role we play, and maybe even how unnecessary we are.

I didn't think we'd have a homestead Thanksgiving, because we didn't do much homesteading this year, mostly because of our work with COUNTRYSIDE.

As a result, our garden shrunk to less than half its usual size — although we did plant about 200 pounds of seed potatoes in the hog pasture, which were promptly swallowed by weeds. Yes, we sold every last pig and sow: the only pork left on the place is in the freezer.

We didn't put down a single chick, or gosling, or turkey poult, whose voracious appetite by this time would make us think of Thanksgiving dinner with anticipation.

Yet we're homesteaders, and we *will* have a real, homestead, Thanksgiving dinner!

I just found out about it last Saturday, and learned two lessons in the process.

It was a beautiful, beautiful, frosty morning, with a sky so clear some stars were still shining even as the sun was rising. Even though it was the weakening washed-out sun of autumn, the temperature quickly reached 40 and kept on climbing. It was much too rare a day to squander by repairing the water line in the barn, which had been my number one priority. I convinced Diane that we should gather hickory nuts.

It was a pleasant walk through the wet pasture, and along the eastern edge of the fencerow to take advantage of the sun's warming rays. And the nuts were so plentiful it was a pleasure to pick them up and drop them into the sack. Actually, we filled our sacks so quickly we went back to the house for more.

Spreading the thick-hulled nuts in the sun to dry, we were really in a homestead mood so, instead of going on to our intended jobs, we checked out the sorely-neglected garden.

I had planted a small patch of potatoes in the early spring, mulched it and then more or less forgot about it. But now, raking aside the moldering mulch, we found a nice crop of spuds. We filled five baskets in no time.

We managed to find some onions, now topless, resting under a thick growth of weeds. They weren't as large as the smaller lot we'd planted in the raised beds and managed to keep somewhat weeded in spite of the voracity of this year's mosquito crop and our time restraints but they were onions, edible and welcome. We filled a large basket with them.

We dug carrots, some of which Diane had kept fairly weed-free by wearing a hat, gloves, jacket and mosquito net in 90-degree weather. They filled two large egg baskets.

The horseradish, in our garden as free and wild as any weed, was as tall and lush as I've ever seen it, and the plant I dug yielded a root as thick as my wrist. We left the others for later.

The Jerusalem artichokes, also "wild," turned their yellow sunflower-like blossoms to the sun on stalks eight and 10 feet high, and experimentally probing one plant, I learned that what was below ground was as bountiful as what was above.

I was surprised to find some volunteer tomatoes hidden under a canopy of weedy grasses and vines, not just because I hadn't known they were there but because they were ripe, and undamaged by frost. Those we'd planted and cared for had been wiped out more than a week earlier.

And then I discovered some pumpkins, perfectly formed and perfectly ripe. We'd have pumpkin pie after all — and we hadn't even planted pumpkins!

In a short while, the root cellar actually looked like a homestead root cellar. And I was surprised to notice that the tomatoes and other things Diane had canned while I'd been busy haying and combining and planting winter wheat took up most of their allotted space on the shelves.

The lessons I learned?

One, which I'd already been studying rather closely in the fields, was that maybe Masanobu Fukuoka was right when he wrote in *The One-Straw Revolution,* "I ultimately reached the conclusion that there was no need to plow, no need to apply fertilizer, no need to make compost, no need to use insecticide. When you get right down to it, there are few agricultural practices that are really necessary."

The other is that perhaps we make homesteading — and other things? — more work than they really should be. Maybe instead of being obsessed with the fable of the grasshopper and the ant (grasshoppers do survive winter, don't they?) we should pay a little more attention to the parable about the lilies of the field.

Something tells me that this year I'll have even more than usual to reflect on when I relax on Thanksgiving day, beyond the sidewalks.

Happy Thanksgiving to you, too!

140. December 1984

Where did you go on your vacation?
"Down to the goose pasture and back into history"

Inspiration comes unexpectedly, at times, in places, and in ways that often startle and delight.

So it was last Saturday, when Diane and I found the stone arrowhead in our goose pasture, which we were touring on our vacation.

But I should explain.

We seldom take real vacations. Sometimes we talk about it, think and dream about it, but that's as far as it goes. You can't put off planting, or making hay, or combining oats, or monthly magazine deadlines. We just never got into the habit of going anywhere.

But we still need some time off, now and then.

We discussed it for more than a week. Maybe a weekend in Minneapolis would be nice, or Chicago, or even Milwaukee? The distance from home isn't important: What we need is a change of pace, mostly. A chance to forget about day-to-day things, and experience something new.

It was fun discussing it, looking at maps, suggesting possible things to do and see, but it ended up like almost all of our vacations.

We went to Madison — not to the airport, but to the classiest supermarket in town — and shopped mostly in the gourmet section. We bought a good bottle of wine. Then we came home to a candle-lit dinner that was as good as any we would have found in Minneapolis or Chicago.

We didn't wash the dishes: People on vacation don't wash dishes.

Mostly we lounged, reading, talking once in awhile, listening to soft music on the radio.

Saturday morning, instead of rushing off to clean the barn or scrub the kitchen floor or to do any of the other 1001 things that "needed" doing, we slept late. Then we enjoyed a leisurely holiday-type brunch, and went back to bed.

Then we went for a walk, and that's when it happened.

The goose pasture, a field that got its name the year we raised 1,000 Embden geese there, is now planted to winter wheat which on Saturday was just beginning to sprout in thin, even lines. It borders the marsh, 3,000 acres of state-owned wildlife area (which, incidentally, makes it a lousy place to try to raise 1,000 geese, which is one reason that was the second-worst business decision I ever made). We both saw the oddly shaped piece of stone at the same time, but I picked it up. We marveled at the arrowhead in my hand. People just don't find arrowheads around here anymore, on land that's been deep-plowed for years and cultivated for years before that.

As I touched it with my hands, running my fingers over the meticulously chipped surface and the feathered edge, I could almost feel myself touching it with my *mind*... almost, perhaps, as some long-dead person had done as he chipped at the stone, shaping a rough rock into his mind's image of what an arrowhead should look like.

I love my land, I have a deep feeling for it, and I've spent hours reading the abstract that sketches tiny portraits in legal prose of the people who farmed it before me. But the maker of this arrowhead predated us all, probably by many, many years.

What was the land like, then? Where was his village, how did he live? How did he feel when he missed whatever he was shooting at and lost his arrow? Was he thinking about an empty pot that night, or about the time and effort it would take to make another arrow, or...?

These thoughts and emotions all flashed across my mind in mere moments. Then I dropped the piece of stone in my pocket and we continued our walk and our weekend.

Sunday afternoon I said, "If we really would have gone someplace this weekend, we'd be on our way home by now."

Diane agreed.

"So I'm going to hook up the chisel plow and pretend we're driving home while I get some plowing done." I'd had enough vacation.

But I kept thinking about that arrowhead. As the John Deere strained to pull the chisel through the grain stubble, I found my eyes scanning the ground around me, more than usual, which was silly, of course.

At the same time, I couldn't help but think of the people and animals who had worked or passed through this particular little plot of Earth in years and centuries past... and what it might be like years and centuries from now...

That night I took the arrowhead out again, and examined it more closely, from different angles, something most people don't do with their vacation souvenirs.

I hope whoever made it wasn't terribly proud of it: It's by no means a perfect arrowhead. It's not even a decent piece of flint, which might be one of his excuses. Maybe he had others. The more I handled the stone and felt its vibrations, the more I felt its maker was just an ordinary guy doing his job, and making the occasional inevitable mistake.

I think I would've liked him. We would've had a lot in common.

Once again I saw him bent over this piece of stone, shaping it... saw him take aim... miss...

What if he missed because he had a future-vision of a thousand fat white geese honking just behind him? Or a subdivision, just beyond his quarry?

I put the arrowhead in a drawer. You can carry these things too far.

It was a good weekend. A good vacation. So good, in fact, that Diane and I are trying to decide where not to go for the holidays. We think either Bermuda or Nova Scotia would be nice places to not visit.

Just as Thoreau "traveled far — in Concord" we can tour even the centuries, right here beyond the sidewalks.

Comments on this could take many different paths. An expert later told us that the arrowhead was probably 5,000 years old, and indeed, some ancient petroglyphs were discovered about a mile away a few years later.

And that "subdivision just beyond his quarry" packs a double whammy not only because today there are many new homes

nearby, but even more incredible, that field is now owned by a stone quarrying company!

The writing was on the wall, and our days on the farm were numbered.

Part XV: 1985

Inflation: 3.55%; Fed year-end interest rate: 10.75%;
Year-end Dow: 1546; Average annual income: $22,100;
Gas/gal: $1.09; Movie ticket: $2.75; Rib eye steak, $3.89/lb.;
Compact discs introduced; Scientists discover hole in ozone layer

141. February 1985

Some helpful hints for homestead carpenters

Livestock and carpentry seem to form a natural combination. While I can't remember the first thing I "helped" my dad build, it was probably a rabbit hutch or chicken coop or pigeon loft. Just a year ago last summer my own sons and I replaced some beams and flooring in the haymow of the old barn (using hydraulic jacks to raise the old beams enough to slip new ones in) and we put up three small grain bins (two of which required cement work as well as carpentry).

Between these two events I've erected miles of fencing, and have built pens, gates, milking benches, goat mangers, pig brooders, sheep feeders, sheds and pasture shelters...and that's not even considering the cold frames, hotbeds, greenhouses, smokehouses and other things homesteaders construct from time to time, let alone the "construction phase" most of us go through somewhere near the beginning of our homestead experience. If we don't already know how to dig footings, finish cement, lay brick and stone, frame in buildings, put up drywall, glaze windows, plaster, do basic wiring and put on roofing, that's where we learn.

There are books, magazines, neighbors and many other sources of information on most construction techniques, but there are some lessons we have to learn for ourselves. For the benefit of anyone who hasn't been there yet (and maybe the nostalgia of those who have) here are a few pointers.

First, don't be shy about talking about your building projects. Be prepared for a completely different reaction when you switch from gushing excitedly about your Nubian quadruplets to casually mentioning the milking stand you knocked together now that your doe is fresh.

Most people think anyone who raises goats, or chickens or rabbits is a mite odd, but anyone who *builds* something, no matter what it is, is a regular American!

How many times have you heard people say, "Why would anyone want to keep those smelly chickens around when they can pick up a dozen eggs at the gas station for under a buck?" Ditto for milking, and butchering, and for that matter even canning pickles and tomatoes.

But did you ever hear anyone say "Why would anyone want to spend all that time building a grandfather clock (or model ship or coffee table or whatever) when they could just go to a store and buy one?" I never have.

So if you have learned to shuffle and bow your head and mumble when talking about your animal-raising pursuits, be prepared to stand up tall and proud when you talk about your latest construction project. Any child can raise a rabbit, so the thinking goes, but it takes a real man to figure out why the toilet keeps running.

Lesson two is, because construction and repair are considered normal, you can find a lot more help and advice and equipment for that than you can for animal-raising. Magazine racks are full of publications dealing with home mechanics (and they're filled with ads) and hardware store owners will be delighted to tell you how to do a job (and then sell you the tools). Contrast this with when you got your first rabbit or goat!

That makes construction much easier than animal husbandry.

Number three: construction is like sex. Lots of people do it even though they aren't very good at it. This is an important lesson on two counts. First, perfection isn't the goal. Second, you get better with practice.

Lesson four applies to dyed-in-the-wool homestead carpenters. Forget about looking for detailed blueprints for most of your projects. In most cases they probably don't exist, and if they do they probably won't suit your needs anyway, and if they do you probably won't have the right materials on hand. Homesteaders don't start out with detailed plans and bills of materials to use as a shopping list. We start out with a somewhat vague idea what we're trying to accomplish, then we measure up what's on the scrap pile and decide how big we can make it.

Lesson five isn't really all that important, but it pays to be forewarned: if you should happen to buy a piece of new lumber some day, don't be alarmed when you saw into it. That aroma is natural, for new wood. You simply aren't used to it, as a homestead carpenter.

There are many other lessons for any kind of construction work, of course. Measure twice and cut once. You can always cut a board shorter but you can't cut it longer. A workman is only as good as his tools. But this is all common advice you're sure to pick up as you talk to others about your projects, or even reading articles in Countryside. What I've tried to do here is present some uncommon advice, which is much harder to come by, and which will stand you in good stead when you start your next construction or repair job beyond the sidewalks.

142. May 1985

Happy birthday to Countryside: A glance back

More than 1,500 issues published, but there's still more to talk about

This is Countryside's 69th or 70th anniversary issue—or maybe the 15th, depending on how you look at it. Some people have been wondering about that, and this is a good month to explain it. You know it's not a simple story if we don't even know how many candles to put on the cake, but to make it seem simpler this *Beyond the Sidewalks* is a combination of that column, the *Publisher's letter* (which lost its page two spot to a paying advertiser: be sure to patronize Stark Bro's Nursery!); and *Country neighbors* (with me being the neighbor this month).

We can put this all in a nutshell. My one-man homestead print shop started a nameless newsletter in 1969. In 1970 we took over *Small Stock Magazine*, which had been started by Wallace Blair in 1917 under the name *The Pet Stock Journal*.

The next year we added *American Small Stock Farmer*, which Edward Stahl had founded in 1916 as *The Journal of Outdoor Enterprises*.

And here we are, still at it.

But that's a pretty stark outline of a richly varied, venerable old family tree. As with all family trees, there are many branches, some of them hidden or little-known, and many stories about them.

Consider how different farming was 70 years ago, and how different magazines were. There were hundreds of small magazines, most of them published by small country printers, on rabbits and poultry alone. (The University of Poultry Department was founded 75 years ago, not for commercial interests, but at the demand of fanciers who wanted more and larger poultry shows.) Most of these publications didn't last very long—some folded after a single issue—they didn't carry much advertising, and unlike most magazines today (except COUNTRYSIDE of course) they were written by their readers and editors. As farming changed, and as small town print shops and their newspapers disappeared, the small magazines they'd been printing faded away too. Many of them were acquired by Blair and Stahl, and merged into *The Pet Stock Journal* and *The Journal of Outdoor Enterprises*... and those two magazines changed to keep up with the changing world and readers' tastes.

In the first issue of *The Pet Stock Journal*, Wallace Blair wrote that the magazine's purpose was to "present better methods of raising and selling pet stock for exhibition and for food." That January, 1917 issue had articles on Belgian Hares, bantams, guinea pigs, Persian cats, pigeons and skunks.

The name changed several times, becoming *Small Stock Magazine* in 1925, when it was "devoted to rabbits, cavies, pigeons and milk goats."

The greatest period of magazine acquisition and growth was during the depression. To give you an idea of the magazines that had been available before that, here's just a partial listing of the titles that were merged into *Small Stock Magazine* alone: *Successful Rabbit Breeding, Rabbit Fancier's Guide, The Reliable Rabbit Journal, The Red Magazine, American Fur Animal, Weidman's Rabbit Farmer, American Rabbit Record*, and many others.

By 1948 *Small Stock Magazine* had evolved into a rabbit magazine, one of only a small handful of survivors. Circulation had reached 25,000, and it was billed as "American's Most Read Rabbit Magazine."

In the January, 1948 issue, Mr. Blair noted his magazine's growth and said, "During this period of time there have been some very strenuous years, and times when, from a financial standpoint, we should have discontinued publication, but we just couldn't do it. This was our 'baby' and we just couldn't give it up." That issue had 46 pages, more than 27 of them advertising.

But it wouldn't last. After the postwar interest in chickens and rabbits and homesteading (as it was called even then) waned, Americans geared up for the age of plastic, the atomic age, an age of prosperity and plenty. Farms became larger, more mechanized and more specialized. National advertising took on increased importance, and magazines expanded to meet the challenge. People migrated from the remaining small farms to the cities and suburbs, interest in autos and tv increased and interest in small stock decreased. The few remaining once-proud magazines serving small stock raisers foundered, and decayed.

When I took over *Small Stock Magazine* in 1970, it was down to 20 pages, with four or five pages of ads, and circulation was about 2,000. *American Small Stock Farmer* was in even worse shape: It hadn't published an issue for more than a year before we merged it into *Small Stock* in 1971.

Beyond the sidewalks

I had a long-term dream and a long-range plan, and everything was on schedule.

The dream was to be a small, diversified, self-sufficient farmer, or homesteader. (I probably shared that dream with Diane the day I met her in 1953 and learned her father owned a farm! Before that there was no one to talk to about it.)

The plan was to earn enough money to buy the land and tools we'd need, and to build up a small homestead business to supply the small amount of cash that would be required on an on-going basis.

By 1970 I was "retired" from a job on a large magazine, we lived on a one-acre homestead, and we had another 20 acres of wooded hillside, with a delightful stream gurgling at the foot of it, where we'd build our dream homestead. We already had goats, sheep, chickens, geese, rabbits, bees and a pig on the one acre. We had a large garden, berries and fruit trees, and a "lawn" planted to alfalfa. We produced nearly all of our own food. We sold a few eggs, some rabbits and a little honey and goat milk, but most of our cash income came from Diane's nursing job and the homestead print shop. The big bucks were going to come when we completed remodeling the once-abandoned creamery we called home, and sold it to make the final move.

In 1970, everything changed. Here's what happened.

Trying to make a living, even a modest one, with a small print shop in a small town (one hardware store, one small grocery and a few taverns and churches) was precarious, as countless other small-town printers before me had learned. Like them, I had to sell printing farther afield, and like them I thought a regular publication would bring in a regular income. I'd worked on magazines and before that in advertising, had been a newspaper reporter and had a journalism degree, so publishing something was a natural choice.

But the publication that worked was one for small independent telephone companies around the country, and it wasn't very exciting to me. I knew there were other people who were living and thinking as we were...wouldn't they respond to a publication that addressed their needs and interests? Besides, just think what I could learn, by having someone to talk with!

We scraped together $25 to test an ad in *Organic Gardening & Farming*, a magazine I'd written some articles for and which seemed most hospitable to the idea of homesteading. I offered a newsletter, printed on one 12" x 18" sheet of paper and folded down to 6"x9" booklet size (I didn't want to get involved in collating and binding and trimming a real magazine) for $1 a year *plus* a letter with a question, an answer or a comment or experience the rest of us could use.

Within a few months there were more than a hundred replies...and I was ecstatic! It was like getting letters from old friends I hadn't met yet, people who were interested in the same things I'd been interested in for years while thinking I was odd and alone. It was exciting and educational and inspirational.

I printed all the letters. The one sheet newsletter (which had no name, but which carried the Countryside Print Shop return address and rooster logo) became a small magazine, which we called COUNTRYSIDE. It was "published in the countryside, by homesteaders, whenever the other chores are done" and therefore had no date—just a number. The post office said this wasn't acceptable. It had to be dated, and it had to have a regular publication schedule. Already we were forced to become a "business."

Diane, the four children and I put the pages together by walking around the dining room table.

COUNTRYSIDE's readers/writers talked about raising goats and rabbits and other animals; we swapped recipes for making soap and vinegar and tanning hides, we discussed the state of the world and our fears for the future.

And when I commented on how hot the water got in the garden hose, and wondered aloud how I could make use of that principle when we got to Stony Brook, we discussed solar heat. When I mentioned that I was trying to hook up a bicycle light generator to a windmill to provide lights to the henhouse, some old-timers told of the wind-electric systems they'd used in the '30s, and electrical engineers offered suggestions on updating those systems.

Everything was falling into place even better than I'd dared to hope. When we did make it to Stony Brook it would be even more utopian than I'd dreamed it would be during all those years!

Then, one day in 1970 a very interesting little magazine with the delightful title "*The Mother Earth News*" appeared in my mailbox. It was satisfying to know that "homesteading" was more common and popular than I'd suspected...but the guy who was putting out this magazine was serious about it. It was clear that my little homemade effort wouldn't last unless I became more aggressive. Besides, I was spending entirely too much time on it—at a loss—and while I thoroughly enjoyed it and benefitted greatly in other ways, the time and money spent on COUNTRYSIDE really should have been going toward making the leap to Stony Brook...

Just a few months later, *Small Stock Magazine* became available when the editor and publisher died.

You know the rest, or you can guess.

Even this is still only a bare-bones outline. The years following were busy, often hectic ones. By 1973 (when we sold the creamery and Stony Brook and bought a ready-made 80-acre farm) circulation had reached nearly 10,000. It was impossible for me to continue printing it myself on my small press, and more economical to farm it out. That was fine with me. I much preferred caring for my 100 hogs and 20 head of cattle and the field crops—and the goats, sheep, chickens, rabbits and garden, of course!

Diane had quit her nursing job to help with the magazine, and when we hired more help, the office was moved to town. When readers asked us where to find unusual hard-to-find homestead tools (such as hog scrapers and, prior to 1973, wood burning stoves) and we weren't able to sell advertising to the people who had those products for sale, we started the Countryside General Store both as a service to readers and as a means of generating additional revenues to keep the whole operation going. Soon the store was putting out 96-page catalogs...and we cranked up the Countryside Print Shop presses again, this time with professional printers. Since they had extra time, we started (or re-started) other magazines: *Rabbits, Backyard Poultry, Dairy Goat Guide* and *sheep!* We later took over *National Stock Dog*, sold *sheep!*, closed the store and made many, many other changes against a wavering backdrop of social and economic change.

And yet, the basic purpose of the business, and my personal goals, have changed very little. While *Mother Earth* went on to reach millions, and other similar magazines appeared (and in most cases disappeared) COUNTRYSIDE reached 30,000 circulation in 1976 and has remained fairly constant at that level. That gives me time for other things... and I now farm 150 acres, and we still try to be self-sufficient in food, at least.

There have been ups and downs, moments of despair and moments of elation. Or, as Wallace Blair wrote here 37 years ago this month..."During this period of time there have been some very strenuous years, and times when, from a financial standpoint, we should have discontinued publication, but we just couldn't do it. This was our 'baby' and we just couldn't give it up."

That's one thing that hasn't changed in 15, 69, or 70 years. Wallace Blair died, in the pressroom, after 37 years at the helm of his magazine. I intend to beat his record, and whether I take my leave in the pressroom or in the barn, you can be sure it'll be beyond the sidewalks.

143. June 1985

You have to be driven—and not by a chauffer!

We're told that none of us use more than a tiny portion of our true abilities, and this is one subject on which the experts don't get much argument. We all know we're better than we usually appear to be! We also know that we could stage an outstanding performance, if we really had to. And it's always fascinating to read about some 95-pound mother who lifts a runaway car off her baby. Even Albert Einstein only used a small portion of his brain, so they say.

On the other hand, when I drive past suburban homes where it seems obvious that the occupants work 40-hour weeks, I often wonder what they do with the other 128 hours. I wonder the same thing about some farmers in the winter, when there's no plowing, planting or harvesting to be done.

The reason for these musings is that I feel very good about what I accomplished in the past month or so. This isn't bragging: rather, there's a sense of amazement, and even some shame when I wonder about all the time I must have wasted over the years.

You might recall that just a few months ago I was more than two weeks behind with COUNTRYSIDE. Now we're right back on schedule. But that's not all.

Our 150-acre farm is in fine shape. I spent some glorious sunny days on the tractor, chisel plowing and harrowing and planting oats, barley, alfalfa, clover, corn and some rape in the hog pasture.

The main garden isn't in yet, but the onions, potatoes, and some other early crops are planted. (Our traditional planting day is May 30.)

I also planted 1,000 pine and spruce trees, cleared some brush out of the orchard, learned to run the computer that takes care of COUNTRYSIDE subscriptions, sheared sheep, and what is hardest of all to believe, went fishing!

I haven't been fishing in years, because I never "had time." But when I found myself working 16 and 18 hours a day, it became obvious that I had to schedule some "off time" just the way I scheduled the work. So I made it a point to spend a few minutes with my mandolin or banjo or bouzouki, or tossing the boomerang, and on Sunday when the grandchildren were here we flew a kite for a few hours (until the string broke).

Of course, it helped that everything just seemed to fall into place. We've had a very dry spring here, so there were no weather-related delays. This isn't normal. And there were no serious machinery breakdowns. That's not normal either, for me. In fact, the only exciting moment was when the tractor caught on fire. It's a John Deere 2630, with the muffler running under the floorboard. A leak developed in the hydraulic system, oil dripped down onto the floorboard, and eventually some dripped onto the hot muffler. A few handfuls of the dry sandy soil I was working with doused the flames and no damage was done. It also helped that I planted as much winter wheat and rye as I did, last fall. That always takes a big springtime load off us part-time farmers.

But even so, I accomplished a great deal. It was one of the most enjoyable springs I've ever experienced.

Of course, I was in a position similar to that of the 95-pound mother: I was *desperate*. All that work *had* to be done, and now! So I did it. And it was easy—and fun—and I feel good about it.

Maybe one reason we don't make use of our full potential is that we aren't pushed enough, usually. From time to time we might be pushed by the weather or the clock, or the boss or banker or personal commitments—or by a child being crushed under a runaway car—and we find strength we didn't even know we had. But ordinarily, most of us do what we think we must do, and no more.

We also have to *want* to do it. I love COUNTRYSIDE and I love my farm, and not only do I not want to see 25 years of work go down the drain, but I enjoy doing what needs to be done. Similarly, people who enjoy homesteading can accomplish ever so much more than those who find it tiresome or troublesome.

And finally, you have to have a dream. I seriously doubt whether any of the farmers we speak of in this issue who are going broke would have much incentive to spend long hours working and to do a better job if they were convinced that they were going to lose everything in the end anyway. I wouldn't have been inclined to put out the extra effort on the magazine if I'd thought people wouldn't subscribe to it and advertise in it. And countrysiders who can't picture their work as polishing a rough stone into a sparking gem, or who can't even dream of themselves with a grand champion animal, who don't have *something* to work toward, they aren't going to have as much incentive as they could either.

We drive ourselves (or are driven) in order to achieve our potential. We have to enjoy what we're doing. And we need a dream. Maybe that's why so many homesteaders seem to achieve more than other people: Where are these three factors as abundant as they are beyond the sidewalks?

Again, the financial problems I was facing are obvious, but I appear to be handling the situation. Was there light at the end of the tunnel?

144. July 1985

It really is "fun to be frugal"

I think it's a lot of fun to be frugal... much more than most correspondents indicated in this month's *Question*. Here are some examples from my experience.

***

When I was in college I lived next to the railroad tracks, where boxcars that had been loaded with wheat were often parked. There was plenty of wheat left in the "empty" cars. I ground it to make flour and cereal... and if I'd had a chicken in my apartment, there would have been enough for her, too.

***

Many people wouldn't stoop to eating carp, or smelt. But when the river recedes in the late spring, leaving big carp flopping in the puddles in the fields along the banks, you can pick them up by the gunnysackful. I fill the smokehouse. And since one night's work can net enough smelt to literally fill a freezer, we eat a lot of smelt. With creative cookery, both carp and smelt are delicious, and they have an extra seasoning that perhaps can only be appreciated by a dedicated frugalist: they're free!

***

A few years ago I was in a posh restaurant in Chicago (business trip), and the waiter informed us that the special of the day was venison, "Which," he added with a phony French accent, "is the meat of a deer."

"Yeah, I know." I said, dismissively, "but I had that last night." You see, there was this doe that got hit by a car, and...

***

Once three young pheasants flew up in front of the truck as I was driving home. It took me only a few seconds to pick them up, and a few minutes to dress them out. No gun, no shells, no tramping through the marsh for hours, and no buckshot in the meat. Truly a frugalist's delight!

***

The trucks that haul sweet corn to the cannery often drop ears along the way. I know where there's a dandy bump in the road where I can pick up a meal in a matter of moments during the season.

***

Of course, gardening is as much fun as being frugal is. It must be, or many of us wouldn't bother with it. Why grow tomatoes or cucumbers when there are so many people who are willing, even eager, to share their surplus? And if you know any gardeners at all there's *never* any need to plant zucchini.

***

As much satisfaction as I get from a meal that was produced entirely on my own homestead, I get even more when Diane says there's nothing in the house to eat, and I make "something out of nothing." (I've considered writing a cookbook, but of course that's impossible because you never have the same kind of "nothing" twice.)

But frugality doesn't cover just food. Once, when I was a very young magazine publisher (before the days of fancy computerized typesetting which we couldn't have afforded anyway) I wanted a headline set in a very large type for a special effect. I found the letters I wanted on a box in the kitchen cupboard, cut them out, rearranged them, and pasted them down.

It's challenging to be frugal: how many words can you make out of "corn flakes"?

***

This is just a small sample. I could offer many others because I feel it's great fun to be frugal. It's a sport, a game, a cross between the mental discipline of chess and climbing a mountain "because it's there." To me, the thrill of making a score in frugalism is akin to catching a trophy fish or making a hole-in-one.

And that, I think, is one of the biggest reasons why I enjoy country life so much. Some people get their tans in a tanning salon or by vacationing in the tropics: I get mine in the garden. They get their exercise at a health club: I get mine cutting wood. They get their gourmet foods at snooty restaurants and expensive specialty shops (and then have the nerve to suggest that my fresh organic eggs and produce and goat cheese etc. are "expensive.") They get their kicks by spending money: I get mine by being frugal.

There have been times in my life when frugality has been a necessity, but it has never been a burden. Maybe it's the way you were brought up, or maybe it's just a character flaw, but when you have the right view of the world, frugality is exciting, challenging, rewarding, satisfying, and yes, it's a whole lot of fun. New cars today are awfully shoddy and outrageously over-priced, most so-called entertainment isn't as much fun as caring for animals and watching things grow, and aren't yachts and swimming pools an awful lot of work to maintain?

I'll take a good game of frugality any old time, beyond the sidewalks.

This might sound like a case of whistling past the cemetery, or at least making the best of a hopeless situation, but I meant it.

145. August 1985

Summer visitors prove you can't go home again
Thomas Wolfe was right

Summer vacations are a time when many people go back to visit the scenes of pleasant memories. But as Thomas Wolfe said, "you can't go home again" because home (or anything else) as you remember it simply doesn't exist any more.

Change is an inescapable part of life.

We country people in particular, I think, are very much aware of small, day-to-day changes. We detect the first slight swelling of the maple buds in spring, notice the first green shoots in the fields, watch for the first ripe strawberry. A goat in heat, a rabbit about to kindle, a cauliflower at its peak of perfection... it takes an observant person to catch such subtleties. But none of those changes are shocking. They're expected, and we anticipate them and watch for them. It's only when we don't see or think about a thing for awhile and then try to "go home again" that change bursts into an explosive force.

When you see a child only infrequently it's easy to imagine that it sprouts an inch or two at a time, instantaneously. When you go home again, it's easy to believe that everything changed with one lightning bolt.

I didn't go anywhere this summer to be reminded of this. I just went about my business beyond the sidewalks, observing changes in the corn so I knew when to cultivate, in the hay so I knew when to mow, and in the grain so I knew when to combine. It was a parade of summer visitors, most of whom were retracing their steps in search of former pleasant times, who reminded me of cataclysmic change.

M y sister, Gretchen, who was formerly a COUNTRYSIDE staff writer but who moved to Salt Lake City several years ago, made a brief visit. We didn't have much time together, but among people who have been close, it doesn't take much time to realize that you can't go home again. Waterloo and COUNTRYSIDE had changed, in her eyes, and she had changed in mine.

Carole Wiley stopped by during one of her infrequent trips to the states. Carole was our advertising manager during the glory days, when the staff was young and energetic and filled with enthusiasm, and the fervor to save the world... and the world seemed amenable. Carole was one of the catalysts in organizing a highly successful farmers market in Waterloo (which has since withered away) and she sold as many as 21 pages of ads in a single issue of COUNTRYSIDE which enabled us to put out the largest issues we ever printed, and she was here when we planted the fruit trees in front of the office, an early demonstration of edible landscaping. Even the trees have changed: they are now loaded with apples, cherries, and pears and plums.

Carole Wiley, who used to run home during the noon hour to add wood to the fire to keep her house from freezing; who kept a great garden and put up tons of produce; who was a firm believer in "homesteading;" left us when her husband got a government job in Kenya; saw most of the civilized world; now resides in Sri Lanka; has a pilot's license and more astounding yet, a baby ("We waited 'til the very last minute," she said).

But all these superficial changes have a deeper connotation. They're mere symbols of how the world has changed and how we've changed with it.

I'd never met Diana Fletcher before I looked up from my desk to see her standing there with her backpack. Diana's from England but she taught in Africa for 20-some years and is now touring the U.S. on behalf of a friend who developed a plow that can be drawn by a single draft animal. It was developed for countries where farmers are too poor to own a team, and where even their single beast may be malnourished and therefore not at full power, but she thinks American homesteaders with a horse or even a pony might be a market. When she got off the bus in Waterloo she'd been told COUNTRYSIDE was out of business, apparently by someone who was thinking of the retail General Store (some people here aren't even aware of the magazine), but was given directions to the Belanger farm. Her route took her past the big green building with COUNTRYSIDE in large letters on the façade, so she stopped in and saved herself about three miles of hiking.

She ended up spending the night with us and during the hours we spent talking it was almost like going "home" to the early 1970s again, the days when Carole and Gretchen and more than a dozen other dedicated activists worked and planned and rapped together here. Fifteen, maybe even 10 years ago, a lady from England getting off a bus in Waterloo and walking three miles with a backpack to talk about a plow that can be drawn by a pony wouldn't have been too unusual. In the summer of 1985 it seemed very unusual... and it made me realize once again how much everything has changed. Our conversation was almost like going back 15 years, and it's startling to think that there are people now reading this who never even heard of the phrase "small is beautiful," much less felt the fervor and excitement and promise that went with it among so many of us just a short time ago. And of course there was the usual stream of people looking for the Countryside General Store. The building, once the crown jewel of downtown Waterloo, now houses Waterloo Auto Parts.

"Why did you close such a wonderful store!" is the almost universal reaction.

Because the world changes. Times change, people change, and as I chatted with these visitors it became obvious that they could see the changes too. One lady admitted that 15 years ago her children were home, they had a large garden and kept livestock. When the children moved out the garden became smaller, she got an outside job, and got rid of the animals. The economic outlook is different, the psychological outlook is different, everything is different.

You can't go home again, even beyond the sidewalks.

146. September 1985

When "less" is "more"

This is a story about man who, like many of those responding to the *Question of the Month* in this issue, is homesteading for the second time around.

Oh, he never left the countryside. He never even completely gave up homesteading. But he grew tired of caring for rabbits, and then goats, and then chickens...and at one time or another gave up on practically every aspect of homesteading.

He's not unusual. Many more people can say, "We used to raise goats (or rabbits or poultry)" than are raising them today. If you distill all their reasons, you'll almost certainly come up with this: "It just wasn't fun anymore."

If you raise animals, or certainly if you're a homesteader, you have to enjoy what you're doing or it simply isn't worth the time and trouble. One of the most common reasons people don't enjoy what they're doing is the often heard lament, "There's so much work, and so little reward!"

That's exactly what this man said to himself. But what happened, to make the fun go out of something he had so thoroughly enjoyed a few years before?

He had started out with a trio of rabbits. They gave him something to do after work in the evenings, they entertained and educated his children. They soothed him and they put meat on the table. They proved to be so worthwhile that he bought some chickens.

It was just a small flock of Rhode Island Reds, but when they were laying they produced far more eggs than his family could use. So he offered to sell the extras to friends, and was surprised at how eager they were to buy his eggs. And he reasoned to himself that it wouldn't be any more work or trouble to feed and water 50 hens than it was to care for a dozen...

Then he found a goat. He'd always been interested in goats, but they were scarce, back in the period this story covers, so when he heard of someone with goats to sell he visited them at once. The goat owner told him that goats need company, that one would be lonesome and noisy and probably wouldn't give as much milk. So he bought three.

They freshened, and he didn't know what to do with the kids. After all, while the does he had purchased were common grades, the kids had purebred sires and would almost certainly be better milkers than their mothers were! But when the people with babies who couldn't tolerate cow milk found out he had goats and wanted to buy milk from him, he decided to keep the doe kids. He was sure his decision was the right one when, at Easter, he sold the buck kids for meat and could have sold many more.

The next year, all six of his goats had twins and he didn't have room for 18 goats so he built an addition. The rabbits were multiplying, and he had more chickens than ever. He also bought a pig, to utilize the whey from cheesemaking and the extra milk and broken eggs and other waste. When there was talk of a rabbit meat processing plant opening in the area, he expanded the rabbitry and when a goat cheese factory started buying goat milk, he bought still more goats.

The rabbit processor went out of business after only a few months, and this homesteader kept on buying pellets for a few more months, but he finally decided that the rabbits were too much work for too little reward. The monetary reward was negative, of course, but even worse, the rabbits no longer soothed him. Instead of giving him something to do after work in the evening, they became an onerous chore. The children, instead of being entertained by the rabbits, avoided them. He sold a few, for far less than he felt they were worth, and put the rest in the freezer.

In the meantime, all his eager egg customers had dropped off. Of course, he hadn't been able to deliver eggs during the winter, when the birds barely laid enough for his own family, and when he called on his former customers in the spring when production increased again they had found other sources and weren't interested.

The chickens, too, became too much work for too little reward, and eventually joined the rabbits in the freezer.

It was several years before the goats went, but again, the fun had gone out of it. So much work... so little reward.

This little story was repeated, countless times and with many variations, across the country during the 70s.

For many of the people involved it was the end of their association with livestock and with other homestead activities. Some of them moved to town to live in apartments and work in offices and factories. Maybe some of them paved the barnyard and made it into a tennis court or built a swimming pool in the garden, I don't know, but they quit homesteading.

But not all of them. Some, looking at the empty rabbit cages and the forlorn goat pens, remembered... They remembered how it used to be. The excitement of a new litter or of kidding, the pleasures of milking and drinking fresh milk, the soothing effect of coming home from work and having something to do...

So they bought a trio of rabbits. Half a dozen chickens. Two goats. And resolved never to fall into the more-is-better trap again.

We can't end this story with "and they lived happily ever after," but we're pretty sure they will, beyond the sidewalks.

147. October 1985

The metaphysics of feeding sorghum

This is about a letter from Elin White and some metaphysical ideas she gave me, and about growing sorghum. First the sorghum.

I planted about four acres of sorghum—actually sorghum-sudan—on a Stony hill that had some severe weed problems. Sorghum, like black walnut, releases chemicals into the soil that inhibit the growth of certain plants, but even without that attribute, the stuff grows so rank and lush and fast that most weeds don't stand a chance of competing with it.

And then you can imagine how organic matter is added to the soil when you disk down the corn-like plants that are 8-10 feet high and growing just a few inches apart in seven-inch rows! I planted about a bushel of seed per acre, in late July.

It also makes wonderful feed for sheep, goats, and steers. I've been cutting a pickup load for the steers every evening, holding back half for the next morning, and they think it's candy. Since we only have four steers, I cut it by hand, which is not only physical exercise, but metaphysical exercise.

But not at first. First you have to get the hang of it.

I experimented with the scythe, two types of sickles, and a machete. A serrated sickle worked best on young, tender plants, but as they grew taller and tougher the machete worked better.

Then there was the loading. Do sorghum cutters hack down a patch, then pick it up and toss it on the truck, or do they cut a handful at a time and load that? The first method resulted in a mess of stalks that were taller than I and lying every which way in the field, and they were almost impossible to gather up. The second method took forever.

Experience showed that the way to cut sorghum is to wrap your arm around a bunch, cut it close to the ground, and lay the bunch against your left leg. Then gather in another bunch, cut it, lay it on the first, and so on until you have a respectable armload to throw on the truck or can't reach out any farther.

After a few days it was easy. All the brain had to do was to stay alert enough to avoid amputating a hand or a foot, and that left plenty of mental capacity to ponder other things.

Such as Elin's letter, which made me think of cutting sorghum, and milking, and weeding the garden.

These are activities that—after you get the rhythm—free your mind and your soul. A beginning milker has to pay attention to the job at hand to avoid squirting milk up a sleeve, and the gardener has to be alert enough to hoe out the pigweed but not the potatoes, but after a while it becomes routine. Some people might even say boring but WHOOPS! As soon as you get bored the cow steps in the pail or you hoe off a potato or, if you're cutting sorghum, you're liable to slice the machete into your boot. Just as when you're driving a tractor round and round and round in a field, as soon as you become too complacent, as soon as you become bored, something will go wrong.

Maybe it's this combination of awareness—often, of danger—with a lulling rhythm—of the swish of milk into the pail or the swish of hay through the mower or the swish of the knife through the sorghum—that often puts so many of us into a trace-like state. The mind wanders, unfettered, through regions it would never consider entering when fully conscious. You think of your kindergarten teacher or the first time you saw your grandchild, or what it's going to feel like to die or about what Elin said in her letter.

She said, "Your August editorial 'going home again' sort of caught me. I haven't had time to let it rattle around upstairs yet, but I have a feeling there's something to what you are saying that applies directly to my life.

"You know, before I dropped out of the rat race and came out here to live, retrospection and introspection just never entered my head. I was too busy keeping the wheels of industry oiled, I guess. Trying to keep the fast lane of life from eating my lunch, actually."

She wrote about her grandparents, who were what most of us would call homesteaders. "They were a real class act," she said. "And as much as I would like to make my own life like theirs, I just can't do it. The world has changed and I can't go back all the way anymore. I just have to do the best with the equipment and the times I have."

And then came some real food for thought while chopping sorghum:

"I sleep outside from May to October and sometimes wake up in the darkest part of the night and feel... friendly, I guess you could say. I just lie there on my pad on the porch and sort of integrate. Let the night sounds and smells mingle with my soul. The brook across the road and the cicadas. A little night breeze will come along from the south and almost blow my essence out across the lawn. When I can't tell me from the night any more I imagine that I have found GOD.

"After a few minutes of such luxury, I pull myself back into my snug sheets and go back to sleep.

"Such thoughts in Grandma and Grandpa's time would have been out of place. So maybe what you were saying, to me, at least, was that there is such value in memories of home and such joy in what we make of the present. We just can't let go of the richness of life. The joy of life."

I like that, very much. And as I cut sorghum I wanted to tell Elin that I disagreed that such thoughts would have been out of place in Grandma and Grandpa's time. Maybe they didn't talk about them, but how many of us talk about them even now? When we fall into a rhythm, a routine, and let ourselves slip away and play while our bodies are happily engaged, we're not making use of any 20th century technology or psychology or science, so how can we assume that our grandparents' or great-grandparents ten times removed didn't feel the same as we do?

Grant Wood, who painted "American Gothic" and was often called American's "Painter of the Soil," once said, "I get my best ideas while milking a cow."

Maybe one of the things wrong with the world today is that not enough people milk cows... or sleep outside... or cut sorghum. Maybe the world would be a better place if more people would "feel friendly," integrate, and let their essences blow out across the lawn once in awhile.
***

The sorghum has been disked in now, adding tons of organic matter to that field. By the way, what I cut for the steers hardly made a dent in it, so if you're looking for some kind of green feed for next summer, even if you only have a few sheep or goats and a few square yards of ground on which to grow forage, I'd certainly recommend scattering some sorghum-sudan seed. Who knows, you might reap even more than you sow, if you get metaphysical while you cut it.

That's funny. Just the other day I was thinking about how often we get back more than we put in, when we live beyond the sidewalks.

148. December 1985

The myth of labor-saving devices

Our favorite family magazine often prints letters from countrysiders who report that their friends and neighbors look at their lifestyle and sadly shake their heads saying, "Why would anyone want to live like that?"

Why, indeed, would anyone choose to live in this modern age without the labor-savings and convenience of a microwave, a garbage disposal or a trash compactor, and how can they even exist without running water or electricity?

The fact is these wonderful "labor-saving" (but energy gobbling), expensive gadgets and devices don't save any more time than does driving 60 miles an hour rather than 55—and on a short trip, at that.

This runs contrary to popular belief, and it's certainly contrary to a lot of advertising, but it's true, according to a household time use study made by the USDA.

People who own microwave ovens spend an average of 83.1 minutes a day on food preparation, according to the study. People who rough it without microwaves spend 87 minutes a day on the same task. The gizmo saves a whopping 3.9 minutes a day.

The savings are the same for a dishwasher. People who use them spend an average of 35 minutes a day washing dishes; people who don't spend 38.9 minutes. Time savings: 3.9 minutes a day.

It takes 2.6 minutes a day to wrap the garbage in a newspaper and take it to the trash can instead of flushing it down the sink with a waste disposer. But of course if you put the food waste in a bucket and carry it out to the compost bin when you're going to the garden anyway, or to the pig or chickens, couldn't we say you spend less time on this daily chore than you would if you had a disposal in the sink?

The average household with these three "labor-saving" conveniences saves one hour and 12.8 minutes a week. So when someone asks me how we can live without these appliances I merely cock one eyebrow and say, "Oh, and what do you do with the hour and 12.8 minutes a week you save?" We never even get around to bringing up original cost, operating costs, maintenance, or the fact that the kitchen space saved can be put to better use by storing such utensils as the Victorio Strainer and bread pans.

"Oh, you bake bread?" My grandmother used to bake bread and it took her *all day*."

There's the fallacy, which is now also applied to microwaves and dishwashers.

It might take a good portion of the day for the flour, water, yeast and honey to become a crusty, warm loaf of bread, but it doesn't take all day to bake bread. The baker doesn't have to stand there and watch the dough rise, or bake.

Similarly, by the time the plates are scraped and rinsed, placed in the dishwasher and taken out again... and the nondishwasher items are washed by hand... the machine offers very little advantage. The microwave might warm or cook food in the twinkling of an eye, while the chicken or roast or stew in the pot on the woodstove takes all day, but the cook isn't constantly standing over that pot while the wood fire works its magic on the food.

My mother used to like to tell the story of the vacuum cleaner salesman who (she said) knocked on the door. He claimed that his machine would cut her housecleaning time in half.

"Wonderful," she said. "I'll take two."

My wife and I got a similar pitch some years ago when we were remodeling the kitchen and debated about adding a dishwasher. The saleswoman pointed out all the time my wife would save with a dishwasher, and tried to overcome my reticence by hinting that she could use the extra time helping me on the farm, perhaps driving a tractor.

But a time savings of 27.3 minutes a week—or worse yet, 3.9 minutes a day, since we wash dishes every day—isn't enough to get a tractor started, to say nothing of checking the oil, fueling it, and driving to the field!

We did buy the dishwasher, but that was many years ago. Now my wife works in town and I do all the cooking—and the dishwashing. But I don't use the dishwasher.

How can I "live like this?" How do I manage to run a farm *and* cook everything from scratch (including baking bread and pies, etc.) and washing the dishes?

While preparing dinner I listen to "All Things Considered" on National Public Radio instead of sitting idle in front of the tv news or reading the newspaper. I start the bread during lunch, punch down the dough during a quick afternoon break, and put it in the oven when I start dinner. Presto, hot, fresh bread. Since I prefer the radio over television anyway, the kitchen radio entertains me while I do dishes. Nothing to it.

However, what I find particularly interesting is that the USDA household time use study that was conducted just a few years ago was a follow-up to some done by the USDA Bureau of Home Economics in the 1920s. At that time, running water and electricity were relatively uncommon in farm homes. As Maude Wilson, who conducted some of the studies back then put it, "Some houses are better equipped than others. What advantage to the well-equipped?"

She found that "well-equipped"—that is, those with electricity, indoor plumbing, electric iron, vacuum cleaner, etc., offered the homemaker "an average net addition to her personal time of about an hour a week." The same as the microwave and dishwasher save today!

By the way, how many hours do you have to work to get the money to pay for such conveniences?

You can draw your own conclusions, but don't make the mistake of thinking kitchen appliances offer fantastic time-savings. They don't, and the USDA confirmed what some of us knew all along.

2014: This column kicked off the "Great Dishwasher War." I loved it! I was surprised to hear that so many homesteaders highly value their dishwashers. We had one in our last home (it came with the house) but not for the past 14 years. Despite months of debate, and the odd situation of *homesteaders* defending such a modern appliance, nobody convinced anybody of anything. I still wouldn't want one. But my computer? That's a different story...

Postscript: 1986-2014

In 1991 the World Wide Web became available to the public. A mere nine years later there were an estimated 295 million Internet users.

The '90s introduced cloning, stem cell research, and the development and growth of genetic engineering and GM foods.

By 2000 average income reached $40,343, a gallon of gas was $1.26, a first-class stamp was 33¢ and a lb. of bacon was $2.97. Mad cow disease caused alarm and brush fires scorched more than 5 million acres in the western US, the worst in 50 years.

Y2K passed without any widespread serious computer failures.

The DotCom bubble burst; thousands of companies went broke.

Sept. 11, 2001: Almost 3,000 died in al-Qaeda suicide attacks.

2009: The Great Recession devastated the American Dream for millions, and in 2010 the BP Deepwater Horizon oil spill was the year's headline environmental disaster.

2014: The first class stamp that was 6¢ in 1970 is now 49¢. The government expects gas to average $3.46/gallon (36¢ in 1971). The 2011 median household income (latest figure) was $50,054. Stocks that were 631 in 1970 are now over 16,000. Extreme poverty (households living on less than $2/day before government benefits) doubled from 1996-2011 to 1.5 million, including 2.8 million children. Unemployment: 6.7% (not including millions who are no longer even looking for work).

Diane and Jd observe their 55th wedding anniversary. Life expectancy of a white American male: 78.7 years.

The late '80s were rough for the Belangers, in many ways. *Backyard Poultry* didn't attract a following, and we scuttled it. (It came back like gangbusters in the 21st century when backyard chickens became the in thing.) We disposed of *sheep!* magazine (which also came home to roost after 2000) and eventually, the entire printing operation. The Countryside General Store had already been folded. Magazine circulation plummeted, as did our income. At one point Diane took a job in a nearby city but too far from home to commute: she stayed in an apartment. At another time I worked in Madison — as a Kelly Girl. (Well, I did have a ponytail.)

Then, after a long and often contentious struggle involving capitalism, government, and unhappy neighbors (what a story that would make!) the farm was sold — not for industrial agribusiness, not for a housing development, but for a stone quarrying company's railroad siding. My carefully tended organic soil, the arrow-maker's hunting grounds, the land I dreamed of nourishing future generations, will never feed anyone again. That, obviously, could be yet another saga.

After scouring much of the Midwest for a new home, in 1990 we settled on 80 acres of woods and water in the Chequamegon National Forest in northern Wisconsin. I had decided I'd rather grow trees than corn, and I loved the seclusion. From the family room that became my office I could look out over the small glacial lake behind the house and see ducks and geese, otters, bald eagles, and the occasional wolf or bear. Porcupines and deer were common, snowshoe hares proliferated, bobcats showed only their tracks, raccoons and weasels ravaged my doves and poultry, and we're sure we saw a pine martin more than once.

The magazine had all but collapsed. Circulation was roughly 4,000, insignificant and uneconomical. Di and I could easily handle it on our own, in our little northwoods hideaway, as a kind of retirement project.

But then, two events changed everything again.

The first came when the giant Hearst Corporation started a magazine called, of all things, *Countryside*. There are many stories related to that, including one about a Hearst writer who contacted me for information on goats, and was startled when I expressed a bit of — let's call it "irritation" — that a massive corporation ($3.6 billion in sales, 20,000 employees) had usurped our name (especially one I'd always considered not very original in the first place) and then had the gall to ask *me* to help *them* write a story for it!

When COUNTRYSIDE readers saw the glossy "new" Countryside on newsstands, many accused us of selling out. Others just got confused. There could be no doubt that our already meager circulation, to say nothing of our goodwill and reputation, suffered greatly. (And note that Hearst had five times as many *employees* as we had *readers*.) I was also upset by their hypocritical search for successful family-run small businesses to highlight while effectively destroying ours.

Their letterhead listed more than a dozen in-house attorneys, and they retained still others everywhere they owned a newspaper, radio or tv station. We couldn't find an attorney who even dared to get involved with such a behemoth, until a lawyer who happened to be a COUNTRYSIDE reader offered his services. (We met him as a Tennessee homesteader, but when the dust settled, he was a professor at Pepperdine University School of Law.) We eventually won a settlement that, although a widow's mite to Hearst, was a vast fortune to us: $75,000.

Recall, we started with a $25 investment. Since then everything had been hand-to-mouth, usually with a very short arm. We never took much in salaries, took out loans only on real estate and the printing equipment (for "a provident and productive purpose") and had very little to budget on promotion. What could we accomplish with $75,000!

For the first time we inaugurated a real business plan, with a focus on acquiring new subscribers.

It worked. We spent what were to us huge sums on direct mail advertising. We soon had to hire help. Judy III's computer was in our den/family room/office.

It was déjà vu all over again: back to where we were in the very beginning. Again, Diane didn't appreciate other people working in her home. Moreover, as circulation grew, we needed still more help and more room.

A small tavern just down the road from us had been for sale for years. We bought it and converted it into an office.

And hired more employees.

By the way, Hearst put out only a few issues of their "Countryside" before folding it. Their millions couldn't match our dedication.

The second momentous event was Y2K, the concern that computers, which by then were involved with virtually everything, would not recognize the year 2000 and would cause widespread havoc. Worst-case scenario: the entire economy would be shut down. Part of the problem was the common practice of representing the year with two digits. The rollover from x99 to x00 became invalid in date-related processing. In addition, although most programmers knew that most years divisible by 100 are not leap years, many were not aware that years divisible by 400 *are* leap years. Perhaps it seemed too far off in the future — like *2001* was when we saw the movie in 1968 — and like most people think about dwindling natural resources: "We'll cross that bridge when we come to it." Y2K was a leap year, and we had come to the bridge.

There were hundreds of stories, from highly reputable business sources, about computer failures discovered through testing. Whether it was this testing, fixing and upgrading that prevented the disaster or whether the problem was overblown is unknowable, but very little happened.

However, *preparing* for the disaster became a big business — one that COUNTRYSIDE was admirably suited for, experienced with and prepared for. Combining the interest in Y2K with our recent surge in promotion, circulation soared to 100,000.

By then, not only was I exhausted: our two eldest children, who had been sporadically involved with the business since its inception, were ready to take over. The January 2000 issue (edited and printed in 1999) was my last.

Since then Diane and I have survived yet another 15-year era, albeit one without much to write about. The home in the forest didn't have adequate sunny garden space, among other shortcomings, and we moved to an even smaller place about 12 miles farther south. During the growing season gardening is a full-time job, much of it devoted to flowers and unusual conifers. And while I went 20 years without writing a book (and thought I was too old to start anew) Alpha, *The Complete Idiot's Guides* publisher, made me an offer I couldn't refuse. I'm not talking about money: writing a book pays far less than minimum wage, for most authors. But these books gave me a unique opportunity to get my message out to a new and different audience. And after writing *The Complete Idiot's Guide to Self-Sufficient Living* and *CIG to Raising Chickens* I was ready to tackle a long-incubating project, *Enough! A critique of capitalist democracy and a guide to understanding the New Normal.* This collection of *Beyond* columns has been simmering even longer. Countryside Publications—consisting of COUNTRYSIDE, *Backyard Poultry, sheep!* and *Dairy Goat Journal*—was sold to Swift Communications in late 2012. Anne-marie still edits COUNTRYSIDE.

It's been a wild ride — enlightening, exhausting, exhilarating, maddening, frustrating and fun, and for the most part, satisfying. But I'm glad it's over. My writing convinced few people to embrace voluntary simplicity. Others accomplished far more. I did my best, and I'm tired.

Since retiring, my reading list has expanded appreciably, and I have taken many college-level courses via computer. I often hear a lecture a day and read 2-3 books at a time on everything from anthropology and history and geology to economics, philosophy, and quantum mechanics, with a little *Fifty Shades of Grey* thrown in for variety. So it's safe to say that not only have I experienced more than twice as much life as the young man who wrote *Beyond the Sidewalks:* I also have much more book learning. What can I add to what he wrote?

Surprisingly little — but that "little" could be of vast importance. *Any changes would center on clarifying the focus and becoming much more outspoken about it.* I couldn't have done that sooner because I didn't fully realize until re-reading these essays that they're actually about *human evolution.* Not mere technological advancement, which is how most people see "progress," but the gradual development of a species. The "yearning" often alluded to is for the next step toward perfection.

Humans have walked the Earth for roughly 200,000 years. But the Earth is 4.54 *billion* years old, in a universe that's 13.8 billion years old. The span of human existence is ridiculously insignificant. One often-used demonstration asks you to extend your arm to represent the age of the Earth. Flick a file across a fingernail at the end of that arm. The amount removed represents the time Man has existed on the planet.

We consider ourselves the epitome of creation, but we are less than infants in the cosmos. As F. L. Boschke puts it, "Creation still goes on," (the English translation of his fascinating book, *Die Schöpfung Ist Noch Nicht zu Ende*). Nothing — not Man, not the Earth, not the universe — is a finished product. We have a long way to go, and we won't get there by increasing the GDP of any nation, or even the world.

Not only do we not recognize or acknowledge this: we mistake mere technological advancement — and wealth — for true evolution. The capability of going farther, higher, faster does not make us better humans, or more intelligent, than Leonardo da Vinci or Socrates. Having access to more medical knowledge and technology doesn't mean we are higher beings or more skilled than Hippocrates. In that same vein, how many PhDs who have simply absorbed knowledge from others could actually discover or formulate new information in the manner of Aristotle, Archimedes, or Galileo? Having access to a supermarket certainly doesn't make us more advanced than our ancestors who produced their own food.

None of this even begins to address the level of human perfection attributed to Jesus of Nazareth or Gautama Buddha.

Again, the problem is mistaking technology for true advancement. Using that technology to destroy ourselves is the ultimate irony. (Make no mistake: the Earth, and many species, will survive even our gravest blunders.) Technology gives us a false sense of superiority ("Jesus and Buddha didn't even have flush toilets or cell phones!") and then we use that technology in ways that endanger both our spiritual and physical survival.

Note that there are two forms of evolution: individuals can evolve over a lifespan, perhaps from racist to anti-racist, from Democrat to Republican, or from the religious upbringing imposed by their parents to atheism. But the evolution of individuals is insignificant when compared to the evolution of a species, which can take place only over generations. To repeat: we are but infants in the universe.

It's certainly true that this affects us individuals about as little as the sun becoming a red giant sometime in the far-distant future, and we have absolutely no control over it anyway. However, if we can intuit that the ultimate perfection of humanity involves what we now, with our limited knowledge and vocabulary, can only call "spiritual" traits, which are being subjugated by technology and materialism, it makes sense to use our intelligence to pursue those higher though unattainable values to whatever extent possible by liberating ourselves from materialism.

I'm more certain than ever that Nature is indeed One. Everything in this universe was present in that one speck that constituted the Big Bang 13.8 billion years ago: not only are all humans related, but all *life* is related, both plant and animal. And since everything came from the same stardust, all living things are also related to the seemingly lifeless elements of the Earth. How interesting that more than 2000 years ago the Roman poet Lucretius wrote, intuitively, "this snow-flake was a flame; the flame was the fragment of a star." In *The Universe, Its Beginning and End*, astronomy professor Lloyd Motz points out that we have direct proof that every atom of every human body (and of everything else, including snowflakes) existed, in a much simpler form, in the deep interior of some long-dead population-II star. With this knowledge, avoiding stepping on ants and worshipping trees and rocks isn't as strange as it might seem. All of creation demands far more respect than our species gives it.

While this is the foundation of my philosophy of homesteading, and indeed, living, there are more practical and immediate aspects. Perhaps my attitudes toward food as portrayed in many of the *Beyond* essays indicate my attraction to the Stoics and Epicurus: used properly, (meaning respecting its production, preparation and consumption), food is a sacrament. What does that make homesteading? Note that this attitude toward nourishment involves none of the luxury associated with "epicurean," and is the diametric opposite of gluttony. It also applies to beauty, in all its myriad forms: what is the purpose of a flower, or a songbird? Do they require one, aside from their beauty?

Stoic doctrine was popular until banned in AD 529 by the Emperor Justinian I, who considered it at odds with the Christian faith: Is that where we got off the track? Epicurus said, "Not what we have, but what we enjoy, constitutes our abundance." When enjoyment was forbidden, the acquisition of material abundance took precedence, which led to capitalism and the Protestant work ethic. It's an interesting thread and just one of many forks in the road that could have altered our destiny, but these are obviously far beyond the scope of this book — which is my final effort.

I no longer believe civilization is going to collapse within the decade, but I'm more convinced than ever that *homo sapiens* is on the road to extinction. The changes of the past 70 years continue to proliferate, snowballing with increasingly dire consequences. It could have been different, and wonderful, had more people eschewed the mindless materialism that rules and is destroying society, civilization, and the character of the planet, and has been for at least the past 200 years of the Industrial Revolution. The only remaining hope is that a global catastrophe on the scale of Noah's flood — such as nuclear Armageddon or climate change — would allow a small contingent to start anew. *Enough!* was my feeble and ineffectual attempt at explaining the problem: that it did not is one of my major failures and chief regrets.

But then, as the Talmud says, "Every man should plant a tree, have a child, and write a book." With four children, ten books, and thousands of trees planted, I should be more than satisfied.

After 76 years of occasionally heavy use, my mind is wearing out: I often have trouble finding the right word, which means it's time to stop writing and start paying more attention to trees and flowers. Flowers don't care if you have lost most of your hearing, your eyesight, your strength, your voice, and even your mental capacity. They bloom for the moment, without any regard for the petty concerns of mankind, and then fade, without regret. They are Stoic. In my old age, I shall be a flower.

To everything there is a season. Everything must end. I accept that, and I'm content.

I thank you for reading, and I wish you peace, from beyond the sidewalks.

Jerome D. Belanger
Lublin Wisconsin
April 2014

~ Finis ~

From the same author:

Country Living, A Guide for City People *(Award Books, 1973)*
The Homesteader's Handbook to Raising Small Livestock *(Rodale Press, 1974)*
Raising Milk Goats the Modern Way, *(Garden Way, 1975; now* **Storey's Guide to Raising Dairy Goats**, *4th Edition, 2010)*
Raising the Homestead Hog *(Rodale Press, 1977)*
Soil Fertility *(Countryside Publications, Ltd., 1977)*
The Place Called Attar *(Countryside, 1990)*
The Complete Idiot's Guide to Self-Sufficient Living *(Alpha, 2009)*
The Complete Idiot's Guide to Raising Chickens *(Alpha, 2010)*
Enough! A critique of capitalist democracy and a guide to understanding the New Normal *(Countryside, 2012)*

Made in the USA
Lexington, KY
30 January 2015